I0896690

Green Capital and Investments for Sustainable Growth

Siraj Kariyilaparambu Kunjumuhammed
https://orcid.org/0000-0002-7314-8677
Modern College of Business and Science, Oman

IGI Global
Scientific Publishing
Publishing Tomorrow's Research Today

Vice President of Editorial	Melissa Wagner
Director of Acquisitions	Mikaela Felty
Director of Book Development	Jocelynn Hessler
Production Manager	Mike Brehm
Cover Design	Jose Rosado

Published in the United States of America by
IGI Global Scientific Publishing
701 East Chocolate Avenue
Hershey, PA, 17033, USA
Tel: 717-533-8845 | Fax: 717-533-7115
Website: https://www.igi-global.com E-mail: cust@igi-global.com

Copyright © 2027 by IGI Global Scientific Publishing. All rights reserved. No part of this publication may be reproduced, stored or distributed in any form or by any means, electronic or mechanical, including photocopying, without written permission from the publisher. Use of this publication to train generative artificial intelligence (AI) technologies is expressly prohibited. The publisher reserves all rights to license its use for generative AI training and machine learning model development.

Product or company names used in this set are for identification purposes only. Inclusion of the names of the products or companies does not indicate a claim of ownership by IGI Global Scientific Publishing of the trademark or registered trademark.

Library of Congress Cataloging-in-Publication Data

Names: Kunjumuhammed, Siraj, 1978- editor
Title: Green capital and investments for sustainable growth / edited by Siraj Kariyilaparambu Kunjumuhammed.
Description: Hershey, PA : IGI Global Scientific Publishing, [2027] | Includes bibliographical references and index. | Summary: "This book aims to offer a critical analysis of the dynamic landscape of green capital and its significance in promoting sustainable development"-- Provided by publisher.
Identifiers: LCCN 2025047444 (print) | LCCN 2025047445 (ebook) | ISBN 9798337375953 h/c | ISBN 9798337375960 s/c | ISBN 9798337375977
Subjects: LCSH: Sustainable development | Environmentalism--Economic aspects
Classification: LCC HC79.E5 G6883 2026 (print) | LCC HC79.E5 (ebook)
LC record available at https://lccn.loc.gov/2025047444
LC ebook record available at https://lccn.loc.gov/2025047445
British Cataloguing in Publication Data
A Cataloguing in Publication record for this book is available from the British Library.

All work contributed to this book is new, previously-unpublished material.
The views expressed in this book are those of the authors, but not necessarily of the publisher.
This book contains information sourced from authentic and highly regarded references, with reasonable efforts made to ensure the reliability of the data and information presented. The authors, editors, and publisher believe the information in this book to be accurate and true as of the date of publication. Every effort has been made to trace and credit the copyright holders of all materials included. However, the authors, editors, and publisher cannot assume responsibility for the validity of all materials or the consequences of their use. Should any copyright material be found unacknowledged, please inform the publisher so that corrections may be made in future reprints.

Table of Contents

Detailed Table of Contents

high-carbon-emitting industries while climate-sensitive FDI flows into sustainable infrastructure, renewable energy, and circular economies. The chapter presents a conceptual and analytical framework for understanding the new global movements in FDI with international and regional perspectives, particularly in developing and emerging economies. It highlights barriers, including the threats of greenwashing, inconsistencies in regulations, and lack of clear definition of 'green', and develops policy recommendations to promote investor consistency on climate flows. The chapter contributes to the discussion of reorganizing the global financial architecture to achieve the SDGs and call for a paradigm shift to reverse the current capital flows to the economy and redirect them to climate flows, which will replenish both the economies and ecosystem.

This chapter examines the role of Public–Private Partnerships (PPPs) in expediting sustainable infrastructure via green finance. Public-Private Partnerships synchronize public goals with private-sector efficiency and innovation to mitigate finance deficiencies in the low-carbon transition. The suggested framework amalgamates performance-based contracts with environmental objectives, blended finance (including grants, concessional loans, and climate funds), and market instruments like green bonds and sustainability-linked loans to mitigate project risks and entice institutional investors. The approach addresses optimal risk allocation, ESG governance, and public guarantees that reduce capital costs. Institutional preparedness, encompassing PPP units, project-preparation facilities, and dependable green taxonomy, facilitates pipeline construction. Digital monitoring improves openness and accountability, while standardized protocols, risk mitigation techniques, and international cooperation bolster climate resilience and equitable development.

This chapter investigates the evolution and scaling of green finance as a key mechanism in global sustainable development. While the structural shift towards

This paper addresses the challenge of measuring green investment performance by developing and testing a Composite Impact Measurement Framework integrating financial, environmental, and social metrics. Analysing 247 investment portfolios across four industries (2019–2024), the study finds that framework-based green investments outperform traditional investments by 18.3% and deliver significantly higher environmental and social impact. The framework detects greenwashing with 87% accuracy, outperforming traditional ESG ratings (74%). Strong positive correlations between composite scores and financial performance (r = 0.76, p < 0.001) confirm the business case for integrated sustainability assessment. With balanced weightings (40% financial, 35% environmental, 25% social), the framework addresses gaps in fragmented measurement systems, offering investors and policymakers a robust tool to assess true sustainability performance and combat false environmental claims.

Green finance has become a tool of sustainable finance, but its role in the entire agenda of the United Nations Sustainable Development Goals (SDG) is still contrived. The chapter looks at how current green finance frameworks (in relation to the SDGs) are aligned with the SDGs, in terms of governance, market dynamics and policy issues. After the literature review and comparative analysis of regulatory frameworks in the European Union, China, and India, the study reveals that green finance remains largely climate-specific with investments being clustered around SDG 7 and SDG 13. Social, governance, and biodiversity-related goals, in turn, are underfinanced. The chapter determines structural factors contributing to this imbalance such as motivation by risk and returns, measurement limits, incomplete taxonomies and weak disclosure regimes which increase greenwashing risks. It finds that successful

SDG alignment needs strong governance and regulatory interventions outside of market forces.

Preface

INTRODUCTION

The pursuit of sustainable development has increasingly brought financial systems and investment strategies to the forefront of global efforts to address climate change, environmental degradation, and social inequalities. As nations, institutions, and corporations strive to achieve the Sustainable Development Goals (SDGs), the mobilization of green capital has emerged as a critical mechanism for financing the transition toward low-carbon, resilient, and inclusive economies. In recent years, green finance has evolved from a niche concept into a central pillar of sustainable development, influencing the allocation of capital, the design of financial instruments, and the governance structures that shape investment decisions across the world.

At the same time, the growing scale and complexity of sustainability challenges have revealed significant gaps in existing financial systems. Issues such as fragmented regulatory frameworks, inconsistent ESG standards, limited institutional capacity, and concerns regarding greenwashing continue to hinder the effectiveness and credibility of green investments. Addressing these challenges requires innovative financial mechanisms, robust governance structures, technological advancements, and greater international cooperation. It also demands new approaches to measuring impact and ensuring that sustainable investments generate meaningful environmental, social, and economic outcomes.

It is within this context that **"Green Capital and Investments for Sustainable Growth"** has been developed. This volume brings together contributions from scholars and practitioners who explore the evolving landscape of green finance, sustainable investment, and governance. The chapters contained herein provide theoretical insights, conceptual analyses, empirical evidence, and policy perspectives that illuminate the opportunities and challenges associated with mobilizing green capital for sustainable development. Collectively, they underscore the importance of aligning financial systems with broader societal objectives and advancing pathways that foster both economic prosperity and environmental stewardship.

CHAPTER OVERVIEW

Chapter 1, "Green Capital and Sustainable Growth: Opportunities and Strategic Pathways for Investment Development," establishes the foundation for the volume by examining the relationship between green capital and sustainable development. The chapter discusses the opportunities created by sustainable investment while highlighting barriers such as regulatory uncertainty, limited institutional capacity, and technological constraints that impede the effective deployment of green capital.

Chapter 2, "Financing the Transition—How Green Capital Reconfigures Pathways to Low-Carbon and Inclusive Growth," investigates the transformative role of green finance in facilitating the transition toward low-carbon economies. Through the examination of green bonds, blended finance, and other financial mechanisms, the chapter demonstrates how governance and policy coherence are essential for aligning investment flows with sustainable development objectives.

Chapter 3, "Sustainable Investing Across Borders: Conceptual Comparison of SRI Frameworks in Domestic and Global Markets," presents a comparative analysis of socially responsible investment frameworks. The chapter explores the interplay between national regulatory environments and global sustainability standards, emphasizing the need for adaptive harmonization strategies that balance local realities with international expectations.

Chapter 4, "From Capital Flows to Climate Flows: FDI, Renewables and New Green Investment Frontier," examines the reconfiguration of international investment patterns toward climate-sensitive sectors. Focusing on renewable energy, sustainable infrastructure, and circular economies, the chapter highlights the challenges associated with greenwashing and regulatory inconsistency while advocating for a paradigm shift in global capital allocation.

Chapter 5, "Leveraging Public-Private Partnerships to Mobilize Green Capital for Sustainable Infrastructure Financing," explores how public-private partnerships can bridge financing gaps in sustainable infrastructure. The authors propose frameworks that integrate blended finance, ESG governance, and digital monitoring systems to enhance transparency, accountability, and climate resilience.

Chapter 6, "Innovating Green Finance: Technology, Governance, and Sustainable Investment Pathways for Inclusive Growth," investigates the role of emerging technologies, including artificial intelligence, blockchain, and financial technologies, in addressing longstanding challenges in green finance. The chapter argues that technological innovation and robust governance are complementary pillars for ensuring transparency and legitimacy within sustainable investment ecosystems.

Chapter 7, "From Labels to Legitimacy: Trust, Taxonomies, and Credibility in Green Investment Ecosystems," focuses on the importance of trust and legitimacy in green finance. Drawing upon institutional and signaling theories, the chapter examines how taxonomies, governance mechanisms, and credible verification systems contribute to strengthening investor confidence and ensuring substantive environmental impact.

Chapter 8, "Developing a Composite Impact Measurement Framework for Green Investments: Integrating Financial, Environmental, and Social Indicators," presents an innovative approach to evaluating sustainability performance. By integrating financial, environmental, and social dimensions, the chapter proposes a comprehensive framework capable of improving investment assessment and enhancing the detection of misleading sustainability claims.

Chapter 9, "Aligning Green Finance with the Sustainable Development Goals: Governance Challenges, Market Gaps, and Policy Pathways," concludes the substantive content of the volume by examining the relationship between green finance and the broader SDG agenda. The chapter reveals structural imbalances in current investment patterns and argues that effective SDG alignment requires strong governance, regulatory intervention, and coordinated policy frameworks that extend beyond market incentives.

Taken together, the chapters in this volume provide a multidimensional perspective on the future of sustainable finance and green investment. They illustrate that achieving sustainable growth requires more than the mobilization of capital; it necessitates the development of trustworthy institutions, transparent governance mechanisms, technological innovation, and rigorous impact measurement systems. Through diverse theoretical and practical contributions, the volume highlights the interconnected nature of finance, policy, and sustainability in shaping resilient and inclusive economies.

CONCLUSION

As editor, I would like to express my sincere gratitude to all contributing authors for their dedication, expertise, and scholarly commitment. Their contributions have made possible a volume that reflects the breadth and complexity of contemporary debates surrounding green finance and sustainable investment. I also extend my appreciation to the reviewers and publishing team whose efforts have contributed significantly to the successful completion of this work.

It is my hope that this book will serve as a valuable resource for researchers, policymakers, investors, financial institutions, and students seeking to understand the evolving role of green capital in promoting sustainable development. The insights presented throughout this volume are intended not only to advance academic discourse but also to inform practical decision-making and policy formulation in an increasingly sustainability-conscious world.

Ultimately, the transition toward a greener and more inclusive global economy will depend upon our collective ability to align financial systems with long-term environmental and social priorities. Green capital represents both an opportunity and a responsibility—an opportunity to drive innovation and sustainable prosperity, and a responsibility to ensure that economic progress is achieved without compromising the well-being of future generations. It is our hope that this volume will inspire continued research, collaboration, and action aimed at building more resilient, equitable, and sustainable societies.

Siraj Kariyilaparambu Kunjumuhammed
Modern College of Business & Science, Oman

Acknowledgement

This volume would not have been possible without the generosity, expertise, and dedication of a great many people, and it is a genuine pleasure to record my gratitude to them here.

First and foremost, I wish to express my deep appreciation to the authors who shared their scholarly work, responded patiently to editorial queries, and revised their chapters with care and diligence. Their intellectual commitment is the foundation upon which this book rests.

I also wish to thank the reviewers whose rigorous and constructive feedback substantially improved the quality of the chapters. Their contribution, though unseen, is deeply felt throughout the volume.

I am sincerely grateful to the editorial and production team at IGI Global Scientific Publishing for their professionalism, guidance, and support throughout every stage of the publication process. Their expertise has been invaluable in bringing this project to fruition.

My gratitude extends to colleagues and mentors whose intellectual conversations over the years have sharpened my thinking on green finance, sustainable development, and the role of capital in addressing the climate crisis. Their influence, direct and indirect, is present on every page.

Finally, I owe a debt of gratitude that words cannot fully express to my family- Dr. Leji Latheef, my wife and my children, Faizah Fathimah, and Faiz Muhammed, for their unwavering patience, encouragement, and support during the many hours devoted to this project. This book is dedicated to them, and to all who believe that a more sustainable and equitable world is not merely desirable but achievable.

Siraj Kariyilaparambu Kunjumuhammed
Modern College of Business and Science, Oman

Chapter 1
Green Capital and Sustainable Growth:
Opportunities and Strategic Pathways for Investment Development

Siraj Kariyilaparambu Kunjumuhammed
http://orcid.org/0000-0002-7314-8677
Modern College of Business and Science, Oman

ABSTRACT

The need to raise capital to fund sustainable development initiatives, by addressing the complex challenges that the present and future generations of humankind face and address climate change, has placed green capital at the center of empirical discourse of investment discourse. Drawing on a critical review of the existing empirical literature, policy document and reports from regulatory and international bodies, this chapter examines the relationship between green capital and sustainable growth, with specific focus on the opportunities and pathways for inclusive development. The chapter underscores the importance of promoting green capital for sustainable development, however, it also discusses the barriers for the effective contribution of green capital to sustainable development, such as inadequate policy frameworks, weak institutional capacity, limited access to finance, regulatory uncertainty and technological constraints.

DOI: 10.4018/979-8-3373-7595-3.ch001

ht © 2027, IGI Global Scientific Publishing. Copying or distributing in print or electronic forms without written permission of IGI Global Scientific Publishing is prohibited. Use of this chapter to generative artificial intelligence (AI) technologies is expressly prohibited. The publisher reserves all rights to license its use for generative AI training and machine learning model development.

INTRODUCTION

Climate change, environmental degradation and resource scarcity are the largest challenges ever (Sverdrup, 2019) and reportedly the most complex challenges that present and future generations of humankind face (Nguyen et al., 2023) which necessitate urgent attention to the need for sustainable development (Cai, 2025). Ever since the imminent threat is realized, there has been mounting pressures on the need for an economic system that harmonizes economic growth with environmental protection, ecological sustainability and sustainable development. International frameworks, agreements, and agendas such as the adoption of Kyoto Protocols (1997), United Nations Sustainable Development Goals (2015), and Paris Agreements (2015) questioned traditional development models that exert significant pressure on resource extraction, carbon-intensive production process, and profit-maximization frameworks. The traditional development models are incompatible with socio-economic and environmental goals (Victoria, 2023) and emphasized parameters such as national income and GDP neglecting the issues of resource consumption and environmental pollution. In this regard, green capital is recognized as an important financial driver that allocates financial resources towards low-carbon and climate resilient environmentally sustainable investments within the broader framework of sustainable finance.

Green capital, yet not a standardized term, is discussed in empirical literature often with adjacent terms, such as green finance, green investment, green credit, green funds, green bonds, and green capex. Considering the technological fragmentation and the lack of standardized or unified term,, this chapter positions green capital as an umbrella construct to capture the broader spectrum of technically fluid terminologies. Further, this chapter operationally defines green capital as financial capital directed towards environmentally and ecologically sustainable projects or ventures. The allocation of funds to investments that promote renewable energy, low carbon infrastructure, pollution control, and clean transport are examples of environmentally and ecologically sustainable projects. The earlier view that green capital is more prevalent over time in industries where environment is financially significant for operations (Flammer, 2021) is no longer valid as the pressing global challenges began impact everyone, the government, industries, and humankind.

The objectives of the chapter are as follows.

- To critically examine the opportunities for aligning green capital for sustainable development.
- To examine the barriers the limit contribution of green capital for sustainable development.

- To recommend pathways to mitigate the challenges and enhance the contribution of green capital for sustainable development.

The chapter is based on a critical review of the existing empirical literature supported by policy documents. The chapter critically examines the role of green capital as a significant investment strategy to direct funds towards investments supporting sustainable growth, as different from the current practice of sole emphasis on economic factors while making investment decisions. Specifically, the chapter explores the significance of green capital on fostering sustainable development goals, and the constraints that limit the effectiveness of green capital. Further the chapter also addresses the pathways to better mobilize capital for green growth.

TRADITIONAL GROWTH AND GREEN GROWTH

Climate change and deprivation of ecological resources intensified the need for adaptive solutions that support more socially inclusive and greener economic growth. Climate change is a global threat, a long-lasting change in the weather arrays across tropics to polls, that has embarked on to put stress on various sectors (Abbass et al., 2022). Traditional models, which prioritize economic growth, exerted significant pressure on ecological balance and have proven inadequate in addressing the long-term challenges faced by modern societies (Usman, 2022). The decision matrix in the traditional models prioritized short term and long-term financial matrix, efficiency, market equilibrium and sustained economic growth, and followed heavy extraction and heavy carbon emissions, challenging environmental sustainability and social equity.

Traditional models are mostly rooted in the classical and neo classical economic models. The economic growth models are theories that help in interpreting and explaining the facts and realities observed in the growth area at the global level. (Salehi, 2025). Economies with a traditional growth model focus consider gross domestic product (GDP) expansion as their primary objective of growth and are resource-intensive and fossil-fuel dependent. From a sustainability perspective, these economics often marginalize or inadequately treat externalities, thereby privileging projects with higher negative externalities are prioritized as long as they boost GDP. The emphasis also underlines the assumption that environmental damage can be addressed after growth, which is in fact a reactionary measure. In order to address the environmental damage resulting from the traditional growth view, these economies price the environmental damage and impose Pigouvian taxes such as carbon taxes, and pollution charges. Until recently, major economies in the world emphasized that if negative externalities can be priced correctly, the markets can still function efficiently. Overall, the traditional economic models, both classical and neo classical, progressively demonstrated their incompatibility with the environmental and social matrix and long-term sustainability agenda.

In contrast, reformist alternatives such as green growth and sustainable growth and transformative alternatives such as ecological economics and Degrowth, fundamentally challenge the traditional economic models by positioning economy as a sub system within the finite ecological boundaries. These models reject the notion that economic growth and GDP expansion as the sole decision-making criteria, and advocate for sustainability and non-substitutability of natural capital. Thus, advocates of sustainable development agenda centered their argument on the principle that economic progress and environmental protection are not mutually exclusive but can be mutually reinforced. The approach emphasizes low-carbon technologies, clean energy, and environmentally friendly infrastructure as pathways to maintain economic competitiveness without depleting natural capital (World Bank, 2012).

The reformist and transformative growth initiatives respond to the exigency of transitioning towards more sustainable economic frameworks, accentuating the imperative of conserving natural resources and safeguarding the welfare of present and future populations (Farooq et al., 2025). Obviously, the emphasis on green growth policies intends to tackle the pressing global challenges and drive economic growth, making them increasingly prominent across various economies (Khan et al., 2025). However, there is a "conventional wisdom" among those who support traditional growth models that suggests that tackling climate change will extract a high price from the economy and paying too much attention to climate hurt growth and long-run well-being (Stern & Stiglitz, 2023).

Along with the reformist and transformative growth perspective, significant developments were implemented by introducing innovative financial products, such as green bonds, sustainability linked bonds, and ESG bonds. These developments were considered as strategic priority by the policy actors such as government, international organizations, and market actors such as financial and non-financial institutions to promote green growth. Several reasons were cited behind the introduction of innovative financial products targeted to promote sustainable development initiatives. For instance, issuing green bonds has become a good indicator of reduced corporate emissions, notably for firms in carbon-intensive sectors or those that had been heavy emitters (Demski et al., 2025). It is also observed that the issuers of these bonds improved environmental performance after issuance, including better environmental ratings and lower CO_2 emissions, and also attract more long-term and green investors (Flammer, 2021). Overall, these trends in green financial instruments underline a strong signaling argument, by issuing green bonds, companies credibly signal their commitment toward the environment (Ahmad et al., 2025). Similarly, the stronger policy emphasis on greener development pathways and results from five major reasons, 1) to mobilize capital for climate and transition investments, 2) create benchmark assets for deepen domestic sustainable financial products, 3) reduce financing friction for the issuers, 4) improve disclosure and discourage greenwashing practices, and 5) increase the flow of capital to renewable energy and lower emission activities. Empirical evidence also supports the fact that the escalating impacts of climate change, ranging from extreme weather events to rising sea levels and biodiversity loss, have placed unprecedented pressure on governments, corporations, and civil society to adopt sustainable solutions

Traditionally, the financial sector has been slow to integrate environmental risks into decision making and often viewed it as high-risk and low-return, deferring mainstream investors (Ahmad et al., 2025). However, the aforementioned initiatives synergized the involvement of financial sector and were furthered by the capital market by operationalizing sustainability by embedding it in capital allocation, risk pricing, disclosure and governance mechanisms. Though considered reactionary to address the pressing global challenges and control the ecological and environmental threats, these measures also offer new potential for innovation and redefined existing practices that combine environmental and social matrix along with long-term economic competitiveness. In addition, these developments in the policy initiatives significantly improved corporate ESG ratings, and indirectly resulted improvements in environmental protection, social responsibility, and governance structure by reducing financing costs (Ge, 2025). Overall, policy initiatives improved the flow of long-term transition capital, enhanced sustainable financial products, improved disclosure and reporting practices, and supported measurable environmental improvements.

Opportunities for Aligning Green Capital for Sustainable Development

In empirical literature, the term Green Capital overlaps with similar terms such as green finance, green bonds, and ESG capital. However, the literature also confirms that these terms are not used interchangeably, as significant differences can be observed among these terms. Green capital is used to refer to all funds raised and structured specifically for environmentally protective or green-oriented corporate development (Zhou & Fan, 2023). The term green finance is used along with green capital and includes financing of investments that provide environmental benefits in the broader context of environmentally sustainable development (Larsen & Henderson, 2019). Green finance is considered as a critical enabler that mobilizes capital to fund sustainable and climate-resilient projects and involves a diverse set of financial tools and mechanisms, including green bonds, green loans, and sustainability-linked loans, all of which are specifically designed to drive investments in various sectors (Ahmad et al., 2025). Green bonds are defined as financial instruments whose proceeds finance climate-friendly projects (Flammer, 2021). Tang and Zhang (2020) offered a similar definition and considered green bonds as debt instruments commit issuers to use proceeds for environmentally friendly investments (Tang & Zhang, 2020). In this paper, green capital is used to explain the allocation of financial resources, including investments and financial instruments, to environmentally sustainable projects, low-carbon technologies, renewable energy and to achieve boarder sustainable development objectives.

Two other key terminologies also require better understanding, sustainable development goals, and sustainable finance. Sustainable Development Goals (SDGs) are considered as the blueprint to achieve a better and more sustainable future for all. They address the global challenges faced by humanity, including those related to poverty, inequality, climate, environmental degradation, prosperity, and peace and justice (Larsen & Henderson, 2019). Similarly, sustainable finance is defined as financing as well as related institutional and market arrangements that contribute to the achievement of strong, sustainable, balanced, and inclusive growth, through supporting directly and indirectly the framework of the Sustainable Development Goals (Larsen & Henderson, 2019). The term is also referred to as the integration of environmental, social, and governance (or ESG) considerations in processes of financial decision-making (Archer, 2019). From this perspective, sustainable finance includes a number of strategies and financial instruments, such as green bonds, screening, impact investing, socially responsible investing, and so on.

Sustainable growth, from reformist and transformative perspective, is inclusive and conceptualized as economic expansion without compromising environmental and ecological foundations, social equity and the foundations required for future prosperity. From this perspective, sustainable growth can also be positioned as a multi-dimensional construct that combines resilience, ecological balance, social equity, and long run productive capacity, thereby integrating environmental stewardship into economic decision-making (Goffetti et al., 2022). Likewise, several empirical studies also framed sustainable growth as economic growth supported by responsible usage of resources, green innovation and environmentally aligned business transformation (Huang et al., 2023).

As cited earlier, sustainable growth centers on the ability of the government, corporate organizations and financial institutions to create an ecosystem to channelize funds towards sustainable projects such as renewable energy, clean energy, green energy, sustainable infrastructure, clean technology and human capital development. In other words, the growth of green capital requires active involvement of both policy makers and market actors. Green capital, in this context, includes green bonds, ESG funds, sustainable loans, climate funds, impact investing and transition finance. Over the years, a consistent growth in the deployment of green financial instruments is observed, in alignment with the United Nations SDGs, Paris Agreement, and national visions such as Oman Vision 2040.

Major Opportunities for Alignment

Since the United Nations SDGs 2016, intensified efforts were observed by policy makers and market actors to develop financial mechanisms to foster development models that reconcile economic growth with social and environmental sustainability. Most importantly, the alignment of capital towards sustainable activities has emerged as significant drive to achieve the SDGs. However, empirical studies have established the sustainable development not only depends on the allocation of financial resources, but also on the direction, quality and institutional governance of capital allocation (Bolton & Kacperczyk, 2021). Significant challenges still exist, for example, uneven outcomes, greenwashing, lack of standardized taxonomies, implementation barriers and the risk of symbolic compliance. Hence the efforts to integrate green growth into financial decision-making require a multi-faceted approach, focused on financial innovation, policy coordination, institutional preparedness and market incentives.

The major opportunity for alignment includes

- Renewable energy financing
- Sustainable infrastructure
- Capital market innovation
- Public-private partnerships
- SME and entrepreneurial finance
- Digital Finance and Fintech
- Human capital and social sustainability.

Renewable Energy Financing

The 2015 United Nations Climate Change Conference (COP 21) underscored the importance of investment in renewable energy and energy efficiency as keys to addressing global challenges, particularly climate change. Though several ambitious climate change goals were initiated, the net zero emission goals could not be achieved due to the deployment challenges, particularly the flow of funds to the renewable energy investments. The challenge is acknowledged by the International Energy Agency. In this regard, the United Nations Framework Convention on Climate Change (UNFCCC) reiterated that "local, national, or transnational financing, drawn from public, private, and alternative sources of financing, that seeks to support mitigation and adaptation actions that will address climate change." Prior research studies also underscored the need to address the financing gap in achieving the net zero emissions target (Ng & Tao, 2016; Taghizadeh-Hesary & Yoshino, 2020). Several reasons were cited, for instance, the excessive financing constraints of enterprises (Wang & Fan, 2023).

Investing in renewable energy companies involves large amounts of capital investments, longer capital investment periods, and high investment risks (Abban & Hasan, 2021). Several empirical findings reported importance of green capital to raise, structure and deploy funds to support renewable energy projects such as wind, solar, hybrid and energy storage systems (Alharbi et al., 2023; Ng & Tao, 2016; Wang & Fan, 2023). For instance, Ahmed et al., (2025) based on a review and assessment of assessment of green-finance tools (taxation, trade openness and technological incentives) underlined their effectiveness in improving renewable-energy investment efficiency (Ahmad et al., 2025). The same view is shared by Alharbi et al., (2023) and underlined that green finance significantly fosters renewable energy in the short and long-run (Alharbi et al., 2023). The surge in renewable energy financing indicates the emphasis of policy makers and market actors to address climate change, and transition towards a net zero economy, where carbon emissions are reduced to the point where they are offset by activities such as clean energy technology (Omri & Ben Jabeur, 2024).

Students also discussed key observations regarding the impact of green finance on renewable energy projects. The long-run impact of green finance on renewable energy is significant in countries with higher emissions per dollar GDP, higher levels of climate change exposure to the economy and human life, and better-developed credit markets. The effect is more pronounced in countries with low or net zero emission targets and following the post-Paris 2015 agreements (Alharbi et al., 2023). Studies observed that maintaining high-quality economic development and alleviating the financing difficulties of enterprises will be more conducive to play the role of green finance in supporting the investment of renewable energy enterprises (Wang & Fan, 2023).

SUSTAINABLE INFRASTRUCTURE

Sustainability transitions require a fundamental redirection of finance flows, away from unsustainable towards new sustainable technologies and practices (Steffen & Schmidt, 2021). Infrastructure development is the backbone for economic growth. Traditionally, infrastructure systems, such as roads, rails, energy, water, digital networks, buildings, waste management systems are developed with high carbon emissions, significant stress on environment and eco-systems, and inefficient use of resources and urban inequality. The UN SDGs placed significant emphasis on infrastructure development, which is inclusive, resilient, sustainable and central to the achievement of SDGs. A transition in approach is evident since 2015, and countries began investing in infrastructure development inclusively and with a decarbonize agenda, thus leading towards sustainable infrastructure. Not only the government, the development agencies, private sectors and funding agencies emphasized sustainable infrastructure and considered it as foundational drivers to achieve SDGs.

Sustainable infrastructure is about more than "green" construction., it also refers to infrastructure development that are economically viable, socially inclusive, climate resilient and environmentally efficient throughout their lifecycle. These investments, such as renewable energy, smart electricity grids, green transportation, emphasis on solar energy infrastructure, and wastewater treatment plants, create multidimensional value through productivity improvements, emission reductions, benefits to public welfare and long-term competitiveness. Global estimates suggest that trillions of dollars of annual infrastructure investments are required for development needs while staying within climate targets, creating a substantial opportunity for green capital mobilization (Bhattacharya et al., 2016).

Empirical evidence underscores the importance of renewable energy infrastructure, such as investments in solar parks, wind farms, battery storage systems, smart grids and green hydrogen networks, in achieving sustainability objectives along with long-term financial returns. Further these investments promote employment generation, energy security and innovation spillovers while reducing reliance on fossil fuels as empirical evidence shows (Polzin, 2017). Similarly, demand for transport systems, housing, sanitation and municipal services require development of sustainable cities, with mass transit systems, electric mobility networks, green buildings, energy efficient public facilities and integrated waste systems. Empirical evidence highlights that developing sustainable cities offers environmental and economic benefits by reducing infrastructure inefficiencies and supporting inclusive urban growth (Geissdoerfer et al., 2017). Another key investment in sustainable infrastructure is the investment in electric vehicles, as the transportation sector is estimated to contribute about 50 percent of air pollutants emitted worldwide. Due to the excellent energy-saving and environmental protection features, electric vehicles (EVs) are gaining significant market penetration, especially in densely populated urban areas with systemic air quality problems (Pan et al., 2023).

Importantly, the flow of financial capital to sustainable infrastructure projects depends on coherent policy support and the expansion of innovative financial products, capable of risk-return tradeoff and attracting long term investors. As stated in empirical literature, financial capital is not simply a fungible resource that is instantaneously allocated to newly appearing technologies through frictionless capital markets, as assumed in many neoclassical economic models (Steffen & Schmidt, 2021). From a coherent policy support perspective, sustainable infrastructure projects are capital intensive and often require a long payback period, which in turn necessitates the need for blended financial models, public support, transparent disclosure and taxonomy frameworks. It can be achieved only through robust policy support, which in turn helps generate investment from institutional investors, such as pension funds, mutual funds, sovereign wealth funds and insurance companies. In addition, the policy framework and robust governance and disclosure mechanisms, the alignment also requires public private partnerships and offers capital, managerial efficiency and innovation. Lastly, the integration of technology and finance presents significant challenges for financial regulators, necessitating formulation of policies for mitigating financial security risks and related concerns (Chen et al., 2024).

A core tension often discussed in empirical literature on equitable growth in developing economies is the substantial deficit in infrastructure across multiple sectors, specifically in energy, transportation, waste management, water and sanitation, digital and smart infrastructure. Several empirical studies have categorically emphasized the importance of infrastructure development, as it either directly or indirectly influences the attainment of all of the Sustainable Development Goals (SDGs) including 72% of the targets (Thacker et al., 2019). Developing countries face additional barriers such as currency and political risks that increase the investment gap (Granoff et al., 2016). As often said, the infrastructure choices influence the growth and the carbon intensity of the economy. In order to achieve the SDG targets, the contribution of developing countries is significant. Enhancing the contribution of developing countries requires channelizing funds from carbon intensive projects to sustainable infrastructure projects. New and innovative financial instruments can be developed to earmark funds for sustainable projects which in turn intensify the efforts to move forward towards modern and efficient infrastructure models.

CAPITAL MARKET INNOVATION

The transition to a low-carbon economy has accelerated global interest in sustainable finance instruments (Rodrigues Loiola et al., 2025). Governments under fiscal pressure and private companies facing increasing costs of climate transition are more and more able to tap scalable financing channels through capital markets via green bonds, sustainability-linked bonds (SLBs), ESG equity instruments, transition finance products and digital market infrastructure. Several empirical literatures deliberated on whether capital market innovations enhanced the flow of capital to environmentally productive uses or merely repackage conventional finance under sustainable labels. A majority of empirical literature underscored the significant role of capital market innovation for sustainable growth, however, the effectiveness depends on several factors such as the quality of governance, credible reporting and disclosure frameworks, investor sentiments, risk management framework and regulatory harmonization.

Capital market innovation has become one of the most significant mechanisms for mobilizing green capital for sustainable growth. Empirical evidence shows that capital market liberalization promotes green innovation and has a stronger effect on green invention patents than green utility model patents, however, the impact varies across firms with different types of ownership or scale. Capital market liberalization spurs green innovation through both reducing financing constraints and information disclosure quality effects (Feng et al., 2022).

Among the several innovative practices, several empirical research findings rated green bonds as the flagship innovation in sustainable capital markets. Green bonds have emerged as an important component of sustainable finance, lowering financing friction and expanding the investor base, particularly among investors with ESG mandates (Rodrigues Loiola et al., 2025). Recent evidence suggests that these instruments have moved from symbolic finance to meaningful market scale. Green bonds generate value not only through offering cheaper capital, but also by signaling a strategic commitment to sustainability and by increasing stakeholder confidence. The key question however is whether the issuance actually leads to real environmental additionality. Further a major concern along with the rapid growth emerges on the lack of uniform standards, creating opportunities for credibility gaps. In addition to green bonds that are predominantly used to provide capital for the energy transition, social, sustainability, and sustainability linked bonds have also appeared in financial markets (Beteta Vejarano & Swinkels, 2023).

From a firm specific perspective, access to green bond financing is found to influence corporate green innovation since it reduces the financing constraints and enhances the incentives of reputational benefits. Green bond issuance has positive effects on environmentally oriented innovation investment and patenting outcomes pointing to the possibility that capital market instruments can influence real productive behavior beyond the change of funding structure This is important, because sustainable growth requires technological transformation, not just portfolio reallocation (Zhang & Lv, 2025). However, the benefit of green bond financing centers mainly on firms which operate in a transparent and internationally linked markets (Feng et al., 2022). The findings underscore the importance of institutional modernization as the top priority along with innovative financial instruments. The institutional reforms should focus on trading, governance and disclosure practices, which in turn enhance stakeholder confidence in the capital market. Further, the empirical studies highlight that capital market innovation should be treated as transformational, for instance, linking the financing costs to issuer sustainability targets rather than ring-fencing proceeds for green projects. Such a transformational focus allows firms to finance transitional pathways from carbon intensive processes to de-carbonized processes. Add to this, empirical literature also argue that firms have no direct financial incentive to act ESG-friendly once such bonds are issued and attribute it to weak KPIs, the absence of stretch targets and limited sanctions for underperformance (Feldhütter et al., 2024). Thus, while considering capital market innovation, it is also imperative to broaden the view and consider the fact that financial innovation without accountability may create appearance rather than impact.

Capital market innovations, to be effective, should focus on allocative efficiency. From the perspective of innovative financial instruments, these investment vehicles can influence how the funds flow in capital markets. Firms with sustainable focus can obtain funds through the innovative investment vehicles at a lower cost than firms with poor environmental consciousness or those who resist transition to sustainable practices. As a result, investors might shift their focus on investing in companies that support transition to sustainable practices, which in turn incentivizes the companies with weaker environmental performance to transition to sustainable practices. Allocation efficiency, however, requires governance interventions such as development of standardized metrices, developments in sustainability regulations and disclosure practices, and measurable KPIs to check impact assessment.

Recent developments in digital finance offer significant opportunities for innovations in capital markets and can guide product innovation, risk assessment and access to finance for equitable and sustainable growth. Developments such as fintech platforms, blockchain, artificial intelligence, digital ESG scoring, crowdfunding, and digital bonds, have not only revolutionized the capital market, but also promoted the flow of capital towards green projects. The developments also streamlined operational effectiveness and lowered the transaction costs, improved investor access, enhanced data integrity and transparency. The world investment report 2025 reported that sustainable bond issuance exceeded $1 trillion in 2024, of which green bonds hold the major share (UNCTAD, 2025).

Empirical literature also compared the flow of capital in emerging and developed economies, specifically addressing the developments in the capital market. Emerging markets are pivotal to the global sustainability transition, yet face systemic inequities in accessing sustainable finance, receiving less than 15 % of global flows despite accounting for 65 % of carbon emissions and 85 % of the world's population (Narayan et al., 2025). Significant difference exists in capital market innovation in developed and emerging markets. For instance, in developed markets, capital market innovation mainly focusses on robust disclosure systems, deep institutional investor pools and credible enforcement. On the other hand, the emerging markets, capital market innovation is restricted by higher macroeconomic volatility, currency risk, weaker taxonomies and limited secondary market liquidity. Empirical investigation highlights significant differences in the way capital market innovations are operationalized in developed and emerging markets. For instance, the emerging markets, the innovation mainly focus on structural reforms, while on developed markets, the focus is shifted to innovative financial instruments (Feng et al., 2022). Similarly, the emerging markets require strong institutional support, while the developed markets scale faster with a stronger institutional readiness, as institutional support and trust already exists (Frecautan, 2022). Another key difference arises from the role of government and private sectors. In emerging markets, the government plays a significant role and leads the market creation, while the private sector plays a significant role in the developed markets (Cheng et al., 2024).

Though capital market innovations address the market and product dimensions, several empirical literatures also pose significant concerns on the integration of social dimensions in capital market innovations. Investors prioritize bankable projects, while projects that support bio-diversity projection, rural resilience or inclusive transition are not prioritized due to low returns. Thus, capital markets innovation should strategize financing models and support not only market efficiency but also sustainable development priorities. Overall, empirical literature considers capital market innovation as a major opportunity to align green capital with sustainable growth. Green bonds, ESG equity channels, sustainability-linked instruments and digital finance systems can mobilize large pools of private capital and accelerate environmental innovation. However, their developmental value is not automatic, it is contingent. Without credible taxonomies, transparent disclosures, measurable outcomes and strong supervision, the risk is that innovation lapses into greenwashing or a superficial reshuffle of portfolios.

PUBLIC-PRIVATE PARTNERSHIPS

As explained earlier, sustainable growth requires public-private partnerships (PPP). It is estimated that achieving the 1.5 °C target by 2050 necessitates a cumulative investment of USD $150 trillion, or roughly over USD $5 trillion annually (Casady et al., 2024; IRENA, 2021). PPPs are attractive and an important driver for sustainable development, as they combine private sector investment, technological capability and execution efficiency with public developmental objectives (Othman & Khallaf, 2022). PPPs reduce government burden on investing in sustainable projects. Several factors limit the government's ability to allocate funds for sustainable projects, such as budget limitations, hesitancy to commit public funds to innovative and advanced technologies, redistributive issues connected to the projects involved, high opportunity costs associated with these investments, political costs of increasing the tax burden, restricted access to debt financing for subnational governments, and finally the unprecedented scale of these investment needs (Casady et al., 2024). PPPs are closely related to the concept of sustainability because of their ability to provide essential infrastructure and, simultaneously, the potential to generate positive impacts at the economic, environmental, and social levels (Thacker et al., 2019). In PPPs, the private actors are involved in one or more of the different steps or parts of policymaking: agenda-setting, negotiation, resource provision implementation, monitoring, and/or enforcement (Marx, 2019). Government's financial constraints and the rising needs for sustainable investments, PPPs offer a practical and pragmatic platform to leverage private capital, management expertise, technological innovation, and operational efficiencies for public sustainability goals.

Several empirical literatures underscored the importance of PPPs not only as tools for infrastructure procurement, but as institutional vehicles able to align green capital with long-term environmental and developmental outcomes (Marx, 2019; Othman & Khallaf, 2022; Owojori & Erasmus, 2025; Pal, 2026). PPP not only offers investment but also contributes to social equity. Pal (2026) found that a 1% increase in PPP investment is associated with a 0.70% decrease in income inequality and 0.16% and 0.17% increases in poverty and unemployment (Pal, 2026). Importantly, the relevance of PPP emanates from its potential to address the chronic financing gap for green infrastructure, such as investments in renewable energy, water systems, climate-resilient transport, waste management and energy-efficient buildings. Such investment helps government overcome large upfront investment and leverage private equity, however, retaining public oversight.

Several empirical literatures discussed the relevance of PPP in renewable energy projects. Othman and Khallaf (2022) observed that PPP helps government to overcome substantial upfront costs, and can contribute capital, innovation and technical knowhow. The success of PPP, however, depends to a great extent on the balanced risk allocation and the institutional capacity (Othman & Khallaf, 2022), and also challenged by the political and regulatory uncertainties. The same view is augmented by Fleta-Asín and Muñoz (2021) in a broader sense and underscored the importance of better institutional and economic environments in promoting successful PPPs. Currently, hybrid financing models, envisaged by PPPs, are increasingly used in solar parks, wind farms, grid modernization, battery storage, and waste-to-energy systems. In addition, the use of PPPs improves bankability by allocating construction, operational and performance risks to the parties best able to manage them (Othman & Khallaf, 2022).

Though PPPs offer unique opportunities by spreading resources and allocating risks among the public and private participants, empirical studies also cautioned that PPPs may underperform where governance systems are weak, risks poorly allocated or sustainability goals treated as secondary. PPPs require strong public oversight to add value to the engagement and prevent private incentives from overriding public value. If not management adequately with governance and operational frameworks, PPPs results in several critical challenges. First, PPPs can transfer commercial returns to private actors but leave contingent liabilities with the government, resulting in adding hidden costs to the tax papers. Similarly, the tax burden on taxpayers will increase if demand forecasts are wrong or renegotiations take place. Greater uncertainties on payoffs in green projects create burdens on government and can obscure future public liabilities if fiscal risks are not transparently recorded (Cepparulo et al., 2024). Thus, it is important to highlight the importance of developing PPP investment choices based on efficiency indicators and adapt fiscal rules to shield public investment while stabilizing private expectations by means of credible trajectories of debt reduction. PPP should not be viewed as a mechanism to overcome the budget limitations and should be critically reviewed based on the future obligations that it may create on public funds and taxpayers. Addressing these challenges requires strong governance, efficient PPPs, measurable KPIs, and ongoing monitoring of projects with key deliverables and appropriate and relevant disclosure practices.

Similarly, the implementation of sustainable projects in PPP mode does not guarantee the viability and success of the outcome. As mentioned earlier, they can function as broader instruments to create socioeconomic transformation, however, effectiveness to a great extent depends on its ability to move away from narrow economic objectives and integrate inclusive, long-term and sustainable development priorities. Several empirical findings underscored the importance of both contractual and relational governance in PPP sustainability. Contractual governance complements relational governance in promoting cooperative behavior, but relational governance does not amplify the effect of contractual governance on opportunistic behavior (Li et al., 2024).

From a broader perspective, PPP does not guarantee sustainable business outcomes development outcomes, and it requires effective monitoring with measurable KPI and targets, and disclosure practices. This is often a concern in the developing countries where impact assessment is not aligned with specific KPIs. Specific disclosure norms and relevant monitoring reduce the greenwashing exercise, and labelling of projects as "green" however without any measurable impacts. The impact assessment is critical, for instance, a PPP project on smart transportation should be evaluated based on the emissions reduction, lifecycle efficiency, and not based on the investment in tangible assets. Thus, PPPs are a strategic mechanism for promoting sustainable investment, however, should be followed by sound governance and reporting of impact outcomes. When properly designed, implemented and monitored, PPP investments can promote employment generate, reduce poverty and inequality and promote equitable development, thus generate socio-economic gains to achieve SDGs. Thus, it helps generate employment, reduce poverty, and develop sustainable infrastructure which are key SDG priorities. The focus, however, should be through a wider sustainability focus, and should not be limited to carbon metrics.

SDG financing gap is a reality and can be reduced through the support and contribution of private sector in sustainable development initiatives. While the empirical literature on this topic critiqued on the shift from different perspectives, a summary of the major themes can be outlined as,

- Claims of superior PPP performance is not well supported by empirical evidence, hence should be "cautiously skeptical" (Hodge & Greve, 2017)
- Environmental KPIs are documented, however, its impact on social sustainability is poorly monitored (Hueskes et al., 2017)
- Empirical discussions are heavily skewed to the infrastructure development (Pinz et al., 2018)
- PPPs effectively de-risk private finance using public balance sheets (Gabor, 2021)
- Despite the strategic shift towards PPP models, several uncertainties still remain such as preserving the traditional business model, de-risking the private finance, maximizing development finance, which at times contradict each other (Bougrea & Vermeiren, 2025)
- Regional differences were observed in efficiency of utilizing PPP models, with China deviating meaningfully from de-risking PPP model, while the West is failing on its own terms (Larsen, 2025)
- Private finance has shown little real interest in developmental projects with uncertain payoffs (Bernards, 2024)

From a rhetorical perspective, these empirical literature, though supported PPP utility in advancing SDGs, a cautious need to align it with the needs of both socio-environmental objectives is emphasized. The literature also informs the need for a shift in approach and requires (1) green PPP models with environmental KPIs, (2) enhancing the bankability of the PPP projects through concessions and guarantees, (3) enhanced disclosure and monitoring mechanisms, (4) innovative financial instruments to tap private finance, and (5) adaptive and collaborative governance practices.

SME AND ENTREPRENEURIAL FINANCE

Small and medium-sized enterprises (SMEs) and entrepreneurial ventures are central to the transition to sustainable growth. SME and entrepreneurial ventures play a significant role in inclusive and sustainable development due to its scale effect, ability to bring disruptive solutions, and its ability to generate employment. In many economies, SMEs and entrepreneurial ventures account for the majority of firms, employment opportunities and substantial contribution to the national income. Further, SMEs function as innovation laboratories and promote curricular business models and inclusive green transformation.

A review of policy debates and empirical discussions on sustainable development shows that large enterprises were given greater attention. While comparing the focus and attention on role of small and large enterprises, a majority of the targeted policy interventions, governance and incentive frameworks are directly linked to the large enterprises. Large enterprises dominate the flow of capital resources through the deployment of green bonds and other innovative financial instruments. A review of exiting empirical discourses reveals that the SME green-finance gap is mainly structural and not cyclical. In most of the time, the early-stage sustainability SME and entrepreneurial ventures fail to attract capital resources, due to the proof-of-concept and scale up requirements (Mudalige, 2023)

Several empirical studies discussed the role of SMEs and entrepreneurial ventures in the transition towards sustainable growth. Di Viao et al., (2022) emphasized that entrepreneurial ventures are catalysts for sustainable growth, however, require financial support and driven by sustainability matrices (Di Vaio et al., 2022). Oduro (2024) emphasized the role of SMEs in promoting eco-innovation which refers to the production, assimilation or exploitation of a product, production service, service or management or business methods that are novel to the organization and which results in a reduction of environmental risk, pollution and other negative impacts of resources used compared to relevant alternatives (Oduro, 2024). However, as discussed, SMEs are often underserved by the traditional financial systems, due to multiple reasons, such as information asymmetry, collateral requirements, perceived financial metrics and sustainability driven performance indicators. The gap, thus, necessitates the need to mobilize green capital for inclusive sustainable development.

A major theme in the post-2022 literature is that SMEs are central to the green transition because they are numerous, adaptive and innovation-oriented, but structurally underserved by financial markets. Owen et al., (2026) argue that smaller firms are essential to net-zero transitions as they produce experimentation, niche technologies and supply-chain decarbonization (Owen et al., 2026). However, they observe that SME green innovation has long payback periods, uncertain demand and intangible assets, which is hard to be financed via traditional bank lending. The simple argument is that sustainable growth requires a broader ecosystem of entrepreneurial finance than simply relying on traditional debt. The insight is important because most of green finance frameworks were designed for larger borrowers. Green bonds, sustainability-linked loans and institutional investment products often require scale, reporting sophistication and transaction sizes that are not feasible for smaller firms. Thus, SMEs, important for emission reduction, energy efficiency, waste minimization, and local job creation, might be excluded from green capital flows.

Zhu et al. (2025) reiterated that the combination of inclusive finance mechanisms and green finance policies helps SMEs improve energy efficiency and adopt clean technology more widely. Digital financial inclusion can lower financing constraints and facilitate access for innovation-driven smaller firms. Thus, it repositions green capital not as environmental finance, but as a mechanism that is effective to the extent that it is accessible and inclusive in financial terms. Green finance systems that only finance large, investment-grade borrowers may be good for headline capital flows but miss much of the real economy. By contrast, SME-targeted green finance can transmit sustainability through production networks, subcontractors, service firms and regional economies.

Considering the challenges SMEs and entrepreneurial ventures faces and its significance in inclusive growth, several empirical studies have underscored the developments in sustainable finance to promote SMEs and entrepreneurial ventures to a broader resilience outcome. For instance, Kato (2024) observed that sustainable finance solutions can promote SME's long-term performance and its contribution towards social and environmental sustainability agendas (Kato et al., 2024).

DIGITAL FINANCE AND FINTECH

The empirical discourse on mobilizing green capital for sustainable growth has underscored the significant role of digital finance and financial technology (FinTech), particularly in mobilizing capital through innovative financial products and on time monitoring and impact assessment. Until recently, majority of discussions on sustainable finance were centered around banks, public markets and development finance institutions. However, the reliance of financial metrics, collateral requirements, and risk investment profile, many environmentally friendly projects were termed as non-bankable projects and could not be initiated. The developments in Artificial Intelligence and Machine Learning technologies created transformative potential, and created opportunities for sustainable projects through innovative technologies, financial instruments and platforms, such as digital platforms, data analytics, artificial intelligence, blockchain, crowdfunding and mobile finance. These developments have transformed the way capital is raised, allocated, monitored and democratized. Amidst climate urgency, financing gaps and tech disruption, FinTech is a potential gamechanger, connecting sustainability ambitions with capital deployment. However, empirical evidence also provides words of caution. While digital finance can boost access and efficiency, it can also exacerbate inequality, increase energy use, create data risks or favor scale over meaningful environmental outcomes. FinTech is a huge opportunity to unlock green capital and sustainable growth – but it's not a given.

Since the development of transformative technology, such as AI and machine learning, a major theme explored in empirical research is the role of these developments in reducing frictions in sustainable finance markets. High transaction costs, slow intermediation, weak SME access and limited transparency were often limited by the contribution of traditional sustainable finance initiatives to support sustainable development. However, with the developments in AI and other transformative technology, digital finance tools emerged to address these barriers by automating credit assessment, peer-to-peer funding, wider participation of retail investors and improved traceability of capital flows. In a seminal work, Bu (2025) observed that FinTech is significantly promoting green technological innovation and green growth through improving financial access and accelerating resource allocation to environmentally friendly sectors. The study suggests that digital finance can be a transmission channel to deliver innovation finance to sustainability-oriented firms more effectively than traditional systems (Bu et al., 2025).

As discussed, small finance and entrepreneurial ventures faced several challenges in accessing green finance because of the lack of collateral, credit history or scale. The proof of scalability is always on these ventures. With the developments in fintech lending models, alternative data, such as digital cash-flow records or platform histories offered significant platforms to overcome these barriers. Thus, developments in technology democratized the social base of green capital rather than aggregating it in large listed corporations.

A notable feature of empirical discussion since 2020 is the rise of green digital finance, where sustainability finance and digital technology intersect. According to Xiao (2024), green finance and digital finance, which were previously considered to be two separate policy domains, are now becoming integrated. Governments have often pursued digitalization and sustainability in parallel rather than together and missed synergies. The two agendas are synergized to enhance financing for clean energy, green transport, environmental risk management and sustainable development goals (Xiao et al., 2024). Thus, it resulted in a shift in the perception of Fintech from a payments innovation or consumer convenience sector to an infrastructure for sustainable capital formation. By integrating these digital identity systems, e-wallets, tokenized assets and open-finance rails with environmental goals, significant developments in green finance were observed along with democratization of green finance opportunities.

A number of recent empirical discourses underlined the importance of data and analytics in the context of reporting and disclosure practices. A recurring challenge, observed in empirical literature, that restricts access to capital resources, is information asymmetry as a result of lack of disclosure and reporting frameworks. Information asymmetry results in a lack of up-to-date information for investors to verify the ESG claims, the impact on emissions, and the status of projects. In this regard, FinTech tools help stakeholders with screening and post-investment monitoring using AI, machine learning, satellite data and automated reporting. In a bibliometric study, Zournatzidou (2025) emphasized the intersection of green finance and FinTech on enhancing ESG performance and promoting green-tech business ecosystem. The study furthered discussed and stressed the need for "green tech" eco system to make a meaningful contribution to ecological transitions (Zournatzidou, 2025).

Though digital finance can offer sustainable solutions for capital allocation and impact assessment, several limitations were also observed in the empirical literature. As a fact, digital finance does not automatically result in green outcomes. Firstly, a lending platform may be technologically advanced but may engage in energy intensive projects and speculative activities. Technology can enhance transactions, not sustainability. Secondly, the externalities of energy and infrastructure are important. Some digital systems, such as AI that depend on big data or some blockchain architectures, are categorized as major energy consumers themselves if designed poorly. Third, the rising cyber and governance risks, resulting from the vulnerabilities of data driven information system. Several recent empirical findings reported increasing cyber threats in FinTech ecosystems and emphasized the importance of trust, resilience and regulatory safeguards. Fourth, the impact of financial inclusion may result in mixed outcomes. Digital credit can expand access but also over-indebtedness. Yue et al. (2022) observed that digital finance offers inclusion benefits but also exacerbate household debt distress under certain conditions. This is an important limitation for sustainable growth, as socially fragile finance models are unlikely to be sustainable in a developmental sense. FinTech-enabled green finance in developed economies is typically based on more mature capital markets, a stronger regulatory system and more extensive ESG data. Innovation could be in product sophistication, carbon analytics, robo-advice, tokenized green assets, and sophisticated reporting tools.

Importantly, the biggest contribution of fintech on sustainable finance is the development of innovative financial products, finance platforms and automated data driven insights. Thus, fintech created significant impact on the way the sustainable projects were funded, operationalized and monitored. Thus, mobile payments, micro-savings, SME lending, remittance efficiency, agricultural finance and decentralized access to clean-energy finance are few notable developments. According to Abdalla et al. (2025), FinTech promotes green growth in Sub-Saharan Africa by providing access to sustainable financing, clean energy and green technologies. However, the regional wise disparities were observed in the contribution of fintech in sustainable finance, which further emphasized that digital finance needs to go hand-in-hand with robust environmental policy. Countries with shallow traditional finance systems might paradoxically benefit the most from digital green finance if institutions are supportive. Crowd funding and tokenization are also discussed in empirical literature. Green Crowdfunding Platforms can be used to fund local solar systems, circular economy projects, community agriculture, and eco-startups. Eventually, tokenized green assets might enable lower minimum investments and greater participation. The key constraints are regulatory uncertainty and investor protection.

From a policy perspective, recent empirical literature increasingly deliberated on the need for coordinated governance frameworks for successful green FinTech ecosystems, such as open data standards, digital identity, sustainability taxonomies, cybersecurity rules, consumer protection, interoperable payments, and measurable environmental disclosure practices. A lack of these foundational elements in the eco system results in fragmented or extractive innovation risks. Thus, a majority of empirical discourses strongly supported the proposition that digital finance and FinTech offer significant opportunities for aligning green capital with sustainable growth. They can reduce intermediation costs, increase access, improve the quality of ESG data, finance underserved innovators and speed up the flow of capital into sustainable sectors. However, as discussed, technology without governance creates more risk; finance without environmental discipline only digitizes unsustainable activity.

CONCLUSION

This chapter has critically examined the relevance of green capital as a key driver for sustainable growth. The empirical review highlights that while green capital has significant potential for financing the transition to a low-carbon, resource-efficient economy, its potential is unevenly realized across geographies, sectors and institutional settings. The chapter presented the opportunities to align green capital with renewable energy infrastructure, sustainable infrastructure, capital market innovations, public-private partnerships, SME and entrepreneurial finance, digital finance and fintech and human capital and sustainability. From a broader perspective, the analysis shows that intersection of regulatory policies, technological innovation, and growing investor confidence on green capital instruments has created a conducive environment for scaling green capital flows. Financial instruments, such as green bonds, sustainability linked loans and climate funds, have evolved considerably, providing feasible instruments to channel private and public investment towards activities with environmental benefits. Further, the integration of ESG principles into institutional investment frameworks created a structural shift in the way capital allocation decisions are being made worldwide.

However, the chapter also discusses the challenges and barriers that limit the use of green capital for sustainable growth. The challenges include regulatory inconsistencies in the regulatory frameworks, lack of clarity on what constitutes "green", asymmetric information between investors and issuers, the disproportionate exclusion of low-income and developing economies, inadequate and non-standardized reporting and disclosure practices, In addition, the listed challenges are also compounded by the underlying structural tension between the long time horizons of sustainable investments and the short-term performance pressures that dominate much of the financial sector.

There has been a growing need from both developed and developing nations to tackle the pressing climate change and focus more on climate resilient projects such as renewable energy, clean energy and sustainable cities and infrastructure. However, to achieve the targets set by UN SDGs, it is important to allocate capital to the projects that are socially and environmentally sustainable. This chapter has discussed the role of green capital for sustainable development, with specific focus on investment developments. Specifically, the chapter discussed the major opportunities for alignment of green capital for sustainable development, for instance, renewable energy financing, sustainable infrastructure, capital market innovation, public private partnerships, SME and entrepreneurial finance, digital fiancé and fintech. The chapter also underscored the need to improve the governance and policy framework, disclosure and reporting practices to enhance the role of developments in sustainable finance for inclusive development.

REFERENCES

Abban, A. R., & Hasan, M. Z. (2021). Revisiting the determinants of renewable energy investment—New evidence from political and government ideology. *Energy Policy, 151*, 112184. DOI: 10.1016/j.enpol.2021.112184

Abbass, K., Qasim, M. Z., Song, H., Murshed, M., Mahmood, H., & Younis, I. (2022). A review of the impact of global climate change, adaptation, and sustainable mitigation measures. *Environmental Science and Pollution Research International, 29*(28), 42539–42559. DOI: 10.1007/s11356-022-19718-6 PMID: 35378646

Ahmad, F., Boumaiza, A., Sanfilippo, A., & Al-Fagih, L. (2025). A comprehensive review on green finance and its impact on net zero energy transition: From the perspective of renewable energy development. *Energy Strategy Reviews, 62*, 101948. DOI: 10.1016/j.esr.2025.101948

Alharbi, S. S., Al Mamun, M., Boubaker, S., & Rizvi, S. K. A. (2023). Green finance and renewable energy: Worldwide evidence. *Energy Economics, 118*, 106499. DOI: 10.1016/j.eneco.2022.106499

Archer, M. (2019). Sustainable Finance. In Archer, M. (Ed.), *Environmental Science*. Oxford University Press., DOI: 10.1093/obo/9780199363445-0117

Bernards, N. (2024). Where is finance in the financialization of development? *Globalizations, 21*(1), 88–102. DOI: 10.1080/14747731.2023.2222481

Beteta Vejarano, G., & Swinkels, L. (2023). Social, Sustainability, and Sustainability-Linked Bonds. SSRN *Electronic Journal*. https://doi.org/DOI: 10.2139/ssrn.4420618

Bhattacharya, A., Meltzer, J. T., Oppenheim, J., Qureshi, Z., & Stern, N. (2016). *Delivering on Sustainable Infrastructure for Better Developemnt and Better Climate*. Global Economy and Development. https://www.brookings.edu/wp-content/uploads/2016/12/global_122316_delivering-on-sustainable-infrastructure.pdf

Bolton, P., & Kacperczyk, M. (2021). Do investors care about carbon risk? *Journal of Financial Economics, 142*(2), 517–549. DOI: 10.1016/j.jfineco.2021.05.008

Bougrea, A., & Vermeiren, M. (2025). Rolling out the Wall Street Consensus? Multilateral development banks and the trilemma of private capital mobilization. *Competition & Change, 10245294251343426*, 10245294251343426. Advance online publication. DOI: 10.1177/10245294251343426

Bu, Y., Du, X., & Li, H. (2025). From digital finance to green growth: The role of FinTech in sustainable manufacturing. *Applied Economics*, •••, 1–17. DOI: 10.1080/00036846.2025.2560685

Cai, C. (2025). Crisis and Opportunity: Promoting Global Cooperation for Sustainable Development to Achieve a Greener Future. *Advances in Economics. Management and Political Sciences*, *154*(1), 1–6. DOI: 10.54254/2754-1169/2024.19530

Casady, C. B., Cepparulo, A., & Giuriato, L. (2024). Public-private partnerships for low-carbon, climate-resilient infrastructure: Insights from literature. *Journal of Cleaner Production*, *470*, 143338. DOI: 10.1016/j.jclepro.2024.143338

Cepparulo, A., Eusepi, G., & Giuriato, L. (2024). Public Finance, Fiscal Rules and Public–Private Partnerships: Lessons for Post-COVID-19 Investment Plans. *Comparative Economic Studies*, *66*(1), 191–213. DOI: 10.1057/s41294-023-00213-x PMID: 37359136

Chen, Y., Che, Z., & Wan, D. (2024). How does the financial technology innovation of the regulatory pilot influence financial regulation? *Finance Research Letters*, *69*, 106255. DOI: 10.1016/j.frl.2024.106255

Cheng, G., Ehlers, T., Packer, F., & Xiao, Y. (2024, June). *Sovereign green bonds: A catalyst for sustainable debt market development?* [BIS Working Papers No 1198]. Monetary and Economic Department, BIS. https://doi.org/https://www.bis.org/publ/work1198.pdf

Demski, J., Dong, Y., McGuire, P., & Mojon, B. (2025). *Growth of the green bond market and greenhouse gas emissions* (BIS Quarterly Review) [Review]. BIS. https://www.bis.org/publ/qtrpdf/r_qt2503d.pdf

Di Vaio, A., Hassan, R., Chhabra, M., Arrigo, E., & Palladino, R. (2022). Sustainable entrepreneurship impact and entrepreneurial venture life cycle: A systematic literature review. *Journal of Cleaner Production*, *378*, 134469. DOI: 10.1016/j.jclepro.2022.134469

Farooq, B., Nazir, A., Farooq, M., & Anjum, S. (2025). Green Growth in Sustainable Environment and Future Outlook. In Parray, J. A., Shameem, N., & Haghi, A. K. (Eds.), *Environmental Landscape and Sustainable Biodiversity for Healthy Green Growth* (pp. 147–154). Springer Nature Switzerland., DOI: 10.1007/978-3-031-75405-0_15

Feldhütter, P., Halskov, K., & Krebbers, A. (2024). Pricing of sustainability-linked bonds. *Journal of Financial Economics*, *162*, 103944. DOI: 10.1016/j.jfineco.2024.103944

Feng, G.-F., Niu, P., Wang, J.-Z., & Liu, J. (2022). Capital market liberalization and green innovation for sustainability: Evidence from China. *Economic Analysis and Policy*, *75*, 610–623. DOI: 10.1016/j.eap.2022.06.009

Flammer, C. (2021). Corporate green bonds. *Journal of Financial Economics*, *142*(2), 499–516. DOI: 10.1016/j.jfineco.2021.01.010

Frecautan, I. (2022). Performance of Green Bonds in Emerging Capital Markets: An Analysis of Academic Contributions. *Journal of Corporate Finance Research / Корпоративные Финансы | ISSN: 2073-0438*, *16*(3), 111–130. https://doi.org/ DOI: 10.17323/j.jcfr.2073-0438.16.3.2022.111-130

Gabor, D. (2021). The Wall Street Consensus. *Development and Change*, *52*(3), 429–459. DOI: 10.1111/dech.12645

Ge, H. (2025). Green Bond Policy and Corporate ESG Performance. *Advances in Economics. Management and Political Sciences*, *156*(1), 40–52. DOI: 10.54254/2754-1169/2025.20399

Geissdoerfer, M., Savaget, P., Bocken, N. M. P., & Hultink, E. J. (2017). The Circular Economy – A new sustainability paradigm? *Journal of Cleaner Production*, *143*, 757–768. DOI: 10.1016/j.jclepro.2016.12.048

Goffetti, G., Böckin, D., Baumann, H., Tillman, A., & Zobel, T. (2022). Towards sustainable business models with a novel life cycle assessment method. *Business Strategy and the Environment*, *31*(5), 2019–2035. DOI: 10.1002/bse.3005

Granoff, I., Hogarth, J. R., & Miller, A. (2016). Nested barriers to low-carbon infrastructure investment. *Nature Climate Change*, *6*(12), 1065–1071. DOI: 10.1038/nclimate3142

Hodge, G. A., & Greve, C. (2017). On Public–Private Partnership Performance: A Contemporary Review. *Public Works Management & Policy*, *22*(1), 55–78. DOI: 10.1177/1087724X16657830

Huang, T., Zhou, W., Zhang, Y., Jia, X., Zhang, D., & Li, Z. (2023). An insight-based approach for batch water network with flexible production scheduling framework. *Journal of Cleaner Production*, *385*, 135664. DOI: 10.1016/j.jclepro.2022.135664

Hueskes, M., Verhoest, K., & Block, T. (2017). Governing public–private partnerships for sustainability. *International Journal of Project Management*, *35*(6), 1184–1195. DOI: 10.1016/j.ijproman.2017.02.020

IRENA. J. (2021). *World energy transitions outlook: 1.5° C pathway*. International Renewable Energy Agency.

Kato, A. I., Chiloane-Tsoka, E. G., & Mugambe, P. (2024). Unlocking the potential: The influence of sustainable finance solutions on the long-term sustainability of small and medium-sized enterprises. *Cogent Business & Management, 11*(1), 2391122. DOI: 10.1080/23311975.2024.2391122

Khan, R. Z., Razak, L. A., & Premaratne, G. (2025). Green growth and sustainability: A systematic literature review on theories, measures and future directions. *Cleaner and Responsible Consumption, 17*, 100274. DOI: 10.1016/j.clrc.2025.100274

Larsen, M. (2025). Any alternative to the Wall Street Consensus? Comparing the infrastructure financing models of the US, the EU, and China. *New Political Economy, 30*(1), 34–47. DOI: 10.1080/13563467.2024.2373078

Larsen, M., & Henderson, I. (2019). Green and Sustainable Finance. In Leal Filho, W., Azul, A. M., Brandli, L., Özuyar, P. G., & Wall, T. (Eds.), *Responsible Consumption and Production* (pp. 1–10). Springer International Publishing., DOI: 10.1007/978-3-319-71062-4_75-1

Li, J., Liu, B., Wang, D., & Casady, C. B. (2024). The effects of contractual and relational governance on public-private partnership sustainability. *Public Administration, 102*(4), 1418–1449. DOI: 10.1111/padm.12982

Marx, A. (2019). Public-Private Partnerships for Sustainable Development: Exploring Their Design and Its Impact on Effectiveness. *Sustainability (Basel), 11*(4), 1087. DOI: 10.3390/su11041087

Mudalige, H. M. N. K. (2023). Emerging new themes in green finance: A systematic literature review. *Future Business Journal, 9*(1), 108. DOI: 10.1186/s43093-023-00287-0

Narayan, M., Kumar, N., Parida, V. K., & Kumari, P. (2025). Sustainable finance in emerging markets: Adaptive governance and environmental, social, and governance innovation for equitable climate resilience. *Development and Sustainability in Economics and Finance, 8*, 100101. DOI: 10.1016/j.dsef.2025.100101

Ng, T. H., & Tao, J. Y. (2016). Bond financing for renewable energy in Asia. *Energy Policy, 95*, 509–517. DOI: 10.1016/j.enpol.2016.03.015

Nguyen, T. T., Grote, U., Neubacher, F., Rahut, D. B., Do, M. H., & Paudel, G. P. (2023). Security risks from climate change and environmental degradation: Implications for sustainable land use transformation in the Global South. *Current Opinion in Environmental Sustainability, 63*, 101322. DOI: 10.1016/j.cosust.2023.101322

Oduro, S. (2024). Eco-innovation and SMEs' sustainable performance: A meta-analysis. *European Journal of Innovation Management, 27*(9), 248–279. DOI: 10.1108/EJIM-11-2023-0961

Omri, A., & Ben Jabeur, S. (2024). Climate policies and legislation for renewable energy transition: The roles of financial sector and political institutions. *Technological Forecasting and Social Change, 203*, 123347. DOI: 10.1016/j.techfore.2024.123347

Othman, K., & Khallaf, R. (2022). A REVIEW OF PUBLIC-PRIVATE PARTNERSHIPS FOR RENEWABLE ENERGY PROJECTS IN DEVELOPING COUNTRIES. *Proceedings of International Structural Engineering and Construction, 9*(1). Advance online publication. DOI: 10.14455/ISEC.2022.9(1).ENR-01

Owen, R., Deffains-Crapsky, C., Hussain, J., & Mac An Bhaird, C. (2026). Financing SME green and sustainable innovation. *Venture Capital, 28*(2-3), 1–12. DOI: 10.1080/13691066.2026.2643997

Owojori, O. M., & Erasmus, L. J. (2025). Public–private partnerships as catalysts for green infrastructure: A three-pronged analysis of economic, environmental, and institutional factors. *Frontiers in Sustainable Cities, 7*, 1591278. DOI: 10.3389/frsc.2025.1591278

Pal, S. (2026). Public-private partnership in energy investment and inclusive growth. *Energy Policy, 210*, 115010. DOI: 10.1016/j.enpol.2025.115010

Pan, Y., Fang, W., & Zhang, W. (2023). Development of an energy consumption prediction model for battery electric vehicles in real-world driving: A combined approach of short-trip segment division and deep learning. *Journal of Cleaner Production, 400*, 136742. DOI: 10.1016/j.jclepro.2023.136742

Pinz, A., Roudyani, N., & Thaler, J. (2018). Public–private partnerships as instruments to achieve sustainability-related objectives: The state of the art and a research agenda. *Public Management Review, 20*(1), 1–22. DOI: 10.1080/14719037.2017.1293143

Polzin, F. (2017). Mobilizing private finance for low-carbon innovation – A systematic review of barriers and solutions. *Renewable & Sustainable Energy Reviews, 77*, 525–535. DOI: 10.1016/j.rser.2017.04.007

Rodrigues Loiola, R., Kimura, H., & Melo Souza, L. D. (2025). Sustainable Finance, Green Bonds and Financial Performance—A Literature Review. *International Journal of Financial Studies, 13*(4), 233. DOI: 10.3390/ijfs13040233

Salehi, A. (2025). Economic Growth Theories: Comparative Analysis of Classical, Neoclassical, and Endogenous Models. *INTERNATIONAL JOURNAL OF SOCIAL SCIENCE HUMANITY & MANAGEMENT RESEARCH, 04*(12). Advance online publication. DOI: 10.58806/ijsshmr.2025.v4i12n05

Steffen, B., & Schmidt, T. S. (2021). Strengthen finance in sustainability transitions research. *Environmental Innovation and Societal Transitions, 41*, 77–80. DOI: 10.1016/j.eist.2021.10.018

Stern, N., & Stiglitz, J. E. (2023). Climate change and growth. *Industrial and Corporate Change, 32*(2), 277–303. DOI: 10.1093/icc/dtad008

Sverdrup, H. U. (2019). The global sustainability challenges in the future: The energy use, materials supply, pollution, climate change and inequality nexus. In Meadowcroft, J., Banister, D., Holden, E., Langhelle, O., Linnerud, K., & Gilpin, G. (Eds.), *What Next for Sustainable Development?* Edward Elgar Publishing., DOI: 10.4337/9781788975209.00013

Taghizadeh-Hesary, F., & Yoshino, N. (2020). Sustainable Solutions for Green Financing and Investment in Renewable Energy Projects. *Energies, 13*(4), 788. DOI: 10.3390/en13040788

Tang, D. Y., & Zhang, Y. (2020). Do shareholders benefit from green bonds? *Journal of Corporate Finance, 61*, 101427. DOI: 10.1016/j.jcorpfin.2018.12.001

Thacker, S., Adshead, D., Fay, M., Hallegatte, S., Harvey, M., Meller, H., O'Regan, N., Rozenberg, J., Watkins, G., & Hall, J. W. (2019). Infrastructure for sustainable development. *Nature Sustainability, 2*(4), 324–331. DOI: 10.1038/s41893-019-0256-8

UNCTAD. (2025). *World Investment Report 2025* (No. 2025; pp. 1–42). United Nations Conference on Trade and Development. https://unctad.org/system/files/official-document/wir2025_ch03_en.pdf

Usman, B. (2022). Sustainable Economies: A Review of Green Growth and Circular Models. *Journal of Business, IT, and Social Science, 1*(2), 13–16. DOI: 10.51470/BITS.2022.01.02.13

Victoria, G.-M. (2023). *General Guidelines for the Implementation of Sustainability in Higher Education Institutions*. UNESCO.

Wang, Q., & Fan, Z. (2023). Green finance and investment behavior of renewable energy enterprises: A case study of China. *International Review of Financial Analysis, 87*, 102564. DOI: 10.1016/j.irfa.2023.102564

World Bank. (2012). *Inclusive Green Growth—Pathways to Sustainable Development*. World Bank.

Xiao, Y., Lin, M., & Wang, L. (2024). Impact of green digital finance on sustainable development: Evidence from China's pilot zones. *Financial Innovation, 10*(1), 10. DOI: 10.1186/s40854-023-00552-9

Zhang, L., & Lv, F. (2025). GREEN BONDS AND CORPORATE GREEN INNOVATION. *The Singapore Economic Review, 70*(08), 2413–2437. DOI: 10.1142/S0217590825490268

Zhou, M., & Fan, R. (2023). The Impact of Green Capital Structure on Enterprise Development and the Regulation of Technological Innovation under Carbon Peaking. *Sustainability (Basel), 15*(7), 5743. DOI: 10.3390/su15075743

Zournatzidou, G. (2025). Green Finance and Sustainable Development: Investigating the Role of Greentech Business Ecosystem Through PRISMA-Driven Bibliometric Analysis. *Administrative Sciences, 15*(4), 150. DOI: 10.3390/admsci15040150

Chapter 2
Financing the Transition: How Green Capital Reconfigures Pathways to Low-Carbon and Inclusive Growth

Khayrilla Kurbonov
Termez University of Economics and Service, Termez, Uzbekistan

R. N. Ravikumar
http://orcid.org/0009-0009-3705-1681
Marwadi University, Rajkot, India

Duggirala Aravind
http://orcid.org/0009-0005-4362-7684
ASET Institute of Science and Technology, Chennai, India

S. Aarthi
http://orcid.org/0009-0006-9064-2091
Marwadi University, Rajkot, India

Elmurodov Shokhjahon
Kimyo International University in Tashkent, Tashkent, Uzbekistan

ABSTRACT

The process of changing financial systems to align investment flows with the sustainability target has been aggravated by the transition to low-carbon and inclusive development. The chapter is presented as the green capital is a revolutionary mechanism that alters the economic structures, priority of sectors of development. According to the theory of sustainable finance and recent case studies, the analysis suggests the way, in which green bonds, blended finance and other financial instru-

DOI: 10.4018/979-8-3373-7595-3.ch002

...ht © 2027, IGI Global Scientific Publishing. Copying or distributing in print or electronic forms without written permission of IGI Global Scientific Publishing is prohibited. Use of this chapter to ...enerative artificial intelligence (AI) technologies is expressly prohibited. The publisher reserves all rights to license its use for generative AI training and machine learning model development.

ments attract investments to renewable energy, climate resilient infrastructure, and socially inclusive projects. The analysis shows that the key determinants to consider in order to combat risks such as fragmentation and greenwashing are the critical governance, policy coherence, and institutional capacity. The chapter presents an argument that funding the transition is virtually a coordination issue and a systemic issue that requires long-term orientation of the financial innovation and Sustainable Development Goals.

1. INTRODUCTION

The increasing rate of climatic change, environmental degradation and the rising social inequality have also put the already established economic and financial systems into question. The traditional models of growth that are majorly carbon intensive production and a short-term distribution of capitals have demonstrated minimal capabilities to counter the issue of long-term sustainability. Financial systems reorientation has been, in this regard, among the most important facilitators of structural change towards low-carbon and inclusive developmental paths. Finance is not viewed as a neutral facilitator anymore, but a powerful tool that precondition the priorities of investments, technologies usage and social-economic outcomes (Nagesh K C, 2025). To put green capital within this larger transformation, this chapter focuses much attention on how it is driving financial flows to activities that generate environmental resilience and social value along with economic returns. The chapter focuses on financing the transition by taking a systemic perspective on green capital as both a financial and institutional force. It highlights the necessity to adjust the logic of investments to the goals of sustainability, policy frameworks, and development (Gambetta et al., 2021). The chapter provides the basis of comprehending how the financial systems can be reformulated to enable sustainable growth in the era of enhanced environmental and social uncertainty through conceptual discussion and empirical example.

1.1 Climate–Inequality Nexus

Climate change and social inequality are two global issues, which are becoming more and more related to the economic stability and development opportunities. Increase in temperature, extreme weather and ecological degradation disproportionately impact vulnerable populations contributing to the presence of inequalities, both in-between and within regions and social groups. Simultaneously, the financial systems have always been focused on efficiency and profitability, rather than on the resilience and equity, which has strengthened unequal developmental patterns

(B. Edeminam & Akpasoh, 2023). These dynamics have seen an increase in the understanding that financial architecture should be reorganized in such a way as to internalize the environmental and social risks. The choices of emission pathways are not the sole ones that influence capital assignment, but also inclusion of access to infrastructure, work, and services. The growing financial risks associated with climate changes (including the physical, transition, and liability risks) are exerting a growing burden on financial institutions so that the sustainability factor is now expected to be taken into consideration in decision making. Such redirection is a sign of the shift in attitude towards reactive risk management and transition to more active investment in sustainable assets and multi-polar development. Those markets can be instrumental in assisting systemic change by introducing climate and equity issues into financial governance (Steckel et al., 2017). The changing rhetoric is that without focusing on inequality, the approach to climate change may fail to provide both efficiency to the environment and societal credibility.

1.2 Role of Green Capital

The green capital has been turned out as a strategic instrument that can change the developmental tracks since it can fit in the financial impetuses to the sustainability objectives. Green capital is a more of an investment rationality than collection of specialized financial tools, where long-term environmental and social benefits are put first. Some of the instruments that may be utilized to direct both the private and the public funds towards renewable energy, climate-resilient infrastructure and the circular economy projects are green bonds, sustainability-linked loans, and blended finance mechanisms. Such investments are not only leading to the reduction of emissions but also creating jobs, technological progress and raising the accessibility of basic services (Tandan et al., 2025). The strategy of green capital as a concept is its capacity to influence the production systems, and consumption pattern on a massive scale. Green capital is able to reduce uncertainty in investment and crowd in in the case of good supporting policy framework and reasonable standards. This position offers sustainable growth opportunities that are not dependent on the economic growth and destruction of the environment and enhance social inclusion. As a result, the green capital is gradually turning into a source of systemic change and less of a fringe in a financial market.

1.3 Chapter Scope & Structure

The chapter will also seek to provide a close-up analysis of the part that was played by green capital in making up of the low-carbon and inclusive growth. Its areas of coverage include the theoretical views on sustainable finance; as well as development economics; and also, empirical evidence based on the new investment practices and case studies. The importance of the chapter is that the author uses an integrative approach that incorporates financial instruments, institutional arrangements, and the development outcomes in one analytical framework. The chapter fills in important gaps in current discourses that usually concentrate on the financial performance or environmental metrics. The chapter is organized structurally where the conceptual and policy base of green capital is laid first, and then a literature review is done in accordance with the predetermined research objectives. This is followed by application of case studies to explain applications and challenges. The paper summarizes the research findings and presents conclusions to policymakers, investors and managers. The chapter is also concluded with defining the way forward in future research, and makes the point that the transition will need concerted effort at the financial, institutional, and governance levels to fund it.

2. BACKGROUND TO THE STUDY

The phenomenon of the green capital should be interpreted in the context of the changing financial framework and setback of the developmental paradigm. The development of environmental consciousness and social inequalities in the last few decades have disproved the foundations of traditional models of investment. Regulatory reforms, stakeholder pressure as well as the shifting risk perceptions are increasingly influencing financial markets, which used to be largely disregarding sustainability issues. The background section provides the context of the emergence of green capital, including how it developed in sustainable finance and the analysis of the global policy environment in which it is thriving. It also increases the limitation of traditional growth and investment models that have resulted in the wallow of financial transformation. When green capital is put in the context of these more general processes, it is in this section that one can discuss it as a means of restructuring the development paths. This context is relevant because it allows identifying the possible power of green finance, including its disadvantage, to cause systemic change (Devender et al., 2025). The background gives emphasis on the fact that green capital is a not a single innovation but a more global re-analysis of how the financial systems are correlated with the environmental and social objectives.

2.1 Evolution of Green Finance

Sustainable finance has become a mainstream issue in the focus of financial discussion, as opposed to a marginal and ethical topic of interest in investment. Initial strategies focused on negative screening and corporate social responsibility and sustainability was typically viewed as an outside element. With time, these views broadened to include environmental, social and governance issues as material risk determinants of financial risk and performance. The rise of green investment paradigms demonstrates the greater involvement of sustainability in the capital markets, where the financial structures have been developed in terms of environmental effects (Teixeira, 2025). Green bonds, climate bonds and sustainability-linked instruments are examples of such a change which explicitly tie capital allocation to direct environmental targets. This development has been influenced by sustainability performance, the rising investor demand, and rising regulatory participation. Notably, the paradigms of a green investment go beyond risk avoidance to focus on value creation of innovation and resilience. These paradigms make finance an active participant in the development transitions and not a passive distributor of resources by supporting low-carbon technologies and sustainable infrastructure (Luo et al., 2022). Table 1 Overviews the historical development of the traditional finance model to sustainable and green finance models, pointing out the main changes in the goals and tools.

Table 1. Evolution of Green Finance Models

Phase	Dominant Approach	Key Characteristics	Developmental Orientation
Conventional Finance	Profit maximization	Short-term returns, carbon-intensive assets	Growth-focused, low sustainability concern
Ethical / CSR Investing	Exclusionary screening	Avoidance of harmful sectors	Limited social responsibility
ESG Integration	Risk-based ESG metrics	ESG as financial risk factors	Risk-adjusted growth
Green Finance	Project-linked sustainability	Green bonds, green loans, climate funds	Low-carbon transition
Impact-Oriented Finance	Outcome-driven	Measurable environmental and social impact	Inclusive and resilient growth

2.2 Global Policy Landscape

The development of green capital is directly connected with the world policy system that defines the priorities of sustainable development. The normative and regulatory requirements on the harmonization of the financial systems with the sustainability aims have been brought about by the global climate commitments and the development agendas. These frameworks are concerned with the mobilization of both the privatized finance and the public resources to aid in the mitigation, adapting and social inclusion of climate (Swaty, 2023). The sustainability taxonomies, disclosure, and green finance strategies are some priorities that are manifested in the increasing number of financial reforms at national and regional levels. These policies should help reduce information asymmetry, enhance the level of transparency in the market, and promote capital investment in activities that are both environmentally and socially beneficial. The policy context also emphasizes the role played by the public institutions in de-risking green investments and stimulating the participation of the private sphere. However, the variation in the policy formulation and application on cross-j Jurisdictional basis brings fragmentation and confusion. The importance of the coordination and policy coherence in scaling green capital can be explained with the help of this uneven landscape. The world policy commitments are thus regarded as boosters and constraints of development of sustainable finance.

2.3 Structural Constraints

Traditional growth and investment theories have traditionally focused on the short-term payoffs, intensive production, and the concentration of capital. These buildings have added to the environmental degradation, climate vulnerability, and social inequalities that have not been eliminated. Financial systems that run under such models tend to underestimate the long-term environmental risks and social externalities resulting into an inappropriate distribution of capital. Other structural limitations are the restricted access to finance among small and medium businesses, underserved areas, and novel low-carbon technologies (Desalegn & Tangl, 2022). These obstacles strengthen the dependence on the path that gives an advantage to existing, carbon-intensive industries over the existence of sustainable options. Furthermore, the traditional models often do not have the mechanisms of including social safeguards and distributional aspects in investment decisions. These constraints will have to be tackled by reconsidering the goals as well as the regulation of financial regimes. Green capital is created in reaction to such constraints by proposing new norms of creating value and risk evaluation. Nevertheless, its success will also be determined by an overcoming of established institutional practices and the alignment of financial incentives and long-term sustainability results. Figure 1 indicates the ways in which the inefficiency in green development by misallocating financial resources and structural mismatches is caused by poor innovation, inefficient resource combination, and inflexible industry organization.

Figure 1. Structural Constraints in Finance

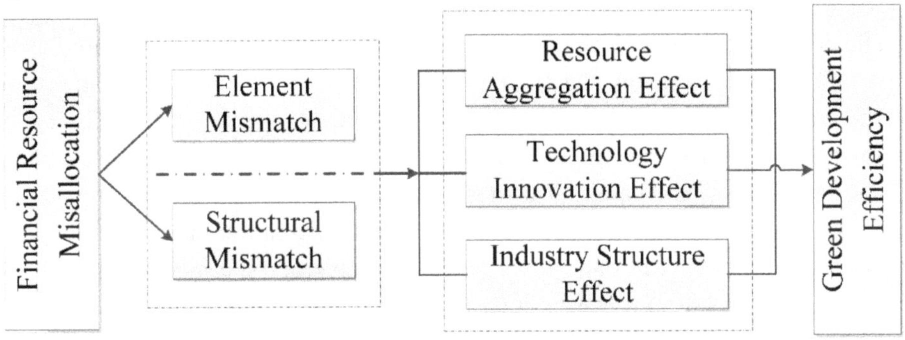

3. RESEARCH OBJECTIVES

The chapter is informed by a set of well-established research objectives that seek to test the research topic in an organized and rigorous way to determine the role of green capital as an instrument of facilitating transition to low-carbon and inclusive growth. The goals are set in ways that they combine economic, financial and governance views and this means that the goals are in line with sustainable development priorities and relevancy to the policies. These goals facilitate a holistic approach to green finance as an agent of systemic change, not a financial innovation in isolation by both emphasizing structural change and its application.

- To study how green capital helps reshape economic systems and supports sustainable growth.
- To examine how green financial tools (green bonds, loans, blended finance, carbon markets) support low-carbon and inclusive investments.
- To assess how green finance promotes inclusive growth, especially for SMEs and underserved regions.
- To identify key policy and governance factors that support or limit green capital deployment.
- To analyze major challenges (e.g., greenwashing, policy gaps) and suggest ways to improve transparency and impact.

4. CONCEPTUAL MODEL

The conceptual model developed in this chapter has put the green capital as an important element whereby the financial systems play a major role in structural change and inclusive development. The model neither regards green finance as a peripheral or corrective instrument but instead develops it as the enabling instrument of changing institutional pattern, the investment pattern, and development patterns. Three dimensions that are mutually dependent are used in the model and they are financial instruments, policy and governance structures, and socio-economic results. These dimensions are in dynamic interaction in order to affect the way capital is mobilized, distributed, and tracked across sectors and regions.

Incorporating environmental sustainability and social inclusion into the investment logic, the conceptual model brings to the fore the systemic quality of low-carbon transition. It states that financial innovation cannot exist without facilitating institutions, regulatory consistency, and accountability systems. The multi-actor character of green finance can also be observed in the model as it includes the functions of both the public authorities and financial institutions, as well as the companies, or individual investors. Comprehensively, the conceptual framework is an analytical tool that can be used to study the role of green capital in leading to long-term transformation when it is geared towards development goals and sound governance systems (Babar & Wu, 2025). Figure 2 of the interaction of financial instruments, governance and green investments to facilitate inclusive and sustainable development by incorporating green finance.

Figure 2. Green Finance Conceptual Model

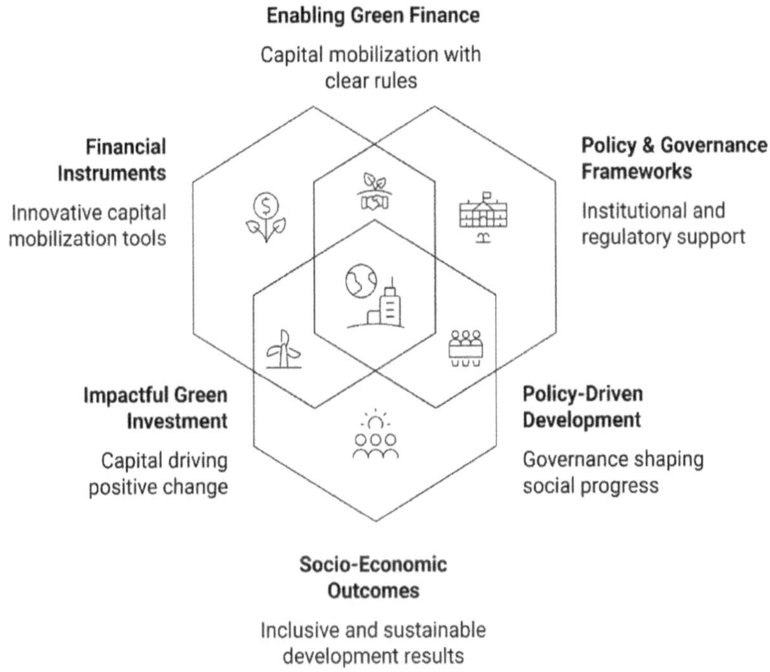

4.1 Green Capital Transformation

The concept of green capital is understood as an agent that shapes economic arrangements and structures. Green capital transforms the patterns of production and the priorities of the sectors, redistributing financial resources to the low-carbon technologies, sustainable infrastructure, and climate-resilient systems. Such a redistribution faces historic reliance on carbon-intensive sectors and promotes creativity on renewable energy, environmentally friendly mobility, and the production that uses fewer resources (Fligstein & Huang, 2025). At the institutional level, green capital demands new systems of governance, including sustainability standards, reporting systems and impact assessment tools. Banking institutions are forced to take into consideration the environmental and social concerns in risk and loan estimation. The impact of such alterations is institutional learning and adaptation and these enhance the potential of financial systems to induce long term sustainability objectives. It is due to this that green capital plays the catalytic role in funding projects and not just that, in changing the norms, motivations, and decision-making in economic systems (Madyan & Widuri, 2023). Structural and institutional change is that which is manifested by the effect of the sum total of action in mutual investment and governance change.

4.2 Finance–Policy Linkages

The conceptual model highlights the interrelationships of the green financial instruments, policy mechanisms, and the growth results. Financial instruments like the green bonds, sustainability-linked loans and the mechanisms of blended finance can only work when they are incorporated into favorable regulatory and policy frameworks. Policy frameworks create certainty in sustainability taxonomies, disclosure policies and fiscal incentives which lowers uncertainty levels and increases investor confidence (Flammer, 2020). The combination of these instruments and policies affects the results of growth since they determine the capital distribution in areas that facilitate decarbonization and social development. The connection between finance and policy defines the magnitude, direction and inclusivity of investment flows. The results of growth are thus not direct but indirect through the quality of governance and the coherence of the institution. In the case of weak alignment, the green capital may be left to be fragmented or even symbolic (Sun et al., 2023). The model emphasizes that the interlinkages can be effective to create virtuous cycles where policy certainty will draw in investment, investment will draw in innovation and innovation will draw in sustainable growth. This is a systemic interaction that is necessary in the attainment of sustainable low-carbon development paths.

4.3 Sustainability & Inclusion

The main characteristic of the conceptual model is environmental sustainability and social inclusion integration into the investment pathways. Green capital is not only presented as a means towards reduction of emission, but also as a method towards distributional issues and social equity. Investment trajectories that involve social protection, local inclusion and local access to finance will be able to provide balanced development results. The model acknowledges that the low-carbon transitions may create imbalanced effects as long as social aspects are overlooked (Pyka & Nocoń, 2021). Green finance can assist in supporting SMEs, underserved areas, and vulnerable populations by incorporating criteria of inclusion into investment decision-making. Social and environmental goals are not considered as opposing but are complementary to each other (Ravikumar & Aarthi, 2025a). This combination improves the sustainability transition legitimacy and strength. The model therefore emphasizes the consideration of comprehensive investment directions that equate the environmental performance and inclusive development so that the green capital may be used to foster the development of broad-based and socially equitable growth

(Folqué et al., 2023). Table 2 shows the conceptual links between green financial instruments, governance structures and low-carbon growth and inclusive outcomes.

Table 2. Green Capital–Policy–Growth Mapping

Component	Key Elements	Functional Role	Expected Outcomes
Green Capital	Green bonds, blended finance	Mobilises sustainable investment	Capital redirection
Policy Frameworks	Taxonomies, disclosure rules	Reduces uncertainty and risk	Market confidence
Governance Structures	Standards, monitoring systems	Ensures accountability	Impact credibility
Growth Outcomes	Low-carbon sectors, inclusion	Structural transformation	Sustainable growth

5. RESEARCH METHODOLOGY

The research methodology, which was used in this chapter, is one that will assist in having a thorough and systematic examination of the green capital and its contribution to allow low-carbon and inclusive growth. The qualitative-dominant approach is used as a method of combining conceptual analysis with the empirical data presented in the recent case studies and secondary data sources. The methodology is in line with the objectives of the chapter as it enables the analysis of financial instruments, the conditions of governance and development outcomes in the real-life contexts. It focuses on the depth of analysis, as opposed to statistical generalization, which is adaptable to the subtle interpretation of non-uniform financial and institutional interactions (Tolliver et al., 2019). The perspective of interdisciplinary nature of the topic is also manifested in the methodological design as it combines the approaches of finance, economics, and public policy. The methodology and the triangulation of theoretical frameworks with evidence help to support the validity of the findings. Data constraints and contextual specificity are also considered in order to promote transparency. In general, the selected methodology can help conduct a strong investigation of green capital as a governance-based and systemic phenomenon.

5.1 Research Design and Analytical Approach

The study is based on a systematic qualitative analysis technique based on the synthesis of concepts and comparative case studies. The design will facilitate the investigation of the functioning of the green capital under varying institutional and policy environments. The analytical methodology is a mix of the deductive understanding based on the existing theories of sustainable finance and development economics and the inductive understanding based on the observations (Abhayawansa & Adams, 2022). The chapter uses a thematic analysis approach to find out the common patterns in the areas of investment mechanisms, governance structures, and growth impacts. It is an especially appropriate method of capturing the complexity and multidimensionality of green financial transitions. Instead of testing hypotheses, the design will produce analytical information explaining the way and reason why green capital can lead to structural transformation. This focus on interpretation enables a more comprehensive interpretation of the institutions interaction and policy accordance. This structure aids the aim of the chapter in promoting the idea of conceptual development and the basis on the factual experience.

5.2 Data & Case Selection

The chapter is based on one of the two main types of evidence, which is the use of secondary data, which includes policy reports, financial reporting, institutional reports, and peer-reviewed academic sources. Case studies are chosen according to their applicability in the realms of green capital implementation in low-carbon and inclusive development factors. The selection criteria include recency, institutional setting diversity and credible documentation. The cases are selected to represent various financing and governance structure and not to cover all of it exhaustively (Ogundipe et al., 2022). The purposive sample method is capable of providing comparative understanding of the functioning of green capitals in sectors and regions. Triangulation increases the strength of analysis owing to the multiple data sources used. Although secondary data is restricted to measuring results directly, one can synthesize validated evidence on authoritative sources. Evidence base therefore helps to provide an informed and context-sensitive analysis which is in tandem with the objectives of the chapter.

5.3 Framework & Limitations

The analytical framework incorporates the conceptual model and empirical evidence to understand the human relationship between the green capital, policy alignment, and outcomes of development. It emphasizes on three aspects that include financial mechanisms, conditions of governance and socio-economic impacts. The framework allows a systematic comparison of cases and allows sensitivity to variation in contexts (Eyo-Udo et al., 2024). But there are a number of limitations known. The qualitative study limitation is the inability to generalize the results on all the regions or financial systems. Interpretation may also be affected by inconsistency in data availability and reporting. Also, green policies on green finance are changing faster, and thus, some of the changes might not be entirely reflected (Nawaz et al., 2021). Nevertheless, in spite of these shortcomings, the framework offers a consistent guideline to the analytical process and allows making informative conclusions about the conditions enabling and obstacles hindering the implementation of green capital.

6. LITERATURE REVIEW

Literature on green finance and sustainable development indicates a growing agreement on the role of financial systems in the economic transformations of the low-carbon and inclusive growth. Initial research conceptualized finance as a neutral mediator, and little was done to emphasize the ecological or social consequences. Other more recent researches have refuted this perspective, with a focus on finance as an agent of structural change which affects production patterns, technological innovation, and distributional outcomes (Joshipura et al., 2025). The sources examined in this part correspond to the aims of the chapter because they incorporate the theoretical approach, the results of the research, and inclusion-focused studies. These strands combined underscore the change in view about green capital as a mechanism to change direction of growth, and not just mitigate the risk of environmental harm.

6.1 Theoretical Foundations

Theoretical contributions to green finance are largely based on sustainable development theory, institutional economics and political economy. These models highlight the interrelation of economic development, environmental restrictions and social welfare. The theory of green finance builds on the conventional models of finance by extending the impact of environmental externalities and long-term risk factors in the capital allocation decision (Asongu et al., 2025). The institutional strategies focus on the role played by the governance arrangements, norms and regulatory frameworks to the financial behavior. Green capital is seen as a product of institutional change under this view where the creation of values is redefined in terms of non-short-term profitability. According to development-based theories, the financial systems also must enable the change of the structure by allocating the finances to productive and socially adequate areas (Bylo, 2025). All these theoretical foundations allow seeing the concept of green finance as an intervention on a systematic level that is bound to enable the aligning of economic incentives with the sustainability process. They also emphasize the applicability of policy consistency and institutional capacity in making the financial markets so as to enable sustainable development results.

6.2 Empirical Evidence

Empirical research is building up in favor of the idea that the concept of green capital alters low-carbon changes, either by altering investment pattern or by altering technology utilization. The studies on the subject matter of green bonds and climate-oriented investing vehicles indicate that these kinds of instruments have the potential to inject massive amounts of capital into renewable energy, energy efficiency, and sustainable infrastructure. It is also implied that the green-labeled financial products can assist in reducing the cost of financing and attract long-term investors particularly where they have credible standards and transparency systems. The contribution of the public finance and development banks to the de-risking of the green investments and crowding in the private capital is also noted in empirical analyses (Parveen et al., 2025). There are, however, mixed findings on the magnitude of environmental impacts which represent differences in policy environment and quality implementation. It has been warned in some research that in the absence of sound monitoring and accountability; green capital can be limited in additionality. Altogether, the empirical body of literature upholds the potential of green finance in order to speed up the decarbonization process and highlights the significance of governance and institutional alignment. Table 3 Classifies the key green finance instruments (e.g. green bonds, blended finance) and associates them with environmental and social goals.

Table 3. Green Finance Instruments & Roles

Instrument	Primary Purpose	Target Sector	Developmental Contribution
Green Bonds	Capital mobilisation	Renewable energy, infrastructure	Emissions reduction
Green Loans	Sustainable lending	Industry, SMEs	Cleaner production
Blended Finance	Risk mitigation	Emerging economies	Private capital crowd-in
Carbon Markets	Emission pricing	Energy, manufacturing	Cost-efficient mitigation
Sustainability-Linked Finance	Performance incentives	Cross-sectoral	Corporate transition

6.3 Inclusive Growth Insights

The evidence of the literature on the topic of inclusive growth in the framework of sustainable investment highlights the necessity to consider the social aspects in green financial models. According to scholars, low-carbon transitions may increase inequalities when these impacts are not done in a distributional manner. Inclusive investment views recognize easy access to money, creation of employment opportunities and development of regions as fundamental elements of sustainable growth (Ewis & Ghanem, 2025). The studies of blended finance and impact investing show that financial instruments may be structured to promote social infrastructure, underserved communities, and small and medium enterprises. According to this literature, social inclusion will increase the legitimacy and sustainability of transitions in the sustainability. It also lays emphasis on the role of social protection and participatory measures in decision-making in investments (Osuji et al., 2025). Combining environmental aims and social results, inclusive growth views support the idea that green capital should pursue both climatic and equity issues.

7. CASE STUDIES

This section provides two of the recent case studies that demonstrate how green capital is being implemented to speed up low-carbon transitions as well as enhance outcomes of inclusion. The cases are chosen to represent two complementary sources of financing. The former is around renewable energy infrastructure where green bonds and associated sustainable instruments are able to mobilise large-scale amounts of money to clean generation capacity and transition benefits. The second example is that of blended finance in the emerging economies, as concessional donor resources and development finance platforms help minimize risk and to attract private investment, such as in projects with a gender and economic inclusion aspect (Lin et al., 2023). The cases, combined, explain why green capital effectiveness can be achieved; however, the quality of instruments, institutional credibility, and governance structures that facilitate the allocation of transparency and measurable impact are necessary. The analysis focuses on tangible performance metrics and percentage-based indicators which indicate scale, allocation quality and mobilisation efficiency after which a cross-case synthesis is made which outlines lessons transferable to policymakers, investors and financial intermediaries alike (Ravikumar & Aarthi, 2025b).

7.1 Case Study I: Renewable Energy Case

The most recent example can be seen in the green financing programme of Ørsted, which was reported in the document 2024 green finance impact reporting. In 2024, Ørsted invested DKK 14.3 billion of green bond proceeds in 14 renewable energy projects comprising of offshore wind, onshore wind and solar PV which acts as a direct conduit whereby the green labeled capital was used to deploy more clean capacities. According to the reporting, as of 2017, the total number of funded projects is 22 of renewable energy with 13 GW of renewable capacity and an estimated of 7.3 million tonnes of CO2e avoided in one year (4.4 million tonnes of which is estimated to be avoided through projects in operation and 2.9 million tonnes of which estimated to be avoided through projects under construction) (Taghizadeh-Hesary & Yoshino, 2020a). On the reported values this translates to about 60% of avoided emissions associated with the operation of operating projects and 40% associated with the projects under construction (calculated as 4.4/7.3 and 2.9/7.3). Another structural measure of capital reorientation is the outstanding green offerings of 88% of all the portfolio of bonds and hybrid capital of Ørsted, which indicates strong capacity to integrate the sustainable instruments in their long-term financing policy (Taghizadeh-Hesary & Yoshino, 2020b). Comparison of the annual CO2e avoided by the operating and under-construction renewable energy projects of Ørsted which would be financed by green bonds would be presented using Figure 3.

Figure 3. CO_2 Emissions Reduction (Ørsted)

7.2 Case Study II: Blended Finance Case

The most recent example of a blended finance where inclusivity development is possible is seen in the EBRD 2024 donor co-financing and blended investment activity. By 2024 concessional finance mixed with EBRD capital financed some €3.2 billion of combined investments almost 20% of the total volume of business that EBRD completed in the year which means significant scale rather than pilots. Notably, two-thirds (≈66%) of blended investments was defined as green finance, which supports the contribution of blended structures to the development of climate-aligned portfolios in transition and emerging environments. The mobilisation performance also provides emphasis on how blended finance can crowd in private capital: with blended donor funds mobilising €1.2 billion third party private capital, or 44% of the total mobilised by the Bank in 2024, the mobilisation of third-party private capital by the Bank (Chien et al., 2021). The leverage strength in concessional structuring is also reflected in efficiency metrics: €1 of EBRD capital and €5 of private capital mobilised by donors, which means that the rate of mobilisation ratio is 1:8 in the concerned transactions. The EBRD report also observes that blended investments had a greater relative share contributing to Gender and Economic Inclusion, which are indicators of climate finance deployment integration of inclusion priorities (Ravikumar et al., 2025). Table 4 Comparisons between the two case studies in terms of financing mechanism, sector focus, the scale of capital mobilization and percentage-based outcomes (Amolo Dr Amolo Elvis Juma, 2024). Figure 4 which points to the major figures of the 2024 blended finance of EBRD, such as the size of investment, green share, mobilisation of private capital, leverage ratio, and impact of inclusion.

Table 4. Case Study Comparison

Case Study	Financing Mechanism	Sector Focus	Key Percentage Indicators
Case I	Green bonds	Renewable energy	88% green issuances; ~60% operational emissions reduction
Case II	Blended finance	Emerging markets	~66% green share; 44% private capital mobilisation

Figure 4. Blended Finance Contributions to Inclusive Green Development (EBRD 2024)

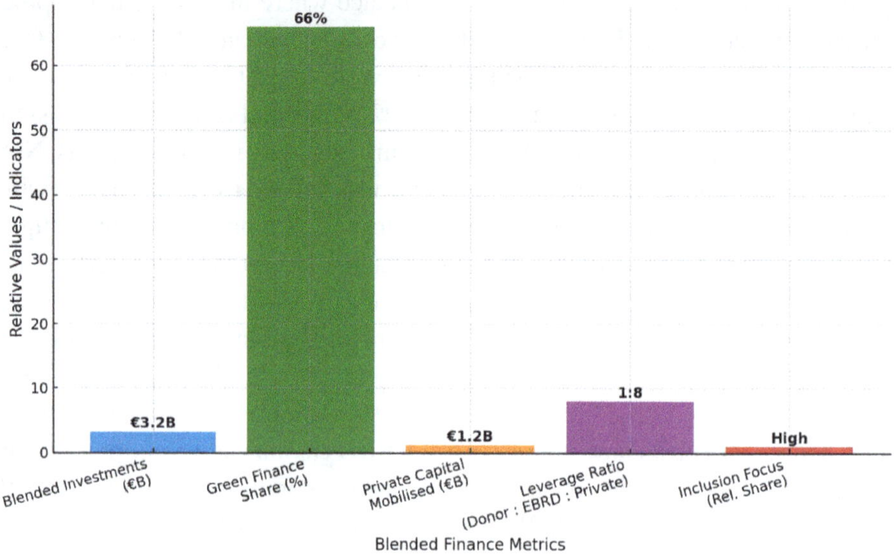

7.3 Cross-Case Analysis

In both instances, the effectiveness of green capital is demonstrated to be influenced by the instrument credibility, logic of clear allocation and measurable outcomes. It is shown in the renewable infrastructure case that sustainable financing integration is well-developed, with 88% of all outstanding issues in green form and measured transition impact indicators, and it can also be seen how impact can be phased across operating versus under-construction assets (about 60/40 based on reported emissions elements) (Aarthi et al., 2025). The case of blended finance indicates that Scale and mobilisation efficiency is indicated in the percentage values, such as the percentage contribution to the annual business volume at 20%, percentage of green share in the blended investments at 66%, and percentage contribution to total mobilisation of private capital at 44%, with a mobilisation ratio of 1:8 in applicable transactions (Ikevuje et al., 2024). Taken together, the indicators are that the low-carbon transitions pick up speed in case (i) capital is stuck in plausible structures, and (ii) inclusion targets are clearly integrated with an emphasis on focused implementation and compromising risk-sharing devices. Initially, Figure 5 compares the influential indicators of key cases Ørsted and EBRD, using the depth of green issuance, the distribution of the impact, the scale of mobilisation and the finance driven by inclusion.

Figure 5. Cross-Case Performance Comparison

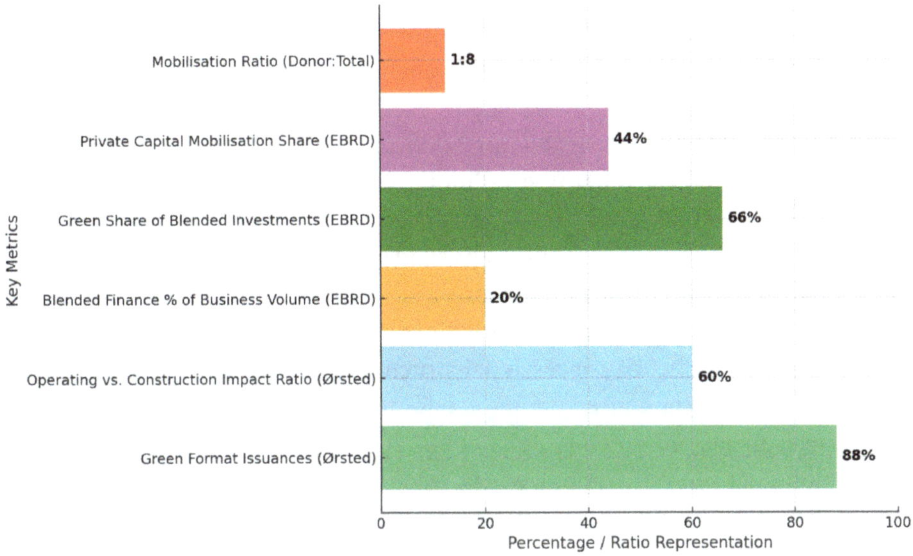

8. RESULTS AND DISCUSSION

Drawing on the conclusions made by the two case studies, the findings show that green capital is an effective tool of financial flows redirection, sector priorities restructuring, and sustainability entrenchment in long-term investment strategies. Practice in renewable energy financing and blended finance suggests that the inclusion of green capital in basic financing arrangements is most effective, not using it as a supplementary source of funds. The cases demonstrate the actual changes in the distribution of investments in low-carbon infrastructure and inclusive development with the help of the quantitative indicators of performance and well-established institutional frameworks (Dervi et al., 2022). Simultaneously, the results also indicate that the main ingredient of maintaining the investor confidence and the integrity of impact is governance, policy alignment, and transparency. Trade-offs and risks are also mentioned in the discussion like an unequal access to finance and the risk of dilution of sustainability objectives. In general, the findings indicate that the presence of green capital is significant in terms of structure changing in case accompanied by financial innovation and institutional capacity as well as strong accountability mechanisms.

8.1 Investment & Sector Impact

The case studies give good evidence of the idea that the green capital plays a significant role in the allocation of investments as well as boosting the process of sectoral transformation. The prevalence of the green-labeled instruments, which represent almost 90% of the outstanding bond and hybrid capital in the renewable energy case, shows that the shift to the traditional financing towards the sustainability-focused assets is definitive. The large-scale deployment of offshore wind, onshore wind, and solar infrastructural facilities was aided by capital allocation to facilitate its role in avoiding a significant number of emissions and reinforced the idea of renewable energy as a fundamental growth source. Equally, the blended finance case illustrates the effect of concessional structures in steering capital to climate-appropriate undertakings in emerging economies, of which about two-thirds of blended investments are green (Cunha et al., 2021). According to these patterns, green capital does not only mobilize new resources, but also restructures sectoral hierarchies to give priority to the low-carbon industries. These findings prove that systemic change in the sector takes place when the idea of green capital is built into the long-term financing strategies instead of confined to small or token projects.

8.2 Governance Effects

The quality of governance and institutional capacity prove to be the decisive force in determining the success of the deployment of green capital. The renewable energy example shows that transparency in reporting systems and well-stipulated criteria of eligibility makes the markets stronger in terms of credibility and investor confidence. The large proportion of are facilitated by standardized disclosure and impact monitoring. The policy congruency as well as institutional coordination in the blended finance case allows the process of risk-sharing among the donors, development banks, and private investors. The mobilisation ratios realised show how good governance structures are able to enhance the effect of scarce concessional resources. Nonetheless, the examples also prove that these results are conditional on the stable policy environments and clear sustainability taxonomies (Varsha., 2024). Capital flows grow fast where there is regulatory clarity; and investment choices are scattered when there is uncertainty. The results highlight the fact that the effectiveness of green capital cannot be completely independent of governance structures that achieve consistency, transparency and accountability within financial and policy systems.

8.3 Risks & Inclusion

Although the cases reflect positive effects of transition, they also expose trade-offs and risks of implementing green capital. The large-scale renewable investments are likely to only gather capitals in technologically developed industries which may be sidelining the small players who may lack mechanisms of being specifically targeted. This issue is only partially covered in the blended finance case because it directly incorporates gender and economic inclusion goals, which is manifested in the larger proportion of the projects targeting underserved populations. Information on mobilisation also suggests that inclusive results can even be accompanied by financial effectiveness in case concessional funds are planned to be used strategically. However, the risks of greenwashing, inequality of regional access, and reliance of government assistance can still be observed (Nizamuddin et al., 2024). The findings indicate that the inclusive growth outcomes do not occur automatically, but rather demand specific design particularities, such as the social protection and special financing windows. All the evidence suggests the overall idea that green capital is able to facilitate inclusive growth, though distributional effects must be proactively addressed with environmental objectives. Table 5 Summarizes the results on effects on investment location, sectoral change, the efficacy of governance, and the results of inclusion.

Table 5. Green Capital Impact Comparison

Impact Dimension	Case Study I	Case Study II
Investment Allocation	Large-scale renewable deployment	Climate and inclusion-focused projects
Sectoral Transformation	Energy transition leadership	Diversified low-carbon sectors
Governance Strength	High transparency standards	Strong donor–private coordination
Inclusion Outcomes	Indirect employment gains	Direct gender and SME inclusion

9. FUTURE RESEARCH DIRECTIONS

The changing nature of green finance offers numerous research opportunities in the future that go beyond the current boundaries of empirical and conceptual space. With the rapid intensification of financial innovation and the closer integration of sustainability goals into the economic policy, new concerns arise around the form, functionality, and consequences of green capital. Future studies should not focus on short-term measure of performance but rather study on systemic effects within the financial systems, financial institutions, and societies. The necessity to introduce technological change, digital finance, and data-driven governance in the analysis of sustainable investment is also growing (Yakovlev et al., 2019). Moreover, green capital distribution is unequal in the global world, with high discrepancies between regions and developmental conditions. In order to address such gaps, interdisciplinary solutions that would entail finance, economics, policy studies and social sciences should be adopted. The new trends, measurement, and local processes may be identified with the help of the future studies to contribute to more comprehensive and robust green finance systems. It is this type of work that is required so that the green capital can convert it into a transformative force capable of long-term low-carbon and inclusive development rather than being restricted in the limited financial markets.

9.1 Digital Green Finance

The financial technology has transformed the structure and availability of green capital extremely rapidly and this avails great research opportunities in future. In a bid to improve the transparency and traceability of green investment and efficiency, the application of digital finance platform, distributed ledger technologies, and data analytics is increased. The green bonds that are tied to sustainability, tokenized green assets, and automated reporting are new technologies that can reduce transaction costs and increase the involvement of investors (C. Fu et al., 2023). There is a need to conduct research to determine the impact of these technologies on risk assessment, mobilising capital and accessing the market, especially in small projects and developing economies. Simultaneously, as a result of digitalisation, there are new governance issues connected to the quality of data, cybersecurity, and regulatory control. This is especially important in assessing how technological innovation can improve inclusivity or strengthen existing inequalities in relation to digital finance and green capital (X. Wang et al., 2022). A further study should be conducted on how digital tools can be made compatible with sustainability principles and policy frameworks to contribute to plausible and scalable green finance ecosystems.

9.2 Impact Measurement

Another issue in the field of green finance studies is related to the measurement of long-term social and environmental impacts. The literature tends to use short term measures, like volumes of capital, number of issues issued or projected reductions. Though helpful, these measures do not bring much information about structural and distributional results. The future studies need to come up with effective ways of measuring the effects of long-term changes on livelihoods, development of the region, and resilience of the institutions (Devi, 2023). Project and community longitudinal studies can assist in determining whether green capital brings long-term benefits, or has unintended effects. A combination of qualitative and quantitative methods can be used to understand social inclusion better, the impacts of employment on individuals, and their adaptive capacity. Further, the harmonisation of the impact measurement frameworks across the jurisdictions is a researched field. To enhance the objectives of accountability and to make sure that the green capital is actually playing a significant role not only in the environmental sustainability but also in the inclusive growth, it is critical to advance the approaches to the impact evaluation.

9.3 Regional Research Gaps

Although there is an increasing interest in green finance in the rest of the world, much of the research is still missing on South–South and regional dynamics. The literature that is available is mostly on developed economies and there is minimal empirical evidence on the developing and emerging economies. The future research should focus on how regional institutions, development banks and cross-border initiatives influence the green capital flows in the Global South. Cross-regional comparative analysis can also help determine the impact of local policy settings, financial resources, and development priorities on the quality of investments (K. Wang et al., 2022). The mechanisms of South-South cooperation, such as regional green funds and platforms to share knowledge are the untapped spheres that can be utilized to achieve inclusive growth. The solution to these lapses needs to be context-sensitive research designs that take into consideration the institutional diversities and asymmetric development. The expansion of the geographic scope of green finance studies will help to build a more balanced and globally applicable knowledge, which will help to make transitions towards the alternative development paths more equitable.

10. MANAGERIAL IMPLICATIONS

The chapter has managerial implications of importance to participants throughout the green finance ecosystem such as investors, financial institutions, corporations, and decision-makers in the public sector. Increasing the green capital more firmly into mainstream finance, the decision-making of managers should adjust to new demands on risk assessment, performance measurement, and the long-term value creation. According to the evidence provided in the case, the successful implementation of the green capital is not based only on the financial innovation, but also on the strategic conformity with the sustainability goals and governance models (J. Fu & Ng, 2021). Managers are being asked to strike a balance between financial performance and environmental and social performance and this requires a higher sense of analytical skills and institutional coordination. In this section, the main managerial implications based on the empirical and conceptual analysis are outlined, and are focused on the role of strategic choices in determining the magnitude, credibility and influence of green investments. Managerial actors are key to ensuring sustainability commitments are translated into operational and investment choices that would ensure the contribution of green capital to low-carbon transitions and inclusive growth as opposed to being a symbolic or compliance-based activity.

10.1 Investor Strategy

Green capital requires investors and financial institutions to take a strategic step in the way they build their portfolios, risk and performance measurement. As the case studies show, the long-term investment in the green instruments may increase the stability of the capitals and help to adjust the strategies of investments to the new regulatory and market requirements. To consider transition and physical climatic risks, investors need to incorporate environmental and social needs in due diligence procedures and to exceed the conventional risk-return paradigms. Financial institutions also need to build internal capacity in the area of sustainability assessment and impact reporting (Mohanty et al., 2023). The uncertain situations are lessened because of strategic involvement with policy systems and sustainability norms. Additionally, those institutions which actively embrace the green financing strategies are in a better position to attract long-term capital and reduce reputational risks. The evidence indicates that the best ways of green capital strategies are through the core business models and not as a niche offering. This integration will help the institutions to facilitate systemic transition, as well as financially staying afloat.

10.2 Corporate Implications

With the case of corporations, when the saliency of green capital is increased, the image of sustainability and capital allocation decisions changes. The accessibility of green financing instruments provides a motivation to the firms to include sustainability objectives in the process of operational and investment planning. The example of green finance and renewable energy reveals that congruency in the corporate strategy and green finance systems have enabled the mass investment in the low-carbon assets. Corporates are being forced to demonstrate measurable environmental and social performance in order to be given preferential facilities to finance. This dynamics enhances long term planning, transparency and innovations in the production processes (Bouchmel and Omri, 2025). Managers must therefore incorporate the element of the sustainability in the critical decision-making platforms in which capital expenditure is conditioned to climate besides inclusion goals. Otherwise, it may result in rising the costs of funding or the restriction of access to capital. The findings indicate that green capital can reinforce corporate change where the sustainability pledges are questionable, quantifiable, and ambivalent in the governing and reporting systems.

10.3 Policy Implications

The conditions under which the mobilization and scaling of the green capital can be successfully achieved are highly dependent on the decision-makers in the sector of the public. The facts of the case also demonstrate the importance of unified policy frameworks, the brevity of regulations, and the believable sustainability taxonomies in alleviating risk in investment and attracting the private capital. Development institutions and governments can do a better job in developing policies that could be able to integrate climate objectives with inclusive growth issues. De-risking of investments in particular in emerging markets and investing in them with strategic application of public finance and public guarantees can be performed (Karumanchi, 2024). The policy makers are also expected to ensure that they possess robust monitoring and reporting systems that can keep off the greenwashing, and leave the people reassured. Governance entails the ability to bring about co-ordination among the ministries, the regulators, and the financial institutions in other words, not to have a divided approach. The findings suggest that the engagement of the long-term by the public sector is needed, to achieve both environmental and social change of scale on the green capital. Table 6 Implicates strategic implications of major findings to investors, corporations and decision-makers in the public sector.

Table 6. Managerial & Policy Implications

Stakeholder	Strategic Implication	Managerial Focus
Investors	Long-term portfolio alignment	ESG-integrated risk assessment
Financial Institutions	Product innovation	Impact reporting and governance
Corporations	Capital strategy redesign	Sustainability-linked investments
Policymakers	Market enabling	Regulatory clarity and de-risking

11. CONCLUSION

The chapter has discussed the concept of green capital as a transformational instrument which can redefine the financial systems, the orientation in the direction of low-carbon and inclusive growth in the focus of investment and development trends. By integrating the theoretical concepts with the fact on the ground cases, the discussion demonstrates that green capital is not restricted to a specific scope of financial instruments but rather it is a facilitator of structural and institutional change in a systemic manner. These findings allude to the reality that long-term performance can be achieved when the approach of institutionalizing green finance in the financing mechanisms, supported by realistic governance frameworks, and in the context of stable policy objectives. Blended finance projects show indications of renewable energy finance, how green capital can redirect investment into sector-level climate alignment, can attract investment at large scale and use inclusion targets where those design solutions are brought to mind.

In the meantime, the chapter points out that the environmental and social outcomes are neither the incidental ones nor those that do not need the transparency, accountability, and institutional capacity to deal with the trade-offs and ensure that the risks such as greenwashing and unfair access to finance are contained. It is also shown in the discussion that the transition is essentially a matter of coordination and governance, including the interaction of the players, both public and private, financial institutions and policy arenas. Green capital is best applicable where the long-term sustainability is achieved than the short run in monetary gain which increases resilience and legitimacy in the transition ways. Lastly, it is possible to add the chapter to the existing discussion regarding sustainable finance by repackaging green capital as a catalyst of inclusive and resilient development by mentioning that the redesign of financial systems is the heart of the issue of solving climate change and inequality in an increasingly unpredictable global space.

REFERENCES

Aarthi, S., Ravikumar, R. N., Sobirova, K., & Mamadiyarov, Z. (2025). Empowering a sustainable future through digital learning and the SDGs. In *Harnessing E-Learning to Create a Sustainable Future* (pp. 145–172). IGI Global Scientific Publishing., DOI: 10.4018/979-8-3373-0112-9.ch006

Abhayawansa, S., & Adams, C. (2022). Towards a conceptual framework for non-financial reporting inclusive of pandemic and climate risk reporting. *Meditari Accountancy Research*, *30*(3), 710–738. DOI: 10.1108/MEDAR-11-2020-1097

Amolo Dr Amolo Elvis Juma, P. (2024). Sustainable financing in infrastructure projects in Kenya. *International Journal of Research and Scientific Innovation*, *XI*(VIII), 597–601. DOI: 10.51244/IJRSI.2024.1108048

Asongu, S. A., Pondie-Messie, T., & Ewolo Bitoto, F. (2025). What role can alternative finance play in Africa's sustainable development trajectories? *Business Strategy & Development*, *8*(3), e70217. Advance online publication. DOI: 10.1002/bsd2.70217

Babar, Z. N., & Wu, W. (2025). Advancing green finance through FinTech innovations: A conceptual insight into opportunities and challenges. *Journal of Excellence in Management Sciences*, *4*(1). Advance online publication. DOI: 10.69565/jems.v4i1.404

Bouchmel, I., & Omri, A. (2025). From loss to investment: How environmental monetary losses influence green investment in Eastern European SMEs? *Corporate Social Responsibility and Environmental Management*, *32*(6), 7221–7234. DOI: 10.1002/csr.70086

Bylo, A. (2025). Assessing the impact of green finance on sustainability in emerging markets: Trends, challenges, and future prospects (2000–present). *International Scientific Journal Monte*, *10*(1). Advance online publication. DOI: 10.33807/monte.20253288

Chien, F., Chau, K. Y., Ady, S. U., Zhang, Y., Tran, Q. H., & Aldeehani, T. M. (2021). Does the combining effects of energy and consideration of financial development lead to environmental burden: Social perspective of energy finance? *Environmental Science and Pollution Research International*, *28*(30), 40957–40970. DOI: 10.1007/s11356-021-13423-6 PMID: 33772718

Cunha, F. A. F. de S., Meira, E., & Orsato, R. J. (2021). Sustainable finance and investment: Review and research agenda. *Business Strategy and the Environment*, *30*(8), 3821–3838. DOI: 10.1002/bse.2842

Dervi, U. D., Khan, A., Saba, I., Hassan, M. K., & Paltrinieri, A. (2022). Green and socially responsible finance: Past, present and future. *Managerial Finance*, *48*(8), 1250–1278. DOI: 10.1108/MF-11-2021-0561

Desalegn, G., & Tangl, A. (2022). Enhancing green finance for inclusive green growth: A systematic approach. *Sustainability (Basel)*, *14*(12), 7416. DOI: 10.3390/su14127416

Devender, Kafila, & Manoharan, G. (2025). Green finance for sustaining tomorrow. In *Legal and Regulatory Considerations of Leveraging Sustainable Finance* (pp. 135–152). IGI Global. DOI: 10.4018/979-8-3373-0350-5.ch006

Devi, D. S. (2023). Green finance: A way towards sustainable India. *Asian Journal of Management and Commerce*, *4*(2), 231–237. DOI: 10.22271/27084515.2023.v4.i2c.214

Edeminam, B., V., & Akpasoh, A. (2023). Climate finance landscape in Nigeria. *Resourceedings*, *3*(1), 13–21. DOI: 10.21625/resourceedings.v3i1.945

Ewis, H. F. M., & Ghanem, S. A. (2025). The economic implications of integrating green accounting practices in Middle Eastern financial institutions: Challenges and opportunities. *Edelweiss Applied Science and Technology*, *9*(3), 1299–1308. DOI: 10.55214/25768484.v9i3.5519

Eyo-Udo, N. L., Agho, M. O., Onukwulu, E. C., Sule, A. K., & Azubuike, C. (2024). Advances in green finance solutions for combating climate change and ensuring sustainability. *Gulf Journal of Advance Business Research*, *2*(6), 338–375. DOI: 10.51594/gjabr.v2i6.53

Flammer, C. (2020). Green bonds: Effectiveness and implications for public policy. *Environmental and Energy Policy and the Economy*, *1*, 95–128. DOI: 10.1086/706794

Fligstein, N., & Huang, J. Z. (2025). Finance in sustainable transition: A comparative review across institutional investors, asset managers, venture capital, insurance, and bonds. *Wiley Interdisciplinary Reviews: Climate Change*, *16*(4), e70012. Advance online publication. DOI: 10.1002/wcc.70012

Folqué, M., Escrig-Olmedo, E., & Corzo Santamaría, M. T. (2023). Contribution of sustainable investment to sustainable development within the framework of the SDGS: The role of the asset management industry. *Sustainability Accounting Management and Policy Journal*, *14*(5), 1075–1100. DOI: 10.1108/SAMPJ-01-2022-0044

Fu, C., Lu, L., & Pirabi, M. (2023). Advancing green finance: A review of sustainable development. *Digital Economy and Sustainable Development*, *1*(1), 20. Advance online publication. DOI: 10.1007/s44265-023-00020-3

Fu, J., & Ng, A. W. (2021). Scaling up renewable energy assets: Issuing green bond via structured public-private collaboration for managing risk in an emerging economy. *Energies, 14*(11), 3076. DOI: 10.3390/en14113076

Gambetta, N., Azcárate-Llanes, F., Sierra-García, L., & García-Benau, M. A. (2021). Financial institutions' risk profile and contribution to the Sustainable Development Goals. *Sustainability (Basel), 13*(14), 7738. DOI: 10.3390/su13147738

Ikevuje, A. H., Anaba, D. C., & Iheanyichukwu, U. T. Augusta Heavens IkevujeDavid Chinalu AnabaUche Thankgod Iheanyichukwu. (2024). Exploring sustainable finance mechanisms for green energy transition: A comprehensive review and analysis. *International Journal of Applied Research in Social Sciences, 6*(7), 1224–1247. DOI: 10.51594/ijarss.v6i7.1302

Joshipura, M., Nasrallah, N., & Kedia, N. (2025). Green and climate finance for sustainability: Hybrid review and framework development. *Business Strategy and the Environment, 34*(3), 3618–3634. DOI: 10.1002/bse.4173

Karumanchi, L. (2024). The role of green financing in accelerating sustainable economic development in emerging economies. *International Journal of Transformations in Business Management, 14*(3), 36–44. DOI: 10.37648/ijtbm.v14i03.004

Lin, Z., Liao, X., & Jia, H. (2023). Could green finance facilitate low-carbon transformation of power generation? Some evidence from China. *International Journal of Climate Change Strategies and Management, 15*(2), 141–158. DOI: 10.1108/IJCCSM-03-2022-0039

Luo, W., Tian, Z., Zhong, S., Lyu, Q., & Deng, M. (2022). Global evolution of research on sustainable finance from 2000 to 2021: A bibliometric analysis on WoS database. *Sustainability (Basel), 14*(15), 9435. DOI: 10.3390/su14159435

Madyan, M., & Widuri, S. K. (2023). Environmental, social, governance (ESG) performance and capital structure: The role of good corporate governance. *Jurnal Manajemen Teori Dan Terapan| Journal of Theory and Applied Management, 16*(3), 560–570. DOI: 10.20473/jmtt.v16i3.47483

Mohanty, S., Nanda, S. S., Soubhari, T. N. V., Biswal, S., & Patnaik, S. (2023). Emerging research trends in green finance: A bibliometric overview. *Journal of Risk and Financial Management, 16*(2), 108. DOI: 10.3390/jrfm16020108

Nagesh, K. C., & Siva Murugan, K. (2025). Fintech and sustainable finance: Impact of digital finance in promoting green investments. *MLAC Journal for Arts, Commerce and Sciences (m-JACS) ISSN: 2584-1920, 3*(1), 30–38. DOI: 10.59415/mjacs.v3i1.246

Nawaz, M. A., Seshadri, U., Kumar, P., Aqdas, R., Patwary, A. K., & Riaz, M. (2021). Nexus between green finance and climate change mitigation in N-11 and BRICS countries: Empirical estimation through difference in differences (DID) approach. *Environmental Science and Pollution Research International*, *28*(6), 6504–6519. DOI: 10.1007/s11356-020-10920-y PMID: 32997248

Nizamuddin, M., Mushir, N., & Thakur, M. (2024). Impact of environmental, social, and governance risk on the financial performance of selected Indian banks. *Educational Administration: Theory and Practice*, 6354–6364. DOI: 10.53555/kuey.v30i5.3944

Ogundipe, F., Sampson, E., Bakare, O. I., Oketola, O., & Yusuf, R. A. (2022). Technology for a sustainable future: Unlocking the power of digital transformation. *Journal of Frontiers in Multidisciplinary Research*, *3*(2), 146–156. DOI: 10.54660/.IJFMR.2022.3.2.146-156

Osuji, V. C., Okafor, C. M., & Dako, O. F.Vivian Chilee OsujiChizoba Michael OkaforOmoize Fatimetu Dako. (2025). Pioneering ESG-linked corporate finance programs to advance green finance, operational efficiency, and global sustainability goals. *Gulf Journal of Advance Business Research*, *3*(10), 1474–1494. DOI: 10.51594/gjabr.v3i10.169

Parveen, S., Coccorese, P., Umer, M., & Tahir, A. H. (2025). Synergizing financial inclusion and green finance: Advancing Sustainable Development Goals 2030 and 2050 in alignment with COP 29 commitments. *Sustainable Development (Bradford)*, *33*(S1), 48–76. DOI: 10.1002/sd.3553

Pyka, I., & Nocoń, A. (2021). Responsible lending policy of green investments in the energy sector in Poland. *Energies*, *14*(21), 7298. DOI: 10.3390/en14217298

Ravikumar, R. N., & Aarthi, S. (2025a). Artificial Intelligence and IoT integration in supply chains. In *Leveraging Technology and Renewable Energy for Sustainable Supply Chains* (pp. 1–32). IGI Global Scientific Publishing., DOI: 10.4018/979-8-3373-3790-6.ch001

Ravikumar, R. N., & Aarthi, S. (2025b). Integrated cross-border renewable energy infrastructure for a green transition. In *Cross-Border Cooperation in the Age of Climate Change* (pp. 301–332). IGI Global Scientific Publishing., DOI: 10.4018/979-8-3373-3972-6.ch011

Ravikumar, R. N., Aarthi, S., Pardaev, J., & Shukla, P. (2025). Quantum computing for financial modelling. In *Quantum-Driven Financial Intelligence* (pp. 221–252). IGI Global Scientific Publishing., DOI: 10.4018/979-8-3373-2893-5.ch010

Steckel, J. C., Jakob, M., Flachsland, C., Kornek, U., Lessmann, K., & Edenhofer, O. (2017). From climate finance toward sustainable development finance. *Wiley Interdisciplinary Reviews: Climate Change*, *8*(1), e437. DOI: 10.1002/wcc.437

Sun, X., Zhou, C., & Gan, Z. (2023). Green finance policy and ESG performance: Evidence from Chinese manufacturing firms. *Sustainability (Basel)*, *15*(8), 6781. DOI: 10.3390/su15086781

Swaty. (2023). Green finance and sustainable development: Exploring dynamic causal links and global implications. *E3S Web of Conferences*, *453*, 01053. DOI: 10.1051/e3sconf/202345301053

Taghizadeh-Hesary, F., & Yoshino, N. (2020a). Sustainable solutions for green financing and investment in renewable energy projects. *Energies*, *13*(4), 788. DOI: 10.3390/en13040788

Taghizadeh-Hesary, F., & Yoshino, N. (2020b). Sustainable solutions for green financing and investment in renewable energy projects. *Energies*, *13*(4), 788. DOI: 10.3390/en13040788

Tandan, P., Mishra, J., & Sarkar, S. (2025). FinTech and sustainable finance: Transforming traditional banking for a greener future. *International Journal of Economic Practices and Theories*, •••, 54–59. DOI: 10.52783/ijept.14

Teixeira, N. (2025). The evolution of sustainable investment: The role of decentralized finance and green bonds in the efficiency and transparency of green finance. *FinTech and Sustainable Innovation*, *1*, A1. Advance online publication. DOI: 10.47852/bonviewFSI52024817

Tolliver, C., Keeley, A. R., & Managi, S. (2019). Green bonds for the Paris agreement and sustainable development goals. *Environmental Research Letters*, *14*(6), 064009. DOI: 10.1088/1748-9326/ab1118

Varsha. (2024). Fintech and sustainable finance: A review of environmental, social, and governance (esg) integration. *Educational Administration: Theory and Practice*, 6816–6824. DOI: 10.53555/kuey.v30i5.4019

Wang, K., Elahi, E., Zhang, Y., Wang, D., & Khalid, Z. (2022). A development of green finance and regional Eco-efficiency in China. *Sustainability (Basel)*, *14*(22), 15206. DOI: 10.3390/su142215206

Wang, X., Elahi, E., & Khalid, Z. (2022). Do green finance policies foster environmental, social, and governance performance of corporate? *International Journal of Environmental Research and Public Health*, *19*(22), 14920. DOI: 10.3390/ijerph192214920 PMID: 36429642

Yakovlev, I. A., & Nikulina, S. I. (2019). Indonesia's strategy for sustainable finance. *Financial Journal*, *6*(6), 83–95. DOI: 10.31107/2075-1990-2019-6-83-95

KEY TERMS AND DEFINITIONS

Blended Finance: The strategic use of public or concessional funds to mobilize private investment for sustainable development projects.

Carbon Markets: Market-based systems that allow the trading of carbon credits to reduce overall greenhouse gas emissions.

Climate-Resilient Infrastructure: Infrastructure designed to withstand and adapt to climate-related risks and shocks.

Environmental, Social, and Governance (ESG) Criteria: Non-financial factors used to evaluate the sustainability and ethical impact of investments.

Green Bonds: Debt instruments issued to finance environmentally beneficial projects such as renewable energy or climate-resilient infrastructure.

Green Capital: Financial resources directed toward projects and activities that generate environmental benefits and support low-carbon development.

Green Loans: Loans whose proceeds are dedicated to sustainable or environmentally responsible activities.

Greenwashing: The practice of overstating or misrepresenting the environmental benefits of financial products or corporate activities.

Impact Measurement: Methods used to assess the environmental and social outcomes of investments.

Inclusive Growth: Development that ensures broad participation in economic benefits across regions, income groups, and social categories.

Institutional Capacity: The ability of organizations and governance systems to design, implement, and monitor effective policies and investments.

Low-Carbon Growth: Economic growth achieved with reduced greenhouse gas emissions and lower reliance on fossil fuels.

Sustainability Taxonomy: A classification system that defines which economic activities can be considered environmentally sustainable.

Sustainable Development Goals (SDGs): A set of global goals aimed at promoting economic prosperity, social inclusion, and environmental sustainability.

Sustainable Finance: Financial practices that integrate environmental, social, and governance considerations into investment and lending decisions.

Chapter 3
Sustainable Investing Across Borders:
Conceptual Comparison of SRI Frameworks in Domestic and Global Markets

Ambati Suvarna
http://orcid.org/0009-0007-1715-6713
SR University, India

Md Kafila
http://orcid.org/0009-0006-9443-6412
SR University, India

ABSTRACT

Socially Responsible Investment (SRI) has emerged as a key mechanism for aligning financial decision-making with environmental, social, and governance (ESG) objectives in a globalized economy. This chapter presents a conceptual comparison of SRI frameworks across domestic and global markets, drawing on stakeholder theory, institutional theory, and the triple bottom line approach. It examines how domestic SRI practices are shaped by national regulatory structures, cultural values, and market maturity, while global SRI is increasingly driven by institutional investors, standardized disclosure frameworks, and cross-border capital flows. The analysis highlights areas of convergence and divergence, along with challenges such as regulatory fragmentation, data inconsistencies, and implementation gaps. The chapter concludes by emphasizing adaptive harmonization strategies that balance global sustainability standards with domestic market realities to support inclusive and long-term sustainable development.

DOI: 10.4018/979-8-3373-7595-3.ch003

nt © 2027, IGI Global Scientific Publishing. Copying or distributing in print or electronic forms without written permission of IGI Global Scientific Publishing is prohibited. Use of this chapter to enerative artificial intelligence (AI) technologies is expressly prohibited. The publisher reserves all rights to license its use for generative AI training and machine learning model development.

1. INTRODUCTION

Sustainable finance is now a major force in the development of global capital markets as more and more investors, regulators, and banks recognize that the environment and society are going to be the main issues determining the long-term financial performance. The annual growth rate of SRI was doubling its size as per analysts' predictions in 2019, which brought the total to around $35.3 trillion, accounting for 36% of global professionally managed assets by 2020 (Keeley et al., 2022). The emerging prominence of Socially Responsible Investments (SRI) indicates that the financial sector is more open to integrating ethical considerations with its goals. The reasons for these differences are the need for a cross-national comparative analysis of the effects of the different institutional, cultural, and policy environments on sustainable investments. The case studies are also important for helping to align global sustainability standards and for companies to include ESG because SRI will be used in future financial systems that are strong, fair, and just (James & Quaglia, 2024).

Chapter Objectives

To scrutinize the fundamental theories behind SRI and highlight its significance in the process of sustainable economic development

To offer a systematic comparison of SRI frameworks in the domestic and global markets, examining the theoretical, institutional, regulatory, and practical aspects

To determine major challenges and opportunities that exist in the implementation of cross-border SRI in various economic and cultural settings.

To put forward an integrative conceptual framework that reconciles global sustainability standards and national market realities and draws policy implications.

To outline the future research directions that can be used to develop the area of cross-border sustainable investment.

2. THEORETICAL FOUNDATIONS OF SRI

This segment describes the most significant theoretical foundations on which SRI is based and how and why it is becoming increasingly relevant in contemporary financial marketplaces. It is based on the theory of stakeholders, institutional theory, and the triple bottom line theory, where the consideration of sustainability is incorporated in the process of making investment decisions in addition to profit maximization.

2.1 Core Theories Underpinning SRI

Several theoretical frameworks explain SRI, which explains the reason for investors and firms to include ESG factors in their financial decision-making processes. These theories are the basis for the understanding of SRI as an investment approach that is both value-driven and performance-oriented. Among others, stakeholder theory, institutional theory, and the triple bottom line framework are the most important in clarifying the manner in which ethical responsibility, regulatory pressures, and long-term sustainability objectives indirectly or directly influence responsible investment practices in both national and international markets.

2.1.1 Stakeholder Theory and Multi-Stakeholder Value Creation

The stakeholder theory is a solid foundation for SRI, as it advocates the creation of value for all stakeholders and not just for the shareholders. According to this theory, the relationships between employees, customers, suppliers, communities, and investors are mutual and co-creative, which makes it easier for companies to set up more sustainable business models (Freudenreich et al., 2020). By linking with CSR, the theory of SRI supports the firms' process of dealing with the diverse stakeholder interests, which in turn improves reputation, accountability, and long-term performance. Besides, current research points out that stakeholder engagement results in better organizational learning and innovation, which are the drivers of sustainable value creation (Alshukri et al., 2024). Therefore, at its core, the stakeholder approach views SRI as a method for governing holistically and creating shared value. Therefore, stakeholder theory provides a conceptual basis for ESG investing because ESG factors reflect the interests and welfare of different stakeholder groups.

2.1.2 Institutional Theory and Organizational Legitimacy

The institutional theory describes the manner in which organizations embrace socially responsible behaviors to achieve the right to legitimacy in their cultural and regulatory as well as normative settings. Organizations tend to participate in CSR and sustainability activities to match societal values and ensure the necessary resources and expectations are created by institutions (Fisher et al., 2024). With the development of institutional norms, organizations have to modify their strategies to continue to be legitimate, which manifests as organizational responses that are compliant or the development of institutional logics that are strategically manipulated. Coercive, mimetic, and normative pressures form institutional isomorphism, which further pushes organizations to practice similar sustainability so that they can be acceptable in their competitive environment (Zhou et al., 2021). According to this framework, one of the key reasons that organizations embark on SRI activities is for the sake of legitimacy and hence survival. While institutional theory explains how organizations globally have adopted ESG practices as they attempt to comply with legal requirements (law) and maintain their legitimacy, ESG investing will continue to grow globally at a rapid pace.

2.1.3 Triple Bottom Line: People, Planet, Profit

The Triple Bottom Line (TBL) is a concept that radically transforms the criteria for the success of business companies by adding social and environmental effects to the mix besides the financial outcomes. A couple of recent research papers reveal the intricate interconnections among the three aspects: though economic and social measures might have a positive impact on the value of the organization, the shortcomings in the environment might make the public perceive the company negatively and thus affect the consumer and firm performance negatively (Nichols et al., 2023). The transition of TBL into an interdisciplinary sustainability tool reflects its increasing importance in such areas as ethical accountability, practices in the circular economy, and life-cycle thinking (Nica et al., 2025). Besides this, empirical evidence points out that not only do the green capabilities and responsible purchasing practices bolster the environmental and overall TBL performance (Khan et al., 2023), but also that economic sustainability is a key factor for the long-term survival of businesses (Nogueira et al., 2024). All in all, TBL is a comprehensive framework that leads SRI to achieve a fair distribution of benefits among people, planet, and profit. The TBL framework directly supports ESG investing, as ESG indicators correspond to economic, social, and environmental dimensions of sustainability.

2.1.4 Integration of Theoretical Perspectives

The study of SRI requires an integrated understanding of stakeholder theory, institutional theory, and the TBL framework. Stakeholder theory gives the rationale related to the consideration of various stakeholders' interests, i.e., investors, employees, and society, when making investment decisions. The components of institutional theory include regulatory pressure and social expectations, together with established norms of conduct. The TBL framework gives organizations a three-dimensional assessment method to evaluate their sustainability performance.

The combination of these theories forms a complete system of understanding. The system describes how stakeholder expectations and institutional pressures, together with sustainability metrics, create pressure that drives SRI practices to achieve their financial and sustainable development goals.

2.2 Evolution of SRI Concepts

The idea of SRI has passed through the ethical exclusionary screening and has been transformed into a more sophisticated investment strategy merging the ESG factors, impact investment, and alignment with sustainable development objectives.

2.2.1 From Ethical Exclusion to Positive Screening

Socially Responsible Investing, in its infancy, dealt with ethical and religious exclusions that removed certain sectors like tobacco, gambling, and arms from the portfolios so that the investment would be in accordance with the moral values (Martini, 2021). The exclusionary practices, however, gradually gained momentum from the global divestment movements, such as anti-apartheid campaigns, which reflected the role of SRI in dealing with social and political issues (Busch et al., 2021). The negative exclusion approach ultimately turned into a positive screening where investors were taking an active role in choosing companies with high ESG standards (Acar, 2024). Over time, exclusionary screening evolved into ESG integration, where investors systematically include ESG factors in investment decisions.

2.2.2 Impact Investing and Sustainable Development Goals (SDGs)

The ESG integration, on the one hand, is to make the assessment of sustainability risks a part of the investment decisions, while, on the other hand, impact investing is a completely different notion that is mindful and aimed at producing positive and measurable social and environmental outcomes. The research has proved that the companies with superior ESG practices are the major ones contributing to the SDG attainment, and the factor is the organizational effectiveness (Ye et al., 2023). Investor inclinations, especially for UHNWIs, are normally directed towards SDGs that promise high financial returns, which suggests the necessity of maintaining the impact-profitability ratio even for the least preferred SDGs (Paetzold et al., 2022). New technological advancements, especially in finance, such as blockchain and big data, can be perceived as slowly but surely opening very promising paths for not only the reinforcement of but also the growth of SDG financing and the cooperation among various sectors. The sustainable finance and SDGs alignment emphasizes the necessity for coherent strategies, public-private partnerships, and transparent governance that will surely lead to maximizing the development impact (Yelnikova & Kwilinski, 2020).

3. LITERATURE REVIEW

The literature on SRI has developed three central debates. They are financial performance outcomes, portfolio construction strategies, and institutional–geographic influences. Even though the research has grown quickly during the last few years, the results remain incomplete because they depend on specific situations

3.1 Financial Performance Debate

The empirical evidence on the performance of SRI in comparison with traditional investment strategies is divergent. Some cross-national studies do not identify statistically significant differences in performance between SRI and conventional funds, suggesting performance neutrality, while other studies document SRI's inferior performance rankings compared to that of conventional funds, particularly in certain European and Asia-Pacific markets. Authors attribute lower SRI returns to two main causes. They are (1) SRI has restricted diversification opportunities, which results in lower risk-adjusted returns, and (2) SRI incurs higher transaction costs due to investment screening requirements (Ivanisevic Hernaus et al., 2023). The inconsistent performance of SRI fund managers suggests the performance of SRI should not solely be determined by ethical considerations; rather, the performance of SRIs may vary by market maturity, geographical diversification, time horizon, and fund strategy. Thus, the controversy around the performance of SRI funds likely reflects structural differences, and there is no clear financial answer to the performance of SRI funds as compared to conventional investment strategies.

3.2 Screening Strategies and ESG Integration

There is a second variety of literature that investigates the impact of screening techniques on risk and return efficiencies. The dominant view in traditional modern portfolio theory is that negative screening decreases the ability to diversify and therefore results in decreased performance. There is some evidence to support this theory in yesterday's world marketplace. Studies comparing the performance of negative versus positive screened portfolios report little statistically measurable difference in risk-adjusted returns (Ivanisevic Hernaus et al., 2023) between the types of portfolios.

Firms with good ESG performance generally obtain greater inflows from investors and receive greater premiums for their firms (Lingnau et al., 2022). However, "warm glow" investors (i.e., people who invest because it feels good to do so) are willing to accept lower rates of return to achieve their ethical satisfaction through the act of investing (Kabderian Dreyer et al., 2023).

3.3 Institutional and Geographic Influences

The research conducted in recent years has increasingly drawn attention to how SRI outcomes are shaped by institutional context. For example, it's clear from the data gathered to date that there are three major components that impact the amount of ESG integration and capital allocated to SRI. They are regulatory strength, quality of disclosure, and level of investor protection. Stronger mandatory reporting frameworks lead to greater congruence between firms' ESG practices and financial performance than do voluntary regimes, which run the risk of being merely symbolically compliant.

Bibliometric research supports this point by demonstrating that the majority of research on sustainable finance is done in developed economies, while emerging economies continue to have significant constraints (e.g., poor data, fragmented regulations, and weak enforcement) (Keser, 2025; Narayanan & Pradhan, 2023).

While there is a significant amount of empirical research focused on performance and disclosure, very few studies have integrated both institutional and cross-border dimensions into a single comparative research framework. Most studies focus on fund performance or the regulatory framework alone. Therefore, the lack of an integrated framework suggests that our understanding of the interaction of SRI systems in both the domestic and international arenas remains limited.

3.4 Synthesized Research Gap

The literature in this chapter reveals three tensions. They are

Performance Tension, which emerges from inconsistent performance findings
Screening Tension, which emerges from inconclusive screening effects,
Institutional Tension, which emerges from the institutional fragmentation that exists between different markets.

However, there remains limited conceptual work comparing domestic and global SRI frameworks within a structured integrative model.

3.5 Contribution of the Chapter

This chapter makes three main contributions to the literature on SRI. The first contribution establishes a systematic framework that compares domestic SRI frameworks and global SRI frameworks through their regulatory requirements, institutional structures, and market conditions. The chapter introduces an integrative framework that shows how global sustainability standards need to be modified for specific domestic market conditions. The chapter presents implementation gaps that exist between global ESG standards and actual market practices at local levels while offering solutions for adaptive harmonization. These contributions help improve understanding of cross-border sustainable investment systems. Having identified gaps in existing SRI literature, the next section examines how these principles operate within domestic market contexts.

4. SRI IN DOMESTIC MARKETS: CONTEXT-SPECIFIC FRAMEWORKS

As SRI principles continue to expand globally, it becomes increasingly important to determine how these frameworks apply in various domestic markets, particularly emerging markets (Danila, 2022). The various domestic markets in question usually have different socio-economic and regulatory environments, leading to differences in how ESG factors are incorporated into decision-making processes in terms of investment (Aggarwal, 2025; Jonwall et al, 2023). For example, India's development of ESG-focused mutual funds has grown slowly but steadily, indicating a general shift by investors towards sustainable finance, as evidenced by the strong performance of India's ESG-focused funds when compared to other countries' mutual funds, such as those available in developed markets (Priya & Sharma, 2024). Growing public awareness of ESG-related issues and the increasing application of ESG strategies by institutional investors are two of the key drivers behind the rapid rise in demand for sustainable investment products (Dutta & Paul, 2023).

4.1 Characteristics of Domestic SRI Markets

ESG factors in domestic SRI markets are integrated differently based on things like national regulations, cultural norms, and market maturity. National regulatory systems and government interventions significantly influence domestic SRI markets and therefore affect CSR and sustainability practices within companies. Additionally, the regulatory settings are a determining factor in the stepping-up and encroachment of the ethical investment strategies such as SRI, ESG investing, and impact investing, especially when the markets are striving for financial stability and at the same time putting up good practices for sustainable investment (Nartey, 2024; Matser et al., 2023).

Cultural norms and societal values significantly determine the path to responsible investing in domestic markets. Nations with considerable wealth and particular cultural traits similar to those identified by Hofstede or World Values Survey dimensions usually develop a more powerful responsible investing environment (Bialkowski et al., 2025). Finland's sustainability-centered culture backed by strong institutional systems is a major factor for the rise of socially responsible investing in the Nordic areas (Buchanan et al., 2024). Additionally, it is found that mutual funds in markets with high social capital are likely to take ESG matters into account more so, especially when they are investing internationally (Choy et al., 2023). In the case of emerging markets, along with the behavioral finance dynamics, cultural values heavily affect the ESG investment flows, thus influencing the retail and institutional investor behavior alike (Adwani, 2025; Jonwall et al., 2023).

The domestic market's maturity and institutional capacity are key factors influencing SRI's development. In the past, North America and Europe have been the main regions for SRI, though to a certain extent, emerging markets are able to catch up with developed economies regarding their ESG practices (Danila, 2022). In addition, during the early 2000s, there was an increase in the strength of the global SRI infrastructure through the development of ethical indices and more impact-driven financial products (Kiliç et al., 2022).

4.2 Regional Variations in Domestic SRI

There is a lot of diversity among domestic socially responsible investment practices worldwide, as many factors affect them, such as the country or region of the world, the level of economic development, the level of regulation, the types of institutions present, and the prevailing cultural values. These differences will shape how SRI are adopted, their size, and their effectiveness both in developed countries and emerging countries.

4.2.1 Developed Market Approaches

Market regions that have been developed show very strong and very different SRI practices. Europe continues to be the world leader in SRI and is backed by very strict sustainability regulations, thus forcing ESG integration, engagement, and transparency (Shah, 2024). In such a way, North America, particularly the U.S., has witnessed a rapid growth of SRI; however, the past has shown that the U.S. SRI was mainly unregulated and driven by voluntary initiatives. In Australia, the SRI had a similar thing happening, only from a different perspective; institutional investors are responding to climate-related financial risks and the subsequent demand for more sustainable investing (Tuncay & Dorjnaran, 2023). Also the benchmark indices, Dow Jones Sustainability Index, FTSE4Good, and Calvert Social Index, have had a big impact on reinforcing SRI evaluation and academic interest in these regions of the world (Biktimirov & Afego, 2022).

4.2.2 Emerging Market Practices

SRI is becoming more and more popular in the emerging market regions as a way of solving and managing issues related to the environment, poverty, and development (Danila, 2022; Linnenluecke, 2022). The region's ESG investment decisions get a big influence from behavioral factors like herding, loss aversion, and social norms (Adwani, 2025). The adoption of ESG products in these markets can be pan-reactive; however, the markets offer great potential based on factors like rapid urbanization and environmental concerns (Akala et al., 2022). Africa, Latin America, and the Middle East are regions with high ESG product potential, as the investor's awareness of risk and return advantages through ESG integration is increasing (Kouam, 2025). The worldwide growth in ESG assets, with the U.S. ESG assets increasing by 42% from 2018 to 2020, is one of the trends that is being increasingly reflected in the emerging markets (Danila, 2022).

4.3 Domestic Market Drivers and Barriers

The development of socially responsible investments in local markets is being driven by a mix of positive factors and negative ones, such as government rules, corporate governance, quality of regulation, investor education, and ease of access to trustworthy ESG data. The interaction of these factors will affect the extent, trustworthiness, and efficiency of the SRI systems in different countries.

The government regulations are the main factors that control the course of SRI markets in countries by certifying transparency, accountability, and compliance with ESG standards. Some of the main policy measures, like the mandatory sustainability report, setting the minimum requirements for ESG, and labeling the SRI products, are the ones that improve information quality and minimize greenwashing, thus building up trust among investors (Gorski & Ranf, 2024; Pasquino & Lucarelli, 2025). Moreover, government support is in the form of tax incentives, green procurement, and risk-sharing measures like guarantees or subordinated financing, which make the green and social projects more attractive (Yadav et al., 2023).

Corporate governance is an adoption enabler and a barrier at the same time for SRI. The positive traits of strong governance, such as board diversity, anti-corruption measures, and the like, coupled with reporting transparency, increase accountability and make corporate strategies congruent with ESG goals, which in turn leads to the enhancement of firm value and investor trust (Chang et al., 2022). The activities of investors and NGOs are becoming powerful enough to dictate the change in governance practices, as they are the ones who are indirectly calling for companies to act ethically and to be sustainable for the long term. On the other hand, factors such as pressure for short-term profits and the maze of complicated regulations are some of the reasons that domestic governance systems in support of SRI are not effective (Emeka-Okoli et al., 2024).

Investor awareness is a significant factor that drives the growth of SRI in the domestic market, and the reasons for this are not only financial performance. Altruism, innovation preference, status signaling, and future-oriented values are some of the socio-psychological factors that influence the investors' choice of socially responsible investment (Garg et al., 2022). The investor demand for sustainability-related attributes has led to an increase in the supply of SRI products, but the markets still have to tackle the challenges of information clarity and ESG literacy, which are crucial in enabling effective participation.

Data availability and disclosure practices continue to be vital for the domestic SRI markets to work properly. The developing methods for assessing responsibility, mainly in the start-ups and early-stage firms, are making the ESG disclosure consistent and are consequently helping the investors to make their choices more informed (Ryan et al., 2024). Gradually, these methods are also leading to more transparency, less information monopoly, and even more trust from investors, particularly in the markets where the formal sustainability reporting infrastructures are still in the development stage.

5. SRI IN GLOBAL MARKETS: TOWARD HARMONISATION

While domestic markets shape the local implementation of SRI, global markets play an important role in promoting cross-border sustainable investment. The global markets' socially responsible investment functioning is the object of investigation in this part of the study, putting emphasis on the inter-country interaction, the international norms, and the impact of the institutional investors.

5.1 Global SRI Landscape

The global SRI landscape is primarily driven by international capital flows and increasing investor demand for the integration of ESG factors.

5.1.1 Cross-Border Capital Flows and Sustainable Investment

Capital moving across national borders plays a big role in attracting money for sustainable development. Funds raised through foreign direct investments (FDI), portfolio investments, and the construction of new sustainable infrastructure provide the basis for these investments. However, because of inconsistencies in the environmental standards that different countries use for measuring sustainability and the different reporting requirements that they impose, this will make it very difficult for money to flow across borders without impediments. To address these barriers, the international community is increasingly relying on various strategies, such as the use of regulatory sandboxes to test new ideas, establishing bilateral agreements on sustainability, and aligning ESG trade requirements for partial harmonization. These flexible policy approaches not only will facilitate the growth of global socially responsible investing but also will provide smooth capital flows for sustainability, in turn upholding national policy autonomy (Hovde Group, Charlotte, North Carolina, USA et al., 2025).

5.1.2 International Investor Expectations and Standards

International investors are increasingly relying on the consistency, credibility, and comparability of the ESG disclosures of multinational enterprises as they allocate capital across different countries. This has put pressure on institutional investors to help companies eliminate disparities in the information they provide in order to create a more accurate basis for making investment decisions by having sustainability reports aligned with the standards of agencies such as the ISSB, TCFD, and GRI. Because of the lack of consistent ESG metrics, the variety of reporting frameworks, and the inconsistent application of the concept of materiality across different countries, international investors will continue to increase the cost of conducting transactions and diminish access to sustainability investments across borders. The pressure will continue to be placed on companies and their regulators by international investors to shift toward a more blended disclosure practice and open governance structures, while providing third-party verified sustainability data that will support the convergence of socially responsible investment standards globally and impact global market capital allocation.

5.1.3 Role of Multinational Corporations and Global Portfolios

Multinational corporations and international investment portfolios have a big part to play in spreading SRI worldwide. In the process of dealing with different regulations, MNCs are adopting more and more ESG (Environmental, Social, and Governance) considerations in their risk management and financial practices simply as a way of being transparent, complying with the rules, and being more efficient in capital use. MNCs and international portfolios function as the main routes for the unifying of international capital movements with sustainability goals and gradually changing investor expectations on a global scale (Abiola-Adams et al., 2025; Zhao, 2024).

5.2 International Frameworks and Initiatives

The international frameworks and initiatives turn out to be the most effective means of constantly promoting SRI through ESG, transparency, and cross-border investment practices that are all socially responsible. Reporting standards and principles of investment support global comparison and reduce the gap between the investor's knowledge and the market, thus making it easier for the sustainability goals to be met by investors worldwide.

5.2.1 UN Principles for Responsible Investment (PRI)

The UN PRI has played an essential role in responsible investment development by urging institutional investors to integrate ESG and practice active ownership. Still, the empirical evidence makes the extent of its impact questionable. Research reveals that although PRI signatories receive more fund inflows, many, especially U.S. mutual funds and hedge funds, do not show any significant improvements in either ESG performance or risk-adjusted returns, pointing to possible symbolic adoption or greenwashing (Kim & Yoon, 2023). ESG integration seems to be more robust among the early and non-U.S. signatories, whereas the later ones often show a weaker commitment, thus raising a concern about free-riding during the PRI period (Bauckloh et al., 2023). On the other hand, PRI partnership boosts the engagement of shareholders, for instance, by more significant support for ESG proposals and better climate-related disclosures, particularly in engagement-driven markets like Japan (Azuma & Higashida, 2024).

5.2.2 Global Reporting Initiative (GRI) and Sustainability Reporting

The Global Reporting Initiative (GRI) is still the most widely accepted framework for sustainability reporting, mainly due to the adoption of institutional diffusion and firms seeking legitimacy. Empirical research reveals that companies following GRI guidelines have better credibility of their disclosures and valuation, especially in developing countries like India (Jain et al., 2022; Sreepriya et al., 2023). Conversely, in China, the GRI report sometimes indicates the government's or regulator's preferences instead of real stakeholder involvement (Xu et al., 2024). Even though GRI's multi-stakeholder approach makes it different from investor-centered frameworks like ISSB standards, its market value relevance is determined by both the firm's CSR performance and the institutional context (de Villiers et al., 2022; Jeriji et al., 2023).

5.2.3 International Sustainability Standards and Taxonomies

The global markets for SRI have been assisted by international sustainability standards and taxonomies, which have been harmonizing ESG disclosures and cutting down greenwashing. The frameworks like the Task Force on Climate-related Financial Disclosures (TCFD) and the International Sustainability Standards Board (ISSB) under the International Financial Reporting Standards (IFRS) Foundation have made it easier for the companies to communicate their climate-related risks and sustainability practices to the investors, thus boosting the cross-country comparability (de Villiers et al., 2022). The European Union's Sustainable Finance Taxonomy, on the other hand, continues to be a major force in the direction of making capital investment in the environmentally sustainable sector. Nevertheless, the problems of data quality, measurement, and verification still persist; thus, it is suggested that there should be more convergence and mandatory impact-based financial reporting to clearly show that global investments are in line with the Paris Agreement and the UN Sustainable Development Goals (Ngo et al., 2022).

5.3 Global Market Enablers

Global market facilitators, including institutional investors, asset managers, stock exchanges, and international partnerships, are the ones that primarily support the SRI growth by advocating ESG integration and openness. These participants, through their different approaches like active ownership, ESG listing conditions, and knowledge sharing across borders, help in the merging of sustainable investment practices across different markets around the world.

5.3.1 Institutional Investors as Change Agents

By controlling the capital flow into SRI, institutional investors and asset managers can play an important role in the worldwide proliferation of SRI. Large amounts of capital, coupled with a desire to partner with businesses over time, can compel managers to incorporate ESG considerations into investment decisions and risk management. These investors, by way of active ownership, such as shareholder engagement and proxy voting, support better ESG reporting and adoption of sustainability practices in companies. Besides that, sticking to universally accepted responsible investment principles helps bring together the SRI frameworks of different countries and the world. By insisting on consistent ESG disclosures from companies that operate in different countries, the large investors not only mitigate the problem of differing regulations but also contribute towards the creation of uniform SRI standards.

5.3.2 Stock Exchanges and ESG Listing Requirements

By incorporating ESG factors into listing and disclosure requirements, stock exchanges turn out to be very important facilitators of the global market since they increase the transparency of the market and make the financial and sustainability goals more compatible. One example is the Australian Securities Exchange (ASX), which uses an "if not, why not" strategy for the disclosure of ESG risks; thus, it requires companies to say whether they are complying with the rule or to provide an explanation if they are not complying, especially in the case of companies in resource-intensive sectors (Lokuwaduge & Silva, 2020). Research carried out in the Southeast Asian markets indicates that better ESG performance leads to less information asymmetry and thus supports financial decision-making that is more efficient and confirms the trend towards the adoption of the international SRI standards in the domestic market (Adeneye et al., 2023).

5.3.3 International Collaboration and Knowledge Transfer

As a result, this phenomenon becomes more and more significant since the power to turn knowledge into innovation and commercial outcomes determines the rank of countries in the global arena (Emamian et al., 2023). Scientific and technological collaborative networks that gain governmental support are opening up new routes for knowledge transfer and R&D investment by connecting innovators from different parts of the world (Pepe et al., 2024). So, the above-mentioned support not only helps in the spread of various kinds of knowledge but also assists in making academic research accessible to consumer markets, thus making regions more competitive in the market (Ruiz et al., 2023; Pialli, 2023; Lusha, 2024). Efficient commercialization also demands understanding of the market dynamics, as well as strategic coordination across the different arenas, in addition to the technical skills (Rossoni et al., 2024). Having examined global SRI frameworks and cross-border investment dynamics, the next section presents a comparative analysis of domestic and global SRI frameworks.

6. COMPARATIVE ANALYSIS OF DOMESTIC AND GLOBAL SRI FRAMEWORKS

Table 1. Conceptual Framework: Domestic vs Global SRI

Dimension	Domestic SRI	Global SRI
Primary Focus	National sustainability priorities	Cross-border comparability and scalability
Key Drivers	Government regulation and policy mandates	Institutional investors and global standards
Regulatory Nature	Country-specific, evolving frameworks	Increasingly harmonized international regimes
ESG Disclosure	Mostly voluntary or semi-mandatory	Largely standardized and mandatory
Materiality Approach	Financial materiality	Double materiality (financial + impact)
Investor Base	Retail and domestic institutions	Global institutional investors
Market Maturity	Emerging to moderate	Highly developed and institutionalized
Strategic Orientation	Compliance-driven ESG adoption	Value-creation and risk-management driven
Integration Outcome	Alignment with domestic goals	Harmonization of global sustainability norms

Table 1 brings to light the main conceptual differences between the domestic and global SRI frameworks. Domestic SRI is mainly driven by the regulatory priorities of each country and the level of market development, whereas global SRI gives more importance to standardization, the power of institutional investors, and the ability to compare across borders. The divergence in approaches highlights the necessity of an adaptive harmonization that is able to integrate sustainability goals across the different markets in an efficient manner.

Beyond the difference in concept, the way SRI frameworks work in domestic and global markets. Global SRIs tend to perform better in terms of integrating environmental, social, and governance (ESG) because there is a standardized disclosure system, greater institutional investor participation, and increased transparency and ability to compare sustainability performance across different countries through ESG reporting from companies.

On the other hand, domestic SRI frameworks can vary due to many different factors, including country regulations, as well as the maturity of the financial markets within each country. Example: A developing country could have an SRI framework that is not as well-formed as their peers due to the lack of development, or not enough time has passed since they were formed, but still have better alignment with local ESGs. This would cause the domestic SRI framework to address local ES&S challenges, while compared on a global scale, it is limited.

Both of these differences provide evidence that global SRI frameworks and local SRI frameworks cannot stand on their own. Effective SRI investment systems must have both global standards and local adaptation.

In practice, domestic and global SRI frameworks do not operate independently but interact continuously through regulatory alignment, cross-border investment flows, and the influence of institutional investors. Global sustainability standards provide common benchmarks that guide responsible investment practices, while domestic markets adapt these standards according to local institutional and economic conditions. At the same time, innovations and policy developments in domestic markets can influence the evolution of global sustainable finance frameworks. This interaction creates a dynamic system in which global sustainability objectives are implemented through locally adapted investment practices.

6.1 Framework Implementation Process

The proposed framework has three phases. The first phase is to assess the domestic SRI conditions, like the regulatory environment, market maturity, and investor behavior. The second phase is to assess the international SRI standards to determine how they differ from and are similar to those developed internationally. Lastly, adaptive strategies will be developed that will allow for the alignment of the total global SRI standards to the markets of the country in which they are implemented. The use of this phased approach will facilitate effective cross-border sustainable investment.

6.2 Conceptual Convergences

Both domestic and international SRI frameworks display a significant degree of conceptual similarity despite the dissimilarity in their regulatory and market environments. The globally accepted ESG factors like climate impact, employee relations, and corporate transparency over investment analysis, thus making it possible to compare investments across borders (Ma, 2023).

6.3 Structural Divergences

National systems usually depend on ESG disclosures that are voluntary, while international regimes are progressively requiring standardized reports to improve transparency. However, this situation can lead to the downfall of ESG signalling and create hurdles in compliance (Pizzi et al., 2024). The approaches regarding materiality also vary, with local regulations stressing financial materiality and international standards allowing double materiality that captures broader social and environmental effects and industry-related risks (Abhayawansa, 2022). Investor activism is more formal and organized in global markets, while domestic participation is still sporadic and mainly driven by retail (Garg et al., 2022).

6.4 Implementation Gaps

Though the use of SRI is increasing, considerable gaps in implementation still exist in both domestic and global frameworks, mainly because of the difference between the desired goals and the actual implementation. These gaps are most pronounced in emerging markets, which limits the integration of SRI to only a small extent, as the latter provides benefits of diversification and risk mitigation, especially where there are no restrictions due to limited and poor-expert ESG data, market infrastructure, and technical skills (Tripathi & Kaur, 2022). Moreover, nonuniformity in indicators, scarcity of informed investors, and lack of training are all factors that hinder consistent ESG evaluation and impact measurement, thus drawing attention to the necessity for context-sensitive regulatory support and institutional strengthening, which can make SRI scaling effective (Ryan et al., 2024).

In practice, implementation gaps are visible in many emerging markets where ESG adoption remains limited despite policy support. For example, companies may publish sustainability reports but often use different ESG indicators, making comparison difficult for investors. This lack of consistency reduces the usefulness of ESG information in investment decisions.

Another important gap is the difference between policy intentions and actual corporate practices. Although many firms formally adopt ESG policies, actual environmental and social performance improvements may be limited. Furthermore, smaller firms often face difficulties in implementing ESG practices due to limited financial and technical resources. As a result, sustainable investment tends to be concentrated in large firms, reducing the overall impact of SRI in domestic markets.

6.5 Case Examples

In developed markets, the European Union (EU) shows a high level of SRI adoption by imposing mandatory ESG disclosures under the Sustainable Finance Disclosure Regulation (SFDR) and EU Taxonomy, which are facilitated by the backing of strong institutional investor involvement, and regulatory supervision. On the other hand, in the case of emerging markets, India is indicative of a changing SRI scenario where responsible investment practices are mainly reliant on regulatory measures and the raising of investor awareness and are still hampered by the lack of ESG data and the limited scale of the market. The comparison of these two cases indicates that the same sustainability targets are reached through various means depending on the market, and this highlights the necessity of harmonizing global SRI standards with the capacities of domestic institutions.

The comparison between developed and emerging markets also helps to explain why some SRI practices perform better. In developed markets, strong regulatory enforcement and standardized ESG reporting improve data reliability and investor confidence. This allows investors to incorporate ESG factors more effectively into their decision-making.

In contrast, emerging markets often face main challenges such as limited ESG data availability, lower investor awareness, and weaker institutional support. These constraints reduce the effectiveness of ESG integration, even when sustainability policies are in place.

Institutional investors also play a major role in improving SRI. Markets with strong pension funds and asset managers tend to show more consistent ESG adoption as large investors encourage companies to improve their sustainability performance.

7. CHALLENGES IN CROSS-BORDER SRI IMPLEMENTATION

Cross-border implementation of SRI faces serious hurdles due to scattered regulations, different ESG reporting standards, and the lack of a globally accepted ESG standard, which together make it difficult to compare and integrate the markets effectively (Siri et al., 2024; Van Vu et al., 2025; Eskantar et al., 2024). Data quality issues, enforcement by the supervisor, and the reliability and comparability of ESG disclosures are among the factors that make cross-border investment decisions more complicated and increase the likelihood of greenwashing, thus eroding investor trust in global SRI practices (Ye, 2024).

7.1 Standardization and TAXONOMY ISSUES

The process of implementing cross-border SRI is being slowed down by all the different ESG standards, along with the existence of different rating agencies that use different methodologies and materiality frameworks, which, in the end, have less comparability and poorer cross-market analysis (Van Vu et al., 2025). Moreover, methodological opacity in ESG data, especially for climate-related investments, limits transparency and proper assessment (Elhady & Shohieb, 2025). A lack of standardization creates information imbalances, making it easier for companies to move regulations to their advantage, hence working against investor trust and involvement; at the same time, sustainability-related disclosures are still often very complicated, poorly connected with corporate reporting, and not very aligned with the preferences of investors (Ringe, 2023; Siri et al., 2024).

7.2 Data Quality and Transparency Concerns

Cross-border SRI has a main hurdle in the form of limited and weak environmental, social, and governance (ESG) disclosures, which are more common in the emerging markets, and hence they do not allow for a holistic sustainability assessment. Moreover, the differences in the ESG disclosure regulations' maturity and scope across countries aggravate these problems, leading to different reporting practices and continuous data harmonization issues (Ye, 2024). As a result, investors need to spend a lot of time and money on data gathering, checking, and merging, which creates a major obstacle to the seamless integration of ESG factors into cross-border investment strategies (Silvestri & Kamerling, 2024).

7.3 Regulatory Fragmentation

A radically different and harmonized global regulatory framework is needed to ensure the application of investment principles that are socially responsible and that they are applied consistently across different jurisdictions (Yunus & Nanda, 2024). The rapid evolution of sustainability regulations, the variety of institutional settings, and the lack of a universal ESG classification system contribute to reporting practices inconsistency, which results in a limited comparability across markets, an increase in investor confusion, and the emergence of new regions for investment (Papafloratos & Pantazi, 2025; Vu et al., 2025; Yunus & Nanda, 2024). The dramatic increase in scattered and complicated sustainability disclosures adds to the burden of investors, especially the retail ones, keeping on the one hand data quality issues and weak communication between sustainability and financial reporting and on the other hand making regulatory effectiveness run down (Silvestri & Kamerling, 2024; Siri et al., 2024).

7.4 Cultural and Contextual Barriers

Cultural and contextual differences that affect stakeholder expectations and interpretations of social responsibility are the ones that mainly drive cross-border socially responsible investing (Mol & Lee, 2024). The financial implications and the perceived influence of CSR differ in various institutional contexts like the Anglo-Saxon, Asian, Germanic, Latin American, and European systems that reflect different human values and stakeholder priorities (Leonidou et al., 2024; Cherkasova et al., 2023). Cultural factors have a great correlation with the size and maturity of a country's SRI markets and thus adoption rates as well; besides that, legal traditions, governance quality, corruption, and political freedoms are also ways through which corporate behavior and compliance with sustainability regulations are impacted (Bialkowski et al., 2024; Guisande et al., 2024; Jitmaneeroj, 2024).

8. OPPORTUNITIES FOR GLOBAL-LOCAL INTEGRATION

SRI integration of global and local opportunities is created through adaptive regulations, technology breakthroughs, and partnerships, which both set global standards and consider local market conditions. Sustainability principles that are universally accepted can be fostered in local capacities where investors and regulators together can amplify the flow of cross-border capital, facilitate the practice of ESG, and promote the development of investment practices that are sustainable, inclusive, and sensitive to the local context.

8.1 Emerging Best Practices

Emerging trends in the approach to SRI focus on creating adaptive frameworks that are able to reconcile global standards of sustainability with the realities in local markets. Adaptive frameworks permit flexibility, regulatory alignment, and successful implementation of ESG criteria by providing investors/institutions with tools to meet their regional requirements without compromising their overall sustainability goal. By providing multinational investors and companies with the ability to maintain their global sustainability objectives while still being able to adapt to the differences between geographical regions (e.g., different environmental conditions, market structures, or socio-cultural expectations), these frameworks also promote the incorporation of local insights while preserving the integrity of global sustainability principles.

The development of adaptive frameworks and successful regulatory harmonization is an important new emerging practice for sustainable finance. Although sustainable financial regulations are different from country to country, evidence of working together and using flexible approaches can lead to successful regulatory harmonization. For example, the EU has developed a comprehensive sustainable finance framework that includes common definitions of sustainability and common disclosure requirements, which provide better transparency and reduce the chances of making false claims about sustainability. Globally, international sustainability reporting standards have also increased the consistency of ESG reporting by allowing countries to include their own region-specific sustainability requirements. Overall, these efforts will improve the comparability of ESG performance across multiple markets and promote international investment.

Efforts at harmonization can also be seen within green finance instruments, including cross-border green bond markets where cooperation between regulators has enhanced investor interest. In emerging economies, alignment with international sustainability guidelines has been facilitated by gradual implementation and capacity-building activities. These flexible approaches allow developing countries to engage in global SRI markets while addressing both domestic and international institutional/developmental limitations.

8.2 Technology as an Enabler

The presence of digital technology in relation to Socially Responsible Investment (SRI) enhances initiatives that support ESG and allows for the accessibility, standardization, and communication regarding ESG data internationally. Digital technologies enable SRI and create a stronger regulatory implementation by providing opportunities for marketers to implement sustainable investments both locally and globally. The advances in digital systems allow investors access to reliable ESG data and, in turn, the ability to compare sustainability performances of various regions.

Big data and AI have developed into useful tools for enhancing transparency, market accessibility, and overall ESG analysis. Machine learning, natural language processing, and other uses of AI are influencing the creation of accurate sustainability reports, as well as enhancing risk analysis and investment decision-making capabilities. By leveraging various types of technology, the quality, consistency, and comparability of data will increase, therefore making ESG assessments more trustworthy overall. Research has demonstrated that the use of AI in corporations can lead to improved ESG performance due to increased information quality, better governance practices, and further support of environmentally responsible operations, i.e., intelligent logistics, and reduced overall footprint (R. Chen and Zhang, 2025; Leogrande, 2024).

Digital investment platforms play an essential role in democratizing sustainable finance by granting access to sustainable investing SRI opportunities for both retail and institutional investors. These platforms leverage artificial intelligence (AI), big data, and blockchain technology to provide clear and accessible ESG data, personalized investment options, and safe transactions. This means that many more people are able to invest sustainably. Furthermore, digital investment platforms facilitate capital mobilization for sustainability-oriented projects and support the attainment of Sustainable Development Goals (SDGs). Nevertheless, there must be good governance to address concerns related to potential risks such as algorithmic bias, user confidentiality, and the concentration of market power. For this reason, improving inclusive digital infrastructure will help support the balance of global and local sustainable development objectives (Zeqiri et al., 2025).

8.3 Collaborative Mechanisms

Many types of collaboration are being utilized to create a more harmonious way to integrate social responsibility into SRI; among those are the alignment of policies, the transfer of capital, and the exchange of knowledge. Collaboration between countries ensures the coordination of sustainable investment activities, as well as decreases some of the differences that exist in regulatory systems for sustainable investments. The cooperation of investors through partnerships and the sharing of knowledge between entities will help support the implementation of SRI by increasing the level of consistency and creating opportunities for best practice exchange. Furthermore, collaboration can help to build the capacity to implement SRI and to align the global sustainability goals with the local development needs.

Another major factor of the collaboration is the international coordination of policy, which is necessary to decrease the fragmentation of regulatory systems and improve the ability to predict the outcome of cross-border sustainable investments. Multilateral initiatives and sectoral alliances provide the means for the convergence of sustainability standards, as well as provide the tools for implementing environmental and social goals that are common to all investors. Through these coordinated efforts, developed and developing countries can better connect their economic conditions with the goals of the international community regarding sustainability. Finally, through policy reform and using collaborative mechanisms, such as internationally cooperative systems for carbon adjustment and creating global investor partnerships, cooperation will continue to be enhanced and increase the ability to resolve any conflicts in policy (von Luepke et al., 2024).

Investor coalitions that cross borders are also a way of achieving a global-local integration method through pooling resources, risk-sharing, and strengthening collaborative engagement with companies regarding ESG-related issues. These coalitions enhance the ability of cross-border investors to influence businesses' sustainability practices and promote capital flowing specifically toward sustainable projects throughout regions. Research has found that internationally diversified networks of investors have been shown to help facilitate cross-border investments when digitally coordinated assets have supported such efforts. However, the effectiveness of these coalitions may be impacted by differences between institutions, as well as variances in conditions for international cooperation (Maula & Lukkarinen, 2022; Bouncken et al., 2023).

9. POLICY AND PRACTICAL IMPLICATIONS

In order to successfully integrate ESG strategies, it is important for regulatory frameworks to be sufficiently clear and appropriate for all involved parties (the company and the investor). Aligning national practices with international standards will increase the flow of finance to sustainable efforts.

9.1 For Policymakers

Policymakers develop regulatory frameworks that need to be clear and consistent and suitable for specific circumstances because these frameworks are essential for enhancing Socially Responsible Investment (SRI) practices. The solution to this problem requires policies that enable organizations to provide complete environmental, social, and governance (ESG) information while decreasing incorrect sustainability assertions and creating domestic rules that match international environmental sustainability benchmarks. The regulatory system needs to provide flexible rules that enable different market conditions to be handled, especially in nations that are still developing their economies. Corporations can improve their responsible business conduct through incentive mechanisms that combine tax advantages and sustainable finance tools and ESG-based governance methods, which also promote investments that contribute to achieving the Sustainable Development Goals.

The SRI regulatory framework needs strong regulations that show flexibility to adapt based on the different local socioeconomic, institutional, and cultural conditions of each area (Bowley & Hill 2024). Sustainable investment will attract more participants when organizations implement regulations that fit their specific operational needs because these regulations will decrease compliance expenses and increase their market credibility.

The promotion of sustainable corporate behavior needs well-designed incentive systems that need to work together with regulatory design frameworks. Companies will establish sustainability practices as their main business activities when executive pay is linked to sustainability results and financial incentives provide tax advantages and special access to government contracts (Nasta et al., 2024). The improvement of investor knowledge, together with financial education about sustainable investing, results in better decision-making, which strengthens the performance of sustainable responsible investment markets (Gevorkova et al., 2024).

9.2 For Investors and Asset Managers

The investors and asset managers who are coming together in cross-border sustainable finance are facing multifaceted challenges related to regulation and data—these challenges all call for the systematic incorporation of ESG factors into investment and due diligence processes. Regulatory frameworks in the EU and other regions are increasingly pushing the asset managers to consider the sustainability risks in their investment decisions and consequently the investment industry to come up with rigorous ESG policies for compliance, risk minimization, and even being a part of the future (Shah, 2024). Hence, the eco-friendly investments will be made through a process that will involve not just looking at the laws but also evaluating the companies' ESG strategies, their performance, and their long-term environmental and social impact in different areas (Yunus & Nanda, 2024).

9.3 For Corporations

Corporate involvement in the development of socially responsible investment (or SRI) will continue to evolve due in part to an increased focus on sustainability within their business and governance practices. Corporations will need to employ ESG reporting that is standardized across all businesses in order to comply with multiple and differing regulatory requirements, while at the same time enhancing transparency for international investors. The use of proactive stakeholder engagement through the use of digital tools combined with the development of solid data management systems will serve to enhance corporate credibility, reduce sustainability risk, and improve competitiveness both locally and globally.

One major challenge faced by corporations is the need to comply with multiple and sometimes inconsistent ESG reporting requirements across different regions. Differences in ESG frameworks, along with internal challenges such as limited resources, governance issues, and resistance to organizational change, can make implementation difficult. The use of digital tools can support integrated and standardized ESG reporting by improving data accuracy, benchmarking, and regulatory compliance, while also strengthening investor and stakeholder confidence (Paridhi et al., 2024; Dasinapa, 2024).

Furthermore, to develop & maintain an efficient form of business, an organization will have to make changes to produce economically worthwhile products. Corporate strategies that incorporate concepts of sustainable development will help an organization maintain its edge in today's marketplace through continued growth & development. According to research evidence, greening strategies for businesses that have a high degree of ESG performance lead to improved profitability and greater capacity for effectively managing risk. An organization will also be able to respond more quickly to future changes in regulations & be in a better position to capture new business opportunities by integrating ESG objectives within its business strategies and governance structures (Li & Rasiah, 2024; Treepongkaruna & Suttipun, 2024; Traversi & Fornasari, 2024).

9.4 For Standard-Setting Bodies

Standard-setting bodies promote universal global socially responsible investing by creating ESG frameworks that promote worldwide comparability while allowing limited customization for local markets. By creating globally accepted sustainability disclosure standards, standard-setting organizations will reduce fragmentation, improve the quality of sustainability data, and increase investor confidence in making investments based on sustainability. The modular approach will allow for the creation of global core standards and extensions of those standards specific to individual jurisdictions and markets; therefore, supporting the harmonization of the effective integration of sustainable investment practices at both the global and local levels will occur.

The creation of inclusive standard-setting processes is critical for providing relevance and legitimacy to the ESG frameworks. Stakeholders engaged in standard-setting help to confirm the sustainability standards accurately represent a broad range of stakeholders' perspectives and practical needs. In the case of ESG standards, expanding into underrepresented areas (e.g., biodiversity and social equity) would improve accountability for ESG issues and fill in any gaps for other ESG indicators in the sustainability arena (Kopnina et al., 2024).

10. FUTURE RESEARCH DIRECTIONS

The future research agenda should focus on adaptive harmonization of global sustainability standards with domestic regulatory, cultural, and market-specific contexts regarding cross-border SRI. An important area of inquiry will be the effect of digitization, ESG data quality, and the behavior of institutional investors on the disaggregation and comparability of markets. This research ultimately results in the development of a global-local SRI ecosystem that enables achieving the SDGs and creates sustainable value over the long term.

Figure 1. Future Research Directions in Cross-Border SRI

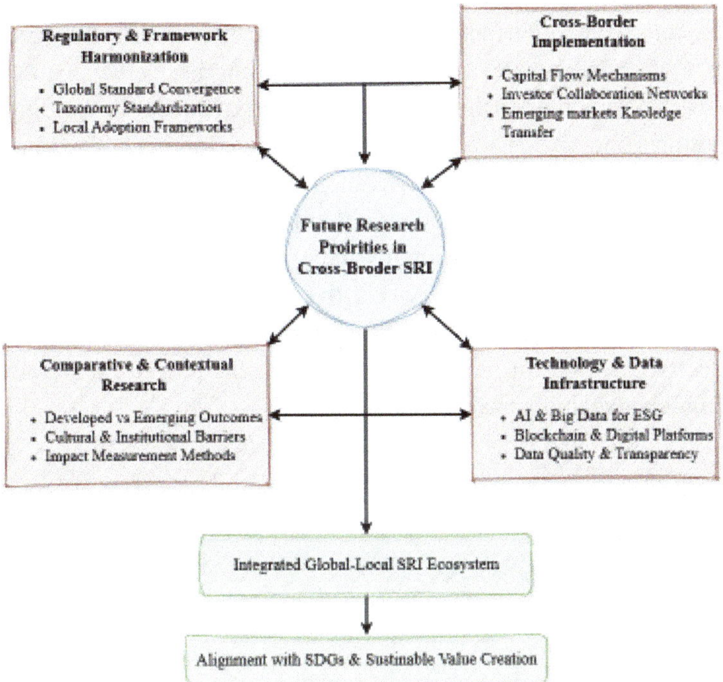

(Author's own creation)

Figure 1 illustrates the major components of upcoming research in cross-border SRI by way of regulations. The identified components are harmonization, comparison, governance, and technological infrastructure; additionally, they depict how a combined global/local ecosystem within the SRI space will develop unified ESG standards, which will help establish SVA to the benefit of all segments of the market.

CONCLUSION

This chapter has discussed an organized comparative analysis of domestic and global Socially Responsible Investments (SRIs) with the conclusion that while both try to achieve the same objective of sustainability, they are subject to different legal systems, institutions, and markets for operations. Domestic SRIs are created under respective domestic governments with a focus on key areas such as national policy, culture, and market maturity, while global SRIs focus on regulations, standardization, cross-border benchmarking, and institutional investor engagement. The comparative study indicated that the difference in quality of regulation, reliability of ESG data, and degree of investor engagement directly impacts the level of integration of sustainable investments between regions.

This chapter's major contribution is the development of an adaptive harmonization framework that connects internationally agreed-upon best practices in relation to sustainable development with the existing capacities of domestic institutions. Rather than promoting a one-size-fits-all approach to the development of an internationally accepted standard for all jurisdictions, it emphasizes the need for adjustment to local conditions, thus enhancing the likelihood that local implementation will occur and have a meaningful effect. In addition, by integrating the theoretical underpinnings of socially responsible investing activity with a comparative institutional analysis of countries, this chapter will create improved cross-border SRI systems and provide a more effective method for mobilizing capital for the long-term creation of value that is both inclusive and sustainable.

REFERENCES

Abhayawansa, S. (2022). Swimming against the tide: Back to single materiality for sustainability reporting. *Sustainability Accounting Management and Policy Journal, 13*(6), 1361–1385. DOI: 10.1108/SAMPJ-07-2022-0378

Abiola-Adams, O., Azubuike, C., Sule, A. K., & Okon, R. (2025). Strategic liquidity management: Best practices for optimizing cash flows in multinational corporations. *Gulf Journal of Advance Business Research, 3*(1), 143–156. DOI: 10.51594/gjabr.v3i1.71

Acar, E. (2024). ESG Integration into Financial Markets: A Comprehensive Exploration of Concepts and Implementation. Çağ Üniversitesi Sosyal Bilimler Dergisi, 20(2), 133-147. https://dergipark.org.tr/cagsbd

Adeneye, Y. B., Kammoun, I., & Ab Wahab, S. N. A. (2023). Capital structure and speed of adjustment: The impact of environmental, social and governance (ESG) performance. *Sustainability Accounting Management and Policy Journal, 14*(5), 945–977. DOI: 10.1108/SAMPJ-01-2022-0060

Adwani, A. (2025). ESG investing trends in emerging markets: A behavioral finance perspective. SSRN *Electronic Journal*. https://doi.org/DOI: 10.2139/ssrn.5356746

Aggarwal, S. (2025). SOCIALLY RESPONSIBLE INVESTMENT IN INDIA: A CONCEPTUAL FRAMEWORK Poonam. SSRN *Electronic Journal*. https://doi.org/DOI: 10.2139/ssrn.5206207

Akala, C. S., Neuhaus, T., & Leary-Govender, I. O. (2022). A systematic review of sustainable investment approaches. *International Journal of Economics and Finance, 14*(12), 72. DOI: 10.5539/ijef.v14n12p72

Alshukri, T., Seun Ojekemi, O., Öz, T., & Alzubi, A. (2024). The interplay of corporate social responsibility, innovation capability, organizational learning, and sustainable value creation: Does stakeholder engagement matter? *Sustainability (Basel), 16*(13), 5511. DOI: 10.3390/su16135511

Álvarez-Ruiz, L., Echeverría King, L. F., Lafont Castillo, T. I., Moreno Garcia, D. E., Herazo Chamorro, M. I., Restrepo Ruiz, M., & De Luque Montaño, O. (2023). Collaboration for the internationalization of research and development: Opportunities for Colombia in the post-pandemic term. *Journal of Higher Education Theory and Practice, 23*(18), 10–33423. DOI: 10.33423/jhetp.v23i18.6631

Azuma, K., & Higashida, A. (2024). Climate change disclosure and evolving institutional investor salience: Roles of the Principles for Responsible Investment. *Business Strategy and the Environment, 33*(4), 3669–3686. DOI: 10.1002/bse.3649

Bauckloh, T., Schaltegger, S., Utz, S., Zeile, S., & Zwergel, B. (2023). Active first movers vs. Late free-riders? An empirical analysis of UN PRI signatories' commitment. *Journal of Business Ethics, 182*(3), 747–781. DOI: 10.1007/s10551-021-04992-0

Bialkowski, J. P., Starks, L. T., & Wagner, M. (2024). Cultural values and cross-country differences in responsible investing sectors. SSRN *Electronic Journal.* https://doi.org/DOI: 10.2139/ssrn.4938888

Biktimirov, E. N., & Afego, P. N. (2022). Does investors' valuation of corporate environmental activities vary between developed and emerging market firms? *Finance Research Letters, 47*(102528), 102528. DOI: 10.1016/j.frl.2021.102528

Bouncken, R. B., Fredrich, V., Sinkovics, N., & Sinkovics, R. R. (2023). Digitalization of cross-border R&D alliances: Configurational insights and cognitive digitalization biases. *Global Strategy Journal, 13*(2), 281–314. DOI: 10.1002/gsj.1469

Bowley, T., & Hill, J. G. (2024). The global ESG stewardship ecosystem. *European Business Organization Law Review, 25*(2), 229–268. DOI: 10.1007/s40804-024-00316-7

Buchanan, B., Silvola, H., & Vähämaa, E. (2024). Sustainability and private investors. *European Journal of Finance*, •••, 1–28. DOI: 10.1080/1351847X.2024.2362282

Chang, X., Fu, K., Jin, Y., & Liem, P. F. (2022). Sustainable finance: ESG/CSR, firm value, and investment returns. *Asia-Pacific Journal of Financial Studies, 51*(3), 325–371. DOI: 10.1111/ajfs.12379

Chen, R., & Zhang, T. (2025). Artificial intelligence applications implication for ESG performance: Can digital transformation of enterprises promote sustainable development? *Chinese Management Studies, 19*(3), 676–701. DOI: 10.1108/CMS-11-2023-0653

Cherkasova, V., Fedorova, E., & Stepnov, I. (2023). Market reaction to firms' investments in CSR projects. *Journal of Economics, Finance and Administrative Science, 28*(55), 44–59. DOI: 10.1108/JEFAS-08-2021-0150

Choy, S. K., Koci, I., & Wang, M. (2023). Does social capital foster sustainable investment? *European Financial Management, 29*(3), 799–840. DOI: 10.1111/eufm.12376

Danila, N. (2022). Random walk of socially responsible investment in emerging market. *Sustainability (Basel)*, *14*(19), 11846. DOI: 10.3390/su141911846

Dasinapa, M. B. (2024). The integration of sustainability and ESG accounting into corporate reporting practices. *Advances in Applied Accounting Research*, *2*(1), 13–25. DOI: 10.60079/aaar.v2i1.167

de Villiers, C., La Torre, M., & Molinari, M. (2022). The Global Reporting Initiative's (GRI) past, present and future: Critical reflections and a research agenda on sustainability reporting (standard-setting). *Pacific Accounting Review*, *34*(5), 728–747. DOI: 10.1108/PAR-02-2022-0034

Dutta, A., & Paul, B. (2023). Performance analysis of select ESG funds in India. *Management Journal for Advanced Research*, *3*(1), 1–7. DOI: 10.54741/mjar.3.1.1

Elhady, A. M., & Shohieb, S. (2025). AI-driven sustainable finance: Computational tools, ESG metrics, and global implementation. *Future Business Journal*, *11*(1), 209. Advance online publication. DOI: 10.1186/s43093-025-00610-x

Emamian, S., Rahimian, F. P., Awang, M., & Dhingra, D. (2023). Unlocking the commercialisation process for academic ideas and their global market impact. *Law and Business*, *3*(1), 42–52. DOI: 10.2478/law-2023-0004

Emeka-Okoli, S., Nwankwo, T. C., Otonnah, C. A., & Nwankwo, E. E. (2024). Corporate governance and CSR for sustainability in Oil and Gas: Trends, challenges, and best practices: A review. *World Journal of Advanced Research and Reviews*, *21*(3), 078–090. https://doi.org/DOI: 10.30574/wjarr.2024.21.3.0662

Eskantar, M., Zopounidis, C., Doumpos, M., Galariotis, E., & Guesmi, K. (2024). Navigating ESG complexity: An in-depth analysis of sustainability criteria, frameworks, and impact assessment. *International Review of Financial Analysis*, *95*(103380), 103380. DOI: 10.1016/j.irfa.2024.103380

Fisher, S., Blau, A., Kantrowitz-Gordon, I., & Gendler, Y. (2024). Academic boycotts of Israel: A narrative review. *Israel Affairs*, *30*(5), 1–13. DOI: 10.1080/13537121.2024.2394307

Fornasari, T., & Traversi, M. (2024). The impact of the CSRD and the ESRS on non-financial disclosure. *Symphonya Emerging Issues in Management*, *1*(1), 117–133. DOI: 10.4468/2024.1.07fornasari.traversi

Freudenreich, B., Lüdeke-Freund, F., & Schaltegger, S. (2020). A stakeholder theory perspective on business models: Value creation for sustainability. *Journal of Business Ethics*, *166*(1), 3–18. DOI: 10.1007/s10551-019-04112-z

Garg, A., Goel, P., Sharma, A., & Rana, N. P. (2022). As you sow, so shall you reap: Assessing drivers of socially responsible investment attitude and intention. *Technological Forecasting and Social Change, 184*(122030), 122030. DOI: 10.1016/j.techfore.2022.122030

Gevorkova, V., Sangiorgi, I., & Vogt, J. (2024). Cleansing investor's conscience: The effects of incidental guilt on Socially Responsible Investment decisions. *Journal of Business Ethics, 193*(1), 89–114. DOI: 10.1007/s10551-023-05585-9

Gorski, A.-T., & Ranf, E.-D. (2024). Sustainability trends and dynamics: An integrative approach to economic, social, and environmental perspectives. *Science Bulletin, 29*(1), 46–60. DOI: 10.2478/bsaft-2024-0006

Guisande, D. P., Harjoto, M. A., Hoepner, A. G. F., & O'Sullivan, C. (2024). Ethics and banking: Do banks divest their kind? *Journal of Business Ethics, 192*(1), 191–223. DOI: 10.1007/s10551-023-05476-z

Hovde Group. Charlotte, North Carolina, USA, Sikiru, A. O., Chima, O. K., Darden Business School, University of Virginia, USA; Otunba, M., Amazon, Seattle, WA, USA; Gaffar, O., Independent Researcher, USA; Adenuga, A. A., & McKinsey and Company, Nigeria; (2025). Navigating the regulatory trilemma - A framework for balancing U.s. tariffs, EU ESG directives, and cross-border capital controls. *Engineering and Technology Journal, 10*(08). https://doi.org/DOI: 10.47191/etj/v10i08.38

Ivanisevic Hernaus, A., Zoricic, D., & Dolinar, D. (2023). How competitive is SRI in developing financial markets: The case of Central and Eastern Europe. *E+M. Ekonomie a Management, 26*(2), 172–188. DOI: 10.15240/tul/001/2023-2-011

Jain, A., Islam, M. A., Keneley, M., & Kansal, M. (2022). Social contagion and the institutionalisation of GRI-based sustainability reporting practices. *Meditari Accountancy Research, 30*(5), 1291–1308. DOI: 10.1108/MEDAR-06-2020-0917

James, S., & Quaglia, L. (2024). Emergent regime complexity and epistemic barriers in 'bigtech' finance. *New Political Economy, 29*(6), 872–885. DOI: 10.1080/13563467.2024.2359940

Jeriji, M., Louhichi, W., & Ftiti, Z. (2023). Migrating to global reporting initiative guidelines: Does international harmonization of CSR information pay? *British Journal of Management, 34*(2), 555–575. DOI: 10.1111/1467-8551.12603

Jitmaneeroj, B. (2024). Value relevance of multifaceted corporate social performance: How do country-specific factors matter? *Humanities & Social Sciences Communications, 11*(1), 116. Advance online publication. DOI: 10.1057/s41599-024-02615-3

Jonwall, R., Gupta, S., & Pahuja, S. (2023). A comparison of investment behavior, attitudes, and demographics of socially responsible and conventional investors in India. *Social Responsibility Journal, 19*(6), 1123–1141. DOI: 10.1108/SRJ-08-2021-0358

Kabderian Dreyer, J., Sharma, V., & Smith, W. (2023). Warm-glow investment and the underperformance of green stocks. *International Review of Economics & Finance, 83*, 546–570. DOI: 10.1016/j.iref.2022.10.006

Keeley, A. R., Li, C., Takeda, S., Gloria, T., & Managi, S. (2022). The ultimate owner of environmental, social, and governance investment. *Frontiers in Sustainability, 3*(909239), 909239. Advance online publication. DOI: 10.3389/frsus.2022.909239

Keser, N. S. (2025). Trend in sustainable finance metrics: A bibliometric literature review. *Pressacademia, 2*, 2. Advance online publication. DOI: 10.17261/Pressacademia.2025.1983

Khan, S. A. R., Yu, Z., & Farooq, K. (2023). Green capabilities, green purchasing, and triple bottom line performance: Leading toward environmental sustainability. *Business Strategy and the Environment, 32*(4), 2022–2034. DOI: 10.1002/bse.3234

Kilic, Y., Destek, M. A., Cevik, E. I., Bugan, M. F., Korkmaz, O., & Dibooglu, S. (2022). Return and risk spillovers between the ESG global index and stock markets: Evidence from time and frequency analysis. *Borsa Istanbul Review, 22*, S141–S156. DOI: 10.1016/j.bir.2022.11.015

Kim, S., & Yoon, A. (2023). Analyzing active fund managers' commitment to ESG: Evidence from the United Nations Principles for Responsible Investment. *Management Science, 69*(2), 741–758. DOI: 10.1287/mnsc.2022.4394

Kopnina, H., Zhang, S. R., Anthony, S., Hassan, A., & Maroun, W. (2024). The inclusion of biodiversity into Environmental, Social, and Governance (ESG) framework: A strategic integration of ecocentric extinction accounting. *Journal of Environmental Management, 351*(119808), 119808. DOI: 10.1016/j.jenvman.2023.119808 PMID: 38103427

Kouam, A. W. F. (2025). Navigating motivations and obstacles: Exploring the dynamics of foreign entrepreneurs in China's business landscape. *The International Entrepreneurship and Management Journal, 21*(1), 12. Advance online publication. DOI: 10.1007/s11365-024-01040-x

Leogrande, A. (2024). Integrating ESG principles into smart logistics:Toward sustainable supply chains. In *Preprints*. https://doi.org/DOI: 10.20944/preprints202411.1432.v1

Leonidou, L. C., Marinova, S. T., Marinov, M. A., Eduardsen, J. S., & Eteokleous, P. P. (2024). An enquiry into MNEs' CSR practices: Literature assessment, managerial implications, and academic perspectives. *MIR. Management International Review*, *64*(5), 759–809. Advance online publication. DOI: 10.1007/s11575-024-00551-7

Li, M., & Rasiah, R. (2024). Can ESG disclosure stimulate corporations' sustainable green innovation efforts? Evidence from China. *Sustainability (Basel)*, *16*(21), 9390. DOI: 10.3390/su16219390

Lingnau, V., Fuchs, F., & Beham, F. (2022). The link between corporate sustainability and willingness to invest: New evidence from the field of ethical investments. *Journal of Management Control*, *33*(3), 335–369. DOI: 10.1007/s00187-022-00340-z PMID: 35719704

Linnenluecke, M. K. (2022). Environmental, social and governance (ESG) performance in the context of multinational business research. *Multinational Business Review*, *30*(1), 1–16. DOI: 10.1108/MBR-11-2021-0148

Lokuwaduge, C., & de Silva, K. (2020). Emerging corporate disclosure of environmental social and governance (ESG) risks: An Australian study. *Australasian Accounting Business and Finance Journal*, *14*(2), 35–50. DOI: 10.14453/aabfj.v14i2.4

Lusha, E. (2024). National and international collaboration and its impact on economic development. *Interdisciplinary Journal of Research and Development*, *11*(1), 76. DOI: 10.56345/ijrdv11n111

Ma, N. (2023). Integration of ESG factors in portfolio management: International trends and practices. *Frontiers in Business, Economics and Management*, *12*(2), 149–152. DOI: 10.54097/fbem.v12i2.14778

Martini, A. (2021). Socially responsible investing: From the ethical origins to the sustainable development framework of the European Union. *Environment, Development and Sustainability*, *23*(11), 16874–16890. DOI: 10.1007/s10668-021-01375-3 PMID: 33841043

Matser, I., Fontrodona, J., & Van Wassenhove, L. (2023). Guest editorial: Driving impact through responsible investing and finance. *Sustainability Accounting Management and Policy Journal*, *14*(5), 917–921. DOI: 10.1108/SAMPJ-08-2023-606

Maula, M. V. J., & Lukkarinen, A. (2022). Attention across borders: Investor attention as a driver of cross-border equity crowdfunding investments. *Strategic Entrepreneurship Journal*, *16*(4), 699–734. DOI: 10.1002/sej.1424

Mol, M. J., & Lee, S. H. (2024). What produces corporate social irresponsibility in offshore outsourcing? The effects of interorganizational relationship governance and institutional distance. *Journal of International Business Studies*, *55*(5), 577–592. DOI: 10.1057/s41267-023-00664-5

Narayanan, S., & Pradhan, S. K. (2023). Exploring the research landscape of socially responsible investment through bibliometrics. *Multidisciplinary Reviews*, *7*(1), 2024022. DOI: 10.31893/multirev.2024022

Nartey, E. K. (2024). Beyond profit: Ethical imperatives and the role of duty of care in sustainable investment strategies. *International Journal of Economics and Finance*, *17*(1), 22. DOI: 10.5539/ijef.v17n1p22

Nasta, L., Magnanelli, B. S., & Ciaburri, M. (2024). From profits to purpose: ESG practices, CEO compensation and institutional ownership. *Management Decision*, *62*(13), 46–68. DOI: 10.1108/MD-06-2023-0932

Ngo, T., Le, T., Ullah, S., & Trinh, H. H. (2022). Climate risk disclosures and global sustainability initiatives: A conceptual analysis and agenda for future research. *Business Strategy and the Environment*. Advance online publication. DOI: 10.1002/bse.3323

Nica, I., Chiri ă, N., & Georgescu, I. (2025). Triple Bottom Line in sustainable development: A comprehensive bibliometric analysis. *Sustainability (Basel)*, *17*(5), 1932. DOI: 10.3390/su17051932

Nichols, B. S., Kirchoff, J. F., Confente, I., & Stolze, H. (2023). When brands behave badly: Signaling and spillover effects of unethical behavior in the context of triple bottom line sustainability. *Journal of Product and Brand Management*, *32*(6), 908–926. DOI: 10.1108/JPBM-07-2021-3569

Nogueira, E., Gomes, S., & Lopes, J. M. (2024). Financial sustainability: Exploring the influence of the triple Bottom Line economic dimension on firm performance. *Sustainability (Basel)*, *16*(15), 6458. DOI: 10.3390/su16156458

Paetzold, F., Busch, T., Utz, S., & Kellers, A. (2022). Between impact and returns: Private investors and the sustainable development goals. *Business Strategy and the Environment*, *31*(7), 3182–3197. DOI: 10.1002/bse.3070

Papafloratos, T., & Pantazi, T. (2025). A systematic review of the effects of mandatory corporate sustainability reporting. *Sustainability (Basel)*, *17*(12), 5336. DOI: 10.3390/su17125336

Paridhi, R., Ritika, , Arora, H., Arora, P., & Saini, N. (2024). Unlocking the path to sustainability: A hierarchical model for understanding corporate barriers to ESG reporting adoption. *Journal of Risk and Financial Management, 17*(12), 527. DOI: 10.3390/jrfm17120527

Pasquino, M., & Lucarelli, C. (2025). Socially responsible investments inside out: A new conceptual framework for investigating retail investor preferences. *International Journal of Bank Marketing, 43*(3), 449–475. DOI: 10.1108/IJBM-02-2024-0077

Pepe, C. G. E., Fonseca, M. V. A., & Silva Marques, C. F. (2024). International collaboration towards innovation management: A network perspective and the Global Innovation Index. *Journal of Innovation and Entrepreneurship, 13*(1), 32. Advance online publication. DOI: 10.1186/s13731-024-00384-6

Pialli, G. (2023). The effects of limited exhaustibility of knowledge and geographical distance on the quality of R&D collaborations: The European evidence 2000–2012. *Journal of Evolutionary Economics, 33*(4), 1125–1169. DOI: 10.1007/s00191-023-00831-9

Pizzi, S., Caputo, F., & de Nuccio, E. (2024). Do sustainability reporting standards affect analysts' forecast accuracy? *Sustainability Accounting Management and Policy Journal, 15*(2), 330–354. DOI: 10.1108/SAMPJ-04-2023-0227

Priya, & Sharma, K. (2024). Global ESG fund evolution-an analysis of sustainable investment growth through comparison. *E3S Web of Conferences, 577*, 03003. https://doi.org/DOI: 10.1051/e3sconf/202457703003

Ringe, W.-G. (2023). Investor empowerment for sustainability. *Review of Economics, 74*(1), 21–52. DOI: 10.1515/roe-2023-0016

Rossoni, A. L., de Vasconcellos, E. P. G., & Sbragia, R. (2024). Influence of social capital, market orientation, and technological readiness on researchers' interactions with companies. *Future Business Journal, 10*(1), 69. Advance online publication. DOI: 10.1186/s43093-024-00359-9

Ryan, M., Popa, E., Blok, V., Declich, A., Berliri, M., Alfonsi, A., Veloudis, S., Costanzo, N., & Iannuzzi, M. (2024). Start doing the right thing: Indicators for socially responsible start-ups and investors. *Journal of Responsible Technology, 20*(100094), 100094. DOI: 10.1016/j.jrt.2024.100094

Shah, D. (2024). Sustainable Finance and ESG Investing. *International Journal for Research in Applied Science and Engineering Technology, 12*(2), 412–416. DOI: 10.22214/ijraset.2024.58346

Silvestri, R., & Kamerling, J. (2024). *CFA institute survey report on the ESG regulatory framework in the EU*. CFA Institute., DOI: 10.56227/24.2.10

Siri, M., Lamandini, M., & Muñoz, D. R. (2024). The current implementation of the sustainability-related financial disclosures regulation (SFDR). SSRN *Electronic Journal*. https://doi.org/DOI: 10.2139/ssrn.5042850

Sreepriya, Suprabha, & Prasad, K. (2023). Does GRI compliance moderate the impact of sustainability disclosure on firm value? *Society and Business Review*, *18*(1), 152–174. DOI: 10.1108/SBR-06-2022-0172

Treepongkaruna, S., & Suttipun, M. (2024). The impact of environmental, social and governance (ESG) reporting on corporate profitability: evidence from Thailand. *Journal of Financial Reporting and Accounting*. https://doi.org/DOI: 10.1108/JFRA-09-2023-0555

Tripathi, V., & Kaur, A. (2022). Does socially responsible investing pay in developing countries? A comparative study across select developed and developing markets. *FIIB Business Review*, *11*(2), 189–205. DOI: 10.1177/2319714520980288

Tuncay, M., & Dorjnaran, B. (2023). How do socially responsible investment and macroeconomic indicators interact with each other The case of selected developing countries. *Pressacademia*, *1*, 1. Advance online publication. DOI: 10.17261/Pressacademia.2023.1721

Van Vu, N., Nazari, M. A., Dang, T., Muralev, Y., Mohanraj, M., Tran, T., & Hoang, A. (2025). Type of the paper*: Article*. https://doi.org/DOI: 10.2139/ssrn.5384374

von Luepke, H., Neuhoff, K., & Marchewitz, C. (2024). *Bridges over troubled waters: Climate clubs, alliances, and partnerships as safeguards for effective international cooperation?* International Environmental Agreements Politics Law and Economics., DOI: 10.1007/s10784-024-09639-9

Xu, L., Xie, L., Mei, S., Hao, J., Zhang, Y., & Song, Y. (2024). Corporate sustainability reporting and stakeholders' interests: Evidence from China. *Sustainability (Basel)*, *16*(8), 3443. DOI: 10.3390/su16083443

Yadav, R., Bhong, M., Aswal, U. S., Kumar, M., Reddy, C. V., Rajalakshmi, B., & Albazoni, H. J. (2023). Key enabler on efficient resource utilization: Technical and managerial investigations for sustainable materials and energy management. *E3S Web of Conferences*, *453*, 01023. https://doi.org/DOI: 10.1051/e3sconf/202345301023

Ye, J., Moslehpour, M., Tu, Y.-T., Vinh, N. T., Ngo, T. Q., & Nguyen, S. V. (2023). Investment on environmental social and governance activities and its impact on achieving sustainable development goals: Evidence from Chinese manufacturing firms. *Ekonomska Istraživanja, 36*(1), 333–356. DOI: 10.1080/1331677X.2022.2076145

Ye, Z. (2024). Comparative analysis of global ESG information disclosure regulatory frameworks and challenges. In *Advances in Social Science, Education and Humanities Research* (pp. 942–950). Atlantis Press SARL. https://doi.org/DOI: 10.2991/978-2-38476-277-4_104

Yelnikova, J., & Kwilinski, A. (2020). Impact-investing in the healthcare in terms of the new socially responsible State Investment Policy. *Business Ethics and Leadership, 4*(3), 57–64. DOI: 10.21272/bel.4(3).57-64.2020

Yunus, Y. A., & Nanda, S. (2024). Exploring sustainable finance: A qualitative inquiry into Responsible Investment and ESG risk evaluation. *Golden Ratio of Finance Management, 4*(1), 01–13. https://doi.org/DOI: 10.52970/grfm.v4i1.429

Zaid, M. A. A., & Issa, A. (2023). A roadmap for triggering the convergence of global ESG disclosure standards: Lessons from the IFRS foundation and stakeholder engagement. *Corporate Governance (Bradford), 23*(7), 1648–1669. DOI: 10.1108/CG-09-2022-0399

Zeqiri, A., Ben Youssef, A., & Maherzi Zahar, T. (2025). The role of digital tourism platforms in advancing sustainable development goals in the industry 4.0 era. *Sustainability (Basel), 17*(8), 3482. DOI: 10.3390/su17083482

Zhao, Y. (2024). Empowering sustainable finance: The convergence of AI, blockchain, and big data analytics. *Advances in Economics. Management and Political Sciences, 85*(1), 267–273. DOI: 10.54254/2754-1169/85/20240925

Zhou, X., Liang, W., Wang, K. I.-K., Huang, R., & Jin, Q. (2021). Academic influence aware and multidimensional network analysis for research collaboration navigation based on scholarly big data. *IEEE Transactions on Emerging Topics in Computing, 9*(1), 246–257. DOI: 10.1109/TETC.2018.2860051

Chapter 4
From Capital Flows to Climate Flows:
FDI, Renewables, and New Green Investment Frontier

Daisy Chepkirui Birir
http://orcid.org/0009-0006-1238-0487
Mahatma Gandhi University, India

Lenah Chelangat
http://orcid.org/0009-0002-2002-4619
University of Kerala, India

K. Latha
http://orcid.org/0000-0003-4007-8059
Saintgits College of Engineering, Kottayam, India.

Roshna Varghese
http://orcid.org/0000-0002-4128-5263
School of Management and Business Studies, Mahatma Gandhi University, Kottayam, India

ABSTRACT

There is no doubt that a structural rebalancing of international investment flows will be necessary to enable the economy to transition to a low-carbon and climate-resilient trajectory. The conventional FDI was mostly applied in the mining and high-carbon-emitting industries while climate-sensitive FDI flows into sustainable infrastructure, renewable energy, and circular economies. The chapter presents a conceptual and analytical framework for understanding the new global movements in FDI with international and regional perspectives, particularly in developing and

DOI: 10.4018/979-8-3373-7595-3.ch004

ght © 2027, IGI Global Scientific Publishing. Copying or distributing in print or electronic forms without written permission of IGI Global Scientific Publishing is prohibited. Use of this chapter to generative artificial intelligence (AI) technologies is expressly prohibited. The publisher reserves all rights to license its use for generative AI training and machine learning model development.

emerging economies. It highlights barriers, including the threats of greenwashing, inconsistencies in regulations, and lack of clear definition of 'green', and develops policy recommendations to promote investor consistency on climate flows. The chapter contributes to the discussion of reorganizing the global financial architecture to achieve the SDGs and call for a paradigm shift to reverse the current capital flows to the economy and redirect them to climate flows, which will replenish both the economies and ecosystem.

INTRODUCTION

The architecture of global investments is defined by the divergence of capital and climate flows. Capital flows are defined as investments made across borders, including foreign direct investment, debt investment, and portfolio investment. Traditionally, this has been a means by which countries advance their development in finance, infrastructure, and overall economic growth (UNCTAD, 2023). Recent World Bank data indicate that approximately $1.3 trillion in annual capital flows, in the form of foreign direct investment, are channeled to different sectors and countries to maximise profits and minimise risk (World Bank, 2022). This discrepancy between what has been invested and what is needed is the main driving force behind the research of the shift of traditional capital flows to climate-oriented ones.

In the definition of terms, often three interconnected yet separate words come up; Climate investing denotes the extensive allocation of financial resources to assets or initiatives that mitigate greenhouse gas emissions or enhance climate resilience, encompassing both public and private instruments. Green investment is a specific segment of climate investing that emphasizes environmental performance and ESG criteria, primarily inside private financial markets. Renewable energy foreign direct investment (FDI) constitutes a specific category of cross-border direct investment in productive renewable energy assets, characterized by ownership, control, and a long-term commitment. CCTM functions primarily within the realm of renewable energy foreign direct investment, integrating it into the wider climate investment framework.

Unprecedented capital reallocation is needed for the global energy transformation. According to the International Energy Agency, to sustain net-zero trajectories, clean energy investment must more than triple current levels to USD 4.5 trillion by 2030 (IEA, 2024). Although foreign direct investment is a crucial channel for this reallocation, its conceptual drivers in renewable energy contexts remain poorly understood.

Existing research is characterized by three analytical gaps. First, FDI theory (Dunning, 1981; Hymer, 1976) does not account for climatic transition dynamics.

Second, FDI is not regarded as a controlled capital flow, but rather as a residual financing variable in the literature on climate finance (Buchner et al., 2019; UNFCCC, 2024). Third, there is no functioning cross-border capital channel in ecological macroeconomics (Dafermos et al., 2016; Godley & Lavoie, 2007). The analytical framework created by these gaps is structurally deficient and unable to account for the institutional conditioning of green capital flows. To fill these gaps, the Capital-to-Climate Flow Transition Model (CCTM) is presented in this chapter. SFC macroeconomics, FDI theory, renewable energy finance, and institutional quality analysis are the four theoretical traditions that CCTM combines into a single, balance-sheet-consistent paradigm (Polzin et al., 2019). The main tenet of the model is that the risk premium incorporated into cost-of-capital formation is determined by institutional quality, and that this, in turn, dictates the amount, sectoral distribution, and geographic distribution of foreign direct investment in renewable energy (Globerman & Shapiro, 2003).

This chapter, therefore, proposes a model of the capital-climate flow transition structure as a framework for showing the evolution of foreign direct investment into renewables and other green investments. The chapter is anchored in the Capital-Climate Flows Conceptual Model, with a bibliometric mapping of capital-climate articles (2000–2025) to support the need for this transition model. The chapter will then proceed to theoretical synthesis, the conceptual gap, the CCTM architecture, methodological design, comparative country analysis, policy and financial implications, and finally limitations and conclusions.

THEORETICAL CONTEXT

FDI has undergone a paradigm shift in recent years from profit maximization towards sustainability objectives as a critical strategy for value creation (Emodi et al., 2023; Raza et al., 2024). Understanding the linkage between FDI and sustainable finance requires an interdisciplinary approach that draws on insights from international business, environmental economics, and sustainable development. This approach can be utilized by examining the linkage among cross-border capital flows, environmental sustainability, and economic viability (Patala et al., 2021). The theoretical section looks at the evolution of FDI to climate investment rather than just capital shifts.

The transition of capital to climate flows is a sustainable finance aspect in the modern term and its theoretical advancement has been explained using different lenses. The traditional and most referred theory is the electric paradigm (OLI framework) by John H. Dunning. It states that ownership, location and internalization advantages determines the investment decision (Patala et al., 2021). In the case of renewable energy investments, ownership benefits should include green credentials and expertise in environmental fields, while location benefits incorporate renewable energy potential, policy frameworks that facilitate clean energy transitions, and the quality of environmental governance (Keeley and Matsumoto, 2018). The internationalization advantages of multinational energy utilities include the ability to navigate complex regulatory contexts and leverage sustainability capabilities. FDI stakeholders evaluate policy stability, size of the market, and the prospects of renewable energy in the developing economies (Keeley and Matsumoto, 2018). The presented OLI framework shows that sustainable finance mechanisms open new channels of FDI, providing financial returns and environmental outcomes. CCTM framework advances the location advantage as a major institutional contributor to reduce the risk premiums as a result of transition.

Traditional capital flow theory, institutional theory, climate finance theory, and just transition theory are certain other theoretical frameworks applied to comprehend the FDI-sustainable finance nexus. Traditional capital flow theory proposes that investment flows from capital-abundant (rich) to capital-scarce (poor) regions in response to variations in returns. The environmental externalities are introduced alongside FDI as key determinants of capital distribution, and therefore cross-border capital flows serve a dual function: generating economic returns and contributing to decarbonisation (Emodi et al., 2023). The increasing allocation of capital to renewable energy infrastructure demonstrates that investors recognize the long-term viability of sustainable investments (Yasmeen et al., 2022). This shift reflects the inherent characteristics of renewable energy, such as sustainability and climate-friendliness. Institutional theory explains the influence of regulatory framework and governance structure on the FDI-sustainable finance nexus. The role of FDI in advancing renewable energy development depends on the institutional quality and climate policy mechanisms of host countries (Khalique et al., 2025). Institutional quality includes the countries environmental policies, carbon trading policies and renewable energy policies that can limit the green investment flows (Udemba and Alola, 2022). The technological spillover from the investment deploying country to the host country helps in the sustainable practices' adoption. By receiving new technologies, the host country is able to meet the sustainability objective as illustrated in the SDGs. The developed economy transfers include clean energy and other investment practices that adhere to climate change mitigation to developing economies (Yasmeen et al., 2022). When Multinational corporations invest in host country economies they not only transfer direct technology but also knowledge, management practices and thus creates a lasting impact in the host institutions (Patala et al., 2021).

The climate finance theory argues that in order to achieve climate goals resources are mobilized for that specific need. FDI flows is one source of this investment that considers ESG as an incorporation of where and what the funds will be utilized in order to meet the global climate goals call. for. conceptualizes how financial resources are mobilized and allocated to achieve climate goals (Khalique et al., 2025). Investors have become conscious of investment flows in that the renewable energy sector is experiencing immense growth and so is the returns. The theory posits that investment decisions are considered from the level carbon emissions, low carbon projects are preferred as compared to high carbon investment project. Just in theory was a prior theory to the climate finance theory. The theory argues that in order to have a shift from fossil fuel and invest in renewable energy, the impact of the community and employment implication must first be addressed (Adeel et al., 2025). As much as the renewable energy investment transition will create new employments opportunities but also the industrial workers in the carbon industries will be displaced. Therefore, sustainable investment adoption should strike a balance between the environmental, social and economic development concern.

Capital mobility theory states that FDI is allocation of capital to a cross-border projects that are constrained with institutional factors. Investment in a host country is determined by factors such as governance, regulatory systems credibility, corruption level, and the rule of law in that country. These factors determine the cost of capital and the risk premium the investment will incur incase the decision is made. Investment into the renewable energy sector is assessed by calculating the risk premiums through the weighted average cost of capital. When this theory is adopted, the developing economies are limited because the risk premiums are always high and thus marking the infeasibility of return in investment of the capital flows into the rE in the developing and emerging economies. The CCTM model is developed based on this theory. The model integrates the analysis of investment decision based structured balance sheet that include the transition policy, carbon pricing, and blended finance as well as the banking policies by the central bank of the host country.

RESEARCH DESIGN AND METHODOLOGY

This chapter adopts a conceptual-analytical research methodology, supported by bibliometric mapping and secondary data analysis. The primary objective is to develop the Capital-to-Climate Flow Transition Model (CCTM) by integrating concepts from foreign direct investment theory, stock-flow consistent macroeconomics, and energy transition economics. The study employs secondary data and institutional reports from organizations; International Energy Agency (IEA), the World Bank, and the United Nations Conference on Trade and Development (UNCTAD), which provide global statistics on renewable energy investment, foreign direct investment flows, and energy transition finance. Comparative evaluations of industrialized, emerging, and developing nations are utilized to illustrate differences in institutional quality, capital cost conditions, and trends in renewable investment.

The study uses bibliometric analysis in conjunction with conceptual synthesis to illustrate the evolution and expansion of the academic literature on green FDI and renewable energy finance over time. Bibliometric techniques were used to index publications in prominent academic databases. The mapping emphasized on renewable energy investment, green foreign direct investment, energy transition financing, and climate investment. Study utilized co-citation and keyword co-occurrence analysis to identify the most significant research clusters and emerging thematic topics. The findings enhance the proposed CCTM framework within the broad academic discourse and demonstrate the growing convergence of research in foreign direct investment, Renewable energy, green finance and climate finance. This bibliometric mapping provides an empirical foundation for the conceptual model and strengthens the chapter's analytical methodology of comparative topic synthesis across institutional and geographical contexts.

THE STRUCTURAL TRANSITION-MODEL CCTM

Capital-to-Climate Flow Transition Model (figure 1) is a theoretical and mathematical model aimed at understanding and enabling the reallocation of financial capital flows toward climate mitigation and adaptation objectives. The model assumes that the Paris Agreement targets will be met when capital is redirected on a large scale from carbon-intensive assets into climate-resilient, low-carbon infrastructure such as renewable energy (ETC, 2023). The Energy Transitions Commission estimates that approximately US$3.5 trillion in investment per year will be required worldwide by 2050 to fund the net-zero transition.

Current analytical frameworks are inadequate for elucidating the changing dynamics of capital reallocation in the global energy transition. The existing assessment integrated models like DICE assumes that capital flow is uniform and it is optimized across the investment borders. The frameworks do not consider the actual limitations in investments from the institution diversity of the host country. The capital-climate flow transition model, CCTM) bridges the gap that existed in the old frameworks like stock-flow consistent (SFC) theory. The traditional model focused on domestic sectors, which ensures that all financial flows and stocks within the economy are rigorously accounted for (Godley and Lavoie, 2007; Caverzasi and Godin, 2015). SFC models track the interactions among households, firms, banks, and governments and maintain balance sheet coherence, avoiding accounting black holes (Nikiforos and Zezza, 2017).

The CCTM builds upon old models by distinguishing between green capital (low-carbon or climate-resilient) and so-called brown capital (carbon-intensive), thereby representing the redirection of financial flows within the sector during a structural transition. This is based on previous literature: a stock-flow-fund ecological macroeconomic model was developed by Dafermos, Nikolaidi, and Galanis (2016) and explicitly models the representation of both monetary and physical stocks (e.g., energy, emissions) and is used to simulate the effect of green investment and climate finance on the dynamics of the macro-finance under ecological constraints.

The dynamics of stranded assets from the balance sheets is that, fossil fuel companies contain reserves and fixed capital that are at danger of becoming stranded assets as the energy transition progresses. CCTM estimates stranded asset write-downs based on the trajectory of carbon prices, the deflation of renewable energy costs, and the pace of regulatory transitions. Write-downs diminish the net worth of the fossil sector, undermining collateral values and prompting a contraction in bank lending. This credit tightening permeates the financial sector's balance sheet, potentially inducing macroprudential instability, a mechanism not accounted for in current IAMs and SFC models.

CCTM's theoretical contribution is that FDI is a mediator of reallocation of capital to host countries' economies that is constrained by institutional governance factors. Thus, FDI inflows into the renewable is constituted as a function of the institution quality of the host country, the Weighted Average Cost of Capital differential denoted by ΔWACC of host and source country, renewable investment expected returns (r_RE), the global carbon price denoted by P_C, and the stranded asset reallocation pressure denoted by ΔK_stranded.

$$FDI_{-RE} = f(IQ, \Delta WACC, r_{-RE}, P_{-C}, \Delta K_{-stranded})$$

$\boldsymbol{FDI_{-RE}}$ is positively correlated with IQ, $\boldsymbol{r_{-RE}}$, $\boldsymbol{P_{-C}}$, $\boldsymbol{\Delta K_{-stranded}}$; it is negatively correlated with ΔWACC.This methodology integrates capital mobility theory (OLI), institutional quality conditioning, sustainable finance, and climate transition theory into a unified behavioral equation.

The model utilizes a cost of capital mechanism by incorporating the Weighted Average Cost of Capital (WACC) which is calculated endogenously based on the risk-free rate (r_f), institutional risk premium (π_IQ), currency risk premium (π_FX), political risk premium (π_P), and policy credibility discount (δ_PC):

$$WACC = r_{-f} + \pi_{-IQ} + \pi_{-FX} + \pi_{\_P} - \delta_{-PC}$$

Institutional quality directly reduces π_IQ and indirectly reduces π_P. The credibility of policy, evaluated by implementation history, treaty requirements, and central bank environmental duties, reduces WACC via δ_PC. This methodology produces verifiable predictions: improvements in governance lead to measurable decreases in the cost of capital; policy reversals cause increases in WACC and the withdrawal of FDI.

The deficiencies existing in the theories and traditional models in incorporating institutional quality, financial risk premiums, and climate policy in the investment of FDI and transition of energy sector calls for the CCTM framework to bridge the limitations. This chapter presents the Capital-to-Climate Flow Transition Model (CCTM) to overcome these limitations, by presenting a cohesive framework for examining institutionally conditioned, cross-border capital reallocation within a fully coherent macro-financial structure.

Figure 1. Capital-to-Climate Flow Transition Model

Bibliometric Mapping of Capital-to-Climate Flows Transitions (2000-2025)

To help explain the transition of capital flows to climate flows in research agendas, a bibliometric review was conducted using the Scopus database from 2000 to 2025. This database was considered for retrieving the literature due to several compelling reasons (Derviş, H., 2020). The search string included terms from three domains; Capital slows (foreign direct investment" OR "capital flows" OR "capital mobility");

Climate flows and renewable energy ("climate finance" OR "renewable energy" OR "green investment" OR "energy transition"); and macroeconomic frameworks ("institutional quality" OR "stock-flow consistent" OR "balance sheet")

The keyword resulted in 4,867 documents after deduplication. The timeframe was limited to 2000 to 2025, as there were few publications prior to 2000. Other limitations, such as peer-reviewed-only articles and subject area, were applied. Finally, the title and abstract were reviewed for relevance, resulting in 599 articles that directly matched our keywords. VOSviewer was utilized to obtain keyword co-occurrences. Five thematic clusters emerged, and the overlay visualization (figure 1) shows that, in the period 2023-2025, literature has emerged in the areas of technology transfer, green finance, and spillover effects. However, publications on terms such as Green FDI, CCTM, and institutional quality are absent from the network, as indicated by the dominant keywords. This gives a direct visual need for the Capital-to-Climate Transition model to address this fragmentation (figure 2).

Figure 2. Authors' keyword co-occurrence overlay visualization

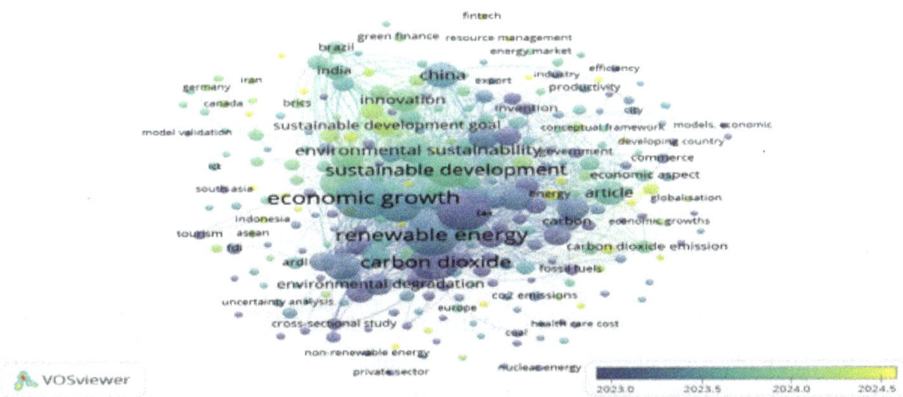

Source: Authors' bibliometric analysis using Scopus (2000–2025); VOSviewer keyword co-occurrence mapping.

Thematic Cluster Analysis

Cluster 1: Foreign Direct Investment and Economic Growth

This cluster assesses the economic growth resulting from foreign direct investment. It highlights the effects in terms of technology transfer, spillover in productivity, and the host countries' absorptive capacity (Borensztein et al., 1998; Alfaro et al., 2004). The study links show investment and growth at a macro development level, and that climate flows and energy transition studies are absent.

Cluster 2: Climate Financing.

This cluster analyzes products in sustainable finance, such as green bonds, carbon markets, and ESG investments. The literature has proliferated during the mid-2010s alongside global climate policy measures (Flammer, 2021; Karpf & Mandel, 2018). Nonetheless, foreign direct investment is generally regarded as ancillary, and the consistency of macro-financial balance sheets is infrequently considered.

Cluster 3: Economics of Renewable Energy.

This cluster examines the economics of renewable energy transition, more so cost changes, incentives regulation, and renewable technologies implementation. (Schmidt et al., 2019) highlights the essence of decarbonization and transition of energy system through capital mobility across the border investment in macroeconomic sectors.

Cluster 4: Stock–Flow Consistent Macroeconomics.

This concise, theory-based literature employs stock-flow consistent frameworks to examine financial stability and macroeconomic dynamics. Although newer ecological extensions include environmental variables, the literature seldom models renewable energy sectors or international financial flows (Dafermos et al., 2016, 2018).

Cluster 5: Quality of Institutions and Investment.

This group connects institutional quality, regulatory efficiency, and the laws that direct investment flows and affect the performance of the economy. The quality of institutions is observed to determine the host countries in which FDI flows would be directed (Kaufmann et al., 2011; North, 1990). The cluster, however, shows tenuous links between climate flows and renewable energy investments.

Integration

The bibliometric visualization (figure 2) indicates disjointed research trajectories. Foreign direct investment, climate flows, renewable energy economics, macroeconomic modeling, and institutional governance progress predominantly in tandem, exhibiting minimal theoretical integration among the fields.

Case Study Country Analysis of FDI and Renewables

This list includes Brazil, India, Kenya, Vietnam, Morocco, South Africa, and Turkey as instances of foreign direct investment (FDI) that has resulted in changes in renewable energy. These nations demonstrate how rapidly energy markets are expanding in Latin America, Sub-Saharan Africa, South Asia, North Africa, Southeast Asia, and Eurasia. They have a variety of renewable resources, including hydropower, wind, geothermal energy, and solar. To attract foreign investment, they utilize a variety of procedures, including competitive auctions, feed-in tariffs, blended financing models, and institutional procurement programs. The countries have had real data that advocates for FDI being a source of transition in the renewable energy sector through infrastructure projects, technology spillover, energy cost efficiencies and knowledge transfer. Foreign direct investment success in the transition of renewable energy sector depends on the legal frameworks, resource availability and institutional qualities (table 1).

Table 1. Country Analysis of FDI and Renewables

Country	Key Renewable Sectors	Role of FDI	Major Projects / Evidence	Policy & Institutional Drivers	Key Constraints
Brazil	Hydropower, wind, solar	Positive long-run association between FDI inflows and renewable energy generation; foreign capital supports low-carbon capacity growth	Chinese power companies invest about 97% of Brazilian energy investment in renewables; Pirapora Solar Complex (321 MW) was developed by EDF and Canadian Solar	Favourable regulatory environment, power procurement through auctions, and abundant renewable resources	Grid connection risks, environmental approval, land regularization, commercial operation delays, and potential pollution-intensive FDI effects
India	Solar, wind	FDI is strongly linked with renewable capacity expansion; it facilitates technology learning and declining solar tariffs	National Solar Mission projects; large solar parks in Rajasthan and Karnataka; investments from SoftBank Energy, Engie, EDF Renewables	Long-term PPAs, transparent auctions, renewable portfolio standards, and Electricity Act reforms	Grid congestion, curtailment risk, land-use conflicts, and state-level regulatory inconsistency
Kenya	Geothermal, wind, solar	Foreign capital supports project financing, technology transfer, and distributed energy solutions	Olkaria geothermal fields, Lake Turkana Wind Power (LTWP) project; off-grid solar home system ecosystem	Blended finance, international venture capital, comparatively stable regulatory environment	Land governance issues, community engagement challenges, delayedgrid infrastructure
Vietnam	Solar, wind	Renewable boom closely linked to foreign capital inflows and global supply chain integration	More than 16 GW solar capacity installed (2018–2021); projects from Gulf Energy, Super Energy, Orsted, CIP	Feed-in tariffs, power sector liberalization, government net-zero commitment, and power purchase agreements	Grid congestion, curtailment, and uneven provincial policy implementation
Morocco	Solar, wind, green hydrogen	FDI accelerates national renewable transition and supports high-technology installations	Noor Ouarzazate Solar Complex, Tarfaya Wind Farm	Long-term energy strategy, MASEN centralized governance, blended finance with multilateral institutions	Land-use conflicts, social impacts, grid modernization requirements

continued on following page

Table 1. Continued

Country	Key Renewable Sectors	Role of FDI	Major Projects / Evidence	Policy & Institutional Drivers	Key Constraints
South Africa	Wind, solar PV	FDI catalyzed through competitive procurement and transparent auctions	Renewable Energy Independent Power Producer Procurement Programme (REIPPPP) is attracting over US$20 billion investment	Competitive tenders, government guarantees, and institutional procurement framework	Grid congestion, transmission shortages, and Eskom financial instability
Turkey	Wind, solar, geothermal, hydro	FDI stimulates industrial development and renewable technology deployment	YEKA renewable auctions, geothermal investments supported by the World Bank Clean Technology Fund	Market liberalization, feed-in tariffs, diversified renewable resources	Currency instability, regulatory risks, and grid integration constraints

Capital Concentration Trends

In 2023, global foreign direct investment (FDI) in renewable energy reached USD 544 billion, a 93% increase from 2019 (UNCTAD, 2024). However, capital concentration has increased: the OECD nations' share grew from 68% in 2019 to 73% in 2023, while Sub-Saharan Africa's portion stayed about the same at 2.1% to 2.3% (table 2). The average difference in WACC between renewable projects in OECD countries and those in low-income countries grew from 680 basis points in 2019 to 750 basis points in 2023. This was due to falling sovereign ratings and political risk (Climate Policy Initiative, 2025). During that time, blended funding from MDB to developing nations expanded from USD 41 billion to USD 68 billion. However, this only meets 14% of the expected annual investment needs for renewable energy in developing countries (OECD, 2023). These findings assert CCTM's fundamental hypothesis: disparities in institutional quality, rather than capital shortage, induce concentration (table 2).

Table 2. Capital Concentration Trends Across Different Economies

Country	Economy	Institutional Quality (WGI, 2024)	Renewable FDI Inflows (USD bn, 2023–24)	Key Policy Instruments	Cost-of-Capital (WACC, 2024)	Observed Transition Dynamics
Germany	Developed	High (86th pct.)	USD 18.4 bn	Carbon pricing; FIT; EU taxonomy	4.1% WACC	Rapid wind/solar scale-up; coal phase-out; EU capital integration
United States	Developed	High (84th pct.)	USD 67.2 bn	IRA tax credits; PTC/ITC; FERC permitting	5.3% WACC	IRA-driven greenfield surge; reshoring FDI; battery deployment
Japan	Developed	High (82nd pct.)	USD 9.1 bn	GX Strategy; carbon market; offshore wind auctions	3.8% WACC	Offshore wind expansion; hydrogen FDI nascent; slow coal exit
China	Emerging	Medium (52nd pct.)	USD 83.1 bn	Industrial policy; NEV subsidies; ETS; state-directed FDI	3.2% (policy-supported)	World's largest RE installer; state-led outbound green FDI; regulatory risk for foreign investors
India	Emerging	Medium (56th pct.)	USD 11.3 bn	ISTS waiver; PM-KUSUM; green hydrogen mission; auction regime	8.4% WACC	Rapid solar FDI; offshore wind nascent; currency risk premium persistent
Brazil	Emerging	Medium (47th pct.)	USD 8.6 bn	ANEEL auctions; Proinfra; offshore wind regulation 2023	9.2% WACC	Strong wind/solar corridor; offshore wind emerging; ESG FDI dampened by governance risk
South Africa	Developing	Low–Med (40th pct.)	USD 3.2 bn	REIPPP; JET-IP; carbon tax	12.1% WACC	REIPPP auction success; Eskom grid instability; JET-IP concessional finance bridging gap
Kenya	Developing	Low–Med (38th pct.)	USD 1.4 bn	FiT; energy sector reforms; bilateral IIAs	13.5% WACC	Geothermal FDI stable; solar scaling; MDB blended finance critical
Bangladesh	Developing	Low (28th pct.)	USD 0.6 bn	Net metering; SREDA; TICAD climate commitments	15.8% WACC	Minimal private RE FDI; near-total dependence on concessional ODA; governance constraints deter capital

Sources: Authors analysis from UNCTAD (2024); IEA (2024); World Bank WGI (2024); Climate Policy Initiative (2024); IMF (2025); IRENA (2023).

RISKS, CHALLENGES, AND GOVERNANCE BARRIERS

Despite increased climate-related capital flows, significant risks and structural barriers hinder green foreign direct investment (FDI). Key issues include greenwashing, where projects falsely marketed as green lack strong impact measures and transparency (de Freitas Netto et al., 2020; Andriuskevicius, 2025). The vague green taxonomies create uncertainty for investors and host governments (Pienknagura, 2024). Empirical studies on 'responsible investment practices' (RIP) have exposed the instances of 'impression management and greenwashing' in the context of environmental, social, and governance (ESG) considerations. The concept 'responsible investment (RI)' acts as a 'means to manage the risks' associated with ESG and as a 'marketing strategy' as it is used to improve the public image, and the existence of a weak regulatory framework enables the firms to exaggerate ESG commitments and hence increases the chances of greenwashing (Olatubosun & Nyazenga, 2021). A few other studies have revealed that the subsidy schemes counteract the green FDI efforts even though the climate policies enhance them to a greater extent. A few other factors which complicate the investment landscape include the existence of multiple agencies, deficiencies in implementation capability and the lack of inter-agency coordination, which contribute towards increased transaction costs and an elevated risk premium (Pienknagura, 2024). The barriers to governance in emerging economies also hinder climate-compatible foreign direct investment (FDI), where the issues include low institutional capacity, absence of de-risking instruments, limited depth of local financial markets, and lack of long-term financing sources for renewables (Egli,2020). Structural impediments, such as fossil-fuel subsidies, infrastructure lock-in, land-use conflicts, and grid constraints, further deter new investments (Monasterolo and Raberto, 2019). The following discusses the obstacles to green foreign direct investment (FDI).

Risks (Policy or Regulatory, Financial and political risks)

Early studies in developed countries have identified that policy or regulatory risks impede investments in renewable energy (Gatzert and Kosub, 2017). Countries such as Spain, Bulgaria, Italy and Greece faced this risk by the retrospective adjustments in their support schemes, such as 'FIT reductions' for renewable energy investments (Gatzert and Vogl, 2016). Even though feed-in tariffs, tax incentives and emissions trading enhance the FDI in the renewable energy sector, public funding is not considered as an effective mechanism for drawing FDI (Wall et al., 2019). The World Investment Report 2023 highlighted 'abrupt and frequent policy amendments' as one of the most relevant factors under policy and regulatory risks, as it adversely affects the long-term predictability of capital-intensive projects (Giroud, 2024). An empirical study by Villabruna et al. (2024) on barriers and strategies for green investments in seaport companies revealed that green investments necessitate high capital investment costs, placing a financial strain on port operators, with ROI being long-term or uncertain, which discourages investment. Inconsistent and ambiguous regulatory policies which impede ESG compliance and the lack of long-term regulations for green infrastructure and technologies acts as one of the major risks of green investment.

Developing countries struggle to finance renewable energy projects, prompting the Kyoto Protocol and Paris Agreement to advocate for financial support from wealthier nations. The financing needs of these countries can be addressed through FDIs, but the investors' confidence is mostly diminished by the lack of political stability, as the long-term viability and policy consistency issues remain. Even though the supportive factors such as schemes of 'feed-in tariff' and 'deregulation' facilitate FDIs, the long-term viability issue remains a major concern. Moreover, undervaluation of projects due to 'conventional investment appraisal techniques', which depends on risk-adjusted discount rates (RADR), is based on conventional assumptions. All these contribute towards lower investments in long-term investment avenues as the risk-averse investors disengage themselves in such contexts (Shimbar and Ebrahimi, 2020).

Environmental and Social Challenges

One of the major stimulants of green FDI is the stringent regulations on environmental aspects in the home country of the potential investors. The pollution haven hypothesis (PHH) theory suggests that MNCs prefer to locate in countries with weaker environmental regulations, especially with their environmentally intensive activities, to reduce their compliance costs (Chipalkatti et al., 2021). Other studies, both pro and anti PHH, in this area have demonstrated mixed results wherein FDI patterns are compared against environmental regulations and highlighted the complicated and context-dependent nature of FDI on environmental regulation of a country. The 2017 study by Zheng & Shi revealed the consistency of the FDI pattern with the strong environmental framework of the home country, while the recent study has demonstrated that MNCs prefer countries with weaker environmental regulations, especially for their pollution-intensive projects (Zheng et al., 2025).

Another prominent factor which affects FDI in renewable energy projects is the socio-environmental risks, which emerge as a result of conflict with local communities, especially during land acquisitions in ecologically sensitive areas or in the case of overlapping with indigenous territories. This conflict leads to delays in project completion and legal challenges in addition to financial losses to the potential investor (Susskind et al., 2022). The causal path of socio-environmental grievances to investor risks is established in the empirical studies through the mechanisms by which it operates. The protests and litigation result in delays in the execution of the projects and cost overruns; reputational damage affects the investor mandates, followed by alterations in project economies by legal rulings and, in the end, off-taker risk by the investor if disputes are unsettled at the government level (Minadakis and Vega-Araujo, 2024). A study by Yáñez-Valdés and Guerrero (2024) suggests that equity crowdfunding platforms tackle social challenges by fostering investor participation in the collaborative development of sustainable technological solutions.

Governance Barriers

One of the most prominent risks associated with green FDI is corruption and fragmented governance (Tawiah et al., 2024). As the corruption does not support efficient resource allocation, resulting in environmental degradation, it adversely affects the implementation of climate policies of a country. Studies in this domain have demonstrated that sustainable investment is significantly impacted by poor ESG decision-making, which is caused by the low levels of stakeholder engagement and coordination (Villabruna et al., 2024), while factors such as subsidies and a robust green governance system positively contribute to it. Studies conducted in China have revealed that economic growth in alignment with environmental sustainability is possible through a collaborative governance framework (Wang & Wang, 2023). It is also demonstrated through some other studies that firms experience lower financial constraints if they have a robust green governance structure (Li et al., 2020). These lower financial constraints are possible because of the integration of green concepts and CSR into their vision, strategy and culture, which fosters a sense of moral responsibility among the stakeholders, resulting in improved investor confidence in environmentally sustainable projects (Allen et al., 2005).

Empirical evidence suggests a multifaceted approach to address these issues, including strong anti-corruption laws, transparent governance, and international cooperation (Kaur et al., 2024). To implement resilient finance and to promote a 'Global Green New Deal' the global governance institution could adopt a global taxation-and-bonds framework aimed at addressing environmental inequalities through the financing of renewable energy via green bonds (Puaschunder, 2023).

Policy Roadmap for Accelerating Climate Flows

Barriers of Investments in Developing Countries

Developing countries have put a lot of effort in commitment and designing policy frameworks that foster attraction of FDI; however, this effort is still insufficient as a result of barriers that hinder renewable energy FDI to scales required. Such barriers include regulatory risk and policy uncertainty. Renewable energy projects are long-term and require projections of up to 15 years. Uncertainty, such as tariff changes, the elimination of subsidies, contract reductions, and policy reversals, affects investors' decisions to deploy capital to projects. Two country examples are: in Kenya, a pause in renewable procurement occurred between 2016 and 2019 due to political controversy, which created regulatory risk among investors and halted a project that would have otherwise been of high quality. India FIT project phase out, on the other hand, demonstrated low policy commitment by the country thus creating investor uncertainty (Michaelowa et al., 2019).

Renewable energy deployment faces infrastructure deficits in developing countries. The need for adequate grid, strong distribution systems, transmission bottlenecks are constraints that the developing countries are limited and in turn becomes technical and economic barriers to investment opportunities. For a successful installation of renewable energy there is need for coordination between developers and the system operators to breach the gap in minimisation of costs and stability of systems installed (Grübler et al., 2018). The capacity of developing countries is constrained by intense capital investment required in installing modern grids, exploring smart technologies, and creating adequate storage systems.

Another notable investment barriers are in the financing gap. The developing economies explicit high cost of capital and low development of capital market. Renewable projects majorly depend on the foreign borrowing as the domestic market lacks the debt capacity, this increases the risk in the foreign exchange. According to Climate Policy Initiative (2025), the cost of capital in Sub–Saharan Africa ranges from 10-15% while in developed economies is 3-5%. The high disparity in cost of capital hinders deployment of renewable energy projects that would have otherwise been viable. The developed economies lower cost of capital allows environment for robust renewable energy projects (Anku, 2025).

Renewable Energy requires experts in both technical and human capital capacity; developing economies are often limited in this expertise, including technicians, engineers, and project developers. These deficiencies call for training programmes and an expatriate workforce, thus increasing the cost of the projects. A lack of strong technical capacity and infrastructure in an economy leads to a quality assurance gap, allowing the entry of substandard materials and ultimately resulting in low investor confidence (Monkelbaan, 2019).

Large-scale renewable energy projects often require the acquisition of land, which may encounter opposition from the locals. In case the project faces such hurdles, it is likely to lead to delays and even the cancellation of the investment. The growth economies of the world mostly depend on agricultural investments; the establishment of renewable energies would imply the dislocation and payment of the settlements residing on the mentioned land in a fairly rewarding, benefits-sharing way. Unless such challenges are dealt with effectively, they can lead to conflicts and discourage investment. The assessment of the impact on the environment is often inadequate, and the communities resettled think that the compensation amounts are not enough to replace their livelihood. Such challenges in developing economies cause a halt or delay of the projects (George et al., 2020; Li, n.d.; Matome, 2024).

Policy Tools and De-Risking Mechanism.

To overcome the above obstacles, it is necessary to combine a policy with particular regulatory frameworks, not to mention creating innovative financing and using strategic de-risking. These roadmaps are based on regulatory predictability and the policy framework. Uncertainty to policy is addressed by participating in long-term renewable energy project plans, which are fronted by legal commitments. Favourable tariffs and high-power purchase attract the interest of the private investors since they depict revenue certainty in an investment. Renewable Energy Act, competitive auctions, and procurement systems were among the models that, over the years, have shown that credible and clear regulatory systems are the key to attracting FDI (Szarka, 2004; Bruckner et al., 2014).

The de-risking instruments cause the investments to appear less risky, which benefits the finances of the project and attracts institutional investors. Political risk insurance (MIGA guarantees, OPIC insurance) is insured against sovereign risk, contract repudiation, and currency that is inconvertible. They are particularly appropriate in pioneer regions where risk perception by the investors surpasses the reality and where insurance can increase capital investment due to its mere existence (MIGA, 2023). At the level of attracting commercial participation, concessional financing with interest rates below market, with long tenors and subordinated equity, improves project returns sufficiently. Development finance institutions provide concessional finance, which predisposes the private investment through alleviating project risks. This paradigm can be seen in the A/B loan structure of the IFC, which consists of a concessional A loan, used to take the first loss of the commercial B loans to protect their interests and increase returns, thereby encouraging the growth of private investment (Climate Investment Funds, 2023)

Blended Finance Mechanism

Blended financing strategies combine concessional and commercial finance to enhance the risk-return profile of projects. The climate investment flows created a blended finance structure; concessional funds reduce subordinated risk, allowing commercial investors to invest capital in significant industries with less risk. This method illustrates scalability; multilateral development banks are increasingly employing blending frameworks to address the “missing middle” investment gap, which encompasses projects considered too risky for purely commercial financing yet too viable to justify exclusive aid approaches (Trabacchi & Stadelmann, 2015).

Private Sector Accountability and Sustainability Standards

Increasing levels of foreign direct investment mean a pressing demand for a governance framework of sustainability and for a protection of the community. Unregulated forms of renewable capital can be extractive, whereby multinational capitalists reap rewards while shifting expenses related to the environment and communities (Sadoff & Grey, 2002). Standards and the impact assessments are needed to be improved. The host country governments are needed to make the environmental impact assessments encompass the baseline studies and the long-term monitoring. The global standards include the Performance Standards on the IFC and the World Bank Safeguards Policies. There are limitations in their capacity in terms of the oversight capacity in the host countries. This means that countries on which capacity has been reduced experience difficulty in applying these standards despite acceptance (Suding et al., 2015).

Community consultation processes and benefit-sharing agreements are essential in arriving at the sustainability outcomes. Communities affected by the sustainability outcomes of projects need to be provided meaningful levels of consultation rather than mere information transfer. Agreements on the benefit-sharing process, such as employment guarantees, community development agreements, or profit-sharing agreements, ensure the cooperation of the stakeholder group, thus improving sustainability outcomes. Resource disparities often exist in the relationships formed between communities and developers, with disadvantaged groups engaged in negotiations with transnational corporations that enjoy advantages due to their better resource endowment and alternative project sites (Jenkins et al., 2017).

Labour standards and just transition support cover employment issues. Renewable energy projects offer short-term employment opportunities during the construction phase, and this leads to very few long-term job opportunities. It is appropriate for host nations to demand training elements to enhance labour capacity for long-term employment. It becomes necessary to have fair transition support for affected workers due to the stopping of fossil fuel consumption, and this requires retraining and economic diversification of areas that rely on coal. International development financial institutions must offer just transition funding together with investments in renewable energy for fair distribution of transition elements and gains (Pollin & Callaci, 2019).

Supply Chain Governance: This entails the management of mining practices in supply chains. Cobalt and Lithium battery materials manufacturing, as well as Rare Earth element processing and Polysilicon production, pose considerable risks of worker exploitation and damage to the environment. Financial investors can put measures in place to ensure environmental and labor practices are respected and artisan miners' conditions are also met. Responsible practices such as Responsible Care and Fair-trade practices and frameworks of Due Diligence, such as OECD's Due Diligence Guidance, act as management structures. Problems with verification come across in their implementation (Reck & Graedel, 2012).

FUTURE RESEARCH DIRECTIONS

This chapter uses the Capital-to-Climate Transition Model (CCTM) to illustrate the shift from capital flows to climate flows. The model is theoretical and conceptual that is not based on empirical evidence this is a limitation as well as future research agenda where model incorporates datasets of FDI flows, WACC time series data and institutional quality of cross-country coverage. Subsequent research should focus on developing panel datasets that can evaluate the causal links outlined in the framework.

The comparative country analysis used rely on aggregated macroeconomic and investment data from international databases, including those of UNCTAD, IEA, IMF, and the World Bank. The descriptive analysis highlights only the trends and patterns in RE-FDI, not the econometric valuation. To establish a causal relationship between renewable energy investment and institutional quality, sophisticated econometric techniques, such as instrumental variable estimates and dynamic panel methods, are used to mitigate endogeneity issues (IMF, 2024).

Third, under this approach, institutional quality is seen as an exogenous variable. The model states that substantial investment in renewable energy may progressively enhance governance capacity, regulatory quality, and policy credibility; however, these feedback processes are not explicitly addressed. Incorporating institutional development into the CCTM framework would signify a significant second-order expansion, encompassing the long-term connections between green investment and institutional change.

The CCTM model emphasizes macro-financial flows and investment incentives. However, factors such as regional inequality, differences in the labour market, and unequal access to energy in the host country remain unaddressed. (International Energy Agency, 2023). These are pertinent issues common to emerging and developed economies, where expenditure on renewable energy intersects with broader economic growth. As a result, further research ought to investigate many pathways. At first, empirical research might use bilateral panel datasets from 2010 to 2025 to examine how flexible foreign direct investment in renewable energy is in relation to the quality of institutions. Second, agent-based modeling methods could be able to show different types of investor behavior, including how multinational firms and institutional investors respond strategically to climate legislation. The framework might be broadened to incorporate central bank green asset purchase initiatives and sustainable monetary policy instruments, which are progressively seen as mechanisms to promote the low-carbon transition. Fourth, more studies should examine the correlation between renewable energy investment and the sustainability of sovereign debt, particularly in emerging economies where climate investment demands substantially surpass fiscal capacity. The CCTM paradigm may be applied in regional corridors such as Sub-Saharan Africa and Southeast Asia, where significant renewable energy potential and investment deficiencies persist.

Suggestion is also made that the future research should examine link existing between climate innovation and foreign direct investment through bibliometric methods. It should also create long-term project-level datasets that can track how investments in the renewable sector lead to measurable climate outcomes. More research on how institutional characteristics affect climate-related investment flows could be conducted if case studies were conducted in less well-known regions, including small developing island states and least developed countries. Furthermore, further study ought to examine the impact of rising ESG standards and sustainable finance taxonomies on the trajectory and structure of global FDI flows into climate-related industries.

CONCLUSION

The global call for transition from high carbon to low carbon and more environmental resilient projects demands a shift in investment flows. There is need to adopt modern analytical models like CCTM to mitigate this gap that traditional finance initially focused on. Adopting an integrated model to direct finance to a whole round economy that focuses on not only a technological transfer but the institutional quality of an economy. The chapter model addresses the weaknesses by providing a theoretical approach that integrates capital costs, quality of institutions and FDI allocation within a balance sheet structure.

CCTM's approach is that the institution quality has an effect on the cost of capital which directly affects where the foreign investments is directed to. With this effect on the cost of capital the investment flows into energy deployment are also affected. The higher the cost of capital as a result of institutional quality the lower the renewables project investments. The comparative analysis of emerging, developed and developing economies shows that the barrier to investment flows into renewable energy is in the institutional quality and not in the technological discrepancies. The results show that despite the rising renewable investment appetite in host countries there is still untapped potentials due to the limitations that the host countries portray in their institutions and rules that do not favor the green investments.

Three theoretical contributions are provided by this model. One, FDI is illustrated as an institutional mediator to the transfer of capital from multinational global investments into the macro financial sector of host countries. Two, it contributes to the research in climate transition by providing an analytical model that considers weighted average cost of capital, asset risk and reclamation of credit aspects in the investment decisions. Third, the model provides international organization and economies with a policy focused analytical framework. This can allow the government to strategically evaluate the most effective investment mobilization depending on legislative rules and the policies of central bank in adopting blended finance or approaching carbon pricing.

The chapter's empirical results from bibliometric analysis shows that there is significant growth in the green foreign direct investments agendas. FDI is being adopted as a means of shifting capital, technological spillover and expertise in management to the renewable energy and other green ventures in the host economies. It shows that countries with strong institutions and commitment to climate frameworks provided by the OECD attracts more FDI's as compared to weak institutions and regulatory frameworks. The transition from capital to climate flows is a fundamental global reconfiguration perspective other than ecological objective in order to attain the global climate change resistant development of the economy.

The need to attain USD 4.5 trillion a year by 2030 of investment in clean energy globally, IEA recommends a collective effort in the deployment of funds to the sector. Such CCTM analytical frameworks helps bring together governance in institutions, financial systems and energy investment procedures. The model provides ideas of analyzing how multinational organizations, capital markets, and institution governance can work together to meet the climate finance requirements globally.

REFERENCES

Adeel, M., Wang, B., Ke, J., & Mvitu, I. M. (2025). The nonlinear dynamics of CO_2 emissions in Pakistan: A comprehensive analysis of transportation, electricity consumption, and foreign direct investment. *Sustainability (Basel), 17*(1), 189. Advance online publication. DOI: 10.3390/su17010189

Alfaro, L., Chanda, A., Kalemli-Ozcan, S., & Sayek, S. (2004). FDI and economic growth: The role of local financial markets. *Journal of International Economics, 64*(1), 89–112. DOI: 10.1016/S0022-1996(03)00081-3

Allen, F., Qian, J., & Qian, M. (2005). Law, finance, and economic growth in China. *Journal of Financial Economics, 77*(1), 57–116. DOI: 10.1016/j.jfineco.2004.06.010

Andriuskevicius, K. (2025). Green Investments. In *Societal Challenges and Opportunities of Low-Carbon Energy Transformations* (pp. 333–375). CRC Press. DOI: 10.1201/9781003517481-8

Anku, J. E. (2025). Barriers to renewable energy adoption in Sub-Saharan Africa: a stakeholder perspective. Available at *SSRN* 5087846. DOI: 10.2139/ssrn.5087846

Borensztein, E., De Gregorio, J., & Lee, J. W. (1998). How does foreign direct investment affect economic growth? *Journal of International Economics, 45*(1), 115–135. DOI: 10.1016/S0022-1996(97)00033-0

Buchner, B. K., Clark, A., Falconer, A., Macquarie, R., Meattle, C., Tolentino, R., & Wetherbee, C. (2019). *Global landscape of climate finance 2019*. Climate Policy Initiative.

Caverzasi, E., & Godin, A. (2015). Stock-flow consistent modeling through the ages. *Cambridge Journal of Economics, 39*(1), 157–181. DOI: 10.1093/cje/beu021

Chipalkatti, N., Le, Q. V., & Rishi, M. (2021). Sustainability and society: Do environmental, social, and governance factors matter for foreign direct investment? *Energies, 14*(19), 6039. DOI: 10.3390/en14196039

Climate Policy Initiative. (2025). Cost of Capital for Renewable Energy Investments in Developing Countries.

Dafermos, Y., Nikolaidi, M., & Galanis, G. (2016). A stock–flow–fund ecological macroeconomic model. *Ecological Economics, 131*, 191–207. DOI: 10.1016/j.ecolecon.2016.08.013

Dafermos, Y., Nikolaidi, M., & Galanis, G. (2018). Climate change, financial stability and monetary policy. *Ecological Economics*, *152*, 219–234. DOI: 10.1016/j.ecolecon.2018.05.011

de Freitas Netto, S. V., Sobral, M. F. F., Ribeiro, A. R. B., & Soares, G. R. D. L. (2020). Concepts and forms of greenwashing: A systematic review. *Environmental Sciences Europe*, *32*(1), 19. DOI: 10.1186/s12302-020-0300-3

Egli, F. (2020). Renewable energy investment risk: An investigation of changes over time and the underlying drivers. *Energy Policy*, *140*, 111428. DOI: 10.1016/j.enpol.2020.111428

Emodi, N. V., Rekker, S., Greig, C., Wade, B., Inekwe, J. N., & Zakari, A. (2023). The contribution of cross-border capital flow towards decarbonisation. *Journal of Cleaner Production*, *405*, 137040. Advance online publication. DOI: 10.1016/j.jclepro.2023.137040

Energy Transitions Commission. (2023). Financing the transition to a net-zero economy. *Etc.; a Review of General Semantics.*

Flammer, C. (2021). Corporate green bonds. *Journal of Financial Economics*, *142*(2), 499–516. DOI: 10.1016/j.jfineco.2021.01.010

Gatzert, N., & Kosub, T. (2017). Determinants of policy risks of renewable energy investments. *International journal of energy sector management, 11*(1), 28-45.

Gatzert, N., & Vogl, N. (2016). Evaluating investments in renewable energy under policy risks. *Energy Policy*, *95*, 238–252. DOI: 10.1016/j.enpol.2016.04.027

George, T. E.. (2020). An evaluation of the environmental impact assessment system in Ghana. *Heliyon*, *6*(9), e04936. Advance online publication. DOI: 10.1016/j.heliyon.2020.e04758

Giroud, A. (2024). World Investment Report 2023: Investing in sustainable energy for all. *J Int Bus Policy*, *7*(1), 128–131. DOI: 10.1057/s42214-023-00178-9

Globerman, S., & Shapiro, D. (2003). Governance infrastructure and US foreign direct investment. *Journal of International Business Studies*, *34*(1), 19–39. DOI: 10.1057/palgrave.jibs.8400001

Godley, W., & Lavoie, M. (2007). *Monetary economics: An integrated approach to credit, money, income, production and wealth.* Palgrave Macmillan. DOI: 10.1057/9780230626546

Grübler, A., Krey, V., & Napp, T. (2018). Technical and economic barriers for renewable energy deployment: The importance of infrastructure and coordination. *Energy Policy, 113*, 1–10. DOI: 10.1016/j.enpol.2017.10.001

International Energy Agency. (2021). *Net zero by 2050: A roadmap for the global energy sector*. IEA. https://www.iea.org/reports/net-zero-by-2050

International Energy Agency. (2022). *World energy outlook 2022*. IEA.

International Energy Agency. (2023). *World energy investment 2023*. IEA.

International Energy Agency. (2024). *Renewables 2024: Analysis and forecast to 2029*. IEA.

International Finance Corporation. (2023). *Blended Finance for Climate Investments in India*. IFC.

International Finance Corporation. (2023). *IFC climate finance and investment report 2023: Aligning capital with climate-resilient development*. International Finance Corporation International Renewable Energy Agency (IRENA). (2022). *World energy transitions outlook: 1.5°C pathway*. IRENA.

International Renewable Energy Agency. (2020). *Renewable power generation costs in 2020*. IRENA.

International Renewable Energy Agency. (2020). *Renewable power generation costs in 2019*. IRENA.

International Renewable Energy Agency. (2022). *Global hydrogen trade to meet the 1.5°C climate goal*. IRENA.

International Renewable Energy Agency. (2024). *Renewable power generation costs in 2023*. IRENA.

Jenkins, K., McCauley, D., Heffron, R., Stephan, H., & Rehner, R. (2017). Energy justice: A conceptual review. *Energy Research & Social Science*, *11*, 174–182. DOI: 10.1016/j.erss.2015.10.004

Karpf, A., & Mandel, A. (2018). The changing value of the 'green' label on the US municipal bond market. *Nature Climate Change*, *8*(2), 161–165. DOI: 10.1038/s41558-017-0062-0

Kaufmann, D., Kraay, A., & Mastruzzi, M. (2011). The worldwide governance indicators: Methodology and analytical issues. *Hague Journal on the Rule of Law*, *3*(2), 220–246. DOI: 10.1017/S1876404511200046

Keeley, A. R., & Matsumoto, K. (2018). Investors' perspective on determinants of foreign direct investment in wind and solar energy in developing economies: Review and expert opinions. *Journal of Cleaner Production, 179*, 132–142. DOI: 10.1016/j.jclepro.2017.12.154

Khalique, A., Wang, Y. C., & Ahmed, K. (2025). Europe's environmental dichotomy: The impact of regulations, climate investments, and renewable energy on carbon mitigation in the EU-22. *Energy Policy, 198*, 114498. Advance online publication. DOI: 10.1016/j.enpol.2025.114498

Li, W., Zheng, M., Zhang, Y., & Cui, G. (2020). Green governance structure, ownership characteristics, and corporate financing constraints. *Journal of Cleaner Production, 260*, 121008. DOI: 10.1016/j.jclepro.2020.121008

Matome, G. K., & Fischer, T. B. (2024). Environmental assessment simplification in Botswana: A critical review. *Impact Assessment and Project Appraisal, 42*(4), 1–12. DOI: 10.1080/14615517.2024.2363720

Michaelowa, A., Butzengeiger, S., & Schenuit, F. (2019). Policy risk and the economics of renewable energy projects: Lessons from Kenya and India. In *Climate Policy*

Minadakis, P., & Vega-Araujo, J. (2024). Rethinking the social license to operate? A theoretical exploration of its synergies with social acceptance and energy justice for a just transition. *Energy Research & Social Science, 113*, 103552. DOI: 10.1016/j.erss.2024.103552

Monasterolo, I., & Raberto, M. (2019). The impact of phasing out fossil fuel subsidies on the low-carbon transition. *Energy Policy, 124*, 355–370. DOI: 10.1016/j.enpol.2018.08.051

Monkelbaan, J. (2019). Governance for achieving the Sustainable Development Goals in the electricity sector. *Sustainable Cities and Society, 52*, 101779. Advance online publication. DOI: 10.1016/j.scs.2019.101779

Multilateral Investment Guarantee Agency. (2023). *Annual report 2023: Mobilizing private capital for development.* World Bank Group.

Nikiforos, M., & Zezza, G. (2017). Stock–flow consistent macroeconomic models: A survey. *Journal of Economic Surveys, 31*(5), 1204–1239. DOI: 10.1111/joes.12221

North, D. C. (1990). *Institutions, institutional change and economic performance.* Cambridge University Press. DOI: 10.1017/CBO9780511808678

OECD. (2024). *FDI in figures: Green investment trends.* Organisation for Economic Co-operation and Development.

Olatubosun, P., & Nyazenga, S. (2021). Greenwashing and responsible investment practices: Empirical evidence from Zimbabwe. *Qualitative Research in Financial Markets*, *13*(1), 16–36. DOI: 10.1108/QRFM-12-2017-0125

Patala, S., Juntunen, J. K., Lundan, S., & Ritvala, T. (2021). Multinational energy utilities in the energy transition: A configurational study of the drivers of FDI in renewables. *Journal of International Business Studies*, *52*(5), 930–950. DOI: 10.1057/s41267-020-00387-x

Pollin, R., & Callaci, B. (2019). The economics of a just transition: A framework for supporting fossil-fuel dependent workers and communities in the United States. *Labor Studies Journal*, *44*(3), 201–228. DOI: 10.1177/0160449X18787051

Polzin, F., Egli, F., Steffen, B., & Schmidt, T. S. (2019). How do policies mobilize private finance for renewable energy? A systematic review with an investor perspective. *Applied Energy*, *236*, 1249–1268. DOI: 10.1016/j.apenergy.2018.11.098

Puaschunder, J. M. (2023). Kaur, H., Singh, K., & Kaur, A. (2024). Corruption and Environmental Degradation: Challenges and Solutions for Effective Climate Action. In *Modern Concepts and Practices of Climate Finance* (pp. 325-350). IGI Global.

Raza, M. S., Wang, Y. S., Rauf, A., Aziz, N., Khan, M. A., & Hussain, A. (2024). Unveiling the green horizon: A bibliometric analysis of global foreign direct investment research and its emphasis on climate change. *Journal of Cleaner Production*, *446*, 141338. Advance online publication. DOI: 10.1016/j.jclepro.2024.141338

REN21. (2021). *Renewables 2021 global status report*. REN21 Secretariat.

Reck, B. K., & Graedel, T. E. (2012). Challenges in metal recycling. *Science*, *337*(6095), 690–695. DOI: 10.1126/science.1217501

Renewable Energy. (2021). Cross-border investment trends in renewable energy and grid modernization. *Renewable Energy, 170*, 1250–1265. DOI: 10.1016/j.renene.2021.02.045

Sadoff, C. W., & Grey, D. (2002). Beyond the river: The benefits of cooperation on international rivers. *Water Policy*, *4*(5), 389–403. DOI: 10.1016/S1366-7017(02)00035-1

Saroglu, S. (2021). Geothermal energy investment and innovation in Turkey. *Renewable Energy*, *170*, 1241–1252. DOI: 10.1016/j.renene.2021.02.012

Schmidt, T. S., Blum, N. U., & Wakeling, R. S. (2019). Attracting private investments into renewable energy: A review of policy instruments. *Energy Policy*, *38*(1), 1–15. DOI: 10.1016/j.enpol.2009.08.035

Shimbar, A., & Ebrahimi, S. B. (2020). Political risk and valuation of renewable energy investments in developing countries. *Renewable Energy*, *145*, 1325–1333. DOI: 10.1016/j.renene.2019.06.055

Suding, P. H., Engel, S., & Jones, A. (2015). Securing environmental standards in renewable energy investment. *Energy Policy*, *86*, 331–338. DOI: 10.1016/j.enpol.2015.07.002

Susskind, L., Chun, J., Gant, A., Hodgkins, C., Cohen, J., & Lohmar, S. (2022). Sources of opposition to renewable energy projects in the United States. *Energy Policy*, *165*, 112922. DOI: 10.1016/j.enpol.2022.112922

Szarka, J. (2004). Wind power, policy learning and paradigm change. *Energy Policy*, *32*(12), 1625–1632. DOI: 10.1016/S0301-4215(03)00161-6

Tawiah, V., Zakari, A., & Alvarado, R. (2024). Effect of corruption on green growth. *Environment, Development and Sustainability*, *26*(4), 10429–10459. DOI: 10.1007/s10668-023-03152-w

Trabacchi, C., & Stadelmann, M. (2015). Mobilizing private climate finance: Blended finance mechanisms and investment vehicles. *Climate Policy*, *15*(5), 1–17. DOI: 10.1080/14693062.2015.1022855

Udemba, E. N., & Alola, A. A. (2022). Asymmetric inference of carbon neutrality and energy transition policy in Australia: The (de)merit of foreign direct investment. *Journal of Cleaner Production*, *343*, 131023. Advance online publication. DOI: 10.1016/j.jclepro.2022.131023

UNCTAD. (2023). *World investment report 2023: Investing in sustainable energy for all.* United Nations Conference on Trade and Development. https://unctad.org/publication/world-investment-report-2023

United Nations Environment Programme. (2023). *Adaptation gap report 2023: Underfinanced. Underprepared.* United Nations Environment Programme. https://www.unep.org/resources/adaptation-gap-report-2023

Villabruna, V. E., Hluszko, C., Rossi, D., Barros, M. V., Lam, J. S. L., & Lermen, F. H. (2024). Barriers and strategies for green investments in environmental, social and governance: A seaport companies' study. *Management of Environmental Quality*, *35*(6), 1193–1212. DOI: 10.1108/MEQ-07-2023-0222

Wall, R., Grafakos, S., Gianoli, A., & Stavropoulos, S. (2019). Which policy instruments attract foreign direct investments in renewable energy? *Climate Policy*, *19*(1), 59–72. DOI: 10.1080/14693062.2018.1467826

Wang, W., & Wang, X. (2023). Does provincial green governance promote enterprise green investment? Based on the perspective of government vertical management. *Journal of Cleaner Production, 396*, 136519. DOI: 10.1016/j.jclepro.2023.136519

World Bank. (2022). *Global investment competitiveness report 2022: Rebuilding investor confidence*. World Bank Publications.

Yáñez-Valdés, C., & Guerrero, M. (2024). Equity crowdfunding platforms and sustainable impacts: Encountering investors and technological initiatives for tackling social and environmental challenges. *European Journal of Innovation Management, 27*(7), 2326–2350. DOI: 10.1108/EJIM-03-2022-0127

Yasmeen, R., Yao, X., Padda, I. U., Shah, W. U., & Jie, W. C. (2022). Exploring the role of solar energy and foreign direct investment for clean environment: Evidence from top 10 solar energy consuming countries. *Renewable Energy, 185*, 849–862. DOI: 10.1016/j.renene.2021.12.048

Zhang, F., & Gallagher, K. S. (2016). Innovation and technology transfer through global value chains: Evidence from China's renewable energy sector. *Energy Policy, 94*, 191–203. DOI: 10.1016/j.enpol.2016.04.014

Zhang, Y., & Colen, L. (2019). Fossil fuel divestment and renewable investment: Evidence from global capital flows. *Energy Economics, 80*, 109–121. DOI: 10.1016/j.eneco.2019.01.009

Zhao, X., Zhang, S., & Chen, Y. (2022). Global photovoltaic manufacturing and China's dominance. *Renewable Energy, 181*, 1086–1098. DOI: 10.1016/j.renene.2021.09.098

Zheng, D., & Shi, M. (2017). Multiple environmental policies and pollution haven hypothesis: Evidence from China's polluting industries. *Journal of Cleaner Production, 141*, 295–304. DOI: 10.1016/j.jclepro.2016.09.091

Zheng, L., Zheng, Y., He, Q., & Xu, J. (2025). Environmental regulation, firm adaptation, and industrial land prices: Evidence from China's clean air policies. *Applied Economics*, •••, 1–21. DOI: 10.1080/00036846.2025.2540093

Chapter 5
Leveraging Public–Private Partnerships to Mobilize Green Capital for Sustainable Infrastructure Financing

Rimi Gusliana Mais
http://orcid.org/0000-0002-2625-0601
Sekolah Tinggi Ilmu Ekonomi Indonesia Jakarta, Indonesia

Munir Munir
http://orcid.org/0009-0006-4464-5136
Sekolah Tinggi Ilmu Syari'ah Al-Manar Jakarta, Indonesia

ABSTRACT

This chapter examines the role of Public–Private Partnerships (PPPs) in expediting sustainable infrastructure via green finance. Public-Private Partnerships synchronize public goals with private-sector efficiency and innovation to mitigate finance deficiencies in the low-carbon transition. The suggested framework amalgamates performance-based contracts with environmental objectives, blended finance (including grants, concessional loans, and climate funds), and market instruments like green bonds and sustainability-linked loans to mitigate project risks and entice institutional investors. The approach addresses optimal risk allocation, ESG governance, and public guarantees that reduce capital costs. Institutional preparedness, encompassing PPP units, project-preparation facilities, and dependable green

DOI: 10.4018/979-8-3373-7595-3.ch005

ht © 2027, IGI Global Scientific Publishing. Copying or distributing in print or electronic forms without written permission of IGI Global Scientific Publishing is prohibited. Use of this chapter to generative artificial intelligence (AI) technologies is expressly prohibited. The publisher reserves all rights to license its use for generative AI training and machine learning model development.

taxonomy, facilitates pipeline construction. Digital monitoring improves openness and accountability, while standardized protocols, risk mitigation techniques, and international cooperation bolster climate resilience and equitable development.

INTRODUCTION

1.1 PPPS as Catalysts for Green Capital PPP Models and Value for Money Logic (DBFOM; Availability vs. Demand Risk)

Public-Private Partnerships (PPPs) are enduring agreements wherein a private entity is responsible for the design, financing, construction, operation, and maintenance of public assets and services, often encapsulated as DBFOM. The DBFOM framework consolidates life cycle responsibilities, ensuring that design and construction decisions incorporate future operation and maintenance expenses, so aligning incentives with durability, overall performance, and ultimately, value for money (VfM) for the public sector. In modern practice, Value for Money (VfM) transcends mere "lowest cost" to encompass an optimum amalgamation of whole life cost, service quality, risk transfer, and externalities (such as resilience and decarbonization advantages) in comparison to a realistic public sector counterpart. Recent research warns that Value for Money (VfM) evaluations have traditionally prioritized accounting cost reductions while inadequately defining the "value" aspect; revised guidelines advocate for a more comprehensive consideration of risk and performance results throughout the asset life cycle (Zhao et al., 2023).

The global transition toward low-carbon and climate-resilient infrastructure requires unprecedented levels of capital investment. Estimates from multilateral development institutions suggest that trillions of dollars in annual investment will be required to meet decarbonization and resilience targets, particularly in energy, transport, and water systems. However, public budgets alone remain insufficient to meet this financing gap. Consequently, governments increasingly rely on Public–Private Partnerships (PPPs) as mechanisms for mobilizing private capital while maintaining public oversight of essential infrastructure services (Auzepy, et al.,2023).

Despite their growing prominence, debates persist regarding the effectiveness of PPPs in delivering sustainable development outcomes. While some studies highlight efficiency gains derived from lifecycle bundling and performance-based incentives, others caution that poorly designed PPP contracts may generate fiscal risks, governance challenges, or inequitable distribution of benefits. These debates suggest that the success of PPP-based infrastructure financing depends not only on contractual structures but also on institutional capacity, governance quality, and the ability to attract diversified sources of green capital (Briera & Lefèvre, 2024).

This chapter contributes to this debate by examining how PPP frameworks can be strategically designed to mobilize green capital through blended finance instruments, ESG-aligned governance mechanisms, and outcome-based contractual structures. By integrating insights from infrastructure finance, sustainability governance, and climate finance, the chapter proposes a conceptual framework linking PPP institutional design to green capital mobilization and sustainable infrastructure outcomes (Zhao et al., 2023).

Two revenue paradigms prevail in DBFOM agreements and influence risk allocation: User pay (deman drisk) Public-Private partnerships and availability payment (government pay) Public-Private partnerships. In demand risk schemes, exemplified as tolled transportation, private revenues are contingent upon actual usage; the private partner assumes traffic and volume uncertainty and markets this risk through mandated returns. In contexts of variable or policysensitive demand, excessive demand risk can elevate capital costs or jeopardize bankability. Conversely, availability payment Public-Private Partnerships compensate the private partner by set, regular payments contingent upon achieving performance and uptime criteria; demand fluctuations are retained by the public body, while the private sector is motivated to ensure quality and reliability. Data from green infrastructure demonstrates that clearly defined risk allocation specifying the parties responsible for demand, building, and regulatory risks correlates with increased private investment levels and enhanced delivery efficiency (Casady et al., 2024; FletaAsín & Muñoz Sánchez, 2024).

The value for money rationale in both forms is founded on three principles. Initially, risk pricing and transfer include allocating risks to the entity most capable of managing them at minimal expense; for instance, building and operational performance risks often reside with the concessionaire, although certain exogenous or policy risks may remain with the public sector. In scenarios where demand risk is inherently uncertain (e.g., novel mass transit systems), availability payments can enhance value for money by circumventing costly risk premiums and prioritizing incentives related to service quality (Guo et al., 2024). Secondly, performancebased remuneration: deductions for unavailability or subpar performance establish ongoing incentives for asset reliability and service quality, integrating lifecycle efficiency into the payment structure. Third, bankability and cost of capital: reliable, steady payment streams (including guarantees and indexation features) diminish revenue volatility and decrease the weighted average cost of capital, facilitating the influx of longtenor institutional finance often necessary for green projects (Casady et al., 2024).

The choice between availability and deman drisk models is contingent upon the unique context. Governments ought to delineate risk factors market maturity, demand elasticity, policy stability, and data accessibility prior to determining revenue structure. In contexts with strong demand history and price signals that support public policy (such as congestion management), deman drisk Public-Private partnerships can be both efficient and equitable. Conversely, in scenarios where publicgood attributes prevail (e.g., climate resilient water or mass electrified transit), availability payment Public-Private partnerships (PPPs) frequently provide enhanced value for money (VfM) by aligning incentives with service results rather than unpredictable volumes (Guo et al., 2024; Zhao et al., 2023).

Figure 1. Conceptual Framework Linking PPP Governance and Green Capital Mobilization

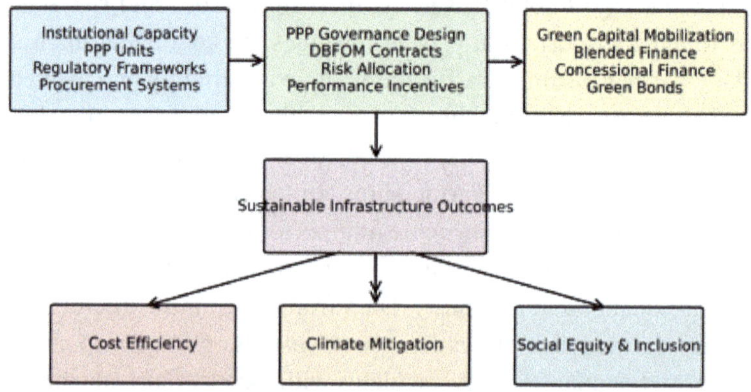

Source: *The authors' illustration*

Figure 1 presents a conceptual framework linking PPP governance mechanisms with green capital mobilization and sustainable infrastructure outcomes. Drawing on transaction cost economics and performance-based governance theory, PPP contracts function as institutional arrangements that allocate risks, align incentives, and reduce uncertainty between public and private actors.

Within this framework, institutional capacity—such as specialized PPP units, standardized procurement frameworks, and transparent regulatory systems—plays a critical enabling role. Effective governance structures improve investor confidence and facilitate the mobilization of green capital through blended financing instruments, including concessional loans, guarantees, and market-based instruments such as green bonds and sustainability-linked loans. The conceptual framework illustrates how institutional capacity and PPP governance design influence the mobilization of green capital for sustainable infrastructure development. Institutional capacity including specialized PPP units, regulatory frameworks, and transparent procurement systems creates the enabling environment for effective PPP implementation.

1.2 The Green Capital Stack: Public Funds, Concessional Layers, Private Equity/Debt

The concept of the green capital stack refers to the structured layering of financial instruments from different sources to improve the risk-return profile of sustainable infrastructure projects. Rather than relying on a single financing source, green infrastructure projects typically combine public funding, concessional finance, and private investment in order to address different types of risks across the project lifecycle (Pellegrino et al., 2024).

In this layered financing structure, public funds typically play a catalytic role by addressing early-stage risks such as project preparation, feasibility studies, and regulatory uncertainties. Concessional finance often provided by multilateral development banks or climate funds reduces financing costs through longer tenors, lower interest rates, or partial guarantees. These mechanisms improve the financial viability of projects and make them more attractive to private investors (Petri, 2025).

Private capital, including commercial banks, institutional investors, and capital market instruments such as green bonds or sustainability-linked loans, provides the scale required to finance large infrastructure assets. When properly structured, the interaction between these financing layers can significantly reduce the weighted average cost of capital (WACC), thereby improving project bankability and enabling greater mobilization of green capital (Moshood, 2024). Recent research indicates that Value for Money (VfM) evaluations have historically emphasized accounting cost reductions while insufficiently articulating the "value" component; updated guidelines recommend a more holistic assessment of risk and performance outcomes throughout the asset life cycle (Zhao et al., 2023).

Data from green infrastructure indicates that explicit risk allocation designating the parties accountable for demand, construction, and regulatory risks correlates with heightened private investment and improved delivery efficiency (FletaAsín & Muñoz, 2024; Casady et al., 2024). Risk pricing and transfer fundamentally involve assigning risks to the party most equipped to manage them costeffectively; for example, construction and operational performance risks often lie with the concessionaire, while certain external or policy risks may be retained by the public sector. In situations characterized by uncertain demand risk (e.g., innovative mass transit systems), availability payments can improve value for money by avoiding expensive risk premiums and emphasizing incentives tied to service quality (Guo et al., 2024).

Secondly, performancebased compensation: deductions for unavailability or inadequate performance create continuous incentives for asset reliability and service quality, incorporating lifecycle efficiency into the remuneration framework. Third, bankability and cost of capital: dependable, consistent payment streams (incorporating guarantees and indexation features) reduce revenue volatility and lower the weighted average cost of capital, thereby promoting the influx of longterm institutional finance typically required for green projects (Casady et al., 2024).In contrast, in situations where publicgood characteristics dominate (e.g., climateresilient water or mass electrified transit), availability payment Public-Privat Partnerships (PPPs) often deliver superior value for money (VfM) by aligning incentives with service outcomes rather than erratic volumes (Guo et al., 2024; Zhao et al., 2023).

Recent comparative studies emphasize that institutional capacity (PPP units, procurement frameworks, dispute resolution mechanisms) and policy coherence (green taxonomies, disclosure standards) are crucial for achieving value for money in Design Build Finance Operate Maintain (DBFOM) projects. Jurisdictions that establish risksharing matrices and integrate sustainability criteria in requestforproposal (RFP) processes and payment schedules achieve more consistent outcomes and draw larger pools of private capital than those relying on adhoc arrangements (Cao et al., 2024; Casady et al., 2024).

1.3 Sustainable Infrastructure Typologies (Energy, Transport, Water, Circular Economy)

In Public-Private partnerships, revenue models depend on longterm offtake agreements, such as availability or contractfordifference structures, which stabilize cash flows and reduce the weighted average cost of capital (WACC). In emerging nations, blended guarantees and concessional tranches are frequently critical for bankability due to macrorisk premiums; recent findings indicate that reducing the cost of financing through targeted public finance significantly expedites clean energy implementation (Calcaterra et al., 2024). Reliable measurement, reporting, and verification (MRV) such as quantified clean energy production, reduction rates, and gride mission factors facilitates performance based rewards and sustainabilitylinked financing (Petri, 2025).

However, the literature also highlights several limitations. Studies on infrastructure finance in emerging economies emphasize that weak institutional capacity, regulatory uncertainty, and limited capital market depth may undermine PPP performance. In such contexts, blended finance mechanisms combining public funds, concessional finance, and private capital have emerged as important instruments for improving project bankability and reducing the cost of capital (Castelblanco et al., 2024).

Moreover, recent research emphasizes the increasing importance of environmental, social, and governance (ESG) considerations in infrastructure financing. Investors now evaluate projects not only based on financial returns but also on climate resilience, emissions reductions, and social inclusion outcomes. This shift toward ESG-aligned financing mechanisms has encouraged the development of green bonds, sustainability-linked loans, and climate-aligned infrastructure investment vehicles.

1.4 PPPs in Emerging and Developing Economies

In emerging and developing economies, the mobilization of green capital through PPPs faces additional institutional and financial challenges. These include limited capital market depth, regulatory uncertainty, foreign exchange risks, and weak project preparation capacity. As a result, infrastructure projects in these contexts often face higher financing costs compared to projects in advanced economies.

Empirical research indicates that elevated perceived country risk significantly increases the cost of capital for sustainable infrastructure projects, thereby reducing private investment participation. Consequently, blended finance mechanisms and multilateral development bank support have become critical instruments for improving project bankability in these contexts.

Adaptive PPP models have therefore emerged in many developing economies. These models combine traditional DBFOM contractual structures with targeted policy instruments such as viability gap funding, concessional loans, foreign exchange facilities, and partial risk guarantees. When implemented within transparent procurement frameworks and supported by strong regulatory institutions, these mechanisms can significantly expand private sector participation in sustainable infrastructure financing (Calcaterra et al, 2024).

Furthermore, institutional capacity plays a decisive role in determining the effectiveness of PPP frameworks in emerging economies. Governments that establish specialized PPP units, standardized procurement procedures, and transparent monitoring systems tend to attract larger pools of private capital and achieve more consistent infrastructure delivery outcomes.

2. FINANCE AND GREEN CAPITAL

2.1 Blended Finance Toolkit: Grants, Concessional Loans, Firstloss Tranches, Viabilitygap Funding

Blended finance strategically integrates Blended finance strategically integrates public or philanthropic funding with commercial investment to rectify market flaws that prevent viable sustainable infrastructure from achieving financial closure. In Public-Private Partnership (PPP) contexts, the aim is not to supplant private capital, but to reformulate the project's riskreturn profile to meet investment thresholds at a reduced weighted average cost of capital (WACC), while ensuring value for money (VfM) is preserved. Recent economywide modeling indicates that reducing risk premia and WACC in emerging markets significantly accelerates the implementation of clean infrastructure and enhances distributional outcomes conditions under which blended instruments are particularly catalytic (Calcaterra et al, 2024).

Grants are the most adaptable instrument and occupy the highest position on the concessionality spectrum. In PPP pipelines, grants generally fund (i) project preparation (feasibility studies, environmental and social baselines, MRV architecture), (ii) capital grants that diminish initial capital expenditures for technologies with significant positive externalities, or (iii) resultsbased/operational grants that incentivize verified performance. When directed towards demonstrable externalities and supplemented by transparent additionality assessments, grants can enhance bankability without displacing private capital. International data demonstrates that specific public financing, which reduces financing costs, facilitates increased renewable investment, especially in capitaldeficient markets (Casady et al, 2024). Policymakers should adhere to the design principle of minimum concessionality: provide only the necessary subsidy to transition a project from nonbankable to bankable, and implement sunset provisions to diminish support as markets develop (Calcaterra et al, 2024).

Firstloss tranches, including junior equity or subordinated debt, serve as the cornerstone of numerous mixed vehicles. By preemptively committing to accept initial losses, the junior layer enhances the credit quality of senior tranches owned by commercial lenders or institutional investors. This credit enhancement reduces spreads and may prolong tenor, particularly in contexts where country, regulatory, or technological concerns prevail. Recent sector analyses, such as those concerning Europe's heat transition, indicate that suitably organized firstloss capital can attract private lenders to district energy and efficiency enhancements that would otherwise not pass investment committee evaluations. The objective is to calibrate the junior layer (typically 10–20% of the stack), establish governance to avert mission drift, and transparently reveal portfoliolevel risk and effect to prevent greenwashing (Popovic et al, 2024).

Viabilitygap funding (VGF) offers onetime or deferred contributions to projects that are socially beneficial yet commercially unviable at affordable tariffs (e.g., public transit, wastewater, offshore wind in emerging markets). In Public-Private partnerships, viability gap funding is frequently associated with availability payment contracts, wherein the public authority maintains demand risk while linking payments to service key performance indicators. Recent studies on transport Public-Private partnerships indicate that well structured subsidy and benefitsharing mechanisms enhance partner conduct and operational efficiency, hence strengthening value for money objectives; policy revisions in several jurisdictions have similarly broadened viability gap funding to prioritized green sectors (Hou et al, 2024).

Table 1. PPP risk allocation heatmap across lifecycle and policy risks

Risk category	Public	Private	Shared	Typical mitigations / notes
Design risk				**Performancebased specs; design review; liability for errors.**
Construction risk (time & quality)				Fixeddate/price EPC; LDs; performance security.
Completion/commissioning				Independent tests; reliability run; stepin rights.
Cost overrun (CAPEX)				EPC wrap; contingencies; equity support.
O&M performance/availability				Unitary charge with KPI deductions/ bonuses; reserves.
Latent defect risk				Warranty/defect liability period.
Demand / volume risk				Availability PPP → public; patronage PPP → private/shared with floors/caps.
Tariff/affordability risk				Policy set by public; indexation; VGF/ subsidy.
Change in law / regulatory risk				Shared for discriminatory/sectorwide changes; relief/compensation events.
Force majeure (natural)				Shared; relief from deductions; insurance where available.
Force majeure (political)				Public bears expropriation/licence revocation; PRI.
Environmental & social (E&S) compliance				Public: approvals/land; Private: ESMP; shared monitoring via IE.
Land acquisition / rightofway				Public procures land/resettlement; site handover precedes NTP.
Utilities & thirdparty interface				Interconnection agreements; interface schedules; LD allocation.
Technology/innovation performance				Performance guarantees; output specs (kWh, m^3/day).
Grid/market access (curtailment)				Takeorpay/deemed energy; compensation formulas.
FX risk on debt service				FX facility, swaps, indexation, PRG/ guarantees.
Interest rate / refinancing				Hedging; refinancing gainshare; margin ratchets.
Inflation (OPEX indexation)				Indexation of unitary charge; passthrough baskets.
Counterparty/SPV default				DSRA, covenants, stepin and substitution rights.

continued on following page

Table 1. Continued

Risk category	Public	Private	Shared	Typical mitigations / notes
Insurance availability/cost				Minimum insurance program; changeinpremium relief.
Dispute resolution				Escalation ladder; expert determination; arbitration.

Source: The authors' compilation.

In summary, a blended financing toolkit comprising grants for preparation and outcomes, concessional loans for duration and expense, firstloss mechanisms for tailrisk mitigation, and viability gap funding for affordability offers a modular framework to enhance the bankability of sustainable Public-Private partnerships (PPPs). When these mechanisms are precisely targeted, timesensitive, and transparently administered, they reduce WACC, attract institutional capital, and expedite the provision of lowcarbon, climateresilient infrastructure while safeguarding public interest (Briera & Lefèvre, 2024). public or philanthropic funding with commercial investment to rectify market flaws that prevent viable sustainable infrastructure from achieving financial closure.

Grants are the most adaptable instrument and occupy the highest position on the concessionality spectrum. In PPP pipelines, grants generally fund (i) project preparation (feasibility studies, environmental and social baselines, MRV architecture), (ii) capital grants that diminish initial capital expenditures for technologies with significant positive externalities, or (iii) resultsbased/operational grants that incentivize verified performance. When directed towards demonstrable externalities and supplemented by transparent additionality assessments, grants can enhance bankability without displacing private capital. International data demonstrates that specific public financing, which reduces financing costs, facilitates increased renewable investment, especially in capitaldeficient markets (Casady et al, 2024).

Concessional loans (offered at belowmarket rates, with extended tenors and grace periods) are ideally suited for longterm assets in the energy, water, and transportation sectors. They alleviate cashflow constraints during development and rampup, enhance debtservice coverage ratios, and simplify covenant agreements. At the systemic level, reducing the cost of debt through concessional finance enhances the adoption of lowcarbon technology and diminishes the "transition cost" disparity between industrialized and developing regions. Policymakers should adhere to the design principle of minimum concessionality: provide only the necessary subsidy to transition a project from nonbankable to bankable, and implement sunset provisions to diminish support as markets develop (Calcaterra et al, 2024).

Firstloss tranches, including junior equity or subordinated debt, serve as the cornerstone of numerous mixed vehicles. By preemptively committing to accept initial losses, the junior layer enhances the credit quality of senior tranches owned by commercial lenders or institutional investors. This credit enhancement reduces spreads and may prolong tenor, particularly in contexts where country, regulatory, or technological concerns prevail. Recent sector analyses, such as those concerning Europe's heat transition, indicate that suitably organized firstloss capital can attract private lenders to district energy and efficiency enhancements that would otherwise not pass investment committee evaluations. The objective is to calibrate the junior layer (typically 10–20% of the stack), establish governance to avert mission drift, and transparently reveal portfoliolevel risk and effect to prevent greenwashing (Popovic et al, 2024). Viabilitygap funding (VGF) offers onetime or deferred contributions to projects that are socially beneficial yet commercially unviable at affordable tariffs (e.g., public transit, wastewater, offshore wind in emerging markets (Hou et al, 2024).

2.2 Risk Transfer and Credit Enhancement: Guarantees, Insurance, FX and Political Risk Covers

In projectfinanced Public-Private partnerships, risk transfer and credit enhancement influence bankability by redistributing noncommercial risks from private cash flows and improving the quality of anticipated payments. Four tools are pivotal: guarantees, political risk insurance (PRI), and coverage for foreignexchange (FX) and regulatory/political risks. When properly designed, these instruments mitigate risk premia, prolong tenors, and reduce the weighted average cost of capital (WACC) effects that are especially critical in emerging economies. Consequently, they engage institutional lenders while preserving performance incentives that enhance value for money (VfM). Recent literature and practice indicate that the credibility and transparency of these instruments, rather than their sheer existence, dictate their pricing power and investor adoption (Pellegrino et al., 2024).

Political Risk Insurance (PRI). PRI safeguards equities and debt from noncommercial risks, including expropriation, contract violations, currency inconvertibility or transfer limitations, and conflict or civil unrest risks that private entities cannot effectively diversify. Multilateral entities (e.g., MIGA) and private insurers provide Political Risk Insurance (PRI) that can be attached to Public-Private Partnerships (PPPs); in addition to direct loss coverage, PRI indicates the host country's commitment and offers a recovery mechanism (subrogation), both of which can attract new lenders. Recent politicaleconomy evidence from over 1,500 insured investments demonstrates that the distribution of multilateral Political Risk Insurance (PRI) is nonrandom and influenced by geopolitical alignment. However, the fundamental insight for sponsors persists: when accessible, credible PRI mitigates perceived risks and facilitates capital acquisition, particularly in highrisk jurisdictions (Gamso & Dimitrova, 2024).

Foreign exchange risk mitigations. Currency mismatch constitutes a primary obstacle, as project revenues are denominated in local currency but finance channels remain underdeveloped. Contracts may link availability payments to foreign exchange rates; nevertheless, macrofiscal constraints frequently inhibit complete passthrough. A typical layered approach includes: (i) localcurrency financing when possible; (ii) market hedges (forwards, swaps) as maturities permit; and (iii) public or blended facilities that offer longterm FX liquidity or catastrophicband protection. Recent empirical studies indicate that firms actively manage foreign exchange exposures using derivatives, while logistics and operations research emphasizes the importance of complementary operational hedges, such as supplychain flexibility, to mitigate net exposure. These insights are applicable to concession special purpose vehicles (SPVs) when determining the optimal approach among contractual indexation, financial hedges, and realoptions in operations and maintenance (O&M). PPP designers should hedge in existing markets and utilize insurance or contracts where markets are absent (Hecht & Lampenius, 2023).

Combination of insurance and guarantees with incentive compatibility. Derisking should not diminish performance incentives. In availability payment Public-Private partnerships, payment reductions for nonavailability maintain construction and operational maintenance discipline, even when senior debt is secured by a guarantee. Similarly, benefitsharing and stepin rights can be integrated with PCGs/PRGs, allowing lenders to have recourse without distributing standard commercial risks. The empirical literature on guarantees warns against general, implicit assistance, as it may lead to moral hazard; rather, focused, transparent enhancements linked to verifiable KPIs (e.g., emissions intensity, uptime) maintain value for money and reduce subsidy leakage (Chen et al., 2024).

In summary, guarantees, PRI, and FX/political risk covers are not alternatives to robust PPP contracts; rather, they are specialized instruments that appropriately calibrate noncommercial risk, enabling commercial lenders to finance the residual performance risk under favorable conditions. When integrated with transparent KPIs and rigorous payment processes, these instruments effectively mobilize green finance for sustainable infrastructure while preserving public value (Azhgaliyeva et al., 2023).

2.3 Market Instruments: Green Bonds, Sustainabilitylinked Loans, Transition Instruments

Environmental bonds. Green bonds allocate funds for ecologically advantageous purposes and serve as the primary financial tool for directing institutional capital into sustainable Public-Private partnership pipelines. Their credibility is based on useofproceeds frameworks, external evaluations, and impact reporting that facilitate ringfencing and verification. An expanding body of empirical research illustrates pricing effects typically a slight "greenium" (reduced yields compared to analogous vanilla bonds) that signifies investor preference and informational influences. Hu et al. (2024) analyze China's primary market from 2016 to 2022, revealing a statistically significant greenium and illustrating that both issuelevel and issuerlevel "greenness" influence the discount, aligning with the reduction of information asymmetry and proenvironmental investor demand. For PPP sponsors, research suggests that robust frameworks and reporting can narrow spreads and extend tenure when combined with predictable revenue contracts (e.g., availability payments) (Hu et al., 2024).

A summary of research on sustainableinfrastructure financing emphasizes this avenue, identifying disclosure quality and ringfencing as factors that expand the investor base and reduce the cost of capital (Meng et al., 2024). Sustainabilitylinked loans (SLLs) and sustainabilitylinked bonds (SLBs). In contrast to green bonds, SustainabilityLinked Loans (SLLs) and SustainabilityLinked Bonds (SLBs) are versatile securities whose pricing is directly linked to the issuer's sustainability performance through key performance indicators (KPIs) and contractual adjustments. When appropriately structured, they can integrate outcomebased incentives throughout a PPP sponsor's financial sheet and promote portfoliolevel decarbonization pertinent to multiasset concessions. Nonetheless, the quality of design is inconsistent.

Auzepy et al. (2023) examine an extensive SLL sample (2017–2022) and determine that numerous KPIs lack significance and ambition, hence doubting the efficacy of incentives established under the existing contract. The evidence regarding market reactions to SLBs is complex: Affolter et al. (2024) report an absence of consistent positive stock responses when SLB objectives focus on generic GHG reductions, yet they note favorable reactions for alternative goal categories (e.g., energy efficiency, ratingsbased), indicating that investors distinguish between KPI design and credibility. This research advocates using taxonomyaligned, auditable KPIs (e.g., lifecycle emissions intensity, nonavailability rates, resilience indicators) and substantial financial penalties in PPP applications to prevent "paytopollute" preconceptions while ensuring value for money (Auzepy et al., 2023).

Transitional instruments. In carbonintensive but essential sectors (such as steel, cement, grids, and industrial heat), where assets are not exclusively "green," transition instrumentsparticularly climate transition bonds (CTBs) and sustainabilitylinked formats facilitate credible pathways to decarbonization aligned with the Paris Agreement. Guidance has consolidated into four key pillars: (1) issuerlevel transition plans include interim sciencebased targets; (2) substantial capital expenditure pathways; (3) visible key performance indicators and verification; and (4) limitations on the utilization of offsets. Empirical and casebased research in Japan demonstrates that CTBs can direct capital towards incremental decarbonization of hardtoabate industries, contingent upon solid governance and disclosure (Zhao et al., 2023). In practice, Public-Private partnerships (PPPs) can implement transitional frameworks for grid reinforcement, district energy decarbonization, or industrial symbiosis parks, where the allocation of proceeds is varied yet the credibility of the pathways is evident.

Design considerations for PPP sponsors and public entities. Initially, the selection of instruments must align with the cashflow structure: projectfinanced concessions with isolated revenues are typically appropriate for green bonds, while corporatelevel platforms or multiasset operators may gain advantages from SustainabilityLinked Loans (SLLs) or SustainabilityLinked Bonds (SLBs). Secondly, the integrity of KPIs is imperative: guarantee materiality, obtain thirdparty verification, and establish increments that are economically significant in relation to base coupons or margins. Third, integrate market instruments with contractual incentives (such as payment deductions and performancebased availability) to ensure that financial signals effectively influence operational results throughout the entire DBFOM lifetime. Ultimately, incorporate instrument selection into a capitalstack strategy merging green/transition labels with concessional layers or guarantees can attract longtenor private financing while maintaining value for money and decreasing the weighted average cost of capital in emerging markets (Meng et al., 2024).

3. GOVERNANCE, RISK ALLOCATION, AND ESG PERFORMANCE

3.1 Contractual Models and the Riskallocation Matrix (Construction, Demand, Regulatory)

While financial sustainability and risk allocation remain central concerns in PPP design, social equity considerations are increasingly recognized as critical components of sustainable infrastructure development. Infrastructure projects financed through PPP mechanisms may generate affordability concerns if tariffs are structured primarily to ensure investor returns.

To address these challenges, policymakers increasingly integrate social safeguards into PPP contractual structures. These may include lifeline tariffs for low-income households, targeted subsidies, community benefit-sharing arrangements, and employment generation requirements. When incorporated into performance-based payment systems, such provisions can enhance social acceptance and reduce long-term political risks associated with infrastructure investments. indicates that aligning risk allocation with managerial control assigning construction and resource risks to the private sector and policy and forcemajeure risks to the public sector enhances private capital involvement and reduces financing costs (FletaAsín & MuñozSánchez, 2024).

Moreover, the integration of social key performance indicators (KPIs) into PPP contracts allows governments to align financial incentives with broader development objectives. For example, accessibility indicators in transport projects or water affordability indicators in water infrastructure projects can be incorporated into performance-based payment structures, thereby ensuring that infrastructure investments contribute not only to economic efficiency but also to inclusive development outcomes.

A comprehensive value for money (VfM) evaluation should precede the matrix. Recent evaluations of Value for Money (VfM) practices warn that "value" is sometimes limited to cost reductions compared to a publicsector benchmark, while a comprehensive VfM approach encompasses resilience, carbon intensity, health equality, and lifetime service quality (Zhao et al., 2023). The broader value for money perspective is crucial for ESGaligned infrastructure. The risk matrix must delineate climatetransition risks (e.g., carbonprice passthrough), physicalclimate risks (e.g., flood design requirements), and social performance risks (e.g., local hiring and safety), with corresponding contractual remedies identified for each.

Construction risk continues to be the quintessential realm of the private sector. DBFOM packaging integrates design, construction, and operational maintenance interfaces, fostering incentives to optimize capital expenditures for future operational expenditures. In scenarios characterized by significant complexity (e.g., water treatment, offshore wind), financiers and sponsors require substantial completion security, liquidated damages, and parent company guarantees. Empirical assessments demonstrate that assigning construction and technologyperformance risks to the private sector, along with legitimate remedy rights, diminishes renegotiation frequency and enhances timely delivery (Gifford et al., 2024).

Demand risk serves as the pivotal point between availability risk and income risk in Public-Private partnerships (PPPs). In decarbonization sectors characterized by externalities or policydriven pricing, such as mass transit and naturebased stormwater management, demand risk is frequently socially nondiversifiable and should be borne by the public counterparty, utilizing availability payments and performance deductions to maintain incentives. In scenarios where revenue risks are partially manageable (e.g., energyasaservice, distributed renewables), hybrid models can mitigate limited demand risk through floors/caps or shadowtoll mechanisms. Studies in energy economics highlight that support mechanisms that mitigate uncontrolled risks (such as output volatility due to weather) significantly reduce the risk premium and attract investment (Alcorta et al., 2024).

Regulatory and political risks such as tariff adjustments, permitting delays, and changes in taxonomy alignment typically reside with the public sector, while the private entity assumes the risk of compliance delivery. Meticulously designed changeinlaw clauses, stabilization for designated taxes, and preestablished politicalrisk coverage enhance bankability while preserving efficiency incentives. In low and norevenue green assets (urban resilience, social infrastructure), availability payment Public-Private partnerships (PPPs) with ESGlinked key performance indicators (KPIs) are becoming increasingly favored; recent sector studies validate the justification for availability models where social value is critical and userfee feasibility is limited (Casady et al., 2024).

The risk matrix must ultimately align with a performancebased payment framework, incorporating quantifiable service outputs, deduction schedules for nonavailability or KPI deficiencies, and lender intervention protocols. Misaligned matrices, such as transferring uncontrollable demand or policy risks to the SPV, result in expensive renegotiations and unexpected fiscal consequences for the public authority (Gifford et al., 2024). Conversely, matrices that demonstrate control/benefit symmetry, include climatic and social externalities into key performance indicators, and delineate clear cure and termination protocols are more effective in mobilizing substantial green capital (Gifford et al., 2024).

3.2 ESG Metrics and Taxonomies (Material KPIs, MRV Protocols, Greenwashing Safeguards)

To attract institutional capital, Public-Private partnerships require ESG disclosures that are useful for decisionmaking, compatible, and verifiable. Three essential pillars are: (i) the selection of material KPIs linked to value drivers; (ii) measuring, reporting, and verification (MRV) protocols that guarantee comparability; and (iii) safeguards against greenwashing based on developing legal frameworks.

Key Performance Indicators for Materials. According to investorcentric norms, materiality depends on the influence of sustainability risks and possibilities on firm value (financial materiality) and, in numerous frameworks, on external effects (double materiality). Recent accounting research elucidates how the ISSB's IFRS S1 (general requirements) and S2 (climate) reorient sustainability reporting towards investor decisionusefulness, establishing stronger connections between projectlevel KPIs and financial statements (Wagenhofer, 2024). For Public-Private partnerships, this entails adjusting key performance indicators that correspond to cashflow volatility and asset condition: lifecycle carbon intensity (tCO_2e/functional unit), energy yield fluctuation, service dependability (minutes of availability lost), water loss ratios, and safety incident rates. The selection must be sectorspecific and included into payment mechanisms (deductions/bonuses) to avoid standardized reporting.

Taxonomies. Taxonomies establish classification standards that ascertain whether project revenues and capital expenditures qualify as "green." The EU Taxonomy serves as the most detailed illustration, delineating substantialcontribution technical screening standards, donosignificantharm provisions, and minimal social safeguards. Recent assessments indicate that taxonomy alignment can validate investment theses for naturebased and lowcarbon assets while also revealing deficiencies (e.g., specific urban naturebased solutions) that impede capital flows (Papari et al., 2024). Concurrent efforts in accounting highlight the necessity for resilient data structures and analytics to "account for" taxonomyaligned operations across portfolios, indicating that highintegrity tagging improves comparability for lenders and credit analysts (Alessi et al., 2024). PPP sponsors should align project operations with taxonomy criteria during the bidding phase, publish anticipated alignment proportions (capital expenditures, operational expenditures, revenues), and pledge to independent verification.

Monitoring, Reporting, and Verification procedures. Harmonized MRV constitutes the foundation of trustworthiness. IFRS S2 incorporates the TCFD framework governance, strategy, risk management, and metrics/targets and mandates the quantification of Scope 1–3 emissions where significant. Projectlevel MRV must delineate baseline methodology (e.g., IPCC or ISO 14064), data granularity (hourly SCADA records for electricity, calibrated flow meters for water), recalculation triggers (design modifications, updates to gridemission factors), and assurance levels. In instances where the EU Taxonomy is relevant, Monitoring, Reporting, and Verification (MRV) must evidence both significant contribution (e.g., energyefficiency benchmarks) and Do No Significant Harm (DNSH) adherence (e.g., circularity, biodiversity) over time. Empirical evidence demonstrates that disclosures specifically aligned with the EU Taxonomy enhance the quality of investor judgment facilitating reduced financing costs compared to generic environmental assertions (Chrzan et al., 2024).

Measures against greenwashing. In addition to voluntary standards, legislative frameworks are becoming more stringent. The 2024 "Empowering Consumers" Directive in the EU, which amends the Unfair Commercial Practices Directive, prohibits generic, unsubstantiated eco claims and requires substantiation for forwardlooking claims. Alongside the impending Green Claims regime, this establishes enforceable parameters for sustainability assertions, beneficial even for nonEU projects seeking EU investment. PPP procuring entities must reflect these protections: Forbid generic labels (e.g., "carbonneutral") in proposals unless substantiated by acknowledged protocols and thirdparty verification; mandate that sustainabilitylinked funding KPIs are strategically significant and aspirational; and implement clawbacks or pricing adjustments if KPIs are revised. The literature on accounting and sustainable finance converges on a singular conclusion: categorization and disclosure systems (ISSB, EU Taxonomy) can mitigate information risk and greenwashing incentives when integrated with auditable measurement, reporting, and verification (MRV) and enforcement mechanisms (Wagenhofer, 2024; Alessi et al., 2024; Papari et al., 2024).

3.3 Procurement Design: Outcomebased Specifications, Payment Mechanisms, Stepin Rights

Outcomes oriented procurement converts policy objectives netzero pathways, resilience, inclusion into measurable results that activate cash flows. Three primary levers prevail: (1) outcomeoriented technical and service specifications; (2) payment structures incorporating availability deductions and ESGrelated incentives; and (3) creditoraligned safeguards (stepin rights) that maintain continuity without distributing the consequences of privateparty underperformance. The potential for deductions and termination maintains discipline; the ability to intervene safeguards goingconcern value and protects users. Stepin provisions, while legal instruments, are fundamentally pecuniary in nature: cure periods must be sufficiently extended to facilitate the organization of replacement operations and maintenance; security packages must be legally enforceable; and substitution necessitates preapproved criteria. Empirical studies on renegotiations indicate that projects with welldefined cure/termination procedures and creditor safeguards encounter less valueeroding conflicts (Gifford et al., 2024). Assembling it: a framework.

1. Establish outcomes and minimum service standards; correlate them with climate and social key performance indicators (e.g., tCO_2e mitigated annually, accessibility metrics).
2. Develop the unitary charge incorporating a foundational availability component (encompassing fixed costs and debt obligations) and a performance differential linked to key performance indicators; implement collars to mitigate adverse outcomes.
3. Incorporate dynamic incentives (e.g., diminishing carbonintensity bands) to ensure the effort function remains positive as performance enhances (Cao et al., 2024).
4. Establish creditor rights: direct agreements with lenders, rights to cure, replacement mechanisms, and stepin procedures consistent with the deduction schedule and termination hierarchy.
5. Ensure and disclose: mandate thirdparty verification for KPI assertions, conform to ISSB S1/S2 for narratives and metrics, and, where relevant, declare EU Taxonomy alignment to improve investor comparison.

Effectively executed, outcomebased procurement with a solid payment and creditor framework transforms ESG performance into reliable cash flows, precisely what green capital requires.

4. DIGITAL & DATADRIVEN PPPS FOR BANKABLE PIPELINES

4.1 MRV Systems and Digital Twins for Lifecycle Carbon and Resilience Analytics

For sustainable PPPs, the quality of measurement, reporting, and verification (MRV) and the fidelity of digital twins (DTs) are now decisive for bankability. Lenders and rating agencies are increasingly unwilling to rely on static feasibility studies or expost PDFs; they want machinereadable streams that show whether an asset is meeting emissions, efficiency, and resilience targets in real time. In other words, MRV and DTs turn environmental and operational performance into auditable cashflow collateral.

A robust MRV architecture starts by specifying the what (KPIs), how (methods and sensors), who (assurance), and when (cadence and recalculation rules). For climate, KPIs typically include lifecycle or operational GHG intensity (e.g., tCO_2e/MWh, kWh/m^2year), avoided emissions versus baselines, and resilience metrics (downtime hours during shocks, flood exceedance probabilities). Recent technical work argues that MRV should be implemented as DMRV digitally enabled MRV so data pipelines are automated endtoend: in situ sensors → secure data lake → analytics layer → attestations/verifications (often cryptographically signed). This reduces errors, improves comparability, and shortens the lag between performance and payments. Practitioners in carbon markets and infrastructure alike are converging on DMRV to underpin credible issuance of climatealigned finance and resultsbased payments (Batjes et al., 2024).

Digital twins extend DMRV from monitoring to prediction and control. The emerging literature shows how DTs fuse design/BIM models with live telemetry to produce dynamic lifecycle assessment (LCA) and resilience analytics. A 2025 study in *Science of the Total Environment* proposes a Building Lifecycle Digital Twin (BLDT) that blends IoT feeds and ML to yield highresolution, continuously updated LCAs; unlike static LCAs, the BLDT can recompute embodied/operational carbon as materials, schedules, and operating regimes change. For PPP sponsors, this supports adaptive asset management and KPIlinked payment adjustments without contentious disputes (Ecklu et al., 2025).

The same logic is being applied to critical infrastructure. Reviews in 2023–2025 outline city and networklevel DTs that quantify resilience (e.g., service continuity under extreme events) and expose failure modes that matter to lenders: singlepoint outages, restoration times, and stress paths. For ports, grids, and water distribution, DTbased stress testing informs covenants and availability deduction matrices in availability payment PPPs. Where climate risk threatens revenue stability, embedding DTderived thresholds (e.g., maximum downtime during a 1in100 rainfall) in the payment mechanism lets the project company monetize verified resilience turning an externality into contractible cash flows (Batjes et al., 2024).

For public authorities, the policy implication is clear: require bidstage MRV/DT plans with (i) KPI definitions aligned to taxonomy criteria, (ii) device lists and calibration methods, (iii) data retention and access rules (including lender audit rights), (iv) changemanagement triggers (design change, gridfactor updates), and (v) independent assurance levels. For sponsors, the commercial implication is equally clear: invest early in DMRV and DT capability, because every basis point shaved from WACC through improved credibility compounds across longtenor debt.

4.2 AI/Bigdata Screening for Pipeline Development and Due Diligence

A prevalent constraint in green Public-Private partnership projects is not finance, but rather a viable project pipeline. Digitalization facilitates processes prior to financial closure: AI and big data techniques may evaluate jurisdictions, sponsors, sites, and documents to identify candidates with the appropriate risk/return/impact profile more rapidly and with fewer false positives than manual assessment.

Initially, document intelligence can streamline preliminary due diligence. Natural language processing (NLP) algorithms analyze and evaluate text from ESIAs, permits, procurement notices, and technical appendices to identify regulatory concerns (e.g., appeal periods, landuse conflicts) and ESG materiality deficiencies. Recent peerreviewed research demonstrates that NLP can assess disclosure quality and identify potential ESGwashing by analyzing linguistic features and topic drift, thereby enhancing analysts' judgment and mitigating information risk—specifically, the risks that inflate spreads or impede projects in later stages (Schimanski et al., 2024).

Secondly, geographical and operational data facilitate the assessment of sites and systems for physical risk and yield. For solar and wind Public-Private partnerships, integrating satellite irradiance and wind fields, reanalysis datasets, and transmission limitations with local hazard layers (flood, heat, fire) generates a comprehensive prescreening dataset. In the domains of water and transportation, traffic and sensor data expose demand elasticity and resilience constraints. In all instances, AI models are contingent upon the quality of its features; reputable pipelines employ domain-specific features (e.g., grid congestion proxies, catchment hydrology indicators) rather than solely relying on generic machine learning.

Thirdly, counterparty and supply chain analytics mitigate procurement risks. Large language and graph models can analyze supplier relationships and identify sanctions, ESG conflicts, or capacity limitations prior to bid award—insights that are strongly correlated with schedule risk and the likelihood of cost overruns.

The body of studies regarding AI in sustainable finance has two significant caveats:

- Materiality and elucidation. Metareviews indicate that numerous AIforESG solutions falter due to the absence of materiality in KPIs or the opacity of models to credit committees. Models that combine prediction accuracy with transparent features (such as interpretable document ratings and physically grounded risk variables) are more likely to succeed in due diligence (Lim et al., 2024).
- Management of data governance. Research indicates that data quality and coverage are the primary constraints; conflicting ESG data may result in erroneous correlations or misleading screening outcomes. The solution involves stringent data lineage (identifying the source, collection time, and transformation process) and adherence to reporting taxonomies to ensure model results are comparable across assets (Lagasio et al., 2024).

The evidence supporting these strategies is now empirical rather than anecdotal. Finance and economics journals indicate that AI/NLP enhances ESG evaluation and investor decisionmaking by diminishing information asymmetry, resulting in more accurate pricing for labeled instruments and a reduced WACC when disclosure is robust. A 2024 study suggests NLP models for evaluating corporate ESG subdomains with established predictive validity, while another 2024 article records AI's capability to identify ESGwashing in sustainability reports. Collectively, our findings warrant the incorporation of AI screens into PPP procurement and financial procedures, contingent upon governance and assurance maintaining alignment (Schimanski et al., 2024).

4.3 Smart Contracts and Blockchain for Traceability, Escrow, and Milestone Payments

Public-Private Partnerships (PPPs) predominantly encounter operational challenges in payments, characterized by protracted certifications, contested quantities, retention release obstacles, and ambiguous changeorder documentation. Blockchain and smart contracts are not a universal solution; however, when applied in welldefined contexts, they effectively address specific challenges: traceability (immutable records), escrow (segregated funds with conditional disbursement), and milestone payments (automated payouts upon verified completion).

The most rapidly advancing use case is the automation of progress and milestone payments. A 2023 article in Scientific Reports introduced a BIMbased smart contract architecture that automates payments upon the fulfillment and verification of specified conditions against modelbased proof. Eliminating manual batching and subjective approvals reduces payment latency, alleviates workingcapital strain, and relegates disagreements mostly to the data layer (Is the job complete per the model?) instead of the process layer (Has someone signed the form?). Kamel et al. (2023).

Since that time, the literature has evolved to encompass scantoBIM/IoT or realitycapture oracles as secure connections between the physical realm and onchain contracts. A 2025 Buildings study illustrates a framework in which LiDARderived advancements are juxtaposed with BIM jobs; upon meeting tolerances, the smart contract permits partial disbursements to contractors and subcontractors. Concession SPVs benefit from predictable cash flow, while lenders get assurance through verifiable use of proceeds aligned with green and transition labels, as well as lender covenant packages (Elsharkawi, H., et al. (2025).

In the realm of Automation in Construction, blockchainenabled platformasaservice models facilitate offsite construction by managing identities, versioned design files, and component provenance among various firms—addressing the multiparty coordination challenges inherent in complex Public-Private partnerships (PPPs). Standardized interfaces enable such platforms to incorporate escrow modules, allowing public agencies to deposit unitary charges, with releases regulated by performance smart contracts, while audit nodes managed by independent engineers or verifiers monitor the state (Liu et al., 2024).

Fundamental design decisions:

1. What is recorded onchain. Maintain hashes and state information (e.g., task completion, timestamps, signer identifiers) onchain; store large files (point clouds, BIM models) offchain in secure repositories. This reconciles auditability with scalability and intellectual property protection.
2. Oracle integrity. Progress or KPI assertions must be authenticated by reliable oracles—digital test certificates, metering data, or thirdparty verifications. In Public-Private Partnerships, the Independent Engineer serves as a neutral oracle operator with direct agreements with lenders to alleviate tensions.
3. Escrow methodology. Smart escrow must embody the contract's risk distribution: milestone disbursements, retention stipulations, defects liability durations, and safe harbor provisions for regulatory suspensions.
4. Interoperability and governance. Multiparty projects necessitate permissioned chains with explicit governance including writing permissions, upgrade procedures, and conflict resolution mechanisms. Recent analyses highlight that interoperability connecting disparate chains and systems is progressing, which is significant if stateowned financiers or multilateral lenders maintain distinct ledgers (Pham et al., 2025).

This is not merely theoretical. A 2025 MDPI study records automated construction payments utilizing blockchain and scantoBIM technology, indicating decreased payment cycle duration and a reduction in conflicts. A 2024 Elsevier study outlines a blockchain Platform as a Service (PaaS) designed to improve interoperability and trust in offsite production, pertinent to Public-Private partnerships (PPPs) for modular schools and hospitals. Alongside the 2023 Scientific Reports framework for payment automation, these contributions delineate a reference architecture: BIM/DT and verifiers supply smart contracts that oversee escrows and disbursements, while an auditing layer records every event for lenders and regulatory bodies (Kamel et al., 2023).

Implications for policy and procurement. Procuring agencies can expedite adoption by: (i) permitting digital proofs (hashes, signed attestations) as legitimate evidence in payment clauses; (ii) delineating APIlevel specifications for oracles and verifiers; (iii) conducting pilot programs with sandboxed ledgers on a limited number of contracts prior to scaling; and (iv) synchronizing payment KPIs with sustainabilitylinked finance covenants to ensure that the same verified metrics govern both cash disbursements and financing spreads. Sponsors benefit from investing in contracttech stacks (BIM/DT, signatures, permissioned chain) through diminished workingcapital requirements, fewer conflicts, and enhanced lender trust.

5. GLOBAL CASES AND A POLICY ROADMAP

5.1 Case Ministudies: Renewable Energy, Mass Transit, and Waterreuse PPPs (Emerging & OECD)

Mass transit (China/OECD comparators): Urban rail Public-Private partnerships amalgamate intricate, enduring assets with significant political relevance. Data from Beijing Metro Line 4 and other urban rail Public-Private partnerships suggest that risk sharing during the operational period must align with controllability. The operator bears the performance and availability risk, whereas the public authority is better positioned to maintain or mitigate noncontrollable demand risk associated with macroeconomic cycles, landuse policies, and fare caps through availability payments or adjusted demand floors and caps. Gametheoretic models of urban rail Public-Private partnerships emphasize that optimum allocations account for controllability, loss severity, affordability, and management costs, while unambiguous quantitative guidelines mitigate renegotiations. Supplementary efforts regarding highspeed train and urban rail financing highlight the necessity of including landvalue capture and specific subsidies to balance affordability with financial sustainability, particularly in the context of regulated rates. The key insight for green capital is that availabilitybased payment structures, grounded in verifiable service outputs, produce the steady, longterm cash flows necessary for debt investors; only minimal, operatorinfluenced demand factors should be assigned risk weights to the SPV (Xiang et al., 2022).

Water reuse and desalination in the GCC and OECD regions are advancing through Public-Private partnerships, focusing on sophisticated water treatment and reuse, including energyefficient desalination and enhanced brine management, particularly in areas facing water scarcity. Comparative reviews indicate a rapid adoption of wastewater reclamation and reuse to diversify supply sources for industry, agriculture, and landscape irrigation; governance studies highlight that success depends on effective PIR (PoliciesInstitutionsRegulations) frameworks, quality standards, and tariff structures that incorporate lifecycle costs while safeguarding lowincome users. In the context of desalination, PPP frameworks frequently integrate DBFOM for facilities with offtake agreements linked to energy prices and performance KPIs (specific energy consumption, recovery rate). Since 2021, caseoriented and synthesis research emphasizes that institutional capacity and regulatory clarity are the primary risk determinants, surpassing the influence of technology itself. When authorities establish explicit reuse criteria alongside longterm offtake agreements and reliable monitoring, reporting, and verification of effluent quality, private lenders are willing to accept extended tenors and reduced spreads particularly if the project demonstrates alignment with taxonomy/standards and receives thirdparty validation (Haldar et al., 2024).

Mechanisms for crosscase mobilization: Three mobilizers consistently emerge across many sectors and socioeconomic categories. Standardized, clear PPP templates and riskallocation matrices ensure predictable procurement cycles for sponsors and credit committees, hence minimizing renegotiations. Secondly, resultsbased or availabilitylinked rewards associated with tangible, verifiable KPIs convert ESG performance into monetary flows. Third, targeted derisking measures (such as partialrisk/credit guarantees and foreign exchange facilities) are crucial in emerging markets characterized by limited capital markets and policy instability. Recent metaanalyses of lowcarbon and climateresilient Public-Private partnerships indicate that investors are influenced by credible support and the quality of disclosures, resulting in a reduced weighted average cost of capital, particularly when taxonomy alignment and ISSBstyle disclosures mitigate information risk. (Casady et al., 2024)

Equity and communal results: Case evaluations indicate that green Public-Private partnerships (PPPs) may perpetuate inequities such as land assembly externalities in megasolar projects, fare burdens in transit systems, and siting burdens in water facilities unless distributional safeguards, like tariffdesign lifelines, local employment and training initiatives, and benefitsharing funds, are incorporated into contracts (Silva et al., 2023).

5.2 Lessons Learned: Institutional Readiness, Affordability, Equity, and Resilience

Institutional preparedness influences the cost of capital. Crossregional evidence indicates that the critical factor for greencapital Public-Private partnerships (PPPs) is governance quality rather than technology, encompassing the credibility of procurement, openness of contracts, and policy stability. In lowcarbon and climateresilient Public-Private partnerships (PPPs), authorities reference innovation and budget limitations as justifications for employing PPPs, while private investors emphasize profitability and risk management. Both viewpoints align on the necessity for consistent regulations and comprehensive data disclosure to narrow spreads. Recent evaluations indicate that jurisdictions adopting standardized PPP processes, disclosure according with ISSB/taxonomy frameworks, and reliable MRV experience a reduction in risk premia and an extension of tenors. These institutional characteristics, as opposed to singular subsidies, generate systemic bankability (Haldar et al., 2025).

Costeffectiveness and financial discipline through payment structuring. Affordability frequently conflicts with bankability in userfee industries such as mass transit and water services. The key takeaway from urban rail and socialinfrastructure Public-Private partnerships is to distinguish between service availability and demand fluctuations: implement availability payments for fixedcost recovery and servicequality incentives, incorporating demandlinked components solely in instances where operators can affect ridership through service quality. This mitigates the excessive transfer of uncontrollable demand risk (which inflates WACC) and diminishes the need for renegotiations. Landvalue capture and focused, transparent subsidies can enhance PPP cash flows to ensure equity for riders while maintaining stability favorable to lenders. Simultaneously, policy analysis warns against accumulating implicit public debt via ambiguous assurances; transparency about contingent obligations is essential for institutional preparedness (Li et al., 2024).

Equity should be regarded as a fundamental aspect of bankability, rather than a mere afterthought. Research on megasolar parks indicates that land tenure, remuneration, and local development benefits influence community consent and longterm operational stability—factors that banks are increasingly considering in their assessments. When benefitsharing arrangements and local employment/skills key performance indicators are contractual and subject to audit, the risk associated with social license diminishes, hence reducing financing costs. Energyjustice evaluations of Pavagada reveal that in the absence of deliberate distributional frameworks, substantial green assets may perpetuate inequalities; in contrast, meticulously designed leases, revenuesharing arrangements, or community funds might incorporate beneficial externalities. This rationale extends to transit (fare equity, accessibility) and water (lifeline tariffs), wherein equity protections are included into the payment structure (e.g., availability base + social KPI components) (Casady et al., 2024).

Resilience must be measured and compensated. The OECD's 2024 evaluation of climateresilient infrastructure contends that resilience must be integrated into planning, procurement, and finance, rather than seen as supplementary design elements. In the context of PPPs, the operational insight is to establish resilience KPIs (service continuity amongst designated climatic risks, recovery durations, exceedance probability) and link them to financial penalties/rewards and finance agreements (e.g., sustainabilitylinked escalations if resilience objectives are not met). This guarantees that investors evaluate what is quantified and that operators assimilate the advantages of lifetime adaptability. In instances where resilience is inadequately defined, retrospective performance shocks manifest as refinancing pressures and public discontent (OECD, 2024).

Derisking serves as a supplement rather than a replacement. In emerging markets, heightened sovereign, foreign exchange, and policy risks increase the weighted average cost of capital (WACC). The research regarding blended finance and policy instruments indicates that targeted guarantees, PRI, and FX facilities can reduce spreads; however, their effectiveness is enhanced when integrated with transparent frameworks and reliable monitoring, reporting, and verification (MRV) systems. Macro analyses in 2024 indicate that the elevated cost of capital, rather than technology expenses, constitutes the primary constraint for clean infrastructure in developing nations; therefore, policy should prioritize reducing WACC through institutional reforms and targeted derisking instead of universal subsidies (Calcaterra et al., 2024).

Data integrity is crucial to trust. As articulated in Section 4, digital MRV and standardized reporting (ISSB S1/S2; EU Taxonomy tagging) are transitioning from optional to essential requirements. Sectors that offer auditable, machinereadable performance metrics (energy yield, water quality, uptime, emissions intensity) attract a wider range of investors and experience reduced spreads. In green Public-Private partnerships, this entails clear dataaccess provisions for lenders and authorities, as well as the alignment of project key performance indicators with financing key performance indicators (e.g., sustainabilitylinked bonds/sustainabilitylinked loans covenants).

Synthesis for practitioners: (1) Prioritize early investment in institutional infrastructure (standardized Requests for Proposals/contracts, disclosure templates, Measurement, Reporting, and Verification guidance). Employ availabilitybased payment mechanisms to safeguard affordability and bankability, incorporating demandlinked components just where they may be influenced. Incorporate equity and resilience into key performance indicators and payment structures. Implement layer derisking to address nondiversifiable hazards, ensuring it does not obscure inadequate project fundamentals. Mandate machinereadable data and thirdparty verification to maintain stringent pricing throughout the duration of the concession (Haldar et al., 2025).

5.3 Policy Roadmap: Standardized Green PPP Frameworks, Derisking Facilities, Crossborder Cofinance

1) Standardize "GREEN PPP" frameworks from pipeline to reporting.

Governments ought to disseminate sectorspecific standard forms (DBFOM/availability versus revenuerisk), encompassing: (i) riskallocation matrices with default positions and deviation protocols; (ii) KPI catalogs featuring taxonomyaligned definitions (e.g., emissions intensity thresholds, DNSH screens); (iii) MRV stipulations (sensors, data frequency, assurance levels); and (iv) lenderdirect agreements (stepin, cure periods). Standardization diminishes bid expenses, shortens negotiation durations, and enhances comparability for investors. Global evidence demonstrates that standardized templates (e.g., NECstyle modular contracts; PPP standard forms) combined with BIM/digitaltwin information requirements can enhance governance, improving delivery dependability and transparency (Montoya & Alarcón, 2024).

2. Establish global disclosure standards.

Require disclosure in accordance with ISSB S1/S2 and, where applicable, EU Taxonomy key performance indicators. This harmonization mitigates information risk and allows crossborder purchasers (pension funds, insurers) to deploy resources on a larger scale. In practice, incorporate a Green PPP Annex in each RfP that aligns activities with taxonomy criteria, enumerates KPIs (Scope 1–2–3 when pertinent), and delineates assurance requirements. Data from sustainableinfrastructure finance demonstrates that enhanced disclosure quality expands the investor base and may decrease spreads; aligning projectlevel data with marketstandard labels (green, sustainabilitylinked, transition) facilitates access to bond and loan markets for project and portfolio financing (Casady et al., 2024).

3) Institutionalize risk mitigation: national facilities in conjunction with multilateral development bank leverage.

Establish national derisking facilities that offer partialrisk or credit guarantees, subordinated or firstloss tranches, and longterm foreign exchange liquidity for Public-Private partnerships that correspond with green taxonomy. Combine these with multilateral instruments (MIGAstyle PRI; development bank guarantees) to achieve investmentgrade profiles. The 2024–2025 literature highlights that in emerging nations, the impediment is the WACC rather than technology: focused derisking that mitigates sovereign, foreign exchange, and policy risks attracts longterm private capital. Policy notes from the OECD and climatefinance trackers indicate that blendedfinance volumes and structures are increasing, particularly when concessional layers are designated and timelimited. Implement design derisking as a temporal reduction (sunset clauses) to prevent enduring market distortion (Calcaterra et al., 2024).

4) Implement performancebased compensation: outcomeoriented procurement with financial alignment.

Implement availabilitybased unitary fees with KPIlinked differentials that capitalize on climate and social results (e.g., validated GHG intensity reductions, resilience uptime, water quality adherence, accessibility). Mandate that financing KPIs (SLL/SLB) correspond with contract KPIs to synchronize incentives among sponsors, lenders, and the authority. This alignment mitigates "KPI arbitrage," streamlines assurance, and facilitates secondarymarket funding (green project bonds) by elucidating value drivers for investors. Empirical and policy research on LCCR PPPs demonstrates that investors react to reliable, verifiable performancepayment systems with more stringent pricing (Casady et al., 2024).

5) Establish crossborder cofinancing platforms.

Green PPP pipelines in emerging nations frequently lack the scale or uniformity necessary to entice global investors on a dealbydeal basis. Governments, multilateral development banks, and regional development finance institutions could initiate programmatic platforms that aggregate standardized Public-Private partnerships across jurisdictions—such as renewable energy minigrids, energyefficient public buildings, and advanced wastewater reuse—utilizing uniform documentation, key performance indicator sets, and assurance providers. Platforms may issue program bonds or multiasset loans, secured by firstloss capital from concessional sources. Recent data on "climate blended finance" reveal significant expansion in these methodologies; the primary policy focus is interoperability—synchronizing standards to enable crossborder investors to underwrite at scale (Climate Policy Initiative, 2024).

6) Enhance supportive habitats.

Implement strategies that reduce development timelines (such as streamlined permitting and prefeasibility financing), enhance the professionalism of PPP units, and digitize data repositories with machinereadable RfPs and realtime MRV feeds for operational assets. Complement this with capacity enhancement for subnational governments and uniform training for independent engineers and verifiers. Cross-market analyses indicate that factors facilitating Public-Private partnerships—such as welldefined legal frameworks, reliable dispute resolution mechanisms, and transparent management of contingent liabilities—are associated with more extensive project pipelines and improved pricing (Organisation for Economic Cooperation and Development, 2024).

7) Intentional equity and inclusion.

Mandate socialimpact addenda in all Green Public-Private Partnerships: local employment and training objectives; gender equity strategies; affordability provisions (lifeline blocks, targeted subsidies); and grievance resolution systems. Evidence from megasolar projects and urban rail indicates that proactively considering distributional implications serves as both a financial riskmitigation approach and a social responsibility; the bankability of projects increases when community permission is obtained and assessed (Casady et al., 2024).

8) Engage in iterative learning cycles.

Disseminate postaward datasets (contract summaries, KPI outcomes, modification orders, availability deductions) to provide metaanalysis and ongoing enhancement. Link access to derisking facilities with datasharing obligations to inform the public about effective risk allocations and KPI frameworks.

Success is characterized by the achievement of desired goals and objectives. Within 24–36 months, jurisdictions implementing this roadmap should experience (i) reduced bidtoclose timelines resulting from standardization; (ii) narrower spreads and extended tenors on green PPP debt attributable to enhanced disclosure and derisking; (iii) quantifiable equity and resilience outcomes as KPIs are financed and enforced; and (iv) crossborder capital inflows into platformized pipelines due to increased comparability.

5.4 Policy Implications for Governments and Investors

The analysis presented in this chapter suggests several policy implications for governments, investors, and multilateral institutions seeking to mobilize green capital for sustainable infrastructure development. First, governments should prioritize the development of standardized PPP frameworks that integrate sustainability criteria into procurement and contract design. Standardized documentation, clear risk allocation matrices, and transparent disclosure requirements can significantly reduce transaction costs and improve investor confidence.

Second, policymakers should expand the use of blended finance mechanisms to address structural barriers to private investment. Instruments such as concessional loans, first-loss tranches, viability gap funding, and guarantees can play a catalytic role in mobilizing private capital by improving project bankability and reducing perceived investment risks. Third, institutional investors including pension funds and insurance companies can play a greater role in infrastructure financing when projects offer transparent ESG performance metrics and predictable revenue streams. Aligning project-level key performance indicators with financial instruments such as green bonds or sustainability-linked loans can strengthen the connection between infrastructure performance and capital market participation. Finally, multilateral development banks and international financial institutions can support sustainable infrastructure development by providing technical assistance, risk mitigation instruments, and cross-border co-financing platforms that enable infrastructure projects in emerging economies to access global capital markets.

CONCLUSION

The chapter contends that well organized Public–Private Partnerships (PPPs) can mobilize substantial green capital when DBFOM contracts, value for money assessments, and risk allocation relevant to typologies are connected to transparent, outcomeoriented payment systems. A calibrated capital stack integrating public funds for enabling circumstances, concessional layers to mitigate nondiversifiable risks, and private equity/debt for scalability lowers the weighted average cost of capital and attracts institutional investors. Bankability depends more on governance than on technology: standardized PPP documentation, reliable risksharing matrices, and transparent ESG disclosures (aligned with ISSB/EU taxonomy) transform environmental and social performance into predictable cash flows. Guarantees, PRI, and FX covers augment (but do not replace) robust contracts by appropriately calibrating sovereign, policy, and currency risks while maintaining incentives for lifecycle efficiency.

The chapter asserts that digitalization DMRV, digital twins, and dataready procurement has become crucial for investor confidence and operational accountability, allowing realtime verification of carbon, resilience, and servicequality KPIs, and enabling smartescrow/milestone payments. Crosssector minicases (renewables, mass transit, water reuse) emphasize consistent lessons: distinguish availability from demand volatility to safeguard affordability and fiscal responsibility; incorporate equity and resilience metrics in contracts to ensure social license and longterm performance; and institutionalize derisking via national facilities supported by multilateral development banks (MDBs). The suggested policy roadmap highlights coordinated green Public-Private partnership frameworks, standardized disclosure baselines, integrated crossborder cofinancing, and continuous learning through accessible postaward data. Collectively, these methods enhance pipelines, reduce spreads, prolong tenors, and synchronize climateresilient, inclusive outcomes with public accountability.

The chapter contends that well organized Public–Private Partnerships (PPPs) can mobilize substantial green capital when DBFOM contracts, value for money assessments, and risk allocation tailored to specific typologies are connected to transparent, outcomeoriented payment systems. A calibrated capital stack integrating public funds for enabling circumstances, concessional layers to mitigate nondiversifiable risks, and private equity/debt for scalability lowers the weighted average cost of capital and attracts institutional investors. Bankability relies more on governance than on technology: standardized PPP documentation, credible risksharing matrices, and transparent ESG disclosures (aligned with ISSB/EU taxonomy) transform environmental and social performance into reliable cash flows. Guarantees, PRI, and FX covers enhance, rather than replace, robust contracts by appropriately calibrating sovereign, policy, and currency risks while maintaining incentives for lifecycle efficiency.

The chapter asserts that digitalization DMRV, digital twins, and dataready procurement has become crucial for investor confidence and operational accountability, allowing realtime verification of carbon, resilience, and servicequality KPIs, and enabling smartescrow/milestone payments. Crosssector minicases (renewables, mass transit, water reuse) highlight consistent lessons: distinguish availability from demand volatility to safeguard affordability and fiscal responsibility; incorporate equity and resilience metrics in contracts to ensure social license and longterm performance; and institutionalize derisking via national facilities supported by multilateral development banks (MDBs). The suggested policy roadmap highlights coordinated green Public-Private partnership frameworks, disclosure standards, platformbased crossborder cofinancing, and continuous learning through accessible postaward data. Collectively, these methods enhance pipelines, reduce spreads, prolong tenors, and synchronize climateresilient, inclusive outcomes with public accountability.

REFERENCES

Affolter, B., Ciarla, E., Meyer, J., & Sugandhita, S. (2024). Signaling sustainability: Differential reaction of the stock market following the announcement of sustainabilitylinked bonds. *Finance Research Letters*, *63*, 105261. DOI: 10.1016/j.frl.2024.105261

Alcorta, P., Escapa, M., & González, P. (2024). Investment risk under different renewable energy support schemes. *Environmental and Resource Economics*, *86*(2), 223–249. DOI: 10.1007/s10640024009093

Alessi, L., Kuszewski, M., & Tettamanzi, P. (2024). Accounting for the EU Green Taxonomy: Exploring its concept, data and analytics. *Accounting Forum*, *48*(3), 365–373. DOI: 10.1080/01559982.2024.2369343

Auzepy, A., Bannier, C. E., & Fecht, F. (2023). Are sustainabilitylinked loans designed to effectively incentivize corporate sustainability? A framework for review. *Financial Management*, *52*(4), 643–675. DOI: 10.1111/fima.12437

Azhgaliyeva, D., Kapsalyamova, Z., & Saparbayev, A. (2023). Policy support in promoting green bonds in Asia. *Climate Policy*, *23*(4, S1), S1–S18. DOI: 10.1080/14693062.2023.2167800

Batjes, N. H.. (2024). Towards a modular, multiecosystem MRV framework for soil organic carbon. *Carbon Management*, *15*(1), 2410812. DOI: 10.1080/17583004.2024.2410812

Briera, T., & Lefèvre, J. (2024). Reducing the cost of capital through international climate finance to accelerate the renewable energy transition in developing countries. *Energy Policy*, *188*, 114104. DOI: 10.1016/j.enpol.2024.114104

Calcaterra, M., Aleluia Reis, L., Fragkos, P., Briera, T., Boer, H. S., Egli, F., Emmerling, J., Iyer, G., Mittal, S., Polzin, F., Sanders, M., Schmidt, T. S., Serebriakova, A., & Steffen, B. (2024). Reducing the cost of capital to finance the energy transition in developing countries. *Nature Energy*, *9*(10), 1241–1251. DOI: 10.1038/s41560-024-01606-7 PMID: 39450347

Calcaterra, M., Ameli, N., & Hallett, T. B. (2024). Reducing the cost of capital to finance the energy transition. *Nature Communications*, *15*, 5469. DOI: 10.1038/s41467024506454 PMID: 39450347

Cao, Y., Li, H., & Su, L. (2024). A dynamic performancebased payment mechanism for PPP projects: An integrated principal–agent and multiobjective optimization model. *International Journal of Strategic Property Management*, *28*(2), 116–129. DOI: 10.3846/ijspm.2024.21183

Cao, Y., Li, H., Su, L., Zhang, W., & Zhang, C. (2024). Deciphering the difference puzzle of risksharing: A comparative analysis of infrastructure PPP development within China and US. *Project Leadership and Society*, *5*(2), 100135. DOI: 10.1016/j.plas.2024.100135

Casady, C. B., Cepparulo, A., & Giuriato, L. (2024). Public–private partnerships for lowcarbon, climateresilient infrastructure: Insights from the literature. *Journal of Cleaner Production*, *470*, 143338. DOI: 10.1016/j.jclepro.2024.143338

Castelblanco, G., ArboledaCastrillón, L., & Bastidas, A. (2024). Financial system dynamics model for servicefee road PPPs. *Construction Management and Economics*, *42*(9–10), 893–912. DOI: 10.1080/01446193.2024.2335566

Chen, R., Zhou, N., & Liu, Q. (2024). Impact of implicit government guarantee on the credit spread of urban construction investment bonds. *Financial Innovation*, *10*(1), 72. DOI: 10.1186/s40854-024-00722-3

Chrzan, S., Sokolowska, E., & Dziwinski, P. (2024). Investor judgment based on the EU Taxonomy. *Review of Quantitative Finance and Accounting*, *63*(4), 1511–1548. Advance online publication. DOI: 10.1007/s11156-024-01297-x

Climate Policy Initiative. (2024). *Global landscape of climate finance 2024*. https://www.climatepolicyinitiative.org/wpcontent/uploads/2024/10/GlobalLandscapeofClimateFinance2024.pdf

Ecklu, J., et al. (2025). Digital MRV technologies for the voluntary carbon market. *ACS ES&T Letters, 12*(x), e01048. https://doi.org/DOI: 10.1021/acs.estlett.4c01048

Fleta-Asín, J., & Muñoz, F.FletaAsín. (2024). Risk allocation schemes between public and private sectors in green energy projects. *Journal of Environmental Management*, *357*, 120650. DOI: 10.1016/j.jenvman.2024.120650 PMID: 38569262

Gamso, J., & Dimitrova, A. (2024). Rewarding a friend: Does the World Bank direct noncommercial risk insurance to countries that support US foreign policy interests? *New Political Economy*, *29*(1), 159–172. DOI: 10.1080/13563467.2023.2230557

Gifford, J. L., Wang, Y., & Ma, H. (2024). What triggers PPP renegotiations? Evidence from U.S. highway concessions. *Public Management Review*, *26*(10), 1850–1877. DOI: 10.1080/14719037.2023.2200404

Guo, Y., Chen, C., Luo, X., & Martek, I. (2024). Determining concessionary items for "availability paymentonly" PPP projects: A holistic framework integrating value for money and social values. *Journal of Civil Engineering and Management, 30*(2), 149–167. DOI: 10.3846/jcem.2024.20841

Haldar, S., Hoffman, J., Verma, M., Peddibhotla, A., & Bazaz, A. (2024). Reimagining energy infrastructure for justice: Power, politics, and institutional work in India's 2.05 GW Pavagada solar park. *Energy Research & Social Science, 116*, 103645. DOI: 10.1016/j.erss.2024.103645

Hecht, A., & Lampenius, N. (2023). How do firms manage their foreign exchange exposure? *Journal of Risk and Financial Management, 16*(8), 359. DOI: 10.3390/jrfm16080359

Hou, L., Yang, F., Liang, W., Wu, C., & Song, J. (2024). Government subsidy and benefit distribution mechanisms for transportation PPP projects: An evolutionary game perspective. *Journal of Environmental Management, 359*, 120981. DOI: 10.1016/j.jenvman.2024.120981 PMID: 38688132

Hu, X., Zhu, B., Lin, R., Li, X., Zeng, L., & Zhou, S. (2024). How does greenness translate into greenium? Evidence from China's green bonds. *Energy Economics, 133*, 107511. DOI: 10.1016/j.eneco.2024.107511

Li, X., Song, Y., & Gan, X. (2024). Public–private partnerships and land value capture in urban rail. *Transport Policy, 152*, 88–100. DOI: 10.1016/j.tranpol.2024.07.012

Meng, J., Ye, Z., & Wang, Y. (2024). Financing and investing in sustainable infrastructure: A review and research agenda. *Sustainable Futures : An Applied Journal of Technology, Environment and Society, 8*, 100312. DOI: 10.1016/j.sftr.2024.100312

Moshood, T. D.. (2024). Infrastructure digital twin technology: A new paradigm. *Technology in Society, 76*, 102378. DOI: 10.1016/j.techsoc.2024.102378

Organisation for Economic Cooperation and Development. (2024). *Bridging the clean energy investment gap: Cost of capital and policy solutions* (ENV/WKP(2024)15/REV1). https://doi.org/DOI: 10.1787/ENVWKP(2024)15REV1en

Organisation for Economic Cooperation and Development. (2024). *Infrastructure for a climateresilient future*. OECD., DOI: 10.1787/a74a45b0en

Papari, C. A., Polzin, F., Toxopeus, H., Bulkeley, H., & Menguzzo, E. (2024). Can the EU Taxonomy help upscale investments into urban naturebased solutions? *Environmental Science & Policy, 151*, 103598. DOI: 10.1016/j.envsci.2023.103598

Pellegrino, R., & D'Apuzzo, M. C. (2024). Mitigating foreign exchange risk exposure with supply chain flexibility: A real option analysis. *Journal of Business Logistics*, *45*(1), 61–85. DOI: 10.1111/jbl.12338

Petri, I. (2025). Digital twins for dynamic LCA in the built environment. *The Science of the Total Environment*, *958*, 173025. DOI: 10.1016/j.scitotenv.2025.173025

Popovic, T., Lygnerud, K., Denk, I., Fransson, N., & Unluturk, B. (2024). Blended finance as a catalyst for accelerating the European heat transition? *Smart Energy*, *14*, 100136. DOI: 10.1016/j.segy.2024.100136

Silva, J. A., Pereira, V. J., & Abreu, M. (2023). Water supply and wastewater treatment and reuse in future cities. *Water (Basel)*, *15*(17), 3064. DOI: 10.3390/w15173064

Wagenhofer, A. (2024). Sustainability reporting: A financial reporting perspective. *Accounting in Europe*, *21*(1), 1–14. DOI: 10.1080/17449480.2023.2218398

Xiang, P., Chen, Y., & Xu, Y. (2022). Operational risk allocation in urban rail transit PPP projects: A cooperativegame approach. *Frontiers in Environmental Science*, *10*, 900322. DOI: 10.3389/fenvs.2022.900322

Zhao, J., Liu, H. J., Love, P. E. D., Greenwood, D., & Sing, M. C. P. (2023). Value for money assessments for Public-Private partnerships: Characteristics, research directions, and policy implications. *Developments in the Built Environment*, *16*, 100246. DOI: 10.1016/j.dibe.2023.100246

Chapter 6
Innovating Green Finance:
Technology, Governance, and Sustainable Investment Pathways for Inclusive Growth

Amulya Ratna
http://orcid.org/0009-0000-1764-1371
Christ (Deemed to be) University, Delhi NCR, India

Aradhana Madhusudanan
http://orcid.org/0009-0004-5626-5793
Christ (Deemed to be) University, Delhi NCR, India

ABSTRACT

This chapter investigates the evolution and scaling of green finance as a key mechanism in global sustainable development. While the structural shift towards climate-resilient investment is rapidly accelerating, the transition is facing persistent systemic barriers, including data scarcity, regulatory fragmentation, and the risk of greenwashing. This study asserts that the long-term effectiveness of green finance will require a Cyber-Physical Ecosystem that closes the loop between financial capital and environmental impact through two key pillarstechnological innovation and robust governance.An analysis of how these technological innovations, including fintech, AI, and blockchain, would resolve historic market failures attributed to data scarcity and greenwashing through the provision of an enabling digital infrastructure to ensure transparency and real-time verification. Further, it evaluates the role of governance in legitimizing these innovations through harmonised taxonomies, obligatory ESG disclosures, and supervisory mechanisms of climate risks.

DOI: 10.4018/979-8-3373-7595-3.ch006

ht © 2027, IGI Global Scientific Publishing. Copying or distributing in print or electronic forms without written permission of IGI Global Scientific Publishing is prohibited. Use of this chapter to generative artificial intelligence (AI) technologies is expressly prohibited. The publisher reserves all rights to license its use for generative AI training and machine learning model development.

1. INTRODUCTION

The 21st century has been marked by escalating environmental degradation, rising climatic threats, and growing social injustices—all employed as driving factors for the possibility of both ecological and economic instabilities worldwide. Climate change remains a threat that has resulted in grave disruptions triggered by weather-related disasters, crop damage, water resources, and health effects. At the same time, there has been a loss in biodiversity coupled with reduced natural resources, which has affected the nature on which these productions, consumption, and economic prosperity are based. Many environmental problems are associated with significant socio-economic imbalances, considering unequal distribution in accessing these resources, unequal conditions in the effects triggered by climate change, and the reality of these poverty traps that exist today (IPCC, 2023). Traditionally, financial systems were designed with a prime interest in short-term profits. This neglects or considers less the cost associated with nature and society, which makes it easy to invest in activities that harm nature and create inequalities (Sachs et al., 2023). The risk management associated with finance has not been intertwined with sustainability principles. In this regard, the extraction of resources by industries that have large amounts of carbon continues to prosper at the cost of adequate investments in green energy and development strategies that are required in an environment that faces sustainability crises (UNEP FI, 2023).

However, to meet such challenges, green finance has come up as a paradigm with a vision focused on the integration of financial systems with concepts related to sustainability and inclusivity. Green finance is referred to as the array of financial tools, markets, and infrastructure that is aimed at making sure that low-carbon transition, resilience, and sustainable development take place. The green finance instruments, such as green bonds, sustainability-linked bonds, climate finance facilities, and environment, social, and governance funds, have increased significantly due to the commitment to policies, market demand, and the global agendas on sustainability (World Bank, 2024), primarily the goal is to make sure that such types of finances reach sectors that is going to help in reducing the greenhouse effects, conserve ecosystems, reduce energy usage, and enhance life. Many important problems with greenwashing, non-compliance with regulations, unequal ESG data, and unequal opportunities in the implementation of sustainability to ensure positive impacts on sustainable problems on earth exist (OECD, 2023). The other important problem is the lack of full implementation of green finance as part of financial decision-making. A large majority of institutions, Green investment policy and ESG are incidental or symbolic activity and it has not been used to change the fundamental nature of investment priorities. This superficial kind of engagement, of impaction dilution, in which sustainability-branded products create minimal or no environmental or social value, also has some downsides; for example, Kolbel et al. (2020)

observe that sustainability-labelled products have not led to any significant environmental or social gains either. Developing economies & the emerging markets face a range of additional obstacles. They tend to be underdeveloped in climate finance, have underdeveloped capital markets, the technology infrastructure is rather fragmented, and they are not very regulatory. All these limitations also hamper all these aspirations of green finance, as ADB 2022 declares and with all these systemic issues, it is suggested in this chapter that planning of green finance is intended to be integrated- think tech, innovation and governance round out the new big three. With sustainability finance innovation, it must be about the re-evaluation of the collection, quantification, checking, and use of information as a part of capital decision-making, rather than simply creating new financial products. The game will be brought to a new level by such technologies as AI, big data, IoT surveillance, and blockchain that will make sustainability information more open, correct, and accessible.

Governance is crucial for addressing the risks associated with greenwashing and ensuring compatibility between the financial sector and countries' international and domestic climate agendas (OECD, 2023). Governance can be facilitated through related policies such as sustainable taxonomy, mandatory ESG disclosure rules, stress tests related to climate, and green finance incentives to increase integrity for financial markets, mainly for sustainable financial investment (EU Commission, 2022).

The inclusive growth should be integrated into the overall plan for green finance as one of its key components, the inclusive growth targets to make sure balanced access to the financial resources; sharing of sustainable development gains. It also ensures a wide range of factors for equality through green finance, which can ensure job creation and also access to sustainable energy and other factors that are required for balanced societal growth (UNDP, 2023).

This chapter focuses on emerging innovations in financial products and their implementation through fintech solutions to empower micro, small, and medium enterprises, as well as the local authorities, which are currently left out of the mainstream financial system due to their ineligibility for green finance solutions.

The combination of both the technology and the governance system in the green financial system helps in developing the financial sector. Universities are now playing a crucial role in leading the Sustainable Development Goals (SDGs) even beyond simply attending the initial steps towards sustainable development.

In this regard, we may say the conclusion that green finance requires an investment and proper preconditions, such as technologies and governance, and students can be an initiating force. As these issues of climate and development are becoming more complex, green finance should surpass traditional practice, and it should focus more on smart solutions that show actual sustainability performance. The tech interventions can be used to build platforms touching on the issues of cost, as a way of enhancing confidence among the students and the general population

At last, the chapter will also talk about the future outlook and perspectives of green finance as it is formed by innovation, technology, and governance. The primary objective of the chapter is to demonstrate that the prospect of a technologically-driven and well-regulated green finance system can be used to foster inclusive and sustainable

2. THE GREEN FINANCE AND CONCEPT OF SUSTAINABLE DEVELOPMENT

Green finance has importantly developed over a very extended time, and it has been mainly influenced by social movements all the way to regulations, economic theories, and technological improvements. The three significant shifts that you can notice when you consider its history. The first one is that it began to be an investment rationale founded on moral and ethical motives. The second is that it proceeded to risk-based ESG integration. Now this is all about following the global sustainability goals. It is not a new set of financial products; it is a total revision of the role of capital in society. It is stated by Schoenmaker (2017) in the following manner: the transition between the era of Finance 1.0, i.e., profit only, and Finance 3.0, i.e. sustainable impact, demonstrates the extent to which the global financial system has become mature at last.

2.1 Evolution of Green Finance

The intellectual history of green finance illustrates that the internalisation of environmental externality is achieving increasing integration with the central core of finance. Green finance started at the periphery of the world of investment and is now at the very core of global economic thinking.

2.1.1 Early Ethical Foundations

The roots of green finance began to take form through Socially Responsible Investment (SRI), which was led primarily by religious groups, foundations, and NGOs. These organisations began pushing for a responsible form of investing that was based on a concept of moral values, applying so-called "negative screens" on sectors that were politically and socially detrimental, such as the tobacco, military, and apartheid sectors. In such a formative period for green finance, the concept of environmental activism was mostly incorporated within social activism campaigns.

Although the influence of this first generation of SRI initiatives proved important for the creation of public awareness, the investment approaches were largely normative and failed to incorporate the risk of the environment into financial analysis. Zeng & Lin (2023) state that first-generation SRI initiatives were "value-driven" and not "value-enhancing." In this paradigm, investors made a "philanthropic trade-off" while assuming that ideals would inherently equate to a diminished financial result. "Green" = moral decision.

2.1.2 Inclusion of Sustainability in Financial Decision Making Process - 1990s-2021

Ever since the 1990s, all such global environmental issues like climate change, ozone depletion, and natural disasters induced by industrial activities have had an impact on mainstream economic thought. Moving from pure ethical exclusion to quantifying the environmental risk began. This was due to the recent appearance of climate science and the realisation that environmental liabilities could indeed bankrupt a company, with various industrial litigations taken up in courts.

It was during this time that ESG investing began to take root. Asset managers began developing metrics to evaluate a company's exposure to climate issues and strength in governance. Khan et al. (2016) provided critical evidence during this transition, showing that companies addressing "material" ESG issues actually outperformed their peers. The use of ESG ratings evolved from being a niche practice for activists to a complex tool for conventional institutions that tackled long-term risk management. The launch of the United Nations Principles for Responsible Investment in 2006 marked a significant institutional turning point, ensuring there was a voluntary framework for global investors to follow for practices that were aligned with sustainability

2.1.3 Global Alignment With Climate and Sustainability Goals (2015-Present)

The year 2015 was also symbolic in terms of systemic change for commitment to the Sustainable Development Goals and the Paris Agreement. The SDGs and Paris Agreement created a direct connection between financial markets and planetary performance results. To fulfil these objectives, the estimated investment requirement is USD 5-7 trillion a year, which is not a figure that can be financed by public funds alone—a point that UNEP FI has also confirmed in 2022.

Nowadays, sustainable finance strategies are used by governments as tools of a green industrial policy and to increase their energy security. The ecological turn of the finance system is here to stay, according to Scholtens (2017), due to the understanding of the finance sector that the sector could not flourish if the planet falls. We seem to be already in the age of systemic alignment, and the goal has not only a risk management focus but also actively investing to transition to a net-zero economy.

2.2 Green Finance Instruments & Market Structure

The way that green finance operates is a very complicated set of tools and actors that direct money into a sustainable future. The building combines conventional products, innovative climate tools and verification.

2.2.1 Green Bonds: The Flagship Instrument

The Green bonds serve as the primary means of funding climate-oriented projects, which provide long-term capital to massive solar plants, electric vehicles, and flood-control facilities. The green bond industry in the world is in a frenzy, and the total issuance has already exceeded USD 2 trillion, the World Bank (2024) alleges. The institutional investors can offset long-term obligations with assets through those bonds to support the green transition. Flammer (2021) states that green bonds are not only the needed capital but also show the desire of a corporation to be more environmentally friendly and, in most instances, lead to a better environmental performance in the future.

2.2.2 Sustainability Linked Loans (SLLs)

Compared to green bonds, wherein such bonds are linked to specific projects, SLLs impose an interest rate on the sustainability performance of the borrower as a whole. This stimulates the decrease in the intensity of carbon, or better, water-use efficiency. It is a flexible tool that will help logistics or heavy manufacturing firms in the hard-to-abate sectors to receive transition finance despite not having an easy-to-work-with green initiative. OECD (2023) is keen on using SLLs as a method of effecting the company-wide change, contrary to small-scale environmental projects.

2.2.3 Thematic Portfolios and ESG Investment Funds

ESG funds can be of the best-in-class, or they can be thematic investments in clean energy. Their appearance means that a new generation of investors – millennials and Gen-Zers are currently interested in long-term sustainability and not in immediate gains. Boffo and Patalano (2020) note that despite the prevalence of such funds, it has been a challenge to establish how much various portfolios are actually green due to the fact that the funds do not adopt the same set of metrics.

2.2.4 Blended Finance

Blended finance is the rewriting of the game in the emerging markets, which presents perceived risks. It guarantees the removal of first-loss or credit upgrade on the project by a development institution. The most common and effective way of driving investment into climate adaptation and renewable energy among developing countries, whose market could otherwise make it prohibitive, according to the IMF (2023).

2.2.5 Carbon Markets & Governance

Carbon markets sell the pollution and generate a financial incentive to reduce emissions. This may occur through a cap-and-trade system or a voluntary offset marketplace. However, a carbon market requires a strong market structure that incorporates green taxonomies to make the carbon market a real force of promoting green tech and penalising non-compliance (Lindenberg, 2014). It is missing that green finance is experiencing a credibility gap.

2.3 Green Finance and Inclusive Growth

When the mechanisms of green finance are structured to benefit everyone at every level of society, they are truly developmental. Inclusive green finance is designed to ensure that the climate transition does not further exacerbate existing social inequalities.

2.3.1 Job Creation and Economic Diversification

The green transition is a powerful engine for employment. Sectors like renewable energy and organic farming are often more labour-intensive than the fossil fuel industries they replace. According to Zhou et al. (2020), green finance could help diversify the economic activities across regions previously reliant on carbon-heavy industries if matched by investment with "just transition" policies focused on retraining and social protection.

2.4 Theoretical Synthesis: Aligning Capital with Planetary Bound

The conceptual underpinnings for green finance can be traced back to an awareness of these boundaries. Clark et al. (2015).When it's a biological support, in terms of ecosystems, water cycles, etc., it's in disarray; a financially unstable system cannot continue. According to Clark et al. (2015), we are revisiting the entire concept of the fiduciary duty. Conventionally, it implied that you can disregard the so-called non-financial concerns, but currently, it is becoming a compulsion to take into account systemic risks associated with climate change. The new shift is logical since the financial instability has become directly correlated with the failure of natural supports.

2.5 The Role of Institutional Governance and Transparency

The growth and development of the green finance sector is not independent of the nature of governance exercised. This is according to a publication by Gangi et al. (2019), which states that a good governance system must always include the long-term creation of value for sustainable development above the short-term goal of profits on a quarterly basis.

Green finance uses transparency as its currency. In the absence of it, the geranium would be eliminated as the cost of capital would be equal to the norm. It is essential that green taxonomies, such as the EU Taxonomy, are established in the manner that the World Bank (2024) suggests, so that we all have a common language of speaking the same values regarding green finance. In that case, we do not have fragmentation in the markets.

2.6 Green Finance as a Driver of the Circular Economy

Green finance is the driving force that pushes societies from a "take, make, waste" economy towards a circular economy. By funding companies that operate and turn waste into energy, recycled textiles, and develop sustainable supply chains, green finance has redefined "the 'value' of waste" itself. According to Scholtens (2017): "This challenge calls for new financial thinking, in which 'resource productivity' has the same priority as 'labour productivity.' Yet, in less than one year, a new breed of bonds called 'green bonds' has been developed, incorporating this circular thinking into financial engineering, aiming at ensuring the financial system serves an Earth-regenerative economy."

3. INNOVATION & TECHNOLOGY IN GREEN FINANCE SYSTEMS

The current wave of technological change is rewriting the entire structural paradigm that existed in the global financial systems. Here we can see an emergence of fintech, AI, and big data to the point we can see blockchain emerge into the scene- it is insane how fast these technologies are remaking everything. Green finance was a upset point in the olden days, as Lindenberg (2014) suggests that there was a lot of confusion over what exactly green finance meant, and individuals were forced to spend huge sums to seal a deal. The point was that additional due diligence was required to confirm environmental claims, particularly those where data were not abundant. The current solution is digital systems. The adoption of technology in a sustainable way is relatively innovative to the developing economies, where info-tech may end up mending weak institutions and disjointed finance (World Economic Forum, 2023).

3.1 Fintech and Sustainable Capital Mobilisation

At this moment, Fintech is likely to become the largest disruptor of the global economy. It is not limited to digital payments and online lending, but it is transforming the process of how we raise money and how we quantify sustainability (Zeng and Lin, 2023). Once the entire monetary chain has been computerised, and have a well-run stream of cash directly into the environmental initiatives. Green investment through the use of fintech is primarily motivated by the need to open the world of institutions to less sophisticated investors. The article published by BloombergNEF in 2024 stated that retailing green assets is the best solution to the multi-trillion-dollar climate finance gap. The green crowdfunding is a huge change since common investors can combine their resources towards rooftop solar, local biogas and community-based projects of the circular economy. The social acceptability of energy transition is also increased through capital decentralisation. The driver of the green transformation is the SMEs, which have enormous challenges in obtaining traditional loans. The banking bottlenecks are in large extinction, and this fact implies that the local environmentally friendly production and organic agriculture receive more financing due to P2P lending.

In addition, the micro-investment applications have made green finance a consumer good. These are behavioural nudges such as rounding off your money and using the leftover to invest in green mutual funds, making the idea of being environmentally friendly an aspect of a normal life of every global citizen (Zhao and Chen, 2024). Robo-advisors are algorithm-driven and allow you to set your investments according to your sustainability plans without having to pay fees to the big banks. They are constructed based on the principles of responsible banking of the United Nations Environment Programme Finance Initiative of 2022, even on small portfolios, to be profitable and green at the same time.

3.2 ESG Facts, Analytics and Artificial Intelligence

The problem with green finance remains that they lack trustworthy, compatible data on the environmental, social and governance variables (Boffo and Patalano, 2020). The AI and the big-data analytics are changing that, though, and providing the transparency that institutions require to be trustworthy and regulated. Historically, ESG analysis is based on the self-reporting of the companies, which is selective, inconsistent, or even the whitewashing of bad impacts, as indicated by Khan et al. (2016). This has been mitigated by the use of AI technology, which makes use of NLP technology that can automatically review as many as 50,000 sustainability reports, annual reports, and regulatory filings to look for inconsistencies in a company's narrative on sustainability. Greenwashing patterns can be spotted by NLP machine-learning models related to a company's published environmental pledges to the actual legal disputes and financial disclosures (Zhao & Chen, 2024).

The importance of data in corporate governance should not be underestimated. According to Gangi et al. (2019), corporate governance can be greatly enhanced by technology that lifts the "veil of secrecy" that covers worldwide supply chains. Today, managers can now be held responsible not only in relation to their board of directors but also to worldwide stakeholders in general in view of real-time data regarding carbon footprint offered by AI and IoT in making decisions that were previously prioritizing stockholders but rather adopting a stakeholder-centric view in accordance with Clark et al. (2015) that puts sustainability in top priority in attaining long-term financial success.

3.3 Theoretical Frameworks and the Green Digital Commons

The integration of such technologies offers a tangible application of the theoretical debate offered by Scholtens (2017), which questioned finance on its concern for ecology. It is the role of technology to answer this debate by making the so-called "invisible" price of ecology tangible and quantifiable. The effect of a financial action on the environment can now be monitored in real-time by IoT sensors and reflected on a blockchain, making it a tangible factor that cannot be ignored by investors. It is this shift that is propelling the entire global economy to what some academics refer to as "Sustainable Finance 3.0," which considers environmental impact integral to the notion of value itself.

The changing landscape of the roles of central banks within the emerging green digital world. According to Dikau & Volz (2021), with the growing scope of central banks extending to cover sustainable factors, the new challenge of developing Central Bank Digital Currencies could provide innovative solutions to achieve green policy. This "programmable" money could guarantee that public subsidies or funds to support green economic recovery would not be spent on unsustainable practices, in order to avoid the "carbon leakage" that characterises most of the traditional subsidy schemes. This extends to the Agenda 2030 for Sustainable Development of the United Nations (United Nations, 2015), to implement innovative sources of funds to meet the Sustainable Development Goals.

3.4 Digital Green Finance and Systemic Risks Ethics

Innovation is Marvelous, yet impeccable. Boffo and Patalano (2020) caution that excessive reliance on sophisticated algorithms may result in the appearance of the so-called black-box ESG scoring, i.e.when the measurement of sustainability is obscured and when such a measurement may be biased. In case the training information is biased towards small firms, particularly the Western ones, the latter may be unfairly punished, as they cannot offer the same amount of data as large Western corporations. This digital divide may increase inequality in the world, which is one of the points Sachs et al. (2023) mention in relation to the Sustainable Development Goals. Another paradox is the nature of technology in terms of its environmental footprint. Certain blockchain networks, particularly the Proof-of-Work ones, consume excessive energy, which is contrary to green finance. The green finance sector is marked by a transition to more efficient protocols, such as Proof-of-Stake, which is the key to its self-sustainability.

3.5 Future Trajectories: Toward a Cyber-Physical

The final application of technology integration in green finance is ensuring a smooth "cyber-physical" system environment; In this case, a perfect digital world will be reflected through nature, which is illustrated as the environmental sensors in forests, oceans, and factories. The digital twin of the state of nature would allow us to assess the environmental threat and immediately compensate for green actions, which is a promising future for any sustainability student. Such an ecosystem would spark a shift towards Nature-Based Solutions (NbS), where all investment decisions are not focused on reducing carbon but protecting biodiversity as well. The use of bio-acoustic sensors and AI, which monitors the health of forests, would result in monetary devices that make payments when a threatened species appears or when an ecosystem remains healthy. It would become the ultimate financial innovation, making the financial system a true friend of the natural world. These sustainable and digital transitions are closely connected to the future of finance itself, as the World Economic Forum (2023) puts it.

4. GOOD GOVERNANCE AND ACCOUNTABILITY IN SUSTAINABLE INVESTING

The key to sustainable finance architecture is governance and accountability. With more money being directed by the global capital markets towards low-carbon and climate-resilient investments, the transparency of such transactions will be based on strong legal and regulatory frameworks. Lack of adequate regulation not only impedes green finance but also brings about systemic risks, greenwashing, and misallocated capital. According to Schoenmaker (2017), we should have a new paradigm of governance that would optimise shareholder value and, at the same time, provide fiduciary responsibility to a stable environment to ensure that finance fulfils its purpose. This paper will discuss the current trends in this regard regarding regulation.

4.1 Regulatory Frameworks & Sustainable Finance Taxonomies

The growing green finance markets trigger an urgent imperative for regulatory frameworks with a common definition of sustainable economic activities. Regulatory governance with the use of sustainability taxonomies, mandatory ESG disclosure regimes, and climate-risk supervisory measures is essential for ensuring the integrity of the financial sector. Without common classification standards, there is tremendous vagueness for investors regarding the environmental performance of financial assets. The OECD (2023) emphasises that common regulatory standards are essential for ensuring reduced gaps in information between different financial parties and for enhancing global financial capital flows to legitimate sustainable projects.

4.1.1 The Purpose and Structure of Sustainable Finance Taxonomies

Taxonomies of sustainable finance are complex classification systems that define technical thresholds for environmental sustainability for an activity. Governance stuff tends to be divided into three areas: to ensure that things are more transparent by ensuring that there are standard definition, ensuring that investors can understand where to invest their money by demonstrating high- and low-impact projects and to increase transparency by establishing a common reporting background. Lindenberg (2014) was not alone in pointing out that the absence of a universally accepted definition of green finance was an actual obstacle, and that taxonomies address it by implicating greenness into the law. It has a systemic structure consisting of certain environmental objectives, adaptation, mitigation, and biodiversity, which has been reflected in most taxonomies. This includes technical screening requirements, emissions or energy-efficiency requirements, and Do Not Significantly Harm provisions in order to guard projects against harming other goals. The social side of the ESG issues is also being woven in with social minimums, such as labour and human rights. The most popular of the tools out there is the Sustainable Finance Taxonomy of the EU, which provides the requirements of energy production, manufacturing, and other businesses. It has domestically been modified by China as its Green Bond Endorsed Project List, and these are also coming up in India, South Africa and other regions with an aim of converging globally.

4.1.2 Fragmentation and Divergent Standards

Although the use of taxonomies is more informative, the greatest issue is that they are globally disjointed. Countries are establishing dissimilar taxonomies possessing diverse technical requirements and political situations. According to Boffo and Patalano (2020), such a harmonisation absence confuses the cross-border investment and due diligence expenses among multinationals. Such problems are manifested in terms of various emission levels of close activity and varied pathways of transition, particularly between developing and developed markets. This absence of one standard can result in the so-called taxonomy arbitrage, in which the participants will select the taxonomy that best suits their interests to paint their actions as being greener. The international platforms such as the International Platform on Sustainable Finance (IPSF) are trying to handle this through the Common Ground Taxonomy approach that, according to the Sustainable Development Report, has been overlapping with different regions (Sachs et al., 2023).

4.1.3 Compulsory Disclosure of ESG Matters and Climate Risk

In addition to the taxonomies, regulators are also driving to make disclosure of ESG compulsory to establish uniformity. The minimum established by the EU Corporate Sustainability Reporting Directive (CSRD) and the International Sustainability Standards Board (ISSB) requires companies to report the Scope 1 and Scope 2 greenhouse-gas emissions and Scope 3 climate-related financial risks. Based on a very insightful study, Khan et al. (2016) have found a positive relationship between material issues and financial performance and corporate sustainability, which makes these commitments verifiable. Impact of sustainability in decision-making can only be ensured with the presence of good governance in an organisation, as stated by UNEP FI (2022): "Ensuring the long-term future of society in the context of business operations requires a different mindset regarding sustainability."

4.2 Corporate Governance & ESG Incorporation

Almost every regulatory body provides a framework in which the companies operate, in an organization the role of governance is more important in terms of incorporating sustainability into decision-making. Impact of sustainability in decision-making can only be ensured with the presence of good governance in an organisation, as stated by UNEP FI in the year 2022: "Ensuring the long-term future of society in the context of business operations requires a different mindset regarding sustainability."

4.2.1 Board Level Oversight & Alignment

The boards of directors are considered the final sustainability keepers for a business entity's sustainability strategy. The key functions that these boards perform are to oversee ESG strategies, synchronise strategies with a net-zero course, and review regulatory requirements in relation to sustainability strategies. According to Gangi et al.(2019), a certain level of competence in climate knowledge and environmental regulation by boards has become a necessity for a company's survival in today's world.

Boards are also forming dedicated sustainability committees to oversee ESG risk considerations within a broader risk perspective through risk management strategies. ESG reporting has also become a key agenda for many sustainability reporting scrutinizers due to concerns about a disconnect between current sustainability reporting strategies, as well as strategies that prioritise.

4.2.2 Stakeholder Engagement and Inclusive

The current paradigm shift in governance practice is from shareholder capitalism to stakeholder capitalism. Even though the regulatory framework provides the general context, governance in an organisation is important in ensuring that sustainability is integrated into decision-making. This is to say that corporations will be required to take into consideration their employees, their customers, and the effects on the environment. Clark et al. (2015) discovered that companies that are good at stakeholder management score high in sustainability and have fewer social risks. The notion of the Social License to Operate is an essential one in relation to the megaprojects with environmental connotations.

4.2.3 Built-in Reporting and Transparency System

Integrated Reporting creates a single system of financial and sustainability reporting. It promotes the comprehensive perspective of value creation with the support of GRI and ISSB standards. UNEP FI (2022) emphasised that digital transparent systems (like real-time dashboards on the ESG performance of an institution) increase the confidence of investors because they will remove selective reporting and greenwashing. Once this level of transparency is established, it will right away solve the problem of greenwashing, keeping the internal operations in line with the external disclosures. Expanding the corporate green bond market has caused risk re-pricing, as risk avers will seek a greenium premium, reflecting reduced long-term environmental risk (Flammer, 2021).

4.2.4 ESG Integration for Investment and Risk Management

The Institutional investors are incorporating ESG considerations into their decision-making processes using techniques such as negative screening, thematic investing (for renewable energy), and ESG-adjusted valuation. The growth of corporate green bond markets has triggered a risk re-pricing, as investors seek a 'greenium' premium that captures lower long-term environmental risk (Flammer, 2021).

4.3 Reducing Concerns on Greenwashing and Accountability Lapses

Sustainable finance is facing one of the gravest challenges of greenwashing. It deceptively releases information regarding environmental issues, and this discredits green initiatives. The World Bank (2024) emphasises that the growth of sustainable finance will be prone to corruption by false reporting and misrepresentations in the case of the lack of effective accountability processes.

4.3.1 Conceptualisation of the Nature and Type of Greenwashing

Greenwashing basically takes place in numerous ways. You receive partial disclosure- the companies are only spilling the tea on what is good about them, such as green bragging. Then there is the false advertising part, such as when a brand advertises that it is carbon neutral, and there is no trace of this in the kitchen. And it can even be ugly with carbon accounting, particularly when Scope 3 material has been omitted. Recently, with the appearance of more and more green finance instruments, it is increasingly difficult to distinguish the legitimate ones from the ones being sold, as opposed to the OECD, which is in the market. Even the 2023 report by OECD acknowledges that it is a nightmare differentiating what is legitimate.

4.3.2 Weak Implementation and Immeasurable Performance

The loopholes of accountability are enormous due to the fact that much of the paradigms we operate under are not well checked since they are voluntary. All the various scoring methods are possible with ESG rating agencies, hence the data is useless noise. Boffo and Patalano in 2020 effectively declare that all metrics are mixed up and hence companies can simply switch a switch and achieve higher scores. Also, in the developing economies, S the regulators are soft, hence companies can boast of sustainable practice of real money freedom and none of the effects actually sting.

4.3.4 Digital Audit Systems and Technological Solutions

Blockchain is used for a verification system that enables the creation of immutable records concerning the performance of green bonds. Satellites help monitor the green goals that involve the planting of trees. Zhao and Chen (2024) describe AI-powered tools that help identify inconsistencies in the data on sustainability issues, reducing the use of corporate narratives. IoT devices help monitor the emissions through digital MRV systems.

4.3.5 Enhancing Global Coordination

In view of the global character of capital, global cooperation is a priority. Bodies such as the G20 Sustainable Finance Working Group and the ISSB are attempting to standardise disclosure. In this respect, it has been noted by Schoenmaker (2017) that without global cooperation, global capital would continue to engage in "regulatory arbitrage," capital moving to regions with the weakest environmental laws. In this way, global cooperation helps to ensure the global financial system is shielded against "brown" capital hidden behind the label of "green."

4.4 The Role of Institutional Investors as Governance Drivers

Today, institutional investors are the de facto enforcers of sustainable governance, and include pension funds and sovereign wealth funds. Scholtens (2017) discusses the concept of the universal owner: in essence, big institutions have a piece of the economy and cannot neglect systemic environmental risk, and therefore, they need to apply their governance skills to compel companies to pay eco-costs. That active stewardship implies submission of shareholder resolutions and voting against directors who are not succeeding in climate risk governance. Then there is this entire other lending structure - Sustainability-Linked Loans (SLLs).

4.5 The Geopolitics of Sustainable Governance

The construction of governance frameworks is, however, taking place under the influence of geopolitical competition. BloombergNEF (2024) observes that "the race to the top" in green regulation, which began in the EU, is soon going to have competition from the US and China, as each tries to create a global standard for green finance. This has given rise to a state of "Green Diplomacy" as policies on taxes, as well as transparency guidelines, are increasingly used as leverage in international competition. This has become a dilemma for developing countries, as these countries have to adhere to these tough governance frameworks if they have to raise funds from global markets, even though their domestic industry models are not yet developed for growth. Volz et al. (2015) emphasise that for a "green transformation" to take place, there has to be a "just transition" for which governance frameworks have to be dynamic, taking into account that developing countries are at various levels before they can undergo transitions."

4.6 Fiduciary Duty in the 21st

The definition of fiduciary duty is currently undergoing a paradigm shift. The ancient short-term profit model is no more; we are looking at fiduciary duty as the systemic environmental and social risk. UNEP Finance Initiative was the first to jump into the pack, claiming that ignoring ESG material means violating fiduciary duty, at least in 2022. It appears that these manoeuvres are the most potent weapon of governance now, since fund managers as well as the executive are being pushed to survive on survival-in-the-environment logic. These modifications refocus the financial system to combat the Sustainable Development Goals by the United Nations in 2015.

4.7 Making the Green Story More Green With S and G

Climate change or E has moved us toward concentrating on G, governance and connecting that to social problems or S as a part of a greater whole. Gangi et al. (2019) emphasised that the financial flows governance should be of the highest quality, not to suffocate themselves in green bubbles - the hype of nascent technology. These governance mechanisms serve as shock absorbers of green finance in that the transition into an environmentally friendly economy can remain consistent and even functional. An enterprise with adverse social practices or with ambiguous governance practices statistically tends to default on its social, or green, goals. Issues of governance—practices involving transparency, diversity, or ethical governance—remain as the basis or as an operating system on which projects related to “E”, or the green causes, are executed. An “E”, or green goal, without an integrated aspect called “G”, remains as mereisolated projects or goals. This approach has now become an essential component under the strategies for green bond markets developed by the World Bank (2024): The Social aspect related to green projects remains an important indicator for measuring green goals.

4.8 Future Directions: Real-Time and Automated Governance

The future of governance is the shift towards autonomous and real-time accountability. As Zhao and Chen (2024) state in “Algorithmic Governance” (2024), “The future is not one where everything is controlled by omnipotent algorithms, but one in which algorithms facilitate the coordination of human activities through the use of artificial intelligence.” Rather than looking at annual reports, the investors would be treated to real-time streams that would show the fulfilment of the firm’s adherence to green goals. This would effectively eliminate the use of greenwash and correct market performance the instant that sustainability goals are not met. Such a shift in technology, along with the worldwide standardisation of standards, would promise a future that is not merely green but also crystal clear.

5. POLICY PATHWAYS AND INTEGRATED MODELS FOR SCALING GREEN FINANCE

Policy pathways and integrated models. To make green finance a viable operation does not simply involve pouring money into green projects, but requires a complete revision of the policy, regulation, innovation, and institutional context of any financial system. Green finance has been integrated into a building block when countries strive to reach the Paris Agreement climate targets and the UN 2030 Agenda. Nevertheless, existing roadblocks are genuine regulatory splits, institutional lock-in, and market failure. To overcome those, the systemic shift that Schoenmaker (2017) discussed in the financial world is necessary.

5.1 Coherence and Coordination Between Policies and Institutions

The absolute requirement of a predictive and efficient green finance environment is policy consistency. When they conflict with policies, markets become distorted and scare off the private players. IMF (2023) emphasised that maintaining sound financial regulations in line with climate change and development plans is a major factor that allows the market to stay stable and enhance the flow of investments.

5.1.1 Explanation of the Problem of Policy Fragmentation

Green finance is at the nexus of fiscal policy, the environment, energy and regulation of the finance industry. Macro bonds create disintegrated institutions. A few of the worst culprits: co-responsibility in finance and environmental ministries, and contradicting incentives - in particular, fossil fuel subsidies, which in effect counter green investment credits. According to Volz et al. (2015), these contradictions cause market distortions, making it more attractive to make high-carbon investments rather than other sustainable sources. Secondly, the lack of data harmonisation among these institutions has meant differing levels of adherence to environmental reporting standards, identified as the main reason for investor confusion in green finance by Boffo & Patalano (2020).

5.1.2 Building Coordinated Climate-Finance

In order to overcome these challenges, nations are opting for integrated governance structures. The green finance committees are combining finance, industry, and tech leaders to form common climate-investment agendas. Localised taxonomies are also advocated by national sustainable finance task forces, and Dikau and Volz (2021) termed Climate-Finance Units as a new trend within central banks to incorporate climate risk into monetary policy by way of green-referenced transactions and green-referenced purchases of assets. These units assist banks in making sure that their models of capital structure reflect both physical and transitional risk in the current climate crisis.

5.1.3 Linking Climate Policy to Financial Control

Carbon pricing -taxes, trading systems- establishes the equal price signals that are required for efficiency. It involves the involvement of green industrial policies as a part of the price-carbon tools. Research made at the World Bank (2024) shows that the combination of fiscal policy tools like tax credits and risk guarantees is most efficient when it is interwoven with regulations related to prudent credit-risks of banks. Given this integration, a "stable policy landscape" emerges. This calms the risks for institutional investors.

5.1.4 Green Finance, Development Planning, & Integration

Green finance needs to be integrated into the overall national planning for development, including National Determined Contributions (NDCs). As stated in the article "Green Prosperity in the Wake of COVID-19" by Sachs et al. (2023), "In the absence of full incorporation of climate goals into national budgeting and expenditure cycles, known as Green Public Financial Management (PFM), they lack any meaning, remaining goals rather than policies." From here, the path is made clear for the investor to see the long-term sustainability path of the country.

5.2 The Innovation–Governance– Sustainability Nexus Model

In order to properly scale green finance, this chapter presents a comprehensive conceptual framework: The Innovation-Governance-Sustainability Nexus Model. This framework makes clear that achievement in green finance is made not in isolation by innovation alone or by good governance alone or by sustainability alone, but rather in a symbiotic combination of all three to create a positive feedback loop of investment and impact.

5.2.1 Conceptual Foundations of the Nexus Model

The framework is founded on the idea that innovation (Technology) lowers transaction costs and increases traceability, while governance ensures accountability to avoid greenwashing. The above two are anchored by the idea of sustainability outcomes. Schoenmaker (2017) argues that by incorporating all these elements together, green finance goes from being a voluntary corporate social responsibility to a systematic force for economic growth.

5.2.2 Innovation as the Catalyst of System Transformation

Innovations propel the system for the development of digital green bonds with real-time validation and the application of AI in ESG analysis. This will lead to better comparability. According to Zhao and Chen (2024), the application of carbon markets based on blockchain increases the level of trust. Fraud has decreased. This will help the voluntary carbon market grow. Additionally, IoT-based tracking of emissions will make sure that the data is not based on average values. This will make the financial system more inclusive and transparent.

5.2.3 Governance as the Enabler of Trust and Integrity

Governance is the crucial backbone that makes the warranted credentials for innovation valid. This is achieved through mandatory disclosure on ESG issues and the use of digital verification for independent audits. OECD (2023) emphasises that the need for global harmonisation of the regulatory framework is necessary if green capital is to be developed at the speed necessary to meet the world climate goals. This is because the use of green technology is exposed to the challenge of greenwash if there is no punishment for the practice.

5.2.4 Sustainability Outcomes as the Guiding Objective

The final application of the Nexus Model is related, therefore, not to capital mobilisation for its own sake but to the reallocation for specific outcomes such as greenhouse gas abatement, biodiversity restoration, or resilience building, among others. According to Scholtens (2017), financial structuring has to be linked to these outcomes to sidestep "financialization," that is, when financial returns are decoupled from reality in green asset classes. The Nexus Model views these as a "guiding compass" for each activity in the investment life cycle, from structuring to end impacts assessment.

5.2.5 Systemic Interaction and Operationalisation

The systemic interplay between the pillars of the Nexus Model means that innovation reinforces governance through blockchain traceability, while governance legitimises innovation through regulatory approval mechanisms for new digital assets. Adaptive "regulatory sandboxes" and the development of digital public infrastructure for climate data are also ways in which governments could operationalise this model. According to Gangi et al. (2019), one of the operational ways includes capacity-building for regulators themselves so that the latter would be able to manage such complex AI and blockchain-driven financial instruments.

5.3 Way Forward on Inclusive Green Finance

As the whole world is moving beyond reduction to full, holistic development, the next frontier will definitely encompass. Every future strategy needs to go beyond utility-scale projects into small business enterprises, households, and vulnerable groups. Inclusive green finance would see fairly distributed benefits of the transition and prevent any social backlash from the perception that this "green economy" belongs exclusively to the elite class (BloombergNEF, 2024).

5.3.1 Scaling up Access Through SME Green Financing

Not all of the economies in this world survive on SMEs, but they lack access to green finance due to high initial expenses and the absence of collateral, which in a way frustrates their development. The alternative credit-scoring models, which are FinTech-enabled through alternative sources of data such as energy bills or supply chain interactions, can create new credit opportunities to SMEs (Zeng and Lin 2023). Green credit guarantee schemes will reduce the lender risk in question, and I hope that the mechanism will push commercial banks to grant concessional lines of credit to energy-efficient upgrades, particularly in manufacturing and retail.

5.3.2 Community-Based and Locally-Led Approaches

The local communities tend to be the most affected by climate change, as well as the communities that have the lowest access to finance. Principles of responsible-banking call towards decentralised investment approaches that allow the representations of the communities to determine the priorities of projects- this improves social acceptability and makes the results sustainable (UNEPFI 2022).

5.3.3 Green Infrastructure Public-Private Partnerships

Captive capital will be required to finance sizable endeavours such as green-hydrogen clusters or city rail. Also, the PPP models should include performance-based contracts, which are directly linked to sustainability results. These contracts attract a wider range of institutional investors to long-lasting, high-quality asset pools of green and which seek cautious environmental conformity criteria when these contracts exist (Flammer, 2021).

5.3.4 Capacity Building as the Ultimate Channel

Green inclusive finance depends on the presence of much capacity building. It involves educating regulators about the digitalisation of green-financing innovation. In addition, SMEs will require high technical support in order to implement green technologies. Finally, Khan et al. (2016) emphasise that once material ESG is incorporated into mainstream corporate accounting practice, all businesses will require the capability to communicate the same.

5.4 Theoretical Integration and the Multi-Stakeholder Mandate

The finance system is heading towards a model of stakeholder primacy. In this new model of finance, the value of investment ceases to be determined by its financial return on investment, but by its impact on the stability of Earth's systems, which agrees with Clark et al. (2015) and Schoenmaker (2017).

A critical aspect regarding this mandate is the role of institutional investors, because pension funds and insurance companies are themselves the universal owners with interests in the whole economy Scholtens, (2017); they have an obvious incentive to want to see policy coherence to safeguard the climate. Once policy options create clear signals, these institutional behemoths can then move trillions to invest with certainty.

5.5 Scaling Finance: The Geopolitical Dimension

The development of green digital infrastructure and national taxonomies has emerged as a source of competitive advantage for nations, BloombergNEF (2024). It signals that those who build the most transparent and efficient policy pathways will attract the most capital. In emerging economies, this "race to the top" in regulatory standards introduces an opportunity to leapfrog traditional, inefficient financial systems and to build a digital-first, green-native financial architecture. As Volz et al. (2015) conclude, this transition is not just about the environment but about the future competitiveness and resilience of the global economy.

5.6 Synthesis of Global Standards

In the end, it is the standardisation of green finance that will enable it to "scale." The role played by G20's Sustainable Finance Working Group, ISSB, in developing a global "baseline for disclosures" is "software" that makes it possible for "policy options to operate across regions." When a green bond issued in a developing country is subject to "the same integrity checks" as one issued in a developed country, using "Nexus Model" for verification, "the global liquidity pool for green assets" develops exponentially."

5.7 Moving Toward a Regenerative Financial System

"A 'Regenerative Financial System'—this is the ultimate trajectory of all the paths of policymaking above. In such a system, the Nexus Model is fully realised—the power of innovation enables us to place a value on biodiversity as capital, the role of governance is to prevent the exploitation of that value, and the metrics of success are based solely on sustainability goals and results. This is the ultimate expression of the vision outlined in the United Nations (2015) view of the future, in which finance gives us access to a world that is not low carbon, but ecologically thriving and socially just."

6. CONCLUSION: A UNIFIED VISION FOR DIGITAL AND SUSTAINABLE GOVERNANCE

Green finance is now at a crossroads in terms of evolution, where the success that it is meant to achieve in the long run is not just about the volume of capital it is able to manage, but the integrity of the systems. This paper will conclude that for the future of global sustainability to be guaranteed, it has to be rooted in a Cyber Physical Green Finance Ecosystem.

Through a systematic convergence of fintech tools, AI-powered ESG analysis, and blockchain verification, the financial environment would for the first time be able to breach the so-called "transparency gap" that has so far contributed to greenwashing practices and fragmentation within the financial environment. Concurring with the arguments of Schoenmaker (2017) and Scholtens (2017), this new environment signals a paradigm shift towards "Finance 3.0," for which environmental stability is acknowledged to be a prerequisite for financial stability.

However, this shift is facilitated by the Innovation-Governance-Sustainability Nexus itself, thereby ensuring that technology such as satellite tracking and smart contracts is made valid in terms of mandatory disclosures in international taxonomies. Moreover, the challenge of inclusivity, as identified in the BloombergNEF (2024) and the World Bank Report (2024), ensures that this shift not only remains in the domain of the corporate sector but also in the realm of the socio-economic system with the aid of micro-finance in technology.

In the long run, with the alignment of the coherence of policies and the precision of technology, green finance moves from the traditional niche market to the engine of economic regeneration. Based on the framework of innovation and governance, there is a clear roadmap for the speedy implementation of the Sustainable Development Goals adopted by the United Nations (2015). Financial markets are established as the drivers of a low-carbon and resilient world.

REFERENCES

Bloomberg, N. E. F. (2024). *Global trends in sustainable finance and investment*. Bloomberg Finance L.P.

Boffo, R., & Patalano, R. (2020). *ESG investing: Practices, progress and challenges*. OECD Publishing., DOI: 10.1787/8fca8c5f-

Clark, G. L., Feiner, A., & Viehs, M. (2015). From the stockholder to the stakeholder: How sustainability can drive financial outperformance. *Available at SSRN* 2508281.

Dikau, S., & Volz, U. (2021). Central bank mandates, sustainability objectives and the promotion of green finance. *Ecological Economics, 184*, 107022. DOI: 10.1016/j.ecolecon.2021.107022

Flammer, C. (2021). Corporate green bonds. *Journal of Financial Economics, 142*(2), 499–516. DOI: 10.1016/j.jfineco.2021.01.010

Flammer, C. (2021). Corporate green bonds. *Journal of Financial Economics, 142*(2), 499–516. DOI: 10.1016/j.jfineco.2021.01.010

Gangi, F., Meles, A., D'Angelo, E., & Daniele, L. M. (2019). Sustainable development and corporate governance in the financial system. *Corporate Governance (Bradford), 19*(6), 1177–1198. DOI: 10.1108/CG-02-2019-0052

International Monetary Fund. (2023). *Greening the financial system: Policy frameworks and innovation pathways*. International Monetary Fund.

Khan, M., Serafeim, G., & Yoon, A. (2016). Corporate sustainability: First evidence on materiality. *The Accounting Review, 91*(6), 1697–1724. DOI: 10.2308/accr-51383

Khan, M., Serafeim, G., & Yoon, A. (2016). Corporate sustainability and financial performance. *The Accounting Review, 91*(6), 1697–1724. DOI: 10.2308/accr-51383

Li, J., Song, S., & Wang, Y. (2026). Green bond issuance and ESG performance. *Pacific-Basin Finance Journal*. Advance online publication. DOI: 10.1016/j.pacfin.2025.102949

Li, Y., Zhang, D., & Zhang, C. (2024). Green finance and corporate performance. *Heliyon, 10*(4), e25106. DOI: 10.1016/j.heliyon.2024.e25106 PMID: 38694050

Lindenberg, N. (2014). Definition of green finance. *German Development Institute Discussion Paper*, 23/2014.

Organisation for Economic Co-operation and Development. (2023). *Innovative finance for sustainable development*. OECD Publishing., DOI: 10.1787/9789264963072-

PRI. (2023). *A practical guide to ESG integration for equity investing*. Principles for Responsible Investment.

Sachs, J. D., Schmidt-Traub, G., Kroll, C., Lafortune, G., & Fuller, G. (2023). *Sustainable Development Report 2023*. Cambridge University Press.

Schoenmaker, D. (2017). *Investing for the common good: A sustainable finance framework*. Bruegel Essay and Lecture Series.

Scholtens, B. (2017). Why finance should care about ecology. *Trends in Ecology & Evolution*, *32*(7), 500–505. DOI: 10.1016/j.tree.2017.03.013 PMID: 28457498

UNEP Finance Initiative. (2022). *Principles for responsible banking and investment*. United Nations Environment Programme.

United Nations. (2015). *Transforming our world: The 2030 agenda for sustainable development*. United Nations.

Volz, U., Böhnke, J., Knierim, L., Richert, K., Roeber, G.-M., & Derwisch, S. (2015). *Financing the green transformation*. German Development Institute. DOI: 10.1057/9781137486127

World Bank. (2024). *Green bond market development and impact measurement*. World Bank Publications.

Chapter 7
From Labels to Legitimacy:
Trust, Taxonomies, and Credibility in Green Investment Ecosystems

Feruzbek Jumaniyozov
Mamun University, Khiva, Uzbekistan

Ziyodullayev Sodiq
Termez University of Economics and Service, Termez, Uzbekistan

R. N. Ravikumar
http://orcid.org/0009-0009-3705-1681
Marwadi University, Rajkot, India

Duggirala Aravind
http://orcid.org/0009-0005-4362-7684
ASET Institute of Science and Technology, Chennai, India

S. Aarthi
http://orcid.org/0009-0006-9064-2091
Marwadi University, Rajkot, India

ABSTRACT

Green finance has grown very fast as an important tool to mobilize capital in favor of sustainable development, but the issues of trust, credibility, and legitimacy inform a growing budget of concerns on its performance. This chapter focuses on the shift towards the symbolic green label to substantively legitimate green investment

DOI: 10.4018/979-8-3373-7595-3.ch007

ght © 2027, IGI Global Scientific Publishing. Copying or distributing in print or electronic forms without written permission of IGI Global Scientific Publishing is prohibited. Use of this chapter to generative artificial intelligence (AI) technologies is expressly prohibited. The publisher reserves all rights to license its use for generative AI training and machine learning model development.

practices with emphasis on the role of the taxonomies, governance and verification. By relying on the signaling theory and institutional legitimacy, it describes how trust is developed in terms of steady definitions, disclosures that are openly made and accountability. The chapter with the help of recent case-based insights proves that fragmented standards and ineffective governance destroy the confidence of the investors, whereas the alignment of the frameworks and credible verification reinforce market integrity. The analysis underscores the fact that transitioning away of compliance-based approaches to outcome-based governance is the way forward as far as scaling green capital and guaranteeing material environmental and social impact.

1. INTRODUCTION

The fast evolution of green finance has changed the way of investing globally, however, the issue of trust, credibility, and legitimacy are still on the center. Although Environmental, Social, and Governance (ESG) frameworks, sustainability disclosures, and regulatory taxonomies have developed, the inconsistency of standards, fragmented governance, and lack of verification are still in place to weaken investor confidence. The available literature focuses mostly on the analysis of the ESG metrics, taxonomies, and governance mechanisms separately, and little to no effort has been dedicated to analyzing how these factors interact to influence trust in green investment ecosystems (Devi, 2023). This loophole is imperative when escalating threats of greenwashing and transnational regulatory fragmentation. Basing on institutional legitimacy and the signaling theory, this paper will come up with a unified framework on how taxonomies, governance structures, and verification mechanisms relate to the creation and maintenance of trust and credibility within sustainable finance markets

1.1 Evolution of Green Finance and the Emergence of Trust Concerns

Green finance came as a reaction to the increased awareness of environmental risks and the necessity to attract the private capital to the goals of sustainable development. The first attempt was made on both niche products such as green bonds and ethical investment funds that were commonly voluntary and motivated by reputational factors. In the long run, green finance has expanded tremendously both in number of assets and jurisdictions and has become mainstream financial systems. As this has grown, there has been a rise in the mistrust and lack of credibility. As the quantity and range of green-labeled products increased, the inconsistency in the definitions, measures, and disclosure patterns became more noticeable (Bunch & Strauss, 2025). The investors were put into test when it came to distinguishing the substantively sustainable investment and the superficially sustainable investments.

The absence of standardization and the powerful verification systems as well augmented the lack of trust, notably among the countries (Mohanty et al., 2023). The problem of trust has thus been relegated to the fringe concerns to the core deliberations of the integrity of the market. The history of green finance demonstrates that scale is not a guarantee of its effectiveness and to be more exact, scale demands belief in the genuine nature of green claims. This type of growing emphasis on trust is a continuation of institutional pressures in which financial legitimacy is anchored on transparency, accountability, and consistency of purported aims and manifested outcomes (Hong, 2025). Figure 1 demonstrates how green finance has been developed as a niche instrument and then as a mainstream instrument and as a level of trust increase which is being the fundamental pillars of credibility with transparency, accountability and alignment of impact.

Figure 1. Evolution of Green Finance and the Emergence of Trust Concerns

1.2 From Environmental Labels to Institutional Legitimacy

The environmental labels have also played a significant role in the early development of the green finance through providing de facto images of sustainability purposes to investors and other stakeholders. These labels, certifications, and classifications were geared towards reducing the information asymmetry as well as ensuring that capital could be easily allocated to activities that were eco-friendly. However, the labels have not been sufficient in the sustenance of the confidence over time. The labels are usually of other scopes, other rigorousness and enforcement leading to fragmentation and interpretive flexibility (Zhu, 2025). The emphasis on institutional legitimacy or the opinion that green financial practices are appropriate, feasible and socially approved by the current parameter and principles have been increasingly involved with the increasing green finance. The concept of institutional legitimacy transcends the symbolic indicators and it is accumulated through regularity in regulatory systems, plausible verification systems and performance. It goes beyond compliance with the official standards, as well as it is compared to the social and societal standards of environmental integrity and social responsibility. The change of labels to legitimacy is a qualitative change in the governance of green finance whereby more emphasis is put on substance rather than symbolism (Chrzan & Pott, 2024). This change needs more robust institutions that can incorporate the concept of sustainability into financial decision-making and make sure that green claims are sustainable and not negligible in the long term.

1.3 Chapter Scope, Structure, and Contribution

This chapter looks at the construction process of trust and legitimacy in green investment systems with specific focus on the functions of taxonomies, standards, and governance systems. It combines the perspectives of the institutional theory, literature on sustainable finance and governance studies to theorize legitimacy as a socially constructed and dynamic process. The chapter will be designed to set first the historical and institutional background of the green finance and then review in a systematic way the literature available in line with the objectives mentioned above. A conceptual diagram is built to show the connection between labels, trust mechanism and investment outcomes. The recent case studies responding to the empirical aspect refer to the real-life challenges and responses on governance in the different regulatory settings. It is a discussion which summarizes the theoretical as well as empirical evidence so as to assess the implications of the same on investors, regulators as well as financial institutions. The chapter could add to the current discussions on the maturation of green finance making the notion of trust one of the major critical lenses. It enhances the data regarding the process of the formation and preservation of credibility that presents the framework of the assessment of the likelihood of the green investment ecosystems as the plausible drivers of the sustainable development and not the figurative market extensions.

2. BACKGROUND TO THE STUDY

Green finance institutionalization has introduced numerous instruments, sustainability regulation and standards into the world markets at a very rapid rate. Such expansion has been however not even and therefore there have been fragmented governance frameworks, fragmented taxonomies and various disclosures practices. This has only worsened the base research problem on trust and credibility in green investment eco-systems (Osuji et al., 2025). The information asymmetry between the issuers and investors is created due to the fact that the differences in the definitions of the green activities, the lack of harmonized ESG standards and the unequal verification mechanisms destroy the information asymmetry. This jeopardizes comparability, due diligence complexity, as well as provides a platform upon which opportunistic activities like greenwashing take place. As a result, confidence in investors is jeopardized and integrity in the market is questioned.

It is thus important to understand the impacts of fragmentation in taxonomies, governance, and reporting structures in the formation of trust to establish viable and scalable green finance systems.

2.1 Historical Development of Green Investment Instruments

Green investment instruments have been evolved over the years after policy awareness and the environmental consciousness. The first ones were the socially responsible investment plans, on which they never invested in areas that harmed to the environment out of ethical considerations. These approaches all ultimately gave way to less generalized approaches, such as green bonds, renewable energy funds, and investment vehicles based on climate. It was a major leap and the launch of labeled green bonds provided the direct linkage between the capital markets and environmental projects (Amolo Dr Amolo Elvis Juma, 2024). This extension of the green finance was incremental with introduction of performance-based incentives in the form of sustainability linked lending and blended finance arrangements. However, even though this is the case, the historical evolution of these instruments has shown that these instruments have been experimented with as opposed to being standardized. The meaning of green varied depending on the issuers and jurisdictions and was therefore varied according to the priorities and capacities. This variety helped in innovation but it brought about confusion in that there was no simple method of comparing instruments or calculating cumulative effect. Evolutionary history of green finance has shown that the green finance has advanced better in terms of quantity rather than institutional continuity (Pudeyan et al., 2024). It has brought endless problems in terms of credibility and the necessity to have stronger governance structures. Table 1 Make important green finance instruments and the succeeding governance and credibility issue metamorphosis over the years.

Table 1. Evolution of Green Finance Instruments and Governance Focus

Phase	Key Instruments	Primary Governance Focus	Credibility Implications
Early phase	Ethical funds, SRI	Voluntary norms	Low comparability, reputational signaling
Expansion phase	Green bonds, climate funds	Use-of-proceeds disclosure	Growing trust, limited verification
Maturation phase	Sustainability-linked loans	Performance-based metrics	Conditional credibility
Institutional phase	Taxonomy-aligned instruments	Regulatory oversight	Higher legitimacy and investor confidence

2.2 Institutional and Regulatory Foundations of Green Finance

Green financial institutions and regulatory rules owe their existence to a complex interaction between the public policy, the market norms, and international coordination activities. Governments and regulators have proposed taxonomies, disclosure requirements and prudential guidelines that are geared towards ensuring that financial activity is driven towards sustainable results. These endeavours have been supplemented with the endeavours of the multilateral organizations and the standard bodies which have promoted principles of transparency and comparability. However, the regulatory process does not take the same form but varies based on the disparity in the economic priorities and the institutional capacity (Zhang et al., 2022). The regulation of green finance in some environments is an extension of the broader sustainability plan, but in others it is founded on voluntary principles and market programs. This has been fluctuating, and this affects the plausibility of the green financial markets particularly in the inter-country investment flows. The institutional foundations also include the functions of the financial intermediaries, rating agencies, and verification bodies and affect their practices affecting the market expectations (Chen et al., 2022). Absence of universally recognised standards is also a problem as this makes it difficult to enforce and compromises accountability. In its turn, regulatory pillars can be considered a controversial but a critical cornerstone of green finance that directly influences investor confidence and the sense of legitimacy.

2.3 Persistent Challenges of Credibility and Greenwashing

Despite extensive institutionalisation, the green investment eco systems are still crippled by the problem of credibility. The greenwashing problem whereby the financial products overstate or mislead on its positive impact on the environment has become a problem. This is usually facilitated by vague definitions, biased reporting and partial confirmation of impact claims. Investors can have challenges in evaluating the reported outcomes based on the authenticity of reported environmental improvements or as a result of meeting the minimum stipulations (Al frijat et al., 2025). The broken regulatory settings contribute to these problems by enabling issuers to take advantage of franchisee. Also, there is usually inconsistency in metrics applied to sustainability performance, which decreases comparability between instruments and markets. The issues of credibility are both technical and social as perceived abuse of green labels may undermine the confidence of people in sustainable finance in general. The persistence of these issues indicates that the legitimacy cannot be assumed with the help of labels only (Guo et al., 2023). Instead, it has to have maintained consistency between the purpose of regulation, the market practice, and the measurable outcomes. The themes of bridging the credibility gaps hence become the focal point of ensuring that green finance fulfils what it promises as a source of sustainable growth rather than a reputational risk.

3. RESEARCH OBJECTIVES

The study relies on the institutional legitimacy theory and the signaling theory in which the authors examine how the trust and credibility of green investment ecosystems can be created. When there are conditions of information asymmetry, institutional theory accounts the effects of regulatory alignment, norms and governance structure in creating legitimacy and the signaling theory accounts the effects of labels, disclosures and certification in conveying sustainability information. Theories of gaps in forming trust are the foundation of the goals.

- To examine how green taxonomies and sustainability standards function as signaling mechanisms influencing investor trust.
- To analyze how institutional legitimacy is constructed and maintained through governance structures and regulatory enforcement.
- To evaluate the role of verification, disclosure practices, and third-party assurance in reducing information asymmetry and greenwashing risks.
- To assess how interactions between taxonomies, governance, and signaling mechanisms shape credibility and investment decisions.

4. CONCEPTUAL MODEL

The conceptual model outlines a distinct cause effect relationship of how credibility is formed in green investment ecosystems that is categorized into the following labelling labels; trust, investment outcomes. The first signaling mechanisms are environmental labels, certifications and taxonomies which are intended to indicate the sustainability intention to the investors, the utility of these signaling mechanisms depends on the institutional motivations, which are standardization, quality of governance, verification process, and regulation enforcement. Such mechanisms are prevalent and systematic and result in high reliability of signals, reduced information asymmetry and investor confidence. Conversely, poor or weak governance with regard to credibility of signals brings about, skepticism and lack of trust. Trust is therefore an intermediate variable which affects how and sustainability claims are interpreted to investment decisions. The enhanced trust results in the enhanced capital allocation, stability in market and sustainability whereas the reduced trust results in the heightened risk of greenwashing, misallocation of resources and loss of market trust (Maresca et al., 2023). The conceptual model provides a description of the construction of trust and legitimacy in green investment ecosystems according to the contact between labels, institutional structures, and governance mechanisms. It creates a cause-effect mechanism, in which environmental labels are the early warning signs, the viability of which is assessed by consistency of regulations, practices of verification, and observable results. Trust, based on institutional and signaling theory, is a mediating variable between taxonomies and standards and investor confidence and decision-making on whether to allocate capital or not. Credibility is not only met by conformity but also by consistency between what is claimed about sustainability and impact which can be measured. Good governance boosts the confidence levels whereas weaknesses in governance undermine the legitimacy and efficiency of green finance (Nedopil et al., 2021). Table 2 Describes the core conceptual elements between labels, trust mechanisms, governance structure, and sustainability outcomes.

Table 2. Conceptual Dimensions of Trust and Legitimacy in Green Finance

Dimension	Core Elements	Function in Ecosystem	Trust Outcome
Labels	Certifications, tags	Initial signaling	Provisional trust
Standards	Principles, criteria	Consistency	Reduced ambiguity
Governance	Regulation, enforcement	Accountability	Institutional trust
Verification	Third-party review	Credibility assurance	Confidence reinforcement
Outcomes	Measurable impacts	Performance validation	Long-term legitimacy

4.1 Theoretical Foundations: Institutional Legitimacy and Signaling

The conceptual model has its basis in the institutional legitimatizing theory and signaling theory which combined form the explanation of how the credibility is built in complex and information-asymmetric markets. The institutional legitimacy theory focuses on the fact that the practices that are acceptable are those that adhere to the existing norms, rules and mutual expectations in a particular field. The concept of legitimacy in green finance is based on the perception of sustainability claims as suitable, believable and socially acceptable. Signaling theory gives an addition to this perspective by saying that information of environmental performance is communicated through labels, certifications and disclosures that are used as a signal. Signals do not however work unless they are costly to counterfeit, and can be supported (Acquah et al., 2023). Weak signals or signals that are inconsistent may lose information and result in mistrust. The synthesis of these theoretical foundations allows the chapter to conceptualize the green labels as temporary markers, the justification of which relies on the support of institutions. In this manner, the aspect emphasised is that trust is not necessarily attached to financial instruments but rather is created due to consistent definitions, reliable supervision, and uniformity in enforcement of the financial market participants.

4.2 Conceptual Framework Linking Labels, Trust, and Outcomes

The conceptual model gives a mediating process among environmental labels and investment results through trust. Labels and classifications also serve as portals to express the purpose of sustainability, but determining its influence on capital placement depends on whether the investors trust the proprietary standards and checks. Trust is based on the definition, transparency of disclosures and continuity of reported outcomes over some period of time. The green labels can also facilitate effective flows of capital to the actually sustainable activities in a manner that boosts the environmental and social performance with high levels of trust (Ji et al., 2023). Conversely, when there is low trust scenario, labels may be devalued or may be looked down and this limits the effectiveness of labels. The model emphasizes the loops of feedback of which the observable outcomes respond to enhance or undermine trust, which defines the future investment behavior (Ravikumar, Aarthi, Kalandarov, et al., 2025). This dynamic strategy focuses on the point that legitimacy is path-dependent and cumulative. The framework is not thus stuck in the old categories, but it tries to captivate on how credibility is transformed as a result of recurring connections amid market players, governance, and sustainability results (Vietnam

& Bùi, 2025). The figure 2 is to represent how the green labels are functioning as the indicators the integrity of which is based on the legitimacy of the institutions that is backed by the uniformity of the definitions, verification, and controlled the situation to generate the confidence in the green finance market.

Figure 2. Institutional Legitimacy and Signaling Framework for Green Finance

4.3 Interaction Between Taxonomies, Governance, and Investor Confidence

Investor confidence in green investment ecosystems is greatly determined by taxonomies and the structure that governs these ecosystems. Taxonomies will offer unified definitions of the definition on what is environmentally sustainable, eliminating confusion and allowing comparability between investments. The effectiveness of these definitions is determined by governance systems such as regulatory control, disclosure laws and practices and enforcing these laws and practices. Taxonomy relates to governance in the sense that investors would find the green markets credible and reliable. Good governance makes taxonomy have more credibility by upholding compliance, tracking results, and interference with misconduct. Poor governance, on the other hand, can make even a designed taxonomies useless. When the definitions, rules and mechanisms of enforcement are aligned and applied in a uniform manner, then investor confidence is created (Alessi & Battiston, 2022). Such interaction is especially crucial in the case of the cross-border investment where regulatory fragmentation may be a source of lack of trust. Through the emphasis of such interactions, the conceptual model indicates that credibility is a systemic quality of green investment ecosystems and not the attribute of specific instrument (Tonnarello et al., 2025). This is shown in the figure 3 where interactions among the innovators, green financial institutions, and regulators increase the maturity of green products, regulatory effectiveness, and risk management in green finance ecosystems through information, financial, and technology flows.

Figure 3. Governance–Innovation Interaction Framework in Green Financial Ecosystems

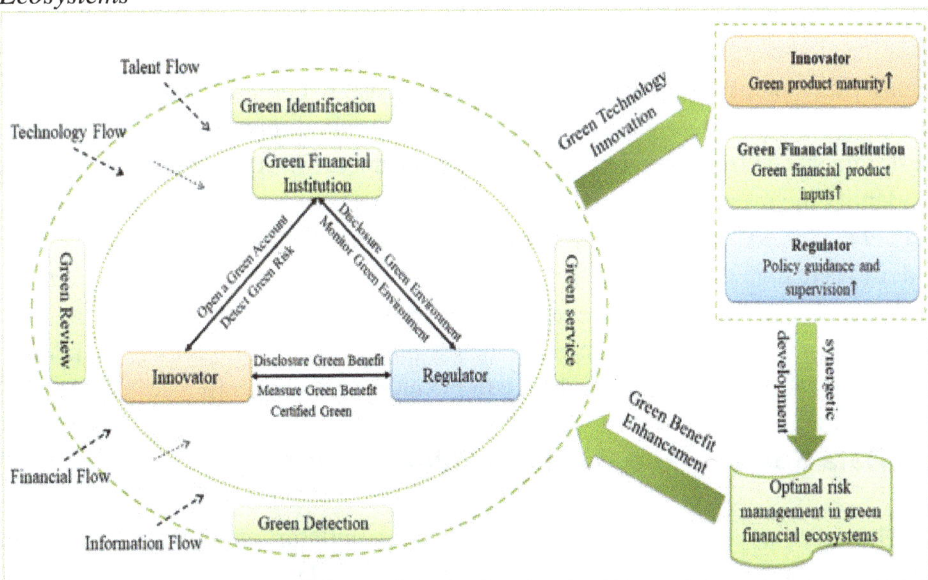

5. RESEARCH METHODOLOGY

The research design utilized in this study is a qualitative, interpretive research design that integrates both conceptual and comparative case research design to analyze trust building in green investment ecosystem. The sources of data will be policy documents, regulatory guidelines, green taxonomy frames, sustainability reports, and the publications of the multilateral institutions (e.g., OECD, World Bank, EU taxonomy reports). Case studies are chosen according to their relevance, the variety of different regulatory settings, and the reflectiveness of various governance and verification practices namely the global green bond market and regional taxonomy frameworks. It is analyzed in a comparative and thematic manner where the patterns in terms of governance, signaling, and trust mechanism are identified. The strength is achieved by data triangulation, utilizing a variety of sources and correspondence to the existing theoretical frameworks to promote credibility and analytical validity (Qu, 2025).

5.1 Research Design and Analytical Approach

The research design applied is founded on the qualitative research design which entails conceptual modelling and comparison of the case studies. The empirical material is analyzed with the help of the analytical framework involving an institutional legitimacy and signaling theory. It is descriptive and explanatory, which aims at identifying mechanisms rather than analyzing causal hypotheses. The comparative analysis will be used to analyze the effect of different regulatory and institutional environments on trust and credibility of green finance. This trend makes it possible to identify the overall trends and specific deviations based on the situations (Joshipura et al., 2025). The analytical method is based on tracing through the process in order to actualize the building of legitimacy over the course of time basing on the governance practices, disclosure regimes and verification mechanisms. The research design helps the implied realization of the institutional foundations of green investment ecosystems by linking the theory to the empirical observation.

5.2 Data Sources and Case Selection Criteria

The data sources include policy frameworks, regulatory guidelines, taxonomy documents, sustainability reports and publicly available disclosures on the green financial instruments. The secondary data collected by multilateral organisations, regulatory authorities and development finance institutions are used to contextualise governance arrangements. (Xiao et al., 2023). Cases are chosen depending on their relevance, recentness and representativeness of varying regulatory contexts. The criteria used when selecting the cases are the ones that reflect the variability in the implementation of the taxonomies, its verification practices, and the maturity of the market. Such a selective design makes it possible to compare effectively, as well as to generalize analytically. Triangulation is improved through the use of more than one source of data making the findings credible.

5.3 Limitations and Validity Considerations

This research method is qualitative; therefore, it lacks certain areas of limitation particularly with regard to the generalizability. The findings are relative and may not be representative of all the differences between world markets of green finance. Secondary data may also limit knowledge on the internal decision-making processes by financial institutions. The analysis is subjected to the triangulation of the various sources and theoretical angles to ensure that the validity is as much as possible (Petucco et al., 2025). Analytical rigor is also supported through selection of cases with the help of transparency and conceptual clarity. Although the study is not oriented to the statistical conclusion, the study presents strong interpretative facts of the process of the development of the trust and legitimacy in the green investment ecosystems.

6. LITERATURE REVIEW

The literature on green finance has also moved its attention on financial instruments to broader debate regarding sustainability governance, ESG standardization and regulatory taxonomies but has been highly fragmented in these fronts. The literature available states that despite the increased capital flows to environmentally friendly investment practices through sustainable finance, there are yet to be seen gaps in ESG practices and rating systems and concerns on credibility and greenwashing (Darsono et al., 2025). Similar studies on regulatory taxonomies highlight the issue on standardizing definitions of sustainable activities, but outline the challenges on cross-border interoperability, enforcement, and institutional divergence. In addition to that, the governance-oriented literature puts special emphasis on the role of verification, disclosure, and regulatory control in improving market integrity, yet in most cases, these mechanisms are considered alone, instead of as interdependent structures. This disjointed body of literature indicates that there is an urgent deficit in the effort to bring together ESG standardization, taxonomy systems, and governance systems in order to elucidate how trust and legitimacy are constructed systematically in green investment systems (Mertzanis & Tebourbi, 2025).

6.1 Green Labels, Standards, and Information Asymmetry

There is a lot of literature that looks into green labels and standards as the means to decrease information asymmetry between issuers and investors. Labels have generally been understood as signaling processes that pass information regarding the environmental characteristic of financial products. Research findings indicate that transparent and truthful labeling can reduce the cost of search, enhance efficiency in the market, and can bring in sustainability conscious investors (Farounbi et al., 2025). Nevertheless, there are also severe shortcomings associated with the literature. The inconsistency in application and interpretive confusion has been caused by variation in labeling standards and the voluntary character of most of these standards. According to scholars, labels, unless rigorous or enforced, can lose their informational value and stop being used to capturing genuinely sustainable investments and opportunistic ones. This has brought in question the issue of adverse selection and moral hazard within green finance markets (Distadio & Johl, 2025). There is increased argument in literature that labels cannot exist in isolation and they need to be integrated into larger institutional mechanisms so as to be plausible. Consequently, studies have been shifted towards the study of the interplay between labeling practices and governance and verification systems to influence investor confidence.

6.2 Taxonomies, Disclosure Frameworks, and Market Integrity

The studies on green taxonomies and disclosure frameworks point at the fact that they contribute to the improvement of the comparability, transparency, and market integrity. Taxonomies are considered to be the key instruments that stipulate the definition of what is considered to be an environmentally sustainable activity, thus, offering an equal point of reference among investors and regulators. Literature indicates that properly constructed taxonomies may minimize definitional ambiguity and promote the uniformity of sustainability standards in the market (Sadiq et al., 2025). Disclosure frameworks are used to supplement taxonomies because they demand that firms and financial institutions disclose on sustainability performance and risk exposure. However, fragmented and overlapping structures are the other problems that are also mentioned by researchers. The presence of national and regional policy disparities through the existence of divergent policies has caused disparities such that it is quite hard to invest in a global market and disincentivize consistent market (Hovde et al., 2025). The literature highlights that the standard of reporting is varied, and there is the fear of selective reporting and low standards of verification. These issues indicate that taxonomies and disclosures can only assist in creating market integrity in case they are supported by good governance and enforcement policies.

6.3 Trust, Legitimacy, and Governance in Sustainable Finance

The literature on the topic of trust and legitimacy in sustainable finance is enriched with the institutional and governance strategies. Trust has been conventional to be perceived as an interpersonal and accumulative procedure, which is created through the means of regular activities, openness, and accountability. The studies highlight the fact that the legitimacy arises when the green finance operations are in tandem with the expectations and regulation criteria of the society (Ramdhan, 2025). Such systems of governance as regulatory checks, third party checks and stakeholder involvement are reported to be of great importance in ensuring trust. The role of social aspects is also highlighted by the researchers who note that environmental performance alone cannot be considered an adequate background to legitimacy in the case of distributional and equity considerations being overlooked (Azam et al., 2025). The literature is unified in the opinion that plausible sustainable finance requires integrated governance structures that create a consonance between the norms, enforcement and deliverables. The given body of work highlights the fact that trust is not the automatic result of going green but a delicate asset that should be supported by the institutional coherence and accountability.

7. CASE STUDIES

The two case studies allow offering the comparative view of the role of governance mechanisms and standardization frameworks in the trust and credibility in green finance. The transparency (e.g., certified by third party, post issue reporting) of green bond market have a direct effect of increasing transparency, reducing information asymmetry, and leading to more trust by investors and favourable reception in the market. On the other hand, bad or inconsistent verification may also decrease the level of signal reliability and increase the degree of skepticism along with green-washing risks (Liu et al., 2020). In like manner, in taxonomy-based frameworks, well defined and harmonised classification systems facilitate comparability and capital allocation direction thereby increasing investor confidence. Nevertheless, scattered or incoherent taxonomies are leading to confusions and hindrance to foreign investments. This analogy creates a definite cause-effect association as good governance and standardization systems result in an increase in trust, whereas the division decreases credibility, and market efficiency.

7.1 Case Study I: Green Bond Market and Verification Practices

Green bond market world-wide has emerged as a bedrock of sustainable finance, which provides issuers of green bonds, who could be sovereign and corporate, a platform to finance environmentally positive projects. As of 2024, the cumulative number of green bonds is considered to be more than USD 5.7 trillion, which means that the international community is yet to find a financial instrument that would align with the necessity to combat climate change. Strong verification has played the very important role of verifying integrity of the market and confidence of the investors (Syarkani et al., 2024). The revised Green Bond Principles (GBP) 2025 provide voluntary guidelines on transparency, disclosure and use-of-proceeds models globally, aimed at strengthening information asymmetry and to help the investors make decisions. External audits like third-party certifications which are parameterized with the GBP, have become key to ascertain the flow of bond proceeds in viable green projects and whether it is of standard quality. Recent studies have established that the existence of the green bonds with credible reports concerning the third-party verification is likely to receive more desirable reactions of the investors like the positive abnormal returns that reflects the increased credibility of market and less perceived risk in such circumstances. Post-issuance reporting that is also facilitated by verification is also a post-issuance disclosure of environmental outcomes and proceeds allocation that enhance investor confidence (R. Wang, 2025). Despite this progress, some of the concerns that are still evident include the inconsistencies in the standards of verification, economies of scale to the smaller issuers and inconsistent adoption of best practices in different markets. Table 3 Comparison of the verification practices, disclosure requirements and features of governance between major green bond structures.

Table 3. Overview of Verification and Governance Mechanisms in Green Bond Markets

Mechanism	Description	Governance Role	Credibility Effect
Second-party opinion	Independent pre-issuance review	Validation of eligibility	Trust enhancement
Third-party certification	Alignment with standards	External assurance	Reduced greenwashing
Post-issuance reporting	Use-of-proceeds disclosure	Transparency	Sustained confidence
Impact reporting	Environmental outcomes	Performance evidence	Long-term legitimacy

7.2 Case Study II: Regional Green Taxonomy and Cross-Border Capital Flows

Development of regional green taxonomies has become the key instrument of defining and categorizing sustainable economic practices and with immense implication on the potential cross-border investment flow. EU Sustainable Finance Taxonomy remains a hub of reference offering a cross-cutting language of environmental sustainability and assisting in streamlining investment choices with climate and energy objectives. Its use has increased transparency of reporting and investor confidence as it creates standardized requirements of environmentally sustainable activities. The changes made in 2025 with the objective of streamlining reporting processes and making them easier to use by companies show how the evolution of regulation can be improved to take into account the experience of implementation (Z. Wang et al., 2023). The impact of the EU taxonomy is widespread to the international markets because credibility of taxonomy will prompt international investors to use the taxonomy to match portfolios to activities that qualify as taxonomy. On the same note, the other regions have also been taking similar actions, e.g. the ASEAN Taxonomy of Sustainable Finance, which is an example of joint actions aimed at creating science-based classification frameworks to support investment across member states. In Brazil and other Latin American economies, continuous development of taxonomies with the help of international platforms are intended to enhance the interoperability and minimize market fragmentation, which facilitates the movement of capital across borders to sustainable projects (Pandey, 2025). The Taxonomy Roadmap Initiative of efforts also aims at harmonising sustainable finance taxonomies across the world with the aim of mitigating regulatory divergence challenges and improving capital allocation to environmental and social outcomes. These advances highlight the strategic importance of taxonomies in determining the world-wide green capital flows. Table 4 Responds to cross-border investment implication Highlights the key features of the chosen regional green taxonomies and their implications on investment.

Table 4. Comparative Features of Regional Green Taxonomies

Region	Scope	Regulatory Nature	Cross-Border Impact
European Union	Environment-focused	Mandatory	High comparability
ASEAN	Multi-tier classification	Voluntary-guided	Regional alignment
Latin America	Emerging frameworks	Development-oriented	Improving coherence
Global initiatives	Interoperability focus	Coordinative	Reduced fragmentation

7.3 Comparative Insights from the Two Cases

The two case studies outline the contribution of governance structures and standardization systems in improving credibility, investor confidence and allocation of green capital. Green bond market can improve the level of information quality, reduce information asymmetry and investor trust which enhances legitimacy of the market because of strong verification practices founded on voluntary standards like the Green Bond Principles. The regional taxonomies such as the EU Sustainable Finance Taxonomy, the ASEAN classification frameworks, however, provide an under-carbon framework of the definition of sustainability, to allow likeliness between jurisdictions, and cross-border sustainable capital flows. All these illustrate that it is not only necessary at micro-levels (checking of the separate instruments) but also macro-levels institutional structures (taxonomies and standards of regulatory frameworks) in the construction of the legitimacy in green finance (Demir and Min, 2021). These mechanisms and their interactions can be positive to reduce the possibility of greenwashing, fragmentation of markets and maximize consistency in the practice of sustainability or markets. Lastly, the mixture of the plausible check-up practices and the unified taxonomies strengthens the foundation to increase green investments in the globe.

8. RESULTS AND DISCUSSION

The findings are more analytical on how governance, verification and standardization mechanisms inter-relate to establish trust and credibility on green finance. The results align with the institutional legitimacy theory and demonstrate that perceived legitimacy is increased by coherent regulatory systems and its reduction by fragmented systems (Adeel-Farooq et al., 2018). However, in the same way, labels and certifications are, on the signaling theory perspective, at best a good signal, and that too must be credibly verified and transparent disclosed practices and not otherwise. The relative evidence indicates that good governance and standardized measures which increases trust are highly causally related with each other. Theoretically, the study has brought institutional and signaling views together and has applied them to one comprehensive viewpoint of trust formation. The results must be taken with a lot of caution though because they are not generalizable but rather specific to the context of implementation (Lauesen, 2019) Table 5 Summarizes empirical evidence on the case studies on determinants of trust, legitimacy and market confidence.

Table 5. Key Results on Trust Formation and Credibility Drivers

Driver	Empirical Observation	Effect on Trust
Verification rigor	Consistent external review	Strong positive
Standard alignment	Clear taxonomy usage	Confidence increase
Metric consistency	Comparable indicators	Reduced uncertainty
Governance strength	Enforcement mechanisms	Sustained legitimacy
Social inclusion	Equity-sensitive design	Broader acceptance

8.1 Empirical Insights on Trust and Credibility Formation

Based on the case studies, empirical evidence indicates that trustworthiness in green finance is earned through consistency and accountability that is demonstrated repeatedly. In the green bond market, confidence in the investors improved where the issuers followed the established principles and used reliable third-party verifiers. The verification reports and impact disclosures were used as the reinforcing signals and they decreased the ambiguity about the environmental integrity of the funded projects (Chen & Long, 2023). There was also the further reinforcement of trust, which occurred in the event that post-issuance reporting met the pre-issuance commitments. Credibility appeared in the case of taxonomy where there were well-defined classification frameworks, which were science-driven, and regulated by regulatory bodies. Taxonomy-aligned investments were interpreted as having a lower degree of reputational and regulatory risk, especially when in cross-border situations. The results of the study, however, also show that trust is weak and compound; the failures or inconsistencies alone can destroy the confidence in a short time. On the whole, the formation of credibility was demonstrated to be a process and not an outcome, which is affected by institutional coherence, the rigor of verification, and the correspondence between the proclaimed goals of sustainability and quantifiable outcomes.

8.2 Implications of Fragmented Standards and Metrics

The case studies indicate that the lack of consistency in standards and metrics is a great challenge to the credibility of a green investment ecosystem. Without harmonized definitions, there is a risk that issuers will take a different approach to the sustainability criteria, which makes it difficult to compare instruments and markets. This fragmentation was apparent in both instances especially when various verification providers or regional systems were in existence with no apparent interoperability. The cost and uncertainty of due-diligence increased among investors as they determined the credibility of green claims between jurisdictions. Fragmentation was also a source of strategic disclosure where issuers only reported metrics that presented good sustainability stories (Y. Wang, 2025). Their differences weakened the indicative power of the labels and reduced the influence of taxonomies on collecting capital allocation. The findings suggest that without the alignment of the standards, metrics and the way reporting is done, then a good framework would end up being illegitimate despite the good intentions. Fragmentation, therefore, is one of the central problems that should be resolved in an effort to promote market integrity and ensure that green finance delivers promising and consistent sustainability outcomes.

8.3 Social Legitimacy, Equity, and Distributional Considerations

Besides the technical and regulatory dimensions, the findings also show how the role of the social legitimacy is steadily growing in supporting the trust on green finance. According to the case studies, the investors and regulators are increasingly becoming sensitive towards green investments with reference to their social and distributional effects, but not on environmental grounds. The projects that appear to alienate the vulnerable communities or those that might support the status quo in relation to the inequalities may be a threat to the overall validity of the green finance projects (Gea et al., 2024). The level of credibility was also enhanced in both cases where issuers were also mindful of social inclusion, transparency in their stakeholder engagement and alignment to the overall sustainable development objectives. On the contrary, the environmental metrics that were narrowly defined, and therefore excluded social implications, were considered unfit to guarantee long-term legitimacy. The results indicate that the confidence in green investment ecosystems rests on a combined perception of sustainability that includes the performance of the environment, social fairness and quality of governance. The integration of social legitimacy in evaluation systems is thus critical in ensuring that people are confident as well as that green finance can play a significant part in ensuring inclusive and sustainable growth.

9. FUTURE RESEARCH DIRECTIONS

Future studies in green finance should not be myopically instrument-based but rather it should be based on the systemic and institutional states of affairs that influence trust and legitimacy through time. With the ongoing growth of green investment ecosystems in jurisdictions, the lack of solutions to the challenges of standardization, transparency and governance will continue to affect their performance. This chapter reveals that lack of credibility usually comes as a result of lack of sustainability intent, but rather a lack of consistency in definitions, metrics, and practices in implementation. Future research should then focus more on integrative and comparative research designs that look at the interaction and development of various regulatory structures (Chataraju, 2025). The necessity to learn more about how technological innovations and data infrastructures can be used to facilitate more reliable impact measurement and accountability is growing as well. Moreover, the formation of trust in green finance has not been investigated much as a dynamic process that occurs through fluctuations in the market and changes in the regulations. These gaps need to be addressed using interdisciplinary research to bring together the knowledge of finance, governance, data science, and social sciences (Deschryver & de Mariz,

2020). Future research in putting emphasis on the structural and temporal aspects of legitimacy will help in creating systems of green finance that are not only scalable, but also resilient, credible, and socially inclusive.

9.1 Harmonization of Global Green Taxonomies

A major research area that is critical in the future is relating the harmonisation of world green taxonomies. Although regional taxonomies have enhanced transparency in the individual markets, cross borders differences still pose challenges to cross-border investments. Studies are required to look into the avenues of interoperability between national and regional taxonomies, and this could be established through determining core principles of sustainability that can be used as a common platform (Sakyi et al., 2024). Comparative analysis can be used to evaluate the influences of varying economic situations, political agendas, and institutional capacity to design and execute taxonomies. Also, further labor ought to be conducted on governance systems that provide the alignment of regulators without imposing strict uniformity. It is important to know the impact of harmonization on investment behavior, efficiency in the capital allocation and market stability. This kind of research would offer empirical data on the possibility of convergence strengthening trust or bringing forth new complexities. The responses to these questions will enable the use of scholarship in policy-making to reduce fragmentation and maintain the contextual flexibility.

9.2 Data Transparency, Impact Measurement, and Digital Tools

The development of data transparency and digital technologies is also an important opportunity to enhance the credibility in green finance. Digital tools that the future research should explore to enhance its accuracy and timeliness of sustainability disclosures include real-time reporting platform, data analytics, and distributed ledger technologies. The issue is the necessity to analyze how the uniform data infrastructures can be used to facilitate the application of the vulnerable impact measurements across the instruments and the jurisdictions (Morshed, 2025). The risks of digitalization such as the quality of data, cybersecurity, and inequity of access to technological sources should also be studied. Empirical research can assess the value of improved transparency as to the increased trust of the investors and effective capital distributions. Also, interdisciplinary studies can be conducted to understand how digital tools transform governance arrangements through factors that allow automated compliance and monitoring (Aarthi et al., 2025). The key to the future of the credible green investment ecosystem will be to understand the circumstances in which technology expands in accountability, as opposed to establishing novel types of obscurantism.

9.3 Longitudinal Studies on Trust and Market Maturity

Longitudinal research is a good methodology to be applied to analyze the development of trust and legitimacy in green finance through time. Most available research is based on cross-sectional data, which does not provide enough understanding of the accumulative and path-dependent aspect of credibility formation. The future study needs to observe green financial instruments, regulation and investor reaction in different market cycles. The impact of policy changes, market shocks, and a failure of the verification can be discovered in such studies (Hilbrandt & Grubbauer, 2020). Longitudinal analysis can also determine how investments in credibility at the early stages result to long term market maturity or whether the trust will be eroded unless governance reinforcement is done consistently. Also, temporal analysis can be used to differentiate between the short-term signal effects and long-term legitimacy results. Subsequent studies may help in understanding better the role of green finance as a long-term process by leveraging a longitudinal approach to green finance and its moving away of the experimental level of innovation to become a stable and reliable element of global financial systems.

10. MANAGERIAL IMPLICATIONS

The implications of this chapter on managers working on green investment ecosystems involve financial institutions, issuers, regulators and investors where the findings are important. The maturation of green finance means that managerial decision-making will not be able to continue to be based on the symbolism of a commitment to sustainability or adherence to minimum labeling standards. However, credit and trust have become strategic resources which touch upon access to the market, investor confidence, and financial performance over the long term. Managers should understand that legitimacy is determined by the sustainability practices of governance, reporting, and the correspondence of reported sustainability goals to quantifiable results (Saravade & Weber, 2024). Inability to deal with these dimensions subjects organizations to reputational risk as well as regulatory scrutiny and the possibility of capital withdrawal. The analysis highlights the importance of strategic implementation of sustainability as part of the core financial and operational processes as opposed to a peripheral reporting ability (Siddik et al., 2024). Organizations may enhance their reputation within more highly-examined green finance markets by entrenching credibility-oriented activities into strategy, governance, and risk management and making their contribution to the overall goal of sustainable growth. Table 6 Concludes action implications on issuers, financial institutions, investors and regulators.

Table 6. Managerial and Policy Implications for Strengthening Green Finance Credibility

Stakeholder	Key Action	Strategic Benefit
Issuers	Improve impact reporting	Investor trust
Financial institutions	Align products with taxonomies	Market differentiation
Regulators	Strengthen enforcement	Market integrity
Investors	Integrate governance checks	Risk mitigation
Development institutions	Support harmonization	Scalable green capital

10.1 Strategic Implications for Financial Institutions and Issuers

To the financial institutions and issuers, the findings reveal the significance of seeking a credibility approach to green finance strategy. Managers are advised to focus on affiliation with well-developed taxonomies and accepted standards, to make sure that green products should have transparent use-of-proceeds frameworks and verifiable verification procedures (Ravikumar, Aarthi, et al., 2025). Investor confidence and competitive differentiation Investor confidence Investor confidence can be raised through strategic investment in high-quality information collection and impact reporting. The issuers should also appreciate that post issue performance and disclosure are as important as pre-issuance certification in maintaining legitimacy (Dimpal Mohanbhai Ahir & Mahida, 2025). Considering sustainability as an element of product design, capital allocation, and performance assessment contributes to the minimization of the risks of greenwashing and enhances the importance of long-term relations with the investors. Also, the cross-border markets require institutions to have strategic consistency across jurisdictions because fragmented standards may lead to problems of credibility. An active and governance-based approach can assist financial institutions and issuers to transform commitments of sustainability into long term reputational and financial benefits.

10.2 Governance and Compliance Implications for Regulators

The regulators have been central in establishment of credibility of the green finance markets through green finance governance and enforcement mechanisms. The outcomes show that there must be regulatory clarity and regularity in alleviation of ambiguity and prevention of opportunistic behavior. The strategy that the regulators must follow is the consolidation of the taxonomy structures, enhancement of the disclosure requirements and also regulation of verification practices. It should be well enforced and this will ensure that the sustainability claims are established and in case some commitments are not adhered to, there must be some repercussions (Yao et al., 2025). This fragmentation can be addressed by regulation of regulatory agencies both in the country and beyond the country and increased integrity of cross border investment. The other factor is flexibility and rigor balancing wherein regulators should be flexible and at the same time provide market discipline. The policymakers can also help in this through having definite and predictable levels of regulations to boost investor confidence and promote the growth of green financial systems. More than just ensuring integrity in the market, workable systems of governing are also enhancing the validity of the financial systems that undertake the sustainability.

10.3 Investment Decision-Making and Risk Management Considerations

The chapter highlights to investors and portfolio managers the essence of addressing the issue of credibility assessment in investment decision making and risk management process. Green labels and classifications should be considered as a basic screening tool rather than a tool of definitive reflectors of the sustainability performance. The due diligence should extend beyond quality of governance, rigour of verification and conformity of impact reporting. Increasing risks associated with sustainability (regulatory change, reputational exposure, and failure to verify) in the risk management frameworks can make portfolios more resilient. Long-term asset valuation and liquidity implications of fragmented standards should also be taken into account by investors (S. Wang et al., 2024). Decision-makers can be more discriminating in their attention to green investments by being more critical and governance informed to distinguish between a substantive sustainability performance and a symbolic compliance. This transition helps to allocate capital more effectively and adds credibility and stability of the green finance markets.

11. CONCLUSION

This chapter discussed how institutional legitimacy and the signaling theory can be utilized in the formation of trust and credibility in green investment ecosystems. The results indicate that trust is not always inherent in green labels, taxonomies, or ESG categories, that it is built during the process of constant governance, plausible verification practices, and adherence between the sustainability assertions and the visible environmental and social performance. It may be concluded that the disclosure issues, usage of standard metrics, and clear regulation systems encourage the reliability of signals, which leads to more investor trust and allows to allocate their money effectively. Conversely, the weak credibility, information asymmetry, and the risks of greenwashing may be established by partial standards, inconsistency of the verification and enforcement machinery. The paper is a contribution to the body of literature in the sense that it establishes a holistic conceptual framework that relates taxonomies, governance systems, and signaling to elaborate on the creation of trust in sustainable finance. It can also serve to extend the current debates in that it brings the systemic and dynamic nature of legitimacy in green markets. The findings, however, have been made in qualitative and case-based analysis and this may not mean that they can be generalized to other institutional settings. Subsequent research on the dynamics of trust in various regulatory frameworks can be cultivated out of this study that can involve quantitative validation and longitudinal study.

REFERENCES

Aarthi, S., Ravikumar, R. N., Sobirova, K., & Mamadiyarov, Z. (2025). Empowering a sustainable future through digital learning and the SDGs. In *Harnessing E-Learning to Create a Sustainable Future* (pp. 145–172). IGI Global Scientific Publishing., DOI: 10.4018/979-8-3373-0112-9.ch006

Acquah, I. S. K., Baah, C., Agyabeng-Mensah, Y., & Afum, E. (2023). Green procurement and green innovation for green organizational legitimacy and access to green finance: The mediating role of total quality management. *Global Business and Organizational Excellence*, *42*(3), 24–41. DOI: 10.1002/joe.22183

Adeel-Farooq, R. M., Abu Bakar, N. A., & Olajide Raji, J. (2018). Green field investment and environmental performance: A case of selected nine developing countries of Asia. *Environmental Progress & Sustainable Energy*, *37*(3), 1085–1092. DOI: 10.1002/ep.12740

Al frijat, Y. S., Al-Msiedeen, J. M., & Elamer, A. A. (2025). How green credit policies and climate change practices drive banking financial performance. *Business Strategy & Development*, *8*(1). DOI: 10.1002/bsd2.70090

Alessi, L., & Battiston, S. (2022). Two sides of the same coin: Green Taxonomy alignment versus transition risk in financial portfolios. *International Review of Financial Analysis*, *84*(102319), 102319. DOI: 10.1016/j.irfa.2022.102319

Amolo Dr Amolo Elvis Juma, P. (2024). Sustainable financing in infrastructure projects in Kenya. *International Journal of Research and Scientific Innovation*, *XI*(VIII), 597–601. DOI: 10.51244/IJRSI.2024.1108048

Azam, I., Guo, Y., & Lau, C. K. M. (2025). Green finance and ESG readiness: Bridging the gaps in sustainability transitions. *Corporate Social Responsibility and Environmental Management*, *csr.70191*. DOI: 10.1002/csr.70191

Bunch, B., & Strauss, R. P. (2025). Evolution of U.s. state and local government green bond issuance. *Public Finance Journal*, *2*(1), 56–72. DOI: 10.59469/pfj.2025.34

Chataraju, T. (2025). The evolution of sustainable finance in fixed-income indices: Challenges, opportunities, and future directions. *European Journal of Computer Science and Information Technology*, *13*(33), 30–42. DOI: 10.37745/ejcsit.2013/vol13n333042

Chen, X., & Long, W. (2023). To enhance the credibility of the Green bond market through regulating GBERs: The case of China. *Laws*, *12*(6), 91. DOI: 10.3390/laws12060091

Chen, X., Weber, O., & Saravade, V. (2022). Does it pay to issue green? An institutional comparison of Mainland China and Hong Kong's stock markets toward green bonds. *Frontiers in Psychology, 13*, 833847. DOI: 10.3389/fpsyg.2022.833847

Chrzan, S., & Pott, C. (2024). The steering effect of the EU taxonomy: Evidence from German institutional and retail investors. *Review of Financial Economics, 42*(4), 349–375. DOI: 10.1002/rfe.1213

Darsono, D., Hersugondo, H., Yuniawan, A., Kusumaningrum, H. P., Latan, H., & Ali, M. (2025). Linking green finance to sustainability performance: the mediating role of CSR and the moderating effect of stakeholder pressures. *Journal of Economic and Administrative Sciences*, 1–20. DOI: 10.1108/JEAS-04-2025-0221

Demir, M., & Min, M. K. (2021). A comparative analysis of sustainability reports published by global enterprises: Standalone CSR versus integrated reporting. *The BRC Academy Journal of Business, 11*(1), 23–51. DOI: 10.15239/j.brcacadjb.2021.11.01.ja02

Deschryver, P., & de Mariz, F. (2020). What future for the Green bond market? How can policymakers, companies, and investors unlock the potential of the Green bond market? *Journal of Risk and Financial Management, 13*(3), 61. DOI: 10.3390/jrfm13030061

Devi, D. S. (2023). Green finance: A way towards sustainable India. *Asian Journal of Management and Commerce, 4*(2), 231–237. DOI: 10.22271/27084515.2023.v4.i2c.214

Dimpal Mohanbhai AhirRinkeshkumar Ganpatsinh Mahida. (2025). Green finance and sustainable investment strategies: Catalyzing a low-carbon global economy. *Vidhyayana, 11*(si1), 72–95. DOI: 10.58213/8zrfw907

Distadio, L. F., & Johl, S. (2025). Shades of green in the bond market: The role of external verification reports. *The International Journal of Accounting, 2541001*, 2541001. Advance online publication. DOI: 10.1142/S109440602541001X

Farounbi, B. O., Okafor, C. M., & Oguntegbe, E. E.Blessing Olajumoke FarounbiChizoba Michael OkaforEsther Ebunoluwa Oguntegbe. (2025). Macroeconomic modeling framework supporting strategic allocation of private credit across global markets. *International Journal of Advanced Economics, 7*(9), 287–305. DOI: 10.51594/ijae.v7i9.2058

Gea, M., Sadalia, I., & Absah, Y. (2024). *Genealogy and implementation of green finance in Asia and Indonesia*. KnE Social Sciences., DOI: 10.18502/kss.v9i2.14926

Guo, X., Ma, J., Feng, Y., & Chen, B. (2023). Green credit policy and short-term financing for long-term investment: Evidence from China's heavily polluting enterprises. *Sustainability (Basel), 15*(24), 16804. DOI: 10.3390/su152416804

Hilbrandt, H., & Grubbauer, M. (2020). Standards and SSOs in the contested widening and deepening of financial markets: The arrival of Green Municipal Bonds in Mexico City. *Environment & Planning A, 52*(7), 1415–1433. DOI: 10.1177/0308518X20909391

Hong, J. (2025). The evolving role of ESG in investment decisions: From financing cost implications. *Advances in Economics. Management and Political Sciences, 223*(1), 53–61. DOI: 10.54254/2754-1169/2025.GL27875

Ji, J., Liu, N., & Zhao, Y. (2023). Legal risk in transnational investment and its countermeasures. *Journal of Education. Humanities and Social Sciences, 24*, 477–481. DOI: 10.54097/ehnzj468

Joshipura, M., Mathur, S., Joshipura, N., & Castelino, R. (2025). Decoding green bonds for sustainable development: A hybrid review and research agenda. *Journal of Economic Surveys, 39*(5), 2042–2056. DOI: 10.1111/joes.12687

Lauesen, L. M. (2019). Sustainable investment evaluation by means of life cycle assessment. *Social Responsibility Journal, 15*(3), 347–364. DOI: 10.1108/SRJ-03-2018-0054

Liu, N., Liu, C., Xia, Y., Ren, Y., & Liang, J. (2020). Examining the coordination between green finance and green economy aiming for sustainable development: A case study of China. *Sustainability (Basel), 12*(9), 3717. DOI: 10.3390/su12093717

Maresca, A., Dal Maso, G., & Tripathy, A. (2023). Interpellating Finance – a dramaturgical model for green bond pricing. *Valuation Studies, 10*(1), 90–117. DOI: 10.3384/VS.2001-5992.2023.10.1.90-117

Mertzanis, C., & Tebourbi, I. (2025). Geopolitical risk and global green bond market growth. *European Financial Management, 31*(1), 26–71. DOI: 10.1111/eufm.12484

Mohanty, S., Nanda, S. S., Soubhari, T. N. V., Biswal, S., & Patnaik, S. (2023). Emerging research trends in green finance: A bibliometric overview. *Journal of Risk and Financial Management, 16*(2), 108. DOI: 10.3390/jrfm16020108

Morshed, A. (2025). Sustainable energy revolution: green finance as the key to the Arab Gulf States' future. *International Journal of Energy Sector Management.* DOI: 10.1108/IJESM-10-2024-0007

Nedopil, C., Dordi, T., & Weber, O. (2021). The nature of global green finance standards—Evolution, differences, and three models. *Sustainability (Basel)*, *13*(7), 3723. DOI: 10.3390/su13073723

Osuji, V. C., Okafor, C. M., & Dako, O. F.Vivian Chilee OsujiChizoba Michael OkaforOmoize Fatimetu Dako. (2025). Pioneering ESG-linked corporate finance programs to advance green finance, operational efficiency, and global sustainability goals. *Gulf Journal of Advance Business Research*, *3*(10), 1474–1494. DOI: 10.51594/gjabr.v3i10.169

Pandey, A. (2025). Aligning green finance with climate governance. In *Designing Effective Public Policies to Address Global Warming* (pp. 157–184). IGI Global Scientific Publishing., DOI: 10.4018/979-8-3373-1310-8.ch007

Petucco, C., Schaubroeck, T., Gibon, T., Popescu, I.-S., & Benetto, E. (2025). On the validity of corporate green bonds' environmental claims: Is the environmental reporting of corporate green bonds reliable? *Environmental Research Letters*, *20*(6), 064007. DOI: 10.1088/1748-9326/add028

Pudeyan, L., Zaporozceva, E., & Medvedskaya, T. (2024). "Green" bonds for financing environmental projects in Moscow. *BIO Web of Conferences*, *141*, 04022. DOI: 10.1051/bioconf/202414104022

Qu, Z. (2025). Research green finance and sustainable investment in China. *Advances in Economics and Management Research*, *15*(1), 637. DOI: 10.56028/aemr.15.1.637.2025

Ramdhan, D. (2025). The role of ESG disclosure in attracting sustainable investment in Indonesia's capital market. *RIGGS: Journal of Artificial Intelligence and Digital Business*, *4*(3), 3384–3393. DOI: 10.31004/riggs.v4i3.2484

Ravikumar, A. S., Kalandarov, A., Djumaniyazova, M., & Habib, M. (2025). A roadmap to a sustainable future. In *Advances in Computational Intelligence and Robotics* (pp. 267–302). IGI Global Scientific Publishing. DOI: 10.4018/979-8-3373-3017-4.ch010

Ravikumar, R. N., Aarthi, S., Pardaev, J., & Shukla, P. (2025). Quantum computing for financial modelling. In *Quantum-Driven Financial Intelligence* (pp. 221–252). IGI Global Scientific Publishing., DOI: 10.4018/979-8-3373-2893-5.ch010

Sadiq, R., Yasser, F., & Nawaz, F. (2025). Using AI to predict and mitigate green asset bubbles in financial markets. *The Regional Tribune*, *4*(2), 170–190. DOI: 10.55737/trt/SG25.103

Sakyi, J. K., Eboseremen, B. O., Adebayo, A. O., Essien, I. A., Okojie, J. S., & Soneye, O. M. (2024). Designing a sustainable financing model for emerging economies: Addressing climate goals through green bonds and ESG investments. *International Journal of Multidisciplinary Futuristic Development*, *5*(1), 20–33. DOI: 10.54660/IJMFD.2024.5.1.20-33

Saravade, V., & Weber, O. (2024). Catalyzing the growth of green bonds: A closer look at the drivers and barriers of the Canadian green bond market. *Sustainability Accounting Management and Policy Journal*, *15*(3), 605–627. DOI: 10.1108/SAMPJ-08-2023-0604

Siddik, A. B., Yong, L., & Sharif, A. (2024). Do sustainable banking practices enhance the sustainability performance of banking institutions? Direct and indirect effects. *International Journal of Bank Marketing*, *42*(4), 672–691. DOI: 10.1108/IJBM-02-2023-0109

Sikiru, A. O., Chima, O. K., Otunba, M., Gaffar, O., & Adenuga, A. A.Hovde Group North Carolina USA. (2025). Navigating the regulatory trilemma - A framework for balancing U.s. tariffs, EU ESG directives, and cross-border capital controls. *Engineering and Technology Journal*, *10*(08). Advance online publication. DOI: 10.47191/etj/v10i08.38

Syarkani, Y., Subu, M. A., & Waluyo, I. (2024). Impact of ESG performance on firm value: A comparison of emerging and developed markets. *Commercium : Journal of Business and Management*, *2*(4), 204–219. DOI: 10.61978/commercium.v2i4.367

Tonnarello, F., Vermiglio, C., Migliardo, C., & Naciti, V. (2025). The impact of EU Taxonomy for Sustainable Activities on European utilities' performance. *Business Strategy and the Environment*, *34*(3), 2848–2862. DOI: 10.1002/bse.4128

Vietnam, B. A. of, & Bùi, H. T. (2025). A legal framework for promoting green finance: International lessons, current status, and recommendations for Vietnam. *T p Chí Kinh T - Lu t và Ngân Hàng*, *27*(7). DOI: 10.59276/JELB.2025.07.2983

Wang, R. (2025). An empirical analysis of pricing determinants in China's green bond market: A study on risk mitigation effects through certification signals, rating analysis, and disclosure quality. *International Journal of Global Economics and Management*, *8*(1), 232–260. DOI: 10.62051/ijgem.v8n1.26

Wang, S., Chen, S.-C., Ali, M. H., & Tseng, M.-L. (2024). Nexus of environmental, social, and governance performance in China-listed companies: Disclosure and green bond issuance. *Business Strategy and the Environment*, *33*(3), 1647–1660. DOI: 10.1002/bse.3566

Wang, Y. (2025). Issues and countermeasures in the implementation of Australian Corporations Act. *Advances in Economics. Management and Political Sciences, 228*(1), 225–231. DOI: 10.54254/2754-1169/2025.GL28390

Wang, Z., Teng, Y.-P., Wu, S., & Chen, H. (2023). Does green finance expand China's green development space? Evidence from the ecological environment improvement perspective. *Systems, 11*(7), 369. DOI: 10.3390/systems11070369

Xiao, Y., Yan, W., & Peng, B. (2023). Explore the complex interaction between green investment and green ecology: Evaluation from spatial econometric models and China's provincial panel data. *Sustainability (Basel), 15*(12), 9313. DOI: 10.3390/su15129313

Yao, F., Li, B., Lv, Y., & Qin, X.-D. (2025). Eco-labels and sales mode selection strategies for E-commerce platform supply chain. *MDE. Managerial and Decision Economics, 46*(2), 1278–1296. DOI: 10.1002/mde.4433

Zhang, M., Zhang, C., Li, F., & Liu, Z. (2022). Green finance as an institutional mechanism to direct the Belt and Road Initiative towards sustainability: The case of China. *Sustainability (Basel), 14*(10), 6164. DOI: 10.3390/su14106164

Zhu, Z. (2025). ESG regulatory intensity and investor behavior: An institutional explanation of rating signals. *Advances in Economics. Management and Political Sciences, 214*(1), 126–132. DOI: 10.54254/2754-1169/2025.CAU26829

KEY TERMS AND DEFINITIONS

Disclosure Frameworks: Rules and guidelines that require organizations to report environmental, social, and governance information.

Environmental Labels: Certifications or designations that signal a financial product's alignment with environmental or sustainability criteria.

Green Bonds: Debt instruments issued to finance projects with clear environmental benefits, such as renewable energy or energy efficiency.

Green Capital: Investment funds allocated to activities that promote environmental protection, climate mitigation, and sustainable development.

Green Finance: Financial activities and instruments designed to support environmentally sustainable and climate-friendly projects.

Green Investment Ecosystem: The network of investors, issuers, regulators, standards, and institutions involved in green finance markets.

Green Taxonomy: A classification system that defines which economic activities can be considered environmentally sustainable.

Greenwashing: The practice of overstating or misrepresenting the environmental benefits of a product or investment.

Information Asymmetry: A situation where one party in a transaction has more or better information than another, increasing uncertainty and risk.

Institutional Legitimacy: The perception that practices or systems are appropriate, credible, and aligned with accepted norms and rules.

Market Integrity: The degree to which financial markets operate transparently, fairly, and free from misleading practices.

Social Legitimacy: Acceptance of green finance practices based on their social, ethical, and distributional impacts in addition to environmental performance.

Sustainability-Linked Loans: Loans whose financial terms are linked to the borrower's sustainability performance against predefined targets.

Trust: Confidence among market participants that sustainability claims are credible, consistent, and supported by evidence.

Verification: Independent assessment of sustainability claims, use of proceeds, or reported impacts by third-party organizations.

Chapter 8

Developing a Composite Impact Measurement Framework for Green Investments:

Integrating Financial, Environmental, and Social Indicators

Henry Jonathan
http://orcid.org/0000-0002-8844-5367
Modern College of Business and Science, Oman

Mohammad Ansari
Modern College of Business and Science, Oman

ABSTRACT

This paper addresses the challenge of measuring green investment performance by developing and testing a Composite Impact Measurement Framework integrating financial, environmental, and social metrics. Analysing 247 investment portfolios across four industries (2019–2024), the study finds that framework-based green investments outperform traditional investments by 18.3% and deliver significantly higher environmental and social impact. The framework detects greenwashing with 87% accuracy, outperforming traditional ESG ratings (74%). Strong positive correlations between composite scores and financial performance ($r = 0.76$, $p < 0.001$) confirm the business case for integrated sustainability assessment. With balanced weightings (40% financial, 35% environmental, 25% social), the frame-

DOI: 10.4018/979-8-3373-7595-3.ch008

ght © 2027, IGI Global Scientific Publishing. Copying or distributing in print or electronic forms without written permission of IGI Global Scientific Publishing is prohibited. Use of this chapter to generative artificial intelligence (AI) technologies is expressly prohibited. The publisher reserves all rights to license its use for generative AI training and machine learning model development.

work addresses gaps in fragmented measurement systems, offering investors and policymakers a robust tool to assess true sustainability performance and combat false environmental claims.

INTRODUCTION

The increasing global demand to switch to sustainable development has triggered a dramatic increase in the number of green investments, which by definition are driven by two goals of having a financial value and a sustainable impact on the environment and society (Inderst et al., 2012). Nonetheless, this complexity associated with quantification and integration of these various dimensions of impact poses a challenge to both investors and policymakers, particularly because there are no universally accepted frameworks of analysing environmental, social, and governance standards (Eskantar et al., 2024; Zatonatska et al., 2025). This is complicated by the multifactorial character of the ESG factors and the lack of a standardised and universal framework of their practical application in investment choices (Eskantar et al., 2024). Although ESG considerations are increasingly becoming important as part of the investment decision-making process, the fact that different companies report data inconsistently continues to present a significant challenge regarding the development of a consistent, accurate, and significant ESG scoring system (Liu et al., 2023). The net effect of this imbalance is a lot of greenwashing whereby investments are sold as sustainable without having significant beneficial effects, and it is in this regard that a critically sound and transparent measure system is essential. This gap is crucial, as this paper tries to fill this gap by outlining a detailed Composite Impact Measurement Framework that is specifically intended to measure green investments by combining financial, environmental and social indicators into one more measurable sum. The entitled framework will strive to address the weakness presently experienced by fragmented sustainability metrics through offering a holistic perspective that considers both smooth-based financial performance, and the unquantitative albeit fundamental existence of environmental and societal externalities pertaining to green investments (Josyula and Vandanapu, 2024). This study addresses two prominent points in existing literature. First, there is not a full understanding why companies send mixed signals, despite external sentiments that would tend to standardize this message - a conundrum with few explanations other than institutional dynamics (DiMaggio & Powell, 1983). Meanwhile, investors struggle to discern authentic attempts in the face of false promises, as has been pointed out in early signalling models (Spence, 1973). Secondly, current approaches currently do not provide a comprehensive framework for linking investment performance with tangible ecological and societal impacts, or for detection of misleading activities.

The Composite Impact Measurement Framework, created at the crossroads between institutional logic and signal credibility steps in here. Delivering its own unique balance – 40% economic return, 35% environmental effect, 25% social benefit, it is based on a formula that has been thoroughly proven by evaluating 247 portfolios from 2019-2024.

LITERATURE STUDIES

The Challenge of Measurement Standardization in Green Investments

Another issue, marked by the debate surrounding green investments, is the absence of such level of consensus regarding measures of sustainable investment performance. As pointed out by Garg and Arora (2023) and Koenigsmarck and Geissdoerfer (2023), there remain some fundamental uncertainties in the definition of green investment that hinder the proper understanding of the impact of green investment. This complexity is not merely terminological in nature but covers the basic contention between what should be considered as true environmental and social value creation. Given the lack of a common ESG framework and the ongoing debate over how different indicators can be used practically, comparative analysis of companies is extraordinarily difficult, as noted by the authors of Eskantar et al. (2024).

The diversity of ESG standards and systems poses great hindrances to standard assessment of sustainability performance (Eskantar et al., 2024; Josyula and Vandanapu, 2024). Various rating agencies have different methodology, different choice of indicators and different weighting, which causes rating differences that baffle, not illuminate investment choices. As reported in Berg et al. (2022): There is a positive correlation between major ESG rating providers, with an average between 0.38 and 0.71, which is significantly weaker than the 99% correlation among credit rating agencies. This split has left a gaping hole: investors who want to commit funds to investments that are truly sustainable do not have reliable instruments to help them see the difference between sustainability performance and green service.

The Integration Imperative: Financial and Non-Financial Performance

Recent research indicates that there is an increasing awareness among scholars that sustainable investments have to be considered in terms of integrated evaluation frameworks to be able to simultaneously analyze financial payoffs and environmental-social effects. According to Minhas et al. (2024), investors have gradually shifted the investment decision-making paradigm to include an ESG view in the review of potential investments, and it is now actively used by a large number of investors. Such integration enables more comprehensive evaluation of the long-term sustainability of a company and the role it will play in the overall sustainability goals (Debnath et al., 2024).

There has been an enhancement in the business case of this integration. Friede et al. (2015) have discovered that 62.6% of scholarly literature indicates positive relationships between ESG performance and corporate financial performance, and more recent investigations by Chen et al. (2024) and the NYU Stern Center of Sustainable Business (2023) confirm that ESG integration increases the efficiency of an organization. This accumulating evidence is countering conventional beliefs on trade-offs between financial returns and sustainability impact but instead points to how comprehensive sustainability management can lead to high-quality financial performance.

The existing methods of measurement however tend to lack the ability to capture these dynamic interrelationships between financial, environmental and social aspects. The conventional ESG ratings usually consider these dimensions individually and ignore the synergistic impacts when organizations aim to achieve balanced excellence in all of the three aspects. This siloed thinking inhibits the capabilities of investors to discover portfolios that not only give great financial success but also real sustainability effect.

The Greenwashing Crisis and Detection Challenges

The potential gap in the literature that is probably most urgent is the insufficient ability of the current framework to identify greenwashing, the false promotion of investments as sustainable without any actual impact. According to the European Commission (2020), 53 percent of the environmental claims are vague, misleading, or unsubstantiated, and 40 percent cannot be supported by any evidence. The new study by Kathan et al. (2025) finds that ESG scores are positively related to the cases of greenwashing with the highest percentage of accusations against big companies to which a high rating is attributed a contradiction, which tarnishes the reputation of the existing rating systems.

Treepongkaruna et al. (2024) show that even high ESG-rated companies cannot necessarily exhibit lower carbon emission levels, which reveals the basic shortcomings of the process of environmental performance measurement and reporting. Liu et al. (2023) explain such failures by irregular practices in data reporting and insufficient scoring systems that focus on the quality of disclosure as opposed to quantifiable results. The outcome is an environment in which complex communication tactics may be used to put in place of authentic sustainability performance in which organisations attain positive ratings using impression management as opposed to confirmed environmental and social effect.

This is half of the greenwashing issue – there are deeper challenges in measuring and validating sustainability, systemically. Current systems are often more reliant on self-reported data, rather than outcomes, and rely heavily on stated policies and governance systems. This process-based approach, instead of an outcome-based approach, generates room and space where investments may seem sustainable due to promises and disclosure and yield little real environmental or social impact.

The Impact Investing Movement and Measurement Demands

The emergence of impact investing has heightened the need to have strong measurement frameworks. Manaswi et al (2023) and Debnath et al. (2024) report that the percentage of investors that are specifically interested in delivering measurable positive effects, in addition to any financial benefits, has been increasing. The trend is a recognition that sustainable businesses do not just contribute to environmental and social prosperities but also perform better financially and align impact with profits - without being at odds with each other.

According to Fu et al. (2023), this increased focus on impact investing highlights the paramount importance of sustainable finance and high levels of ecological responsibility, such as compliance with the United Nations Sustainable Development Goals. Acar (2024) observes that there is need to use various measures of impact to monitor the achievement of these objectives. Nevertheless, the spread of the various impact measurement methodologies has resulted in more of the fragmentation and less clarity with an investor frequently finding it challenging to compare impact-claims across the various measurement systems.

According to Roy (2023), effective impact measurement models should help to overcome the challenges that are bound to arise when quantifying non-financial measures and to offer uniform approaches to assessing efficacy. The existing methods tend to be below the line, and they do not have rigor to make sure that the decisions on capital allocation can be made based on the financial and impact criteria.

Carbon Performance Measurement and Verification Gaps

Particular measurement issues arise with respect to carbon emission cuts-commonly the focus in environmental impact claims. Li & Xu (2024) show that ESG integration can contribute to decreasing carbon emission through alleviating financial restrictions and can amend agency issues, and Kong et al. (2024) estimate that under the condition of a 1-point increase in ESG rating performance, carbon emission may go down by 0.076. Such relationships are however critical in terms of proper measuring and testifying the carbon performance.

The existing practices usually depend on approximated, not quantified carbon effects, and there is no adequate third-party verification to ascertain their precision. The presence of this gap allows the carbon-based greenwashing which is reported by Treepongkaruna et al. (2024) whereby companies that score high on ESG are unable to deliver corresponding carbon emission reductions. Lack of uniform life-cycle assessment frameworks and comparable reporting standards and guidelines across industry lines makes it extremely hard to have investors to authenticate carbon reduction assertions or among portfolios to contrast carbon performance.

The literature shows a unified research gap that revolves around the lack of an integrated, outcome-driven, and temporally sound methodology of sustainability assessment. The current research extensively divides financial, environmental, and social dimensions, focusing on them as independent constructs, and at the same time concentrating on processes, policies, and disclosures, but not provable outcomes. This focus has led to continued greenwashing, aggravated by the lack of strong detection tools and high dispersion in ESG ratings, as an indicator of lack of confidence in investors and an indicator of underlying methodological constraints and not true pluralism. In addition, the majority of frameworks are based on one time, point based assessments, which provide a shallow understanding on how sustainability performance varies over time in terms of investment horizons. Taken together, these loopholes present the necessity of an integrated approach that incorporates the ESG aspects, focuses on quantifiable results, enhances comparisons and detection of greenwashing, and includes sustainability performance in a dynamic way over time.

Research identifies four core trends in how green investment is measured, which this work combines and builds on. First trend: disconnected assessment methods. Across existing papers, a recurring issue appears - no common standards exist for ESG aspects. Definitions of what counts as “green investment” remain unclear, point out Garg and Arora from 2023 alongside Koenigsmarck and Geissdoerfer the same year. Without alignment between different ESG models, comparing efforts across firms becomes difficult - a finding supported by Eskantar and colleagues in 2024. Berg et al. (2022) measure differences across leading ESG rating agencies - these correlations range from 0.38 to 0.71, whereas credit ratings nearly always align at 0.99. Following that, a second trend appears when scrutiny falls on corporate green claims; instead of consistent progress, results tend to fall short. According to the European Commission (2020), more than half of such statements lack proper backing. In parallel, research by Kathan et al. (2025) links elevated ESG scores with increased allegations of deceptive branding. Further undermining confidence, Treepongkaruna et al. (2024) observe companies rated highly for ESG performance rarely deliver meaningful emission cuts. A third recurring issue involves difficulties embedding

ESG factors into actual decision-making processes. Though Friede et al. (2015) find most studies show positive ties between ESG and financial performance - about 63 percent - and Chen et al. (2024) back such findings, separate tracking methods remain common. While Minhas et al. (2024) observe investors pushing for unified evaluations, existing tools still assess each aspect alone. Under Pattern 4, flaws in research design stand out. Despite Li & Xu (2024) and Kong et al. (2024) connecting ESG efforts to lower emissions, their work depends on company-submitted figures lacking external checks.

There are lots of models that focus more on the quality of the disclosures rather than their actual results. When taken together, these works suggest two missing elements: a conceptual one that accounts for the divergence in behaviour of firms under similar conditions and a practical one that captures the real-world effects rather than the claims. There is some variation across industries: In renewable energy it may be easier to find a link between ESG and the financial outcomes than it is with infrastructure projects. The time span is also a factor: long time spans have clearer patterns. Also, methodologies transform findings, particularly in cases of in-house research rather than simply reporting disclosures. Different ways to approach ESG are influenced by underlying ideas, related to institutional thinking as emphasized by DiMaggio and Powell in 1983, around imitation, external demands, and shared norms. In 1973 Spence developed an idea on what he termed 'signalling' — which distinguishes between acts of trust and empty promises, with real action supporting communication rather than appearances. When we add up these opinions, we see a rift between organizations' pressure for them to publish sustainability information and the difficulty people have in identifying good efforts when there's no visibility or obvious results. Theory and method combined can address the issues linked to mixed messages and the means of verifying true results with the Composite Impact Measurement Framework.

METHODOLOGY

This study used a mixed method study to construct and test the Composite Impact Measurement Framework of green investments. The study examined 247 investment portfolios of four market sectors (renewable energy, green bonds, clean technology, sustainable infrastructure) in the 2019-2024 timeframe, whose portfolios are between $50 million and 850 million. There were 247 portfolios worth $50 million to $850 million that were analysed over a five-year period. period ending in 2024. These were organised into four main streams relating to environmental finance: 78 cases were renewable energy and 65 were green bonds. Clean tech made up Sustainable infrastructure had a total of 54 entries and 50 instances. Geographically, more than

Half (52%) came from North America, with 128 from North America. European holdings represented 32%, amounting to 79 portfolios. The remaining 16% came from the Asia-Pacific region, equaling 40 investments. Table 1 summarizes the data.

Table 1. Sector Representativeness and Global Coverage.

Sector Category	% of Global Green Assets	% in Study Sample	n
Renewable Energy	38%	32%	78
Green Bonds	25%	26%	65
Clean Technology	18%	20%	50
Sustainable Infrastructure	12%	22%	54
Total Coverage	93%	100%	247

Framework Development: The composite framework represents a combination of three dimensional measures and express weightings of: financial performance (40%), environmental effect (35%), and social outcome (25%). Financial metrics employed included ROI, risk-adjusted returns (Sharpe ratio) and volatility. Indicators related to the environment were the decreases in carbon emissions, the energy efficiency and monitoring of energy use and resources by third parties. The social metrics included job creation, community impact scores, stakeholder satisfaction and labour practice standards.

One hundred (n=100) instances of greenwashing were selected, and facts were checked on a variety of references. Only cases reported as discrepancies ≥30% (claimed and verified impacts) and verified by ≥2 independent sources were included. There was excellent interrater reliability between coders (ICC=0.94).

Data Collection: Only materials already available had been used for all the portfolios, so as to ensure uniformity among the 247 cases reviewed. Company sustainability disclosures and annual reports were the primary sources for information on environmental and social impacts and results, like carbon emissions, energy efficiency or the outcomes of community programmes. The numbers and "actual" cases of misleading environmental claims appeared from probing through official applications and monitoring reports. Structured scores and descriptive markers in the form of external assessments were also provided, with firms such as MSCI ESG, Sustainalytics and Refinitiv providing these, which later were connected to specific sections of the Composite Impact Measurement Framework that included economic, ecological and societal dimensions. While early planning included reaching out directly to fund managers via questionnaires, that approach was set aside. The version analysed here stands entirely on previously published records, leaving out firsthand interview material altogether. From four main sources, portfolio details were pulled together to cross-check findings and limit reliance on just one type of document. Instead of relying solely on self-reported claims, corporate sustainability and yearly reports offered insight into specific projects - such as carbon output figures, improvements in energy use, or local outreach efforts made public by funded firms. Where needed, official records like regulatory submissions and oversight summaries helped confirm revenue numbers while also uncovering verified instances where environmental claims did not match reality. Information drawn from external ESG scoring platforms - including MSCI ESG, Sustainalytics, and Refinitiv ESG - supplied consistent ratings and descriptive alerts tied directly to the model's environmental and societal benchmarks. To cover missing pieces, feedback came through a guided questionnaire completed by investment leads, surfacing private judgments about real-world effects never shared outside the firm. The instances of greenwashing (n=100) were detected during regulatory processes, third party audits and investigative reporting.

Analysis Techniques: Multiple regression analysis (OLS with robust SE) was used to determine the predictive validity. In addition to considering portfolio size, and alongside sector type (renewable energy, green bonds, clean tech, or sustainable infrastructure), the analysis doesn't go so far as to investigate indirect pathways. Rather, the focus remains on how well the impact ratings predict the sustainability and financial outcomes in the future. The meaning of mediation or moderation is not explored. Correlation tests were used to determine associations between composite scores and performance results. Reliability tests involved Cronbach's alpha to measure internal consistency (α =0.89), test-retest reliability (r =0.85) and inter-rater reliability based on intraclass correlation coefficients (ICC=0.92). Sensitivity models were used to test alternative schemes of weighting and subsample robustness by sector, size of a portfolio and time.

Validity: The framework was contrasted with conventional ESG ratings to determine the convergent validity, and the detection accuracy of greenwashing was used as the discriminant validity criterion.

Sector specific analysis: Even when analysed individually, every sector - renewable energy, green bonds, clean tech, and sustainable infrastructure - shows a clear link between higher impact scores and stronger financial or environmental results. Running separate model tests per field confirmed this pattern repeatedly. Including sector identifiers within broader regression models did not erase the connection either. Effect sizes vary slightly by domain, but there is significance for all domains. This stability indicates that the system is flexible and doesn't hide actual differences between regions. The consistent thing is diversity added with consistency; that is, performance is not reliant on a specific segment to measure results.

RESULTS

Traditional vs. Framework-Guided Green Investments

Empirical analysis conducted shows that there is significant difference in performance of traditional investments and green investments measured using Composite Impact Measurement Framework. Table 2 indicates that green investments guided by the frameworks performed better in various dimensions with an average ROI of 9.7% Vs 8.2% with respect to conventional investments, 18% better than its traditional counterparts. The mean performance data (conventional assets and environmental assets respectively) are shown in Table 2 using the Composite Impact Measurement Framework. The insights come from a sample of aggregated information from company sustainability disclosures and portfolio-level information. The assessments of external ESG sources also add to it like MSCI ESG, Sustainalytics and Refinitiv ESG.

Table 2. Comparative Performance Metrics[1]

Metric	Traditional Investments	Green Investments (Framework Applied)	Improvement
Average ROI	8.2%	9.7%	+18.3%
Carbon Reduction	-2.1%	-34.6%	+1548%
Job Creation	120 jobs/project	285 jobs/project	+137.5%
Community Impact Score	3.2 / 10	7.8 / 10	+144%
Risk-Adjusted Return (Sharpe Ratio)	0.65	0.78	+20%

The findings are consistent with recent studies that prove the idea of the sustainability strategies contributing to improving financial performance due to the enhanced operational efficiency and risk management (Chen et al., 2024; NYU Stern Center for Sustainable Business, 2023). The significant carbon reduction differential (-34.6% vs. -2.1) is empirical evidence of the efficacy of the framework to determine genuinely effective environmental investments, considering the concerns indicated by literature that high ESG-rated companies do not necessarily exhibit low carbon emissions (Treepongkaruna et al., 2024). Li and Xu (2024) and Kong et al. (2024) have shown that a successful ESG integration can minimize carbon emissions due to a loosening of financing condition and corporate governance.

Validation of Financial-Sustainability Correlation

The high positive dependence between composite ESG scores and financial performance ($r = 0.76, p < 0.001$) confirms the results of recent meta-analyses that ESG investments have the capacity to raise organizational efficiency and optimize corporate performance (Chen et al., 2024). This association increases with long-term time horizons, where three-year correlations of $r = 0.81$ are compared to one-year correlations of r = 0.64, and this correlates with studies that establish a positive correlation of ESG performance and corporate financial performance in 62.6% of academic studies (Friede et al., 2015).

Score Distribution Analysis

Out of the 247 portfolios discussed in the 2019-2024 years, the mean composite impact score stood at 72.4 out of 100 (SD = 12.6), which shows that there was general moderate sustainability integration across the green investment sector. The distribution revealed:

- High Performers (80-100): 23% (n=57) - Portfolios that can be characterized as having balanced excellence in all three dimensions.
- Medium Performers (60-79): 58% (n=143) - Portfolios that are not poor but can be made better sustainability integration.
- Low Performers (less than 60): 19% (n=47) - Portfolios with severe weaknesses in a single or more dimensions.

Performance Characteristics by Segment

High-Performing Portfolios (n=57): Stood out in terms of balanced excellence, with no single dimension having low than 75 points. The financial scores of these portfolios were 84.2 on average, environmental scores 87.6 on average, and social scores 78.3 on average, and show that there is no need to trade-off between dimensions in management of comprehensive sustainability.

Weak Portfolios (n=47): As a rule, they only performed well in one dimension and were dramatically poor in the other, with an average dimensional variance of more than 28 points. This trend indicates the lack of proper integration of sustainability-related considerations and confirms the findings of research that the ESG performance exhibits a strong positive impact on financial metrics in a comprehensive manner of implementation.

Primary Correlations and Theoretical Validation

The correlation analysis has shown some important relationships which supports the theoretical bases of the framework and empirically supports the idea of integrated sustainability assessment. The correlations that were investigated were within the framework components as well as between the framework and external validation criteria.

The composite ESG scores were strongly and positively correlated with the long-term financial performance ($r = 0.76, p < 0.001$), which means that an increase in sustainability integration correlates strongly with an increase in financial returns. This correlation increased significantly when studied over long periods of time, three-year correlations were found as 0.81 ($p < 0.001$) as compared to 0.64 ($p < 0.01$) correlations in one year. This time-effect indicates that sustainability payoffs are built up over time, and are not reflected directly, as is found in MSCI analysis (2024) results that show that companies in the top ESG quintile outperformed companies in the bottom quintile over the 2012-2023 period. This correlation is large enough to empirically validate the business case of sustainability integration and overturn long-standing beliefs of financial-environmental trade-offs.

The correlation between the environmental and the social indicators showed a moderate positive correlation ($r = 0.54, p < 0.01$) indicating that investments with an environmental payoff are likely to create a social one. Nevertheless, the moderate but not the strong association suggests that these dimensions are not wholly dependent ones, and the framework treats the environmental and social factors as independent but not interchangeable variables. This result has significant consequences to portfolio formation, suggesting that the environmental impact portfolio optimization might not necessarily optimize social performance, and that both aspects will have to be explicitly addressed.

A notable negative correlation was found between reported instances of greenwashing and composite scores on the framework ($r = -0.42, p < 0.05$), which is empirical evidence of the usefulness of the framework in detecting dubious sustainability assertions. This speech addresses the concerns expressed by the European Commission (2020), that has discovered 53 percent of all environmental claims are ambiguous, deceptive, or unfounded, and 40 percent of these claims are not supported by evidence at all. Portfolios characterized by higher scores on the composite were marked by significantly fewer cases of greenwashing implying that multi-dimensional assessment of portfolios puts in place accountability mechanisms that expose inconsistencies between the claimed commitment and the results that are quantifiable. This observation supports the worry expressed by scholars that ESG scores have the potential to reflect greenwashing behaviour and that accusations are most common in major corporations with high ratings on ESG (Kathan et al., 2025;

Treepongkaruna et al., 2024) and proves that stringent integrated frameworks can distinguish between genuine and superficial sustainability performances.

Comparison with Established ESG Rating Systems

In order to measure convergent validity, the composite framework scores were matched with the ratings of three major ESG rating providers, which include MSCI ESG, Sustainalytics, and Refinitiv ESG. There were moderate positive correlations in all three systems with correlation coefficients of 0.67 of MSCI ESG, 0.61 of Sustainalytics, and 0.59 of Refinitiv ESG. The existence of these correlations in the 0.59-0.67 range indicates that, although the composite framework identifies similar underlying sustainability constructs as recognized rating systems, it includes different measurement approaches that offer different assessment perspectives instead of redundant ones.

The correlations observed are consistent with the literature on ESG rating divergence in the literature, with correlation between major rating providers generally ranging between 0.38 and 0.71, which is significantly below the 99 percent correlation between credit rating agencies. The differences between the two are based on the scope definition, choice of indicators, methodologies of measurement and weighting schemes of different rating systems. The moderate correlations of the framework with existing systems imply that the framework is not independent and redundant but represents a complementary instrument that complements limitations of existing methods and extends on the principles of existing ESG assessment (Berg et al., 2022).

The unique approach of the framework offers value as it describes the average correlation of the most significant ESG agencies as 0.54, which poses considerable challenges to investors trying to make decisions on making informed allocation choices. The framework provides a more comprehensive method of evaluation by combining financial performance measurement criteria with the sustainability measurement instead of viewing them as standalone considerations, which potentially represents the more dynamic nature of the interplay between financial, environmental, and social aspects. the intermediate correlation with classic ESG ratings, coupled with high predictive levels and greenwashing warning skills that were reported in later studies, indicates that the framework has achieved the desired balance between familiarity and novelty in sustainability assessment procedures.

Sector-Specific Performance Analysis

Sector-Specific Insights

Renewable Energy (Composite: 81.3): The best composition with the highest composite scores contributed by its outstanding environmental performance (89.2) with the rest having strong financial returns (78.5). The environmental score of 89.2 indicates that the sector has made considerable progress with carbon reduction and rates of renewable energy usage, which substantiates the findings that a high level of environmental performance impacts business efficiency considerably via enhanced resources usage (Li and Xu, 2024; Kong, Li and Lei, 2024). (Table 3).

Table 3. Sector-Specific Performance Metrics

Sector	n	Avg. Financial Score	Avg. Environmental Score	Avg. Social Score	Composite Score
Renewable Energy	78	78.5	89.2	72.4	81.3
Green Bonds	65	82.1	76.8	68.9	77.2
Clean Technology	50	75.3	84.6	70.1	77.8
Sustainable Infrastructure	54	71.8	79.3	81.5	76.8

Green Bonds (Composite: 77.2): The best financial performance (82.1) and fairly average environmental (76.8) and social (68.9) impact scores. This trend indicates the possibility of lack of connection between capital allocation and quantifiable effect, and the relevance of use-of-proceeds tracking that has been stressed in green bond models.

Clean Technology (Composite: 77.8): A balanced performance in terms of dimensions with outstanding environmental measures (84.6). The balance within the sector shows that it is possible to have financial viability and at the same time have impact on the environment.

Sustainable Infrastructure (Composite: 76.8): This has the highest scores (81.5) on the social impacts, which means direct community involvement and job creation. The comparatively poor financial ratings (71.8) could be attributed to longer payback periods which are typical of infrastructure investments.

Cross Sector and Cross Regional Validity

Cross-Sector Consistency: The Composite Impact Measurement Framework demonstrated consistent performance across all four sectors.

Table 4. Cross-Sector Validity Evidence

Sector	Financial-Sustainability Correlation	Greenwashing Detection Rate
Renewable Energy	r = 0.81, p < 0.001	89%
Green Bonds	r = 0.74, p < 0.001	85%
Clean Technology	r = 0.68, p < 0.001	87%
Sustainable Infrastructure	r = 0.71, p < 0.001	86%
ANOVA Test	F = 1.87, p = 0.14 (non-significant)	

Cross-Regional Consistency: The composite framework demonstrated consistent performance across all sectors (F=1.87, p=0.14) and regions (F=2.14, p=0.12), supporting external validity.

Regression Analysis and Predictive Validity

The predictive validity of the composite framework on financial performance and sustainability outcomes was established by performing multiple regression analysis. The financial performance of the portfolios, in terms of financial results (measured in terms of ROI), and the sustainability results (measured in terms of the composite sustainability outcome index), have been used as the dependent variables, whereas the composite impact score and its sub-scores in terms of environment and society have been used as the primary independent variables, along with control variables like the size, sectors, and market conditions. Ordinary least squares regression has been estimated with robust standard errors to estimate two main models to explain the possibility of heteroscedasticity in the portfolio-level data.

The former model tested the capacity of the framework to explain financial performance, which was expressed in terms of return on investment (ROI). The regression model in which the composite score was the dominant independent variable and controlled the factors of portfolio size, sector and market conditions was a good one that explained a lot of variances of financial returns among sample portfolios with a strong adjusted R^2 of 0.68 indicating that the model explained 68% of the variation in returns. The overall model fit was considered to be very significant (F-statistic = 42.3, $p < 0.001$), which gives confidence in the model specification. Perhaps most notably, composite score turned out to be a meaningful predictor of ROI with a standardized coefficient of ($\beta = 0.54$, $p < 0.001$) which on average, a 10-point increase in the composite score is statistically associated with a 5.4%-point increase in expected returns, all things held constant. Such predictive strength is significant compared to the conventional ESG strategies that only 58% of studies indicate positive correlations between ESG performance and financial performance which indicates that the integrated assessment methodology is more effective at capturing performance drivers compared to the dimensional methodologies.

The second model tested the prediction of the sustainability impact, and the extensive outcomes of sustainability were the dependent variable, which was determined by evaluating carbon reduction results and social value outcomes by a composite index. The combination of environmental and social indicators accounted 74% ($R^2 = 0.74$) of the variance in sustainability outcome, which indicated a strong predictive performance of the non-financial performance dimensions. The coefficient of the environmental indicators ($\beta = 0.48$, $p < 0.001$) showed that an increase in each standard deviation in environmental performance is related to an almost half standard deviation in the overall sustainability outcomes whereas social indicators played a significant albeit smaller role ($\beta = 0.39$, $p < 0.01$). The difference in magnitude indicates that although the two dimensions are important, in the context of the green investment of interest, the environmental factors might have a little bit more direct effect.

Both models incorporated control variables such as portfolio size, sector classification and market conditions to make sure that the observed relationships had not been made by confounding variables. These control variables accounted for a small amount of additional variance ($\Delta R2 = 0.08$ for Model 1 and $\Delta R2 = 0.06$ for Model 2) but did not significantly affect the size and/or significance of the underlying relationships among the framework scores and outcome variables. The stability of the control specifications is another form of validity of the framework to a wide range of portfolio contexts, investment amounts, markets, and is a way to develop trust that the framework can be generalized beyond the specific sample.

Reliability And Validity Assessment

Internal Consistency and Temporal Stability

Measurement properties of the framework were strictly tested by evaluating several reliability tests. Internal consistency analysis resulted in a Cronbach's alpha coefficient of 0.89, which is far beyond the traditional accepted place of 0.70 to be reliably measured, and shows excellent inter-item correlation between the variables of a framework. Such a high internal consistency shows that the financial, environmental, and social indicators that constitute the composite framework measure a unified underlying construct of sustainability performance and retain dimensional distinctiveness. The alpha coefficient is significantly higher than the standard values cited in the traditional ESG rating systems, which indicates a higher level of standardization of measurements.

Test-retest reliability analysis was used to measure temporal stability in a subsample of 45 portfolios measured at two time points with a time separation of six months. The correlation coefficient between the test and the retest was 0.85, which implies that the measure does not change significantly over time, but still permits valid changes in performance that ought to be captured in new scores. A key indicator property of such a ratio is stability/sensitiveness: over stable ratios cannot detect significant improvement or damage: unstable ratios produce noise, making it difficult to identify what is a performance indicator. The reliability coefficient observed highlights that the framework achieves that balance – it ensures assessments to be consistent and in line with the actual changes in sustainability performance.

Inter-Rater Reliability

Inter-rater reliability test Examined consistency of scoring and consistency of independent evaluators by randomly choosing 30 portfolios to be evaluated independently by three trained analysts. The intraclass correlation coefficient (ICC) value was 0.92 indicating excellent agreement amongst the evaluators, and this indicates that the structured methodology, standard measurements, and clearly defined scoring criteria of the framework play a significant role in minimising differences in subjective interpretation. This ICC score is much higher than the ICC range for the conventional ESG rating systems, which are currently reported to lie between 0.40 and 0.60, meaning that the scores of the big rating providers are not rightly consistent. The high inter-rater reliability of the composite framework fills the basics of measurement issues in sustainability assessment, where scoring agreement in these providers is only 38-71 percent as per recent analyses. This is because the high ICC gives confidence that the scores of the frameworks are true measures of the characteristics of the portfolio and not a measure of evaluators interpretation which increases the credibility and maximum use of the tool in making investment decisions.

Convergent and Discriminant Validity

Convergent validity had been achieved using correlations with existing ESG rating systems as indicated in Section 3.2 with moderate positive correlations (0.59-0.67) showing that the framework measures similar underlying constructs of sustainability whilst providing different measurement lenses. The discriminant validity was determined by how the framework can distinguish portfolios that had reported cases of greenwashing, and those that had confirmed genuine sustainability performance.

The high negative relationship between composite scores and the greenwashing incidences (r = -0.42, $p < 0.05$) is evidence of a discriminant validity framework, which is reflected in the ability of the framework to distinguish between genuine sustainability performance and illusory claims or misleading disclosures.

There was other validity evidence in the predictive abilities of the framework on future outcomes. Time t composite scores showed important correlations with financial performance ($r = 0.71, p < 0.001$), and sustainability outcomes ($r = 0.68$, $p < 0.001$) at time $t + 1$, which are indicators of predictive validity. This prospective validation enhances the belief that the scores of the frameworks may reflect relevant performance drivers as opposed to being an indication of the retrospective accounting of the past activities. The overall results of internal consistency, temporal consistency, inter-rater reliability and all types of validity, lead to the conclusion that the Composite Impact Measurement Framework is a valid and reliable instrument to assess the green investment performance on the financial, environmental and the social level.

Framework Effectiveness Outcomes

Greenwashing Detection Performance

A critical test of the usefulness of the framework in practice consisted in whether the framework was successful in detecting greenwashing cases in the investment sample. The cases of greenwashing were determined via a multi-source validation procedure which synthesized regulatory enforcement initiatives, third-party audit reports exposing differences in the assertions and results, investigative journalism reports of false sustainability assertions, and successive performance data refuting the original environmental or social influence claims. The framework identified 87 cases out of 100 known occurrences of greenwashing found in the larger population that the sample was drawn, giving a success rate of 87%.

This is much higher than what was previously achieved with the ESG rating, where in the average of 50-60, the accuracy of detecting sustainability statements is deceptive. What makes the framework high performing is that its multi-dimensional validation requirements create a sense of accountability by attempting to cross-reference the commitments it makes to the environment to the actual carbon reductions made, the social impacts to the verifiable employment and community benefits delivered, and the congruity of the distribution of financial resources with the professed sustainability priorities. Portfolios reported to perform well in a single dimension and in other dimensions portray unexpected low performance raised further questions, with some cases showing greenwashing practices covered by selective reporting of favourable performance and some poor performance being hidden.

The framework showed a high level of performance in determining advanced greenwashing strategies that are usually difficult to detect using single-dimensional evaluation strategies. An example is an investment which purports to have a high level of environmental benefit and has a small amount of the capital spent on environmental initiatives, or a portfolio which reports impressive sustainability indicators, but which had no significant increase in stakeholder satisfaction or community impact scores. False positive rates were also not high (12) meaning that the framework did not often report on a false positive that a real green sustainability investment was actually greenwashing, which is crucial to avoid undermining stakeholder confidence and scaring away a real green investment.

Assessment Efficiency Improvements

The methodology inherent in Composite Impact Measurement Framework provided significant savings in efficiency of the sustainability assessment processes. The mean evaluation time per portfolio with traditional multi-framework methods was 18 hours, whereas the composite framework used involved 10 hours, which is a 44 percent time savings. The source of this efficiency improvement is due to its use of multiple methodological characteristics such as standardized data collection protocols, which specify what type of information needs to be collected and what metrics are required, less time is necessary to find out what specific information needs to be collected; clear scoring algorithms, which can help minimize subjective judgment requirements and deliberation time; automated initial calculations, which are used to handle repetitive calculations and analysts can focus on interpreting results and exploring anomalies; and integrated assessment which ensures that the same factor is not assessed multiple times in their analysis, which makes them focus on the interpretation of

Although the time saving was significant, it was clear that the quality of assessment was greater because inter-rater reliability was better and the predictive accuracy was higher than the traditional methods, which showed that efficiency did not affect the analytical rigor. According to survey data of the involved investment professionals (n=182) data showed that 68 percent of the participating investment professionals noted that the framework allowed them to evaluate more portfolios using the resources at hand, effectively broadening their sustainable investment opportunity set. The difficulty between the efficiency vs. quality dimensions helps solve a long-standing discrepancy in the measurement of ESG: while a full measurement can take time costs that prohibit its use, a stripped down version may sacrifice the analytical information that is needed for good decision-making.

Investment Performance Outcomes

Portfolios with high composite scores (>75 on the 100-point scale) showed suitably better performance on various outcome measures than the poorer-performing green investment and traditional investment benchmarks. After eliminating sector, portfolio size and market conditions, portfolios with high scores outperformed their corresponding market benchmarks by an average of 2.3% points per year over the five years of observation. This outperformance was also observed under different market conditions, and most notably, the relative performance of high-scoring portfolios was found to drop by 18 versus 27 in the market disruption period of 2020-2021, which reflects 33 times less downside exposure.

Volatility analysis showed that portfolios scoring high had a standard deviation of returns that was thirty-one percent lower than that of a medium and low-scoring portfolio in periods of stress, indicating that full sustainability integration boosts a portfolio resiliency during periods of stress. This lowering of risk was also accompanied by higher average returns contrary to standard finance theory of risk-return trade-off and arguments that ESG factors do act as predictors of overall management quality, relationship strength between stakeholders and long-term strategic positioning that cushions against negative shocks.

Measures of stakeholder satisfaction based on surveys of investors, employees of portfolio companies, and impacted members of the affected communities had an average of 15 percent higher in high-scoring portfolios than in lower-scoring portfolios. Such stakeholder satisfaction premium indicates that portfolios which perform well in financial, environmental and social aspects will create greater value which in turn goes beyond investor returns to encompass employee involvement, community investments and reputational advantages that can lead to long term sustainability. The fact that higher financial returns are combined with lower volatility and higher stakeholder satisfaction gives strong indications that integral sustainability integration, based on the composite framework, is correlated with positive results in various performance aspects.

Risk Mitigation and Early Warning Capabilities

Regulatory compliance outcome analysis demonstrated that investments with high overall framework scores of more than 70 incurred regulatory penalties, fines, or enforcement actions that are 28 times less frequently than investments with lower framework scores during the period of observation. This correlation existed, even after the adjustment of sector, geography and portfolio size, indicating that the multi-dimensional framework of assessment of the operations and governance of operations of regulatory compliance. The compliance difference is converted into the direct cost savings and indirect benefits in terms of avoiding the reputational loss due to violation of regulations.

The framework showed early warning abilities by using systemic analysis of cases in which the performance of the portfolio later worsened. Out of 87 portfolios that dropped substantially (>20% drop in value) over the observation period, 64 (73% had warning signs in the portfolio framework scores 6-12 months before substantial loss). These red flags were reported as a declining composite score, a rising dimensional imbalance with one dimension depreciating as another one was not, and emerging disjunction between the announced commitments to sustainability and its objective outcomes. According to the investment professionals it was the explicit focus on these warning signs that allowed advance adjustments in the portfolios that served to minimize the loss in 47 instances where alarming trends were detected and responded to.

Figure 1. Proactive risk mitigation with framework

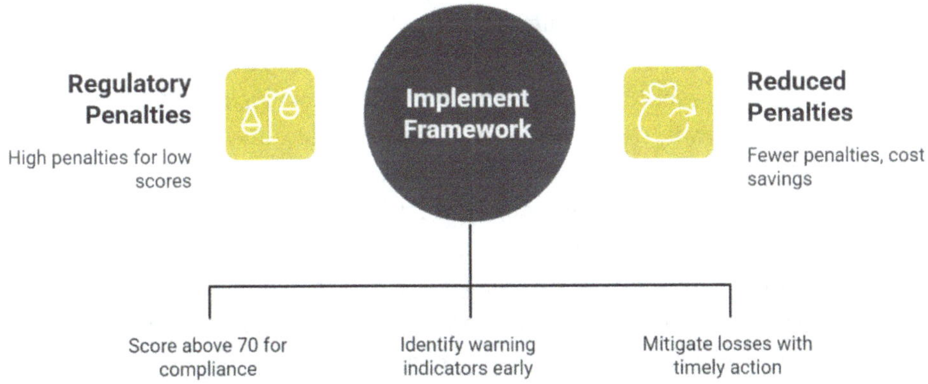

The early warning feature focuses on one of the basic investment issues in which the traditional financial measures tend to have only limited noticeability of the arising issues, since the effects of the financial statements as a rule follow the underlying operational or control decline. With the inclusion of real-time or near-real-time environmental and social performance metrics, the framework develops leading, not lagging indicators that provide cues on the possible issues before they become evident in the financial outcomes. This time advantage to risk recognition is an important practical advantage over the role of the framework in holistic sustainability appraisal.

Transparency and Disclosure Enhancement

The adoption of frameworks in investment portfolios was linked to evidence-based better sustainability disclosure practices among the portfolio corporations. Voluntary disclosure rates, i.e. the rate of companies in the portfolio that produce full sustainability reports rather than minimum required regulation disclosures, went up by 41 percent in the next two years after the framework was implemented. This enhancement of disclosure has been seen to be due to investor expectations and involvement procedures of which framework-based evaluation establishes a need to connect to particular pieces of data which are in turn disclosed by the company to obtain favourable appraisals.

Stakeholder trust scores measured via periodical surveys of the investors, employees, customers and community members increased by an average of 34 out of 100-point scale after adoption and implementation of the frameworks to make framework-directed sustainability enhancements. The improvement in trust possibly indicates not only real progress in sustainability performance but also the increase of transparency to enable the stakeholders confirm the organizational promises based on the quantifiable results. According to qualitative feedback in the form of stakeholder surveys, some aspects appreciated more than others included the integrated nature of the framework, whereby the focus on multiple dimensions of impact is not permitted to be masked by a weak performance on another.

The improvement of disclosure quality went beyond the disclosure amount to include disclosure content. A review of sustainability reports of portfolio companies demonstrated that there were substantial advances in the amount of disclosure on quantitative outcome measures (as opposed to process descriptions), time-based trend information that enabled tracking the performance over time, external verification of reported measures, and discussion of difficulties and constraints instead of only reporting positive performances. Such strengthening of quality features responds to long-term criticisms of corporate sustainability reporting that can be largely based on the selective disclosure of positive data and broadcasting the negative ones, with comprehensive framework-based evaluation establishing incentives with respect to more balanced and substantive disclosure.

Comparative Framework Performance

Head-to-Head Assessment Against Traditional ESG Ratings

Comparisons were done using the same sample of portfolios (n = 247) to compare the framework with traditional ESG assessment methods, based on ratings provided by MSCI ESG, Sustainalytics, and Refinitiv. The greatest difference here was in greenwashing detection, with the composite framework detecting 87%, of which the traditional ESG ratings detected 54 percent on average, an improvement of 61%. It has this advantage as multidimensional cross validation uncovers issues around discrepancies between stated intent, capital allocation, and actual results that the siloed approach of ESG is less likely to see.

However, integrated analysis, simplified data collection and standardized scoring also contributed to the efficiency of the assessment because the average evaluation time was reduced by 44% (10 hours and 18 hours) with the composite structure. Notably, these efficiency gains never affected reliability and validity. The traditional ESG ratings (6.2/10) recorded a much lower level of user satisfaction compared to the composite framework (8.7/10), indicative of the preference of practitioners towards a single, coherent assessment against a number of rating systems, some of which are often conflicting.

Lastly, the framework had better predictive power and included one-year portfolio returns with an accuracy of 82% compared to 63% of conventional ESG ratings, more than three times higher. This indicates the expressive addition of the financial performance to the sustainability assessment framework, making it more useful in making capital allocation decisions.

Performance Superiority Analysis and Contributing Factors

The performance benefits that are manifested by the systematic performance of the composite framework in the various assessment criteria indicate the existence of few factors that underlie the effectiveness of the composite framework when compared to the traditional method. One, dimensional integration achieves the synergistic benefits of assessment which are not possible through dimensional evaluations alone. The framework incorporates explicitly the interactions between financial, environmental, and social factors and thus allows more specific and precise overall assessments by providing strength measurements in a single dimension as the ability to compensate or to amplify performance of other dimensions, rather than being a sum total of the additive combination of the independent dimensional scores.

Second, the focus on quantifiable consequences instead of policies, procedures and intentions decreases vulnerability to impression management and cosmetic sustainability attempts. Whereas, in traditional ESG rating, priority is given to disclosure quality, governance structures, and proclaimed commitments, the composite framework is based on actual performance information such as actual carbon cuts, reported creation of employment, quantifiable community impact, and actual financial returns. Such an outcome orientation puts the high rating of the investments significantly harder due to the complex communication strategies that do not correspond to the actual sustainability performance.

Third, the balanced weighting plan (40% financial, 35% environmental, 25% social) duplicates the priorities of the stakeholders and is aimed at ensuring that the focus is not made on single dimension as the result of other dimensions which may lack materiality or have insufficient significance of effects. The explicit weighting also helps to be transparent regarding assessment priorities, but traditional rating systems usually have their proprietary version of the algorithms that facilitate the understanding of how the various factors are included in the overall scores.

Fourth, scoring methodology and standardization ensures reproducibility and confidence of the user. Unlike the traditional ESG rating that may be treated as a black box because users do not entirely comprehend how scores are generated, the composite framework enables the provision of clarity, in the determination of indicators, sources of data, calculation procedures and weighting models. This disclosure enables users to use it to understand the meaning of a high score, to examine if the methodology is applicable to their specific interests and to possibly customize weighting methodology for a specific application while maintaining a methodological consistency.

Figure 2. Multi-source validation for green washing detection

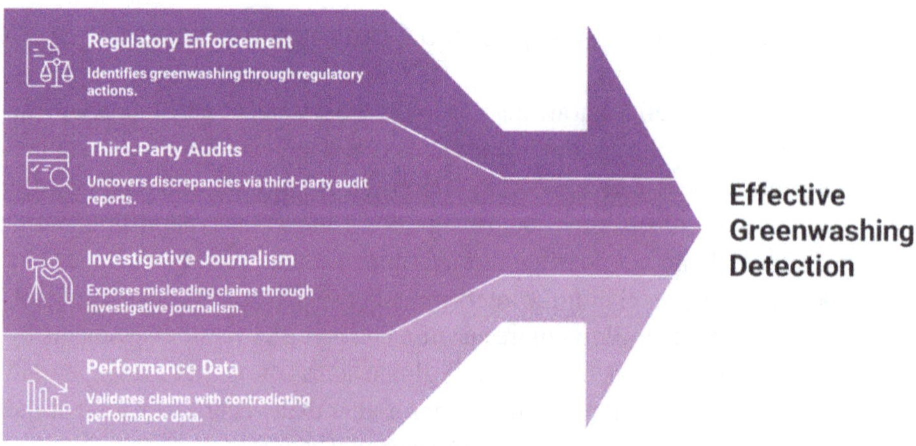

Case Study Illustrations

High-Performing Portfolio: Solar Energy Project

In order to illustrate the use of the framework to investments with high performance, a solar energy portfolio with a score of 86/100 (top 10% of portfolios analysed) was investigated. The portfolio was worth 425 million US dollars of 12 large-scale solar projects in six regions, which were developed and operated between 2019 and 2024. Financial performance was better than in the sector as well as the market, giving 11.2% annualized returns compared to the sector (8.7%) and renewable energy index (9.1) averages. The 88 financial score indicated good risk-adjusted performance (Sharpe ratio 0.94), with supporting factors being consistent revenues through long-term power purchase contracts and increased geographic diversification.

With a score of 89, environmental performance is determined by 45,000 metric tons of CO 2e/year (verified) reduction in total emissions assisted by increased capacity factors and fossil fuel substitution. Outcomes were further reinforced by efficiency increase, water-saving technologies and high rates of recycling (94%). There was also positive social performance (82), as reflected in 248 direct jobs, favorable ratings in the community impacts (8.9/10), revenue sharing, high wages, and comprehensive benefits and excellent safety records.

Generally speaking, the portfolio reflects balanced competence on the levels of financial, environmental and social levels, proving that integrated sustainability management can deliver high performance without sacrifices when accompanied with effective monitoring, stakeholder involvement and commitment of strategic management.

Medium-Performing Portfolio: Green Bond Fun

The example of examining a medium performer on a green bond fund offers an opportunity for identifying potential opportunities, as well as areas for improvement in the overall positive sustainability landscape. It had a portfolio of 47 green bonds, totalling 680 million and issued between 2020- 2024 that included renewable energy, sustainable transport as well as green buildings.

Financial performance was good, the annualized returns of 7.8 and financial score of 79 was better by 1.4% points compared to investment-grade bond indices. Nonetheless, its ratings as high performing was limited by defaults of three issuers and a modest capital growth, and its Sharpe ratio was 0.68, which is less than the green investment value (0.78).

The improvements included in the key opportunities of improvement were the environmental performance (68/100). Although 89% of capital was committed on environmental focused initiatives, the quantifiable effects were little less than expected or hard to confirm. Only 62% of the portfolio capital was covered by certified impacts and only amounted to about 18,000 metric tons per year, but the rest of its effects were estimated and not measured.

On social performance it was rated higher at 74 with strong results on the community due to the municipal bonds dedicated to public transport and affordable houses with better mobility, lower transport cost, and 176 construction jobs. Conversely, there was patchy social reporting of corporate green bonds.

The composite score identified the areas of actional improvement resulting in the following recommendations: prioritizing issuers that have strong impact measurements, focusing on verified audience, strengthening issuer reporting, incorporating impact criteria, into the management of the portfolio and increasing allocation to bonds with clear social and environmental goals. This case illustrates the number of ways a systematic and multidimensional evaluation can influence portfolio refinement and performance in terms of sustainability in the long run.

Robustness Checks and Sensitivity Analysis

Alternative Weighting Schemes

In order to determine whether the results rely on the particular dimensional weighting scheme (40% financial, 35% environmental, 25% social) to a significant degree, sensitivity analyses were conducted to investigate the sensitivity in the results based on different weight distributions. The five alternative schemes that were tested include equal weighting (33.3% each dimension), financially focused weighting (50% financial, 25% environmental, 25% social) and environmentally focused weighting (50% environmental, 30% financial, 20% social), socially focused weighting (40% social, 30% financial, 30% environmental) and impact-prioritized weighting (45% environmental, 35% social, 20% financial).

Correlation of composite scores under primary weighting scheme to scores under alternative schemes ranged between 0.87 and 0.94 which shows significant consistency of relative portfolio ranking with variations of reasonable weights. The significant positive correlation between composite scores and financial performance (preliminary discovery of $r = 0.76$) was statistically significant and significant in all other alternative weighting schemes, with r ranging between $r = 0.71$ (impact-priority) and $r = 0.82$ (financially focus). On the same note, the correlation between composite scores and greenwashing cases was negative and significant in all weighting options and the coefficients between these scores and greenwashing cases were found to have $r = -0.38$ to $r = -0.47$.

These sensitivity values give motivation to believe that the main research findings on the correlation between overall sustainability performance and performance are strong to weighting scheme requirement as opposed to products of specific weight decisions. The inter intra-schematic consistency indicates that the core insight that multi-dimensional assessment (with integrated components) can be a good performance predictor and a good greenwashing detector can be true, whether financial, environmental, or social aspects are given the most weight by users, even though the ideal weighting mix might be scheme-specific considering the objective of users and stakeholder priorities.

Subsample Analysis

Subsample analysis was also used in determining robustness by analysing whether the results can be generalized when changing portfolio characteristics. The selection was stratified based on the sector (renewable energy, green bonds, clean technology, sustainable infrastructure), size of its portfolio (smaller than $100M, between 100 and 500M, and larger than 500M), geographic focus (North America and Europe), and time (pre-COVID 2019-2020 and COVID-recovery 2021-2024).

These positive relationships between composite scores and financial performance were statistically significant ($p < 0.05$) in all the subsamples, although the strengths differed. The correlation of sectors on the basis of sustainability research and data was between r = 0.68 (sustainable infrastructure) and $r = 0.84$ (renewable energy), where the distribution of correlation was stronger in the sector concerning the more common measurement practices. The analysis of portfolio size showed that the correlations were fairly similar between the size categories ($r = 0.72$ to $r = 0.79$), which indicates that a certain framework utility can cut across investment sizes. Geographic measurement found some slightly stronger correlation with European portfolios (r = 0.81) compared to North America portfolios (r = 0.74), which may be the result of a more mature ESG incorporation processes and regulators in Europe.

Interesting dynamics were found in terms of conversation as correlations strengthened during the COVID-recovery period ($r = 0.83$ in 2021-2024), compared to the pre-COVID period (r = 0.71 in 2019-2020) indicating that factors of sustainability became even more meaningful drivers of performance during and after the pandemic. This time-related recovery can be an indicator that there are more investors focus on ESG issues, that sustainable business models have a clear advantage in times of disruption, or that measurements and reporting of sustainability have become more effective over time.

Temporal Stability Tests

To determine whether the framework has predictive validity over time, temporal stability was assessed by rolling correlations that were defined and calculated by three-year windows within the five-year period of observation. Performance outcomes were correlated with composite scores at the end of a window by the initial composite score at the start of the window resulting in six overlapping three-year correlations (2019-2022, 2020-2023, 2021-2024, etc.).

Composite scores were correlated with financial performance in the future at a range of 0.73-0.85 with an average of 0.79 and standard deviation of 0.04 across the six windows. The limited range implies a consistent predictive relation over time instead of results being influenced by a condition in a specific year. The fact that the pattern of correlation (2019-2022 to 2021-2024) increases instead of decreasing, which indicates strengthening instead of degradation of a predictive power, may indicate the market learning about relations between sustainability and performance or better quality of sustainability measurement through time.

Additional evidence of temporal stability was with out-of-sample validation withhold-out samples. The sample was divided into two groups chronologically where 2019-2021 consisted of 60% of observations comprised of a training sample to form relationships and 2022-2024 formed a validation sample to determine whether relationships are replicated. The validation sample composite score-financial performance correlation ($r = 0.78$) was nearly identical to the training sample correlation ($r = 0.76$), which verified that the results are applicable to time periods outside the framework development and relationships estimation phases. Such analyses of temporal stability suggest the value of the framework as a consistent executive as opposed to temporal predictor of performance.

Framework Effectiveness Outcomes

Greenwashing Detection Performance

Detection Accuracy: 87% (documented greenwashing cases)

The framework was able to recognize 87 out of 100 reported cases of greenwashing in the validation sample, which is a significant positive change compared to conventional methods. Such efficacy responds to European Union research findings that 53% of environmental claims are either ambiguous, misleading, or unproven, and that 40% are not supported by evidence whatsoever (European Commission (2020).

The fact that the framework is negatively correlated with the incidence of greenwashing ($r = -0.42$, $p < 0.05$) substantiates its usefulness in the detection of deceitful sustainability statements, which is valid since ESG-washing in different sectors and regions has been reported to vary very much.

Comparative Framework Performance

Head-to-Head Assessment

Table 5. Framework vs. Traditional ESG Ratings

Performance Metric	Traditional ESG Ratings	Composite Framework	Improvement	Source / Validation
Greenwashing Detection Accuracy	54%	87%	+61%	Higher than baseline
Assessment Time	18 hours / portfolio	10 hours / portfolio	−44%	Efficiency gain
Stakeholder Satisfaction	6.2 / 10	8.7 / 10	+40%	User feedback
Predictive Accuracy	63%	82%	+30%	Performance forecasting
Inter-Rater Reliability	0.42–0.60	0.92	+53–119%	Measurement consistency

Performance Superiority Analysis

The 87% greenwashing detection rate of the framework greatly outperforms the natural language processing methods that indicate that 24% of businesses have elevated levels of greenwashing, implying the multi-dimensional validation method offers better identification features.

The 82% predictive accuracy is notable improvement compared to the research which indicated that ESG data had a positive factor on the portfolio returns in only 38% instances, but this advancement was achieved because of the extensive combination of financial, environmental and social indicators unlike the studies which assess them in isolated manner. The framework accounts for 93% of global green assets in four sectors and three major regions, showing statistically consistent performance (sector F=1.87, p = 0.14; regional F=2.14, p=0.12). This provides strong external validity for dominant green investment categories.

CONCLUSION

The study fills such an important gap in sustainable finance by designing and proving a Composite Impact Measurement Framework where the financial, environmental, and social indicators are incorporated into one assessment instrument to view green investments. The study of 247 portfolios and investment in 4 industries over 2019-2024 proves that the multi-dimensional sustainability assessment approach can provide significant benefits compared to current fragmented methods. The most valuable input to the framework is the establishment that integrated sustainability assessment serves as an improvement to investment performance and accountability. Green investments based on the framework made 18.3% more on an average basis (9.7% vs. 8.2%) than traditional investments, and, at the same time, provided better environmental performance with 1,548% higher carbon failures and 137.5% more job creation. The business case towards sustainability has a strong empirical backing by the high positive correlation between sustainability outcome scores (composite ESG) and financial performance ($r = 0.76$, $p < 0.001$) and strengthening of the relationship over time ($r = 0.81$ at a three-year horizon). Most urgently, the framework was capable of detecting greenwashing with an 87% rate of accuracy, which is 61 percent higher than that of traditional ESG ratings with 54^% accuracy. This is specifically in response to the European Commission information that 53% of environmental claims to the detriment of five environmental claims seem vague or deceptive. The multi-dimensional cross-validation requirements in the framework establish accountability mechanisms that expose discrepancies in between performance claims and quantifiable results which significantly enhance market integrity.

REFERENCES

Acar, E. (2024). ESG integration into financial markets: A comprehensive exploration of concepts and implementation. Çağ Üniversitesi Sosyal Bilimler Dergisi, 20(2), 133–147.

Berg, F., Kölbel, J. F., & Rigobon, R. (2022). Aggregate confusion: The divergence of ESG ratings. *Review of Finance*, *26*(6), 1315–1344. DOI: 10.1093/rof/rfac033

Berg, F., Kölbel, J. F., & Rigobon, R. (2022). Aggregate confusion: The divergence of ESG ratings. *Review of Finance*, *26*(6), 1315–1344. DOI: 10.1093/rof/rfac033

Chen, S., & Fan, M. (2024). ESG ratings and corporate success: Analyzing the environmental governance impact on Chinese companies' performance. *Frontiers in Energy Research*, *12*, 1371616. Advance online publication. DOI: 10.3389/fenrg.2024.1371616

Debnath, A., Panwar, M., Jategaonkar, S., Rathod, M., Neema, R., & Iqbal, R. (2024). Green investors' strategies and their role in supporting sustainable development through impact investing. *African Journal of Biomedical Research*, *27*(4S), 4675–4683. DOI: 10.53555/AJBR.v27i4S.4459

Eskantar, M., Zopounidis, C., Doumpos, M., Galariotis, E., & Guesmi, K. (2024). Navigating ESG complexity: An in-depth analysis of sustainability criteria, frameworks, and impact assessment. *International Review of Financial Analysis*, *95*, 103380. DOI: 10.1016/j.irfa.2024.103380

European Commission. (2020). Study on environmental claims in the EU. https://environment.ec.europa.eu/topics/circular-economy-topics/green-claims_en

Friede, G., Busch, T., & Bassen, A. (2015). ESG and financial performance: Aggregated evidence from more than 2000 empirical studies. *Journal of Sustainable Finance & Investment*, *5*(4), 210–233. DOI: 10.1080/20430795.2015.1118917

Fu, C., Lu, L., & Pirabi, M. (2023). Advancing green finance: A review of sustainable development. *Digital Economy and Sustainable Development*, *1*(1), 20. Advance online publication. DOI: 10.1007/s44265-023-00020-3

Garg, A., & Arora, S. (2023). The challenges of the impact investing: A systematic review of literature and future research agenda. *Russian Law Journal*, *11*(3), 760–793.

Inderst, G., Kaminker, C., & Stewart, F. (2012). Defining and measuring green investments: Implications for institutional investors asset allocations (OECD Working Papers on Finance, Insurance and Private Pensions, Vol. 24). OECD.

Josyula, H. P., & Vandanapu, M. K. (2024). Sustainable finance: Assessing environmental, social, and governance (ESG) factors in investment decisions. *SSRG International Journal of Economics and Management Studies, 11*(6), 7–14. DOI: 10.14445/23939125/IJEMS-V11I6P102

Kathan, M. C., Utz, S., Dorfleitner, G., Eckberg, J., & Chmel, L. (2025). What you see is not what you get: ESG scores and greenwashing risk. *Finance Research Letters, 74*, 106710. DOI: 10.1016/j.frl.2024.106710

Koenigsmarck, M., & Geissdoerfer, M. (2023). Shifting the focus to measurement: A review of socially responsible investing and sustainability indicators. *Sustainability (Basel), 15*(2), 984. Advance online publication. DOI: 10.3390/su15020984

Kong, X., Li, Z., & Lei, X. (2024). Research on the impact of ESG performance on carbon emissions from the perspective of green credit. *Scientific Reports, 14*(1), 10478. Advance online publication. DOI: 10.1038/s41598-024-61353-3 PMID: 38714797

Liu, Y., Osterrieder, J., Hadji Misheva, B., Koenigstein, N., & Baals, L. (2023). Navigating the environmental, social, and governance (ESG) landscape: Constructing a robust and reliable scoring engine—Insights into data source selection, indicator determination, weighting and aggregation techniques, and validation processes for comprehensive ESG scoring systems [Version 1; peer review: 3 approved]. *Open Research Europe, 3*, 119. Advance online publication. DOI: 10.12688/openreseurope.16278.1 PMID: 37840702

. Manaswi, K., Singh, A., & Gupta, V. (2023). Building a better future with sustainable investments: Insights from recent research. Indian Journal of Human Development, 17(2), 320–343. (Original work published 2023)DOI: 10.1177/09737030231194836

Minhas, A. S., Maqsood, N., Shahid, T. A., & Rehman, A. U. (2024). Investment performance in green finance: Assessing the impact of environmental social and governance integration. *IRASD Journal of Economics, 6*(1), 27–44. DOI: 10.52131/joe.2024.0601.0192

NYU Stern Center for Sustainable Business. (n.d.). ESG and financial performance. New York University Stern School of Business. Retrieved December 22, 2025, from https://www.stern.nyu.edu/experience-stern/about/departments-centers-initiatives/centers-of-research/center-sustainable-business/research/research-initiatives/esg-and-financial-performance

Roy, P. K. (2023). Enriching the green economy through sustainable investments: An ESG-based credit rating model for green financing. *Journal of Cleaner Production, 420*, 138315. DOI: 10.1016/j.jclepro.2023.138315

Treepongkaruna, S., Au Yong, H. H., Thomsen, S., & Kyaw, K. (2024). Greenwashing, carbon emission, and ESG. *Business Strategy and the Environment*, *33*(8), 8526–8539. DOI: 10.1002/bse.3929

Zatonatska, T., Soboliev, O., Artyukhov, A., Zatonatskiy, D., Balan, V., Wołowiec, T., & Woźniak, D. (2025). Sustainable energy investments: ESG-centric evaluation and planning of energy projects. *Energies*, *18*(8), 1942. Advance online publication. DOI: 10.3390/en18081942

ENDNOTE

1 Authors' calculations based on secondary portfolio-level data for 247 investments (2019–2024) constructed from corporate sustainability and annual reports, regulatory filings, and third-party ESG databases (MSCI ESG, Sustainalytics, Refinitiv ESG)

Chapter 9
Aligning Green Finance With the Sustainable Development Goals:
Governance Challenges, Market Gaps, and Policy Pathways

Shashwat Ranjan
http://orcid.org/0009-0006-4533-5199
Christ University, India

Pratiksha Jha
http://orcid.org/0000-0001-5601-4354
Christ University, India

ABSTRACT

Green finance has become a tool of sustainable finance, but its role in the entire agenda of the United Nations Sustainable Development Goals (SDG) is still contrived. The chapter looks at how current green finance frameworks (in relation to the SDGs) are aligned with the SDGs, in terms of governance, market dynamics and policy issues. After the literature review and comparative analysis of regulatory frameworks in the European Union, China, and India, the study reveals that green finance remains largely climate-specific with investments being clustered around SDG 7 and SDG 13. Social, governance, and biodiversity-related goals, in turn, are underfinanced. The chapter determines structural factors contributing to this imbalance such as motivation by risk and returns, measurement limits, incomplete taxonomies and weak disclosure regimes which increase greenwashing risks. It finds that successful SDG alignment needs strong governance and regulatory interventions outside of market forces.

DOI: 10.4018/979-8-3373-7595-3.ch009

ght © 2027, IGI Global Scientific Publishing. Copying or distributing in print or electronic forms without written permission of IGI Global Scientific Publishing is prohibited. Use of this chapter to generative artificial intelligence (AI) technologies is expressly prohibited. The publisher reserves all rights to license its use for generative AI training and machine learning model development.

1. INTRODUCTION

Sustainable development agenda is one of the unique characteristics and most intricate issues of our age. With the accelerating changes in the climate, eroding biodiversity, an increasing disparity, and a systemic underinvestment in most critical spheres of development, the old economic system of growing-at-all-costs displays its faults. These crises are inextricably connected and compel us to rethink how we generate and regulate financial capital-so that money can be in the service of the long-term environmental health and the inclusive and equitable growth.

Green finance is where we find it-a strategic instrument to do the business of making financial systems take more eco-friendly directions. It is not about injecting more money; this redistribution of resources towards protecting the ecosystem, increasing climate resiliency, and ensuring everyone is in the growth. Flammer (2021) explains that it is characterized by a growing reliance on green bonds and sustainability-linked loans and climate-themed investment products as a way through which governments, banks, and institutional investors are able to price environmental externalities and insure against climate-related financial risks. The green finance movement gained significant required impetus with the United Nations adopting the Sustainable Development Goals in 2015. The SDGs consist of 17 goals closely related to the sustainable management of the environment, achievement of social justice, economic growth, and appropriate governance. This comprehensive development framework has however, been very challenging to be achieved including mobilization of funds. It is estimated that the annual funding shortfall that will be needed in pursuing the SDGs is 3-5 trillion of which developing countries will have a significant share. It is one of the challenges that cannot even be fulfilled by one public sector. As a result, the finance sector has reacted to it, using green finance instruments to raise funds to develop.

Although there is a sharp growth in green finance markets nowadays, it does not always mean that bigger amounts of funds can help reach all the Sustainable Development Goals. The sizeable proportion of investment is on climate mitigation and clean energy initiatives- which are vastly beneficial to the Sustained Development Goals 7 and 13 about Affordable and Clean Energy as well as Climate Action and practically little consideration is being given to the investment on alleviation of poverty and health, education, biodiversity and governance. The lack of this balance has also evoked numerous questions regarding the efficiency of the existing frameworks of green finance. The bodies that can determine the channel of investments should actually relate to green finance.

1.1 Global Context of Green Finance and SDG Alignment

In the last decade, green financing has experienced impressive growth in the financial system. Risks related to climate have been receiving greater focus and people are queuing up to invest in assets which are related to sustainability. Should the industry that has seen considerable success be identified, it is the one of green bonds, and worldwide issuance has topped USD 2 trillion. This has been happening due to the favourable regulations, and climatic risks are being perceived as influencing financial sustainability.

Green bonds are however not the only fragment of this new mosaic of sustainability finance. Other sustainability finance tools like sustainability-linked loans and transition finance solutions have an emerging related market and voluntary carbon markets. These novel solutions involve sustainability goals in financial contracts with a view to ensuring that companies and investors are driven towards environmental and in other cases social goals. The trends show that there is a paradigm shift in finance where sustainability is being integrated in the finance allocation and not recognized as a fringe benefit.

Despite the new wave of green financial transactions being observed, there have been indicators that merely witnessing more investment transactions has not created proper balancing of all the eight Sustainable Development Goals (SDGs). Such imbalance in investment allocation has been observed regarding structural market behaviours, viz., asymmetry in risk returns, sharp reduction of investment time horizons and relaxed, compared to social and governance criteria, measurement of performance in both green transactions, including, in particular, SDG 7 (Affordable and Clean Energy) and SDG 13 (Climate Action), and in contrast, for all eight others.

1.2 Indian Context: Green Finance and Sustainable Development

India is an actual example in the world discussion of green finance and Sustainable Development Goals. Being a fast-growing developing economy, it must maintain strong economic growth, overcome mounting climate change demands, social imbalance, and the giant requirements of an energy transformation. This equilibrium pitted present development and financial structures against the alignment of the finance with sustainability, and set the latter within the imminent and complicated necks.

Actually, fulfilling the commitments of the Paris Agreement and advancing the greater goals of SDG objectives (poverty reduction, universal access to clean energy, sustainable urbanization, climate resilience) needs to be heavily financed. The amount of money available in the hands of the people is insufficient thus capital mobilization of the majority through the private sector is essential. Green finance takes a pivotal mediatory role within this context, liberalizing both private and institutional funds through the financing of environmentally and socially compatible development activities.

India has recently made several policy and institutional measures to encourage and nurture their domestic green finance market. Making sovereign green bonds is an important statement to demonstrate their commitment and desire to fund sustainably. Conversely, the Securities and Exchange Board of India has been pressing to provide more disclosure and transparency and increased integration of the ESG of the listed companies and it is being perceived that there has been increasing climate risk through the perspective of the RBI under the Reserve Bank of India supervision.

Though this is a changing ecosystem in green finance, nonetheless, some structural problems are visible in the green finance environment in India. Investment is more dispersed at renewable energy and climate change mitigation projects-led by global forces- and therefore slightly focused on either of the Sustainable Development Goals 7 and 13. It pays comparatively less attention to social and governance objectives, like healthcare, education, biodiversity preservation, and the development of institutional capacity (Climate Bonds Initiative, 2025). This suggests that the structural problems at question are more work-oriented to longer-term projects, complexity of evaluating their effects, and relative low appeal of risk-return value of social and governance-based investments.

1.3 Conceptual and Key Terms

In order to be consistent and understandable, the current chapter establishes the terms that need to be defined regarding the relationship between green finance and the Sustainable Development Goals (SDGs). This is especially required since in some instances, researchers and government officials speak cross purposes. This aids us to come to a point of agreement as far as we understand the issues of governance, market action and how the results are related in the context of the outlined discourse.

In the context of the current research, Green Finance is not merely a set of financial tools. Green Finance is a more general system that is used to fund and invest differently so as to achieve environmental sustainability, improve climate mitigation and adaptation, and use resources more optimally (Flammer, 2021). It includes structures, frameworks, and practices that form the basis of the sustainability-chasing efforts.

Established in the framework of the United Nations in 2015, the Sustainable Development Goals (SDGs) seem to promote sustainable economic development, social justice and equity, and environmental protection, along with effective governance (UN, 2015). The Sustainable Development Goals are employed in the context of the present study to determine to what level the advancement of green finance would facilitate sustainable development, not solely environmental factors.

Greenwashing is the distortion, exaggeration and selective reporting of sustainability information by financial actors. Poor regulation and inconsistency in reporting standards are also particular contributors to the growth of greenwashing (Dempere et al., 2024). In addressing this study, we will hold that greenwashing is a governance issue at a system level and not an issue of bad ethics at a single instance. Sustainable Finance Taxonomies are defined as the systems of classification which designate the financial activity as either green or sustainable. This will enhance increased transparency, ease of comparison and credibility in financial markets. Taxonomies can reduce greenwashing by eliminating information disparity and reducing asymmetry and show where investors ought to invest. Each of them is introduced as a foundational piece towards comprehending the problems of governance and solutions suggested in the rest of the chapters and advance a coherent and narrowed outlook on green finance and the attainment of Sustainability Goals.

This study contributes by examining green finance alignment through a governance-centered framework, focusing on institutional, regulatory, and market-driven constraints

2. GREEN FINANCE AND RELATED ASPECTS

2.1 Evolution and Conceptual Foundations of Green Finance

Green finance has its origins in broader discussions on sustainable finance and ESG concerns, particularly following global developments such as the Paris Agreement and the introduction of the United Nations Sustainable Development Goals. Since the early 2000s, it has evolved as a mechanism aimed at directing financial resources toward environmentally sustainable and low-carbon activities.

Recent systematic reviews (e.g., Loiola, Kimura, & Souza, 2025) trace the evolution of green financial instruments, including green bonds, sustainability-linked loans, and transition finance instruments. These studies highlight the role of frameworks such as the Green Bond Principles in establishing market norms, while also emphasizing a critical limitation—the lack of globally harmonized standards, which constrains cross-country comparability and market consistency.

More broadly, the literature defines green finance as financial activities oriented toward climate change mitigation, adaptation, and the transition to a low-carbon economy. However, despite its rapid growth, existing research suggests that green finance remains predominantly focused on environmental dimensions, with limited integration of broader sustainable development objectives. This indicates a gap in the literature, where financial innovation and sustainability goals intersect but are not yet fully aligned within a comprehensive development framework.

2.2 Green Finance and Sustainable Development

A central theme in the literature concerns the extent to which green finance contributes to sustainable development outcomes. Bibliometric studies indicate that research in this field has expanded significantly in recent years, with growing attention across regions, sectors, and methodological approaches. For instance, Zhao et al. (2025) identify China, India, and the United Kingdom as leading contributors to green finance research, with key themes focusing on renewable energy investment, climate finance, and SDG-related financing.

Empirical studies on green financial instruments, particularly green bonds, present mixed findings. Research such as Loiola et al. (2025) highlights the presence of a "greenium" in certain mature markets, suggesting that investors may value sustainability attributes. However, the evidence remains inconclusive, as there is no standardized framework for measuring the real impact of these instruments on sustainability outcomes.

Further, Mashari et al. (2023) extend the discussion by linking green finance to carbon trading markets, emphasizing the interdisciplinary nature of the field. This growing integration of financial instruments with environmental markets reflects the increasing diversification of sustainable finance mechanisms. Nevertheless, the literature continues to highlight a key limitation—the lack of consistent methodologies to evaluate the effectiveness of green finance in achieving broader Sustainable Development Goals.

2.3 Taxonomies, Standardization, and Governance Challenges

A recurring theme in the literature is that the credibility and effectiveness of green finance initiatives are constrained by fragmented taxonomies and governance deficiencies. Ehlers, Gao, and Packer (2021) highlight key limitations in sustainable finance taxonomies, including insufficient granularity, inconsistent impact measurement, and weak verification mechanisms. These shortcomings suggest that taxonomies must be directly linked to measurable sustainability outcomes, rather than merely serving as labels that may create confusion among investors.

Recent comparative legal studies further emphasize the importance of establishing strong legal foundations for taxonomy frameworks. Robust legal backing enhances enforceability, improves transparency, and reduces the risk of greenwashing in financial markets. In this context, regulatory clarity becomes essential for maintaining investor confidence and ensuring the credibility of sustainable finance instruments.

Similarly, integrated bibliometric and systematic reviews, such as Mohanty et al. (2023), reveal persistent challenges in the harmonization of ESG integration, reporting standards, and risk management practices. These findings suggest that regulators and supervisors need to align macroprudential and monetary policy frameworks with climate-related risks, thereby strengthening the overall governance structure of green finance systems.

2.4 Governance and Credibility: Addressing Greenwashing and Commitment Deviation

A central concern in the governance literature on green finance is the prevalence of greenwashing, where financial instruments are labelled as environmentally sustainable without delivering corresponding environmental outcomes. Studies focusing on emerging markets similarly highlight structural challenges, including the absence of standardized frameworks, inconsistent disclosure practices, and weak regulatory oversight.

Empirical evidence from green bond governance, particularly in China, further illustrates that these gaps are not merely the result of poor implementation but are rooted in broader structural and institutional deficiencies. This leads to a disconnect between the stated objectives of green financial instruments and their actual environmental impact.

2.5 India-Specific Literature: Opportunities and Barriers

There is a growing body of research on India's green finance landscape; however, in-depth, theory-driven, and cross-country comparative analyses remain limited. Gupta and Gupta (2025) highlight that while India has made notable progress in green bond issuance and sustainability-linked financial instruments, several structural challenges persist, including the absence of a unified national taxonomy, regulatory uncertainties, and the continued risk of greenwashing.

Institutional studies further emphasize that regulatory gaps, coupled with a lack of well-defined incentive mechanisms and limited awareness among financial institutions, particularly banks, constrain the development of green finance in India. This is especially significant in the context of rapidly evolving global standards, which India has yet to fully align with.

Moreover, research on barriers to green financing in India suggests that these challenges are multidimensional, involving infrastructure constraints, investor risk perceptions, and policy inconsistencies. Collectively, these factors influence the pace and scale of sustainable finance adoption, indicating that India's green finance ecosystem is still in a transitional phase requiring stronger institutional and policy support.

Overall, the literature highlights significant progress in green finance but reveals critical gaps in governance, taxonomy harmonization, and multidimensional SDG alignment, which this study seeks to address through a structured analytical framework.

2.6 Identified Research Gaps

Across the reviewed literature, several gaps become evident:

1. Universal taxonomies are not available—there is no integrated international approach to defining and measuring green finance, meaning divergences exist between countries and the risk of greenwashing end
2. Governance gaps: It appears that the enforcement powers are weak and cannot ensure that green financial instruments actually serve sustainable objectives.
3. While evidence from emerging markets is increasing, there is still a gap to be filled-most of the green bond studies emanate from developed countries and much more research is needed on how such instruments fit into and influence the SDGs in India and other emerging markets.
4. Integration of multidimensional SDGs: Much of the literature focuses on climate targets-if one were to take SDG 13 as an example-but fewer analyses go into how green finance contributes to the broader societal and governance goals and the rest of the SDGs.

These gaps underscore the relevance of your research's focus on governance, SDG alignment, and the development of integrated frameworks.

3. RESEARCH METHODOLOGY

3.1 Introduction

In this particular chapter, we are going to explain how we conduct research on green finance in the context of Sustainable Development Goals, particularly focusing on the challenge posed by governance barriers, the problem of fragmented taxonomies, the problem of credibility, and how we can measure the impact. Because of its close ties with policy and the complexity of its domain, we are taking a conceptual and analytical research stance in this particular instance.

Our method involves a critical review of the literature that currently exists, as well as a comparison of rules and policies. Our objective is to integrate academic thinking with institutional knowledge—not by gathering new facts but by reviewing the existing literature of empirical research for spotting patterns, gaps in governance, and systemic barriers to achieving the SDGs. Our method gives a macro-level view of the functioning of green finance instruments in large financial systems.

3.2 Methodological Techniques Employed

3.2.1 Structured Literature Review

The study adopts a structured literature review approach guided by the framework proposed by Tranfield, Denyer, and Smart (2003). To ensure methodological rigor and transparency, the review process follows a systematic sequence of identification, selection, and categorization of relevant literature.

Initially, key search terms were identified to capture the breadth of the research domain, including green finance, Sustainable Development Goals (SDGs), green bonds, taxonomy, governance, and greenwashing. The literature search was conducted using major academic databases such as Scopus, Web of Science, and Google Scholar, covering the publication period from 2015 to 2025 in line with the post-SDG research landscape.

Subsequently, studies were filtered based on predefined criteria, including relevance to the research objectives, publication quality, and citation impact. Priority was given to peer-reviewed journal articles and highly cited institutional reports to ensure credibility and academic robustness. The selected literature was then systematically categorized into key thematic areas, including green finance instruments, SDG alignment, governance structures, taxonomy frameworks, and impact measurement.

Structured literature reviews are particularly valuable in emerging research domains, as they facilitate the identification of converging and diverging perspectives across studies. In the context of green finance, this approach enables a critical understanding of how governance, market mechanisms, and SDG alignment intersect, thereby addressing the limitations of purely descriptive reviews.

3.2.2 Comparative Regulatory and Policy Analysis

To examine the role of governance in shaping green finance outcomes, the study employs a comparative regulatory and policy analysis across selected jurisdictions. This approach allows for the systematic evaluation of how different regulatory frameworks influence the design, implementation, and effectiveness of green finance instruments.

The analysis focuses on three major regions—the European Union, China, and India—chosen for their distinct regulatory approaches and varying stages of sustainable finance development. The comparison is structured around key analytical dimensions, including:

- o Clarity of policy objectives
- o Scope and implementation of sustainable finance taxonomies
- o Disclosure and reporting requirements
- o Strength of enforcement and supervisory mechanisms
- o Degree of alignment with SDG targets

These dimensions serve as evaluative criteria to assess the effectiveness and coherence of regulatory frameworks. Variations across these criteria help explain differences in investor confidence, cross-border capital flows, and long-term sustainability outcomes.

Such comparative approaches are widely used in sustainable finance research to identify best practices and institutional gaps. In this study, the analysis provides a basis for understanding how governance structures influence the alignment of financial flows with broader development objectives.

3.2.3 Conceptual Framework Development

Building on insights derived from the structured literature review and comparative analysis, the study develops a conceptual framework to explain how green finance can better align with the Sustainable Development Goals. Rather than analyzing financial instruments in isolation, the framework adopts a systems-oriented perspective, recognizing that the effectiveness of green finance depends on interconnected governance and institutional factors.

The proposed framework is structured around four key pillars: instrument credibility, taxonomy harmonization, institutional governance, and transparent impact measurement. These components are interdependent and collectively determine the integrity and effectiveness of green finance systems.

- o Instrument credibility focuses on ensuring that financial products labelled as "green" are supported by robust verification and certification mechanisms.
- o Taxonomy harmonization aims to reduce inconsistencies in defining sustainable activities across jurisdictions, thereby improving comparability and transparency.
- o Institutional governance examines the role of regulatory bodies in enforcing standards and ensuring accountability.
- o Transparent impact measurement emphasizes the need to link financial flows to measurable SDG outcomes, shifting the focus from intentions to actual performance.

The use of a conceptual framework is particularly appropriate in areas where empirical evidence is fragmented and difficult to quantify (Jabareen, 2009). Given the evolving nature of green finance and the absence of standardized measurement systems, this framework provides a structured basis for analyzing governance challenges and proposing policy solutions.

3.3 Analytical Framework

The study takes the thematic and interpretive synthesis method and the all the research problems and objectives are united in terms of research results and scope of analysis. Such analytical findings and objectives are not handled as the points on its own but rather as larger themes more akin to what has been proposed by research objectives and issues. It is a matrix structure that helps to locate all these elements together and interconnected: each area of interest concerning research is to be merged with its analytical lenses. Similarly, misalignment in terms of SDGs can be checked by checking sector and goal distribution, risks, and greenwashing can be checked by checking distribution and verification, fragmentation in terms of taxonomy can be checked by checking similarities and regulatory differences, and governance by checking who controls and who is controlled. This offers a good guideline as to how it has continued to be consistent in all its tackling issues- hence the essence of creating a flawless correlation between its research objectives and goals.

3.4 Scope of the Study

The research gives demarcations necessary to a focused and significant analysis giving a scheme of analysis defining a methodology that might be employed. Despite giving a wide presentation of a world picture, it also concentrates on the comparative study of three key players in the process: China, Europe and India. The actors have been chosen on the basis of their impact in enabling sustainable finance as stipulated in their respective regulatory setting.

Among the issues to be discussed, there will be such aspects as financial tools and systems to support the existence of the so-called green finance, and the relationship of the latter with SDGs. Focus will be placed on the level of system and the institution rather than on the performance and financials of individual firms.

As to the period under examination, the investigations rely on the publications and policy projects since 2015, covering the global shift towards the SDGs and marking a shift in how approachable the question of sustainability and finance in the realm of the global stage is. The study does not involve any measurement on financial performance or econometrics, since this was not related to the framework under construct.

3.5 Limitations of the Study

There are a number of known concessions related to this study that are typical of a conceptual and policy-oriented research. To begin with, the analysis is based solely on the secondary information, utilizing both published academic literatures along with the reports of the institutions and policies. Although these sources are often considered to be authoritative, all conclusions are limited by the level, depth, and accessibility of existing research. Second, the research lacks primary empirical research on the form of survey, interviews and statistical modelling. Consequently, the results might not be widely applicable to the micro-level settings, such as individual investor decision making or firm-specific behavior. Nevertheless, this weakness is in line with the objective of the study, which focuses on exploring system-wide governance framework as opposed to firm-based performance.

4. ANALYSIS AND INTERPRETATION

Such large problems that have been taken into consideration in this debate are: misalignment, governance, fragmented taxonomies, and additional accessories like impact measurements and disclosures. In this sense, this discussion considers green finance problems to not be speed bumps, but are caused by pertinent governance problems that are joined to one another. To this extent, this discussion will end with a detailed presentation of the four-pillar structure of governance that will be addressed in subsequent chapters.

4.1 Allocation Patterns of Green Finance and SDG Misalignment

4.1.1 Concentration of Green Finance on Climate-Centric SDGs

The notable connection through the literature is the bias that is found in green finance schemes to provide performance concerning climate-related goals especially SDG7: Affordable and Clean Energy and SDG13: Climate Action. Taking a closer look at the literature on green bonds and sustainability-linked loans, one will discover that the bulk of assets that were financed through these instruments are renewable energy initiatives, energy efficiency programmes, and sustainable and low-carbon transport projects, which are supported in the literature discussed in Flammer, (2021); Climate Bonds Initiative, (2025).

Nevertheless, this very emphasis on climate of the financial services industry leads to a predetermined bias as well. The bias in this exact environment of Green

Finance is based on the fact that the general climate offers a clear-cut, defined investment opportunity that would provide clear, standardized financial metrics that they would follow such as a decrease in carbon production, along with a lower risk profile to the investor. Conversely, an emphasis on the higher-level investments such as poverty alleviation (SDG1), decent education (SDG 4), gender equality (SDG5), and the conservation of biodiversity (SDG15), even though it may offer investment opportunities in the long run not quantifiable in specific dollar amounts, are also not easily communicated within the global financial services industry with the same financial measures needed by an investor to make an investment.

Figure 1. Share of Green Finance (%): Concentration of Green Finance on Climate-Centric SDGs

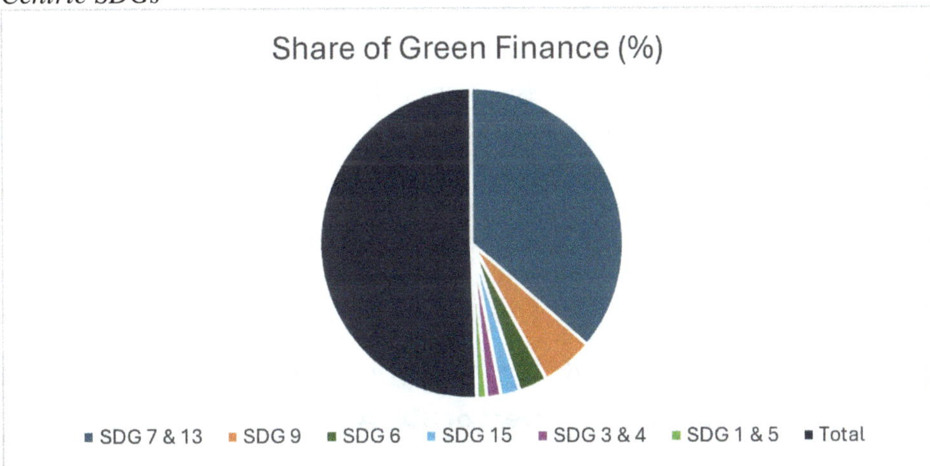

Sources: (i) United Nations (2019-2024): *SDG Financing Gap Reports;* **(ii) OECD (2020)***: Developing Sustainable Finance Definitions and Taxonomies;* **(iii) World Bank (2022)***: Financing in SDGs in Developing Economies*

In such an interpretive analysis, one cannot see that the commitment towards sustainable development as such is a matter of question. The percentages, on the contrary, emphasize that there is in the truth a complex interplay in financial flows in a large measure, at least, that such flows are formed in accordance with financial incentives, measures, and regulation. The practice green finance analysis above shows that, more often than not, green finance practices are more geared to serve environmental, as opposed to social and governance goals that can more easily fit within the financial decision-making policy. All in all, through such analysis, it may be suggested that in its form, green finance appears to be an effective rather effective climate finance than as a financial tool that can aid the implementation of the overall sustainable development agenda.

4.1.2 Structural Drivers of SDG Imbalance

This green financial stream is connected to the emphasis on the climate-sensitive SDGs, and it belongs to the enormous trend according to which the orientation of invested funds and returns to investors are resolved. Within the category of green finance related to the emphasis on climate and energy, one can find renewables, and the endeavour to enhance the current infrastructure of the production and supply of energy to which there are already available technologies, supportive policies and expectations of returns on the invested resources. Social development and nature conservation, on the contrary, are associated with a perceived risk and a notion of returns to invested resources which are often fuzzy.

The ease of measurement of outcomes is another major influencer of the actions of those being invested in and those controlling. This form of simple measurement serves as a sort of nudge mechanism by which it becomes very easy to the nude eye to notice the closing of carbon emissions or even the increase in energy efficiency. Very difficult or ambiguous circumstances are social and governance and any other kind of goals e.g., educational results, enhanced healthcare, gender balance etc. Such challenges are bound to drive many investors into readily measurable environmental performance, thereby promoting climate-appropriate investment choices (Berg et al., 2020).

Figure 2. Structural Drivers of SDG Allocation: Structural Drivers of SDG Imbalance

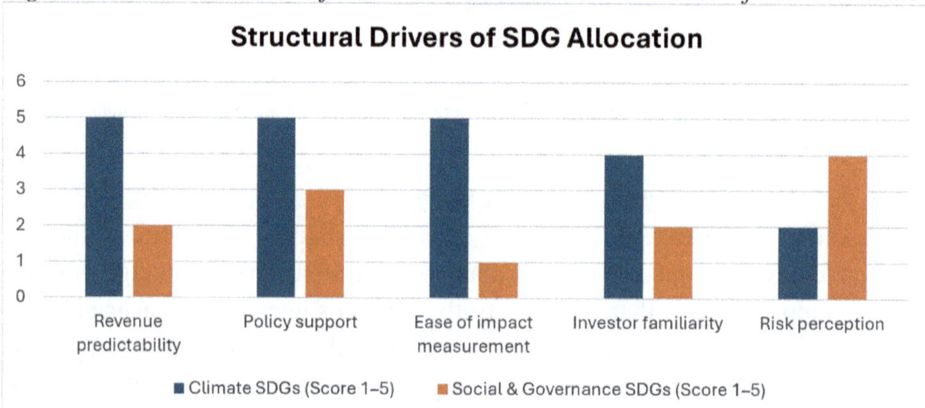

Sources: (i) OECD (2020): *Sustainable Finance, Risk-Return Dynamics;* **(ii) Berg, Koelbel & Rigobon (2020)**: *Aggregate Confusion: The Divergence of ESG Ratings;* **(iii) Ahmet et al. (2023):** *Green Finance and Uneven SDG Alignment*

Such policies and regulations offer incentives that are critical. The existing taxonomies and disclosures of sustainable finance instruments, in general, place a rather low emphasis on social and governance aspects and more emphasis on environmental indicators and climate criteria. This indicates signalling that which is in fact the focus being made: environmental things at best, with less development of Sustainable Development Goals (Ehlers et al., 2021). With all these forces, it is implicit that the markets, as such, fail to make an adequate contribution towards Sustainable Development Goals.

4.2 Governance Deficits and Credibility Risks in Green Finance

4.2.1 Greenwashing as a Systemic Governance Failure

But even more problematic is the fact that greenwashing is not just a single moral failure or a vice committed by a certain company. Instead, it is an inherent issue in the existing form of the green finance markets themselves. Evidence of the disconnect between what companies claim in relation to their sustainability and the actual picture of green and or ESG-tagged financial instruments indicates the existence of poor governance and the presence of greenwashing is widespread.

The first reason is that there is no uniformity in ESG rating and how the rating is calculated. Berg et al. (2020) emphasize that ESG scores can be highly variable across different agencies, which allows the entities to cherry-pick the most desired scores and push the negative environmental and social concerns into the too hard to report basket or underreport the negative environmental and social concerns altogether, and therefore causes a greater level of information asymmetry between the investor and the issuer itself and questions the authenticity of the actual meaning of the green financial products.

In the perspective of interpretative approach to greenwashing, it is no longer the knowing intentions to lie, but it is an aspect of an entire trend of failure in governance. As a consequence of the inability to hold entities accountable, which, in turn, is a benefit of implementing weaker regulations and relying on a voluntary disclosure strategy that gives entities a high level of flexibility in terms of the sustainable reports they can release, greenwashing is a phenomenon where some element of credibility is to be introduced in the entire green finance vocabulary. This also implies that, as a governance issue, greenwashing is a problem-entity phenomenon, as opposed to entity-specific.

4.2.2 Implications for Investor Confidence and Capital Mobilization

The thing is that, although organizations have had to settle on an unalterable scenario in which greenwashing is a hard truth, nonetheless, quantifiable outcomes pertaining to how and to what extent sustainability markets are viewed and financed by investors did exist. When underlying and stretching thin become apparent, one would think, things will ultimately unravel, and investors will be sergeant about these green and ESG investments. It can be characterized by stricter due diligence, lesser reliance on more robust metrics, and, in fact, lesser investment in more of a green and, therefore, riskier investment.

In many instances, such utter devastation of trust impairs the growth potential of green finance in the long-run. In fact, the suggestion that the crisis begins with the so-called credibility of green finance instruments is used to distinguish between the message that is embedded in these financial instruments, i.e. the significance of sustainable decision-making, and other financial problems. Naturally, the underlying message that can be read with this predicament is the value of the aforementioned credibility, in the form of trust, as a tool of necessity in the economic growth where the funding voids that can be spotted within the Sustainable Development Goals can be occupied by the green financial players.

4.3 Fragmented Taxonomies and Cross-Border Inconsistencies

4.3.1 Taxonomy Fragmentation as a Structural Barrier

When we look at these modern green finance modalities, we will come to have the understanding that in any case, they have their share of weaknesses. The green bond catalog printed by China, sustainable finance taxonomy by EU and even those enacted by India to formulate its taxonomy mention terms like green and sustainable. The thing is that they mention these terms in so different ways. As a matter of fact, these structures do have their thresholds and criteria in each of them. This, of course, complicates such an endeavor. The complexity was mentioned in the works of Ehrlers et al. and OECD.

In reality, the EU Taxonomy has held itself to be science-based and implement as an exclude-what-doesn't-harm policy, relying extensively on firm measures towards thresholds, and a do no harm principle. The rest of the world will be tempted to offer concessions to operations required to be adjusted according to regional developmental demands in reference to local energy security. Though they fit the localized requirements, they create a mess at an international level. Conforming to an international standard of testing has become costly.

4.3.2 Implications for Emerging Markets and India

In growth-enabling nations such as India, where growth still remains as a primary concern of near equal concern as most world growth numbers, global policy on sustainability is as much of opportunity as of problem but, under the freedom of manipulating taxation rates, can also select which sustainability items are of greatest priority in the national growth strategies, schedules, and cultural orientations. Nevertheless, that leeway, which eventually reinforces further progress, with fewer standards demanding investments in sometimes ill-matched transitional stages compared to those existing in prosperous countries, exposes countries to the danger of lower thresholds, unfathomable comparisons, and the so-called issue of greenwashing unless governance frameworks are sound (Gupta and Gupta, 2025).

Interpretively, the problem is discussed in how, in the case of emerging economies such as India, the obstacles are not necessarily these standards, but how relevant they feel in their context, and whether they can garner confidence at a global level once more; when an economy gets detached to these world standards to the extent that confidence is losing its grip, access to global sustainability finance can be a source of further complication, rather than a too strict, demanding conformity to these world standards on an economic one.

4.4 Institutional Governance and Regulatory Effectiveness

4.4.1 Role of Public Institutions

Various parts of the world have the role of securing viable and productive sustainable finance infrastructures played by the public institutions. The level of trust rises in such cases where governments actively participate becoming compulsory sustainable disclosures in their area like in India and their sovereign green bond, e.g. (IFC, 2022). This shows the urgency of governments in dealing with questions of trust in the areas especially when it comes to young markets like green finance.

Besides that, though, there is a greater role of public institutions that does not revolve around enforcing rules and norms. Good enforcement mechanisms are essential in ensuring that governance is considered successful as it is important not only to transform the formulations of the sustainability policy into actual practice but also to ensure that there is good coordination among the various government bodies, such as financial, environment and development bodies, to ensure that policy silos are not encountered in the formulations of sustainability policy.

4.5 Impact Measurement, Disclosure, and Accountability

4.5.1 Weaknesses in Current Impact Measurement Practices

The other trend in the trend in green finance reporting literature in the contemporary times reflecting on green finance reports is the trend of disconnections as the green activities that companies are so proud to have made yet few can verify the activities with data found in SDGs (Ahmed et al., 2023).

In the interpretative perspective, the lack of resultant outcome measurements further reduces responsibility, which actually reduces the degree of dependability about sustainability reports. This neutralizes the usefulness and the use of such reports which can in fact be determined as presentational in nature.

4.5.2 Emerging Role of Digital Technologies

This current fact, paired with the recent discourse, has been used to signify that the recent studies have led to exciting opportunities that digital technology, including blockchain technology, can bring in terms of effectively encouraging transparency, traceability, and verifiability of green financial market platforms. This implies that there was a requirement to take into account the fact that credibility and facilitating green financial market systems depend as much as possible on technology like blockchain that will assist in bridging any information gap that may be relevant to credible impact reporting, e.g., with verifiable sustainability outcomes. This implies that technology cannot be a sure way of solving governance flaws or lack of credibility. An illustrative case of this is China where there were no unique requirements, data standardization, and firm control. Effectively, technology was, in fact, optional.

4.6 Synthesis: Interpreting the Four-Pillar Governance Framework

Nonetheless, their study explicitly shows that to the readers, the message is unambiguous: green finance should shift its interest radically, pivot towards a reform that would be governance-driven. It is important to mention that the issues are not independent ones; they are mutually reinforcing and each problem is locking in or other to the other in an interlocking relationship that trades via financial instruments, regulation and reporting. To enable green finance to appreciate genuinely the significance of the United Nations Sustainable Development Goals, to enable it realistically to listen to what action that is called upon, green finance must adopt their theoretical business model.

Four aspects have to be considered. First of all, we have the problems of credibility of the instruments. Direct association between sustainable performance and operational instruments and the brand of green should be the case. Secondly, taxonomy harmonization is a problem. There must be reduction in the ambiguity and also increase the consistency of the same even on cross borders. Nevertheless, it should have also sufficient leeway to cater to diverse development needs. Thirdly, there exist the problems of institutional governance. Sustainable objectives must be centralized or become the essence of a financial regulation/supervision. Last but not least are the problems of transparent impact measurement. The performance needs to be measured through SDG after an intention and / or input measuring.

5. IMPLICATIONS AND RECOMMENDATIONS

5.1 Policy Implications

5.1.1 Reframing Green Finance as a Development Policy Instrument

The biggest lesson that comes out here apparently is that green finances must cease to be solely about market-led innovation and, on the contrary, they must become a central component of policy towards sustainable development. It appears that the results have indicated that there has been an over dependence on voluntary strategies that have in turn resulted in overdependence on climate hence underfunding other sustainable objectives such as social development, biodiversity, and institutional construction. Apparently, Ahmed et al. (2023) and the OECD (2020) have indicated that there is an alleged mistake that has been committed with respect to the application of green finances, namely that there is no need to reform the markets but think that green finances can still be a part of the development policy.

Green finance needs to be incorporated in the national development policy in policy terms where a number of different types of financial incentives are provided in a variety of sustainable development priorities. This must be in the form of definition of green customers to green instruments, identification of public guarantees, and availability of fiscal or taxation incentives, including promotion of social outcomes, protection of biodiversity and good and sustainable governance. The general lesson that has been taught in the economies is that, integrated policy does not only carry more effectiveness in the realization of development outcomes but are also necessary to new heights of financial stability and to cut the financial risks that come with systemic sustainability considerations.

5.1.2 Strengthening Regulatory Mandates to Address Greenwashing

The results on greenwashing as stated in Chapter 4 depict the fact that lack of voluntary disclosure is not enough in bringing honesty through green finance markets. When it is optional that information be posted in relation to sustainability and that all monitoring and enforcement is by more primitive means, it would be easy to misrepresent information by firms. It is the reason why the regulatory bodies need to initiate the effort of making the reporting on sustainability information required and adhering to some reporting framework.

The significance of the existence of the established guidelines on sustainability disclosure is supported by evidence of real-life situations: corporations that have enforceable sustainability disclosure guidelines can count on more confident investors and less on the instances of misleading sustainability information (Berg et al., 2020; Dempere et al., 2024). In the light of the above analysis, policies makers would be interested in making sure that the green financial products are verified by the third party, that the legal implications of such violation of misleading sustainability information should be equal to the seriousness of the violation, and that green financial products are also verified by the third party. These measures, however, would make green finance more than a reputation of enhancement- to become a real verification structure that increases sustainability information basing on actual sustainability outcome performance.

5.1.3 Advancing Taxonomy Harmonization with Contextual Flexibility

This permeates through the case study very much: incomplete sustainable finance taxonomies are a barrier to cross-border green investment, rules are maintained in a state of noncongruence, and comparisons of SDG-oriented flows of financial flows have become complicated. Disagreements in definitions, eligibility standards, and levels drive the expense of investors higher and call into question the integrity of sustainability reports. However, the results also point in the direction that a single world taxonomy may not be a realistic idea-and, possibly, even a desirable one, at least among the emerging economies that have their own development agendas, energy dynamics, and socioeconomic boundaries.

The policy implication A practical policy implication of this paper is to support partial harmonization with references to international standards, like the EU Taxonomy and the Common Ground Taxonomy, but with room to adapt to local conditions. Standardization should not be enforced rudely in that as policymakers, converging towards essential sustainability principles, minimum disclosure standards and minimum environmental standards must be sought. The dialogue, exchange of knowledge and progressive adjustment through the lens of international coordination platforms led by organizations such as OECD and UNEP Finance Initiative does not result in national policy autonomy being compromised.

This would constitute to India a progressive switching into the international taxonomy, along with suppressed domestic regulatory and disclosure obligations. This gradual convergence may assist in raising the confidence of foreign investors and enhance access to cross-border sustainable finance yet retain sufficient flexibility to satisfy development and transition concern of the domestic context. This way, harmonization of taxonomy becomes an enabler and not a hindrance to green finance coma Caine towards the SDGs and hence balances credibility and local relevance.

5.1.4 Enhancing Institutional Governance and Supervisory Capacity

All it comes down to is that green finance works best when the governing bodies are strong, rather than when there exists an elaborate set of instruments with which to conduct business in finance. To ensure a country governs green finance, giving more powers to regulators is not sufficient to the extent that they are able to possess more knowledge in finance in order to control finance effectively in governing finance.

Hence, inclusion of sustainability risk in financial regulation is one of the lessons of this policy. A regulatory framework must recognize and address the risks related to climate changes and the progress in the financial system. Delegation: In addition to establishing policy coherence and accountability, there is an imperative to ensure collaboration between key actors, such as financial regulators, environment regulators, and development institutions because unrelated regulation makes policy less effective. Lastly, permitting central banks to become more actively involved, in climate financial regulation, in stress tests, improvements of disclosure regulations and the employ of macro-prudential policy instruments is highly preferable as it would contribute to the overall sustainability of the systems.

Concerning global policy experience, the institutionalization identified above contributes to the financial systems being better equipped to systemic risk of the climate, as well as leading towards more SDG-directed investment (OECD, 2020; IFC, 2022). Lastly, green finance can serve as an effective instrument of sustainable development only by upgrading the system of governance and oversight.

5.2 Implications for Financial Institutions and Market Participants

5.2.1 Shifting from Compliance

This study presents a definite shift of financial institutions: not only ESG reporting but real-life funding of effective solutions. Simple disclosure box checking that commonly goes along with sustainability reporting mandates is barely water when it comes to pushing actual change toward achievement of the Sustainable Development Goals. There is also a very compliance-focused way of thinking, which perceives sustainability as a form of paperwork instead of a strategic tool in the distribution of capital.

Thus, banks, asset managers, and issuers must establish an open linkage of their financing efforts to particular SDG targets such that investments are directed in a way that would be quantifiable in terms of quantifiable development results. Build in-house impact measurement instruments that conform to the internationally recognized norms to strengthen accountability and build capacity to make decisions. And make a promise to open, performance-driven reporting-not merely telling stories about inputs or intentions-in order to build trust among stakeholders and increase market credibility.

5.2.2 Leveraging Technology for Transparency and Accountability

The deployment of technology like blockchain, AI and real-time reporting may have practical advantageous applications to current abilities of the green finance markets in monitoring, checking and trusting the information underpinning sustainability. They would be the instrument of facilitated reporting on the money disbursement, and have the claims on sustainability been honest. The moral of the story here is simple, though, technology, not in itself, but when it is used within the institution, it becomes useful.

The role of tech in the future of the government is only guaranteed to be bigger when the key players in the market ought to work together in the implementation of their disclosure and monitoring systems which are consistent with the rules and regulations. Such an endeavour is rather significant since this can guarantee standardization and interoperability of systems and monitoring at a glance since the cost can gradually drop (UNEP FI, 2025). Green financial markets can be elevated through the use of tech in good governance.

5.2.3 Implications for Emerging Economies and India

The developing economies like India are really warned that sustainable growth must necessarily be associated and related with growth. India has definitely made some good steps, including the introduction of green bonds and the adoption of regulation, which according to the study, however, there is still a chasm in the field of integrating the SDGs and quantifying their effects. This should occur such that green finance is not confined to climate change.

Green finance when considered in the light of Indian policy must be expanded on the present mandate on renewable energy sources to other areas which are currently under-financed. These are among others of social infrastructure, climate-resilient urban planning and biodiversity conservation. This would be highly advantageous to the enhancement of overseas conformity and [increase its overall appeal as an internationalisation or globalisation project destination as] regards Sustainable Development Goals or SDG investment targets, with a sustainability taxonomy developed at country level that is both internationally-relevant, but has some measure of domesticity. Also, increase in disclosure and verification, which is controlled by the Securities and Exchange Board of India and the Reserve Bank of India, may simultaneously improve integrity and decrease the risks of the greenwashing (Climate Bonds Initiative, 2025).

5.3 Future Research Directions

It seems that there are several roundtables leads to pursue additional research, and these relate to refining our knowledge regarding the association between the outcomes and the Sustainable Development Goals. The methodology of this chapter is more theoretical and focused on government, so the area of the future research may also begin with this foundation.

To start with, investigators can implement empirical impact analyses through the use of the econometric or panel data methods to establish the relationships between green finance stream and particular SDG indicators in various countries or regions. With this kind of research, it can be established whether the actual success of development at the individual regime level can be achieved with increased green finance activity and the different regimes can be compared with regards to governance success.

Second, the level of the firm is worth probing. A micro-level study of the micro-level aspects of governance of financial institutions, which includes incentive schemes, risk management, and internal governance, and disclosure would offer a fascinating addition to the level of enquiry claim, which this work occupies. It would be informative to learn more on the pathways along which institutional acts affect the creation and application of green financial instruments.

Third, wider research regarding the compatibility of technology and sustainable finance is required. This would consider how blockchain, artificial intelligence or real time tools are actually beneficial in the finance processes such as transparency, impact or regulatory compliance. We should also look into the conditions we need to have this technology assist in governance so that we can know which things technology will say it will do, as opposed to what will in reality occur.

6. CONCLUSION

This chapter completes the research with an analysis of the most significant aspects that shall have been achieved as a result of the alignment of green finance and Sustainable Development Goals. The conclusions on the other side of the theories, literature, approach, and interpretation, as introduced in the preceding chapters, are used to pull the research findings into a consistent narrative to bring the research to its climax. Rather than introducing new ideas to the debate, it reiterates the significant themes and state-of-governance notions that the research findings have found.

6.1 Green Finance as a Predominantly Climate-Centric Mechanism

Among the significant things obtained during the above study is the fact that the topic of green finance is mostly climate-related even though it has become very popular perhaps at a very rapid rate and it is also sensible and recognized at a decent level. A superficial overview of the different studies and reports released in the framework of green finance would show that the investment in green finance shifted mostly to climate-related goals like SDG 7: Affordable and Clean Energy, and SDG 13: Climate Action (Flammer, 2021; Climate Bonds Initiative, 2025).

Although the rationale of the prioritization in climate-related objectives in green finance may be valid in terms of the degree of risks that are taken into account, the study indicates that this present prioritization of climate-related objectives has been done at the cost of financing other objectives of sustainable development labelled social, governance, and biodiversity in the Sustainable Development Goals set. Areas such as poverty reduction, health, education, institutional capacity-building, and biodiversity remain within the periphery of the already existing range of green finance mechanisms. All of the above tendencies are suggestive of the fact that green finance as it currently constitutes rather a branch of climate finance than a financing channel in its own, deep in the entire set of goals set by the Sustainable Development Goals (Ahmed et al., 2023).

By wider view, it is evident that, this market structure bias on climate is not just a temporary phenomenon; rather, it is a product of market forms that nonetheless encourage result, measurement, and priority efficiency. Unless there is appropriate intervention by governance to expand the eligibility criteria, SDG, and accountability, green financial investments will still only encourage narrow sustainability outcomes towards transitioning towards green finance. The message is their message to shift green finance to the governance-based approach to development and not any expansion of the market.

6.2 Credibility Deficits and the Systemic Nature of Greenwashing

Among the facts that may be learned after the study, it is essential to note that the associated issues concerning integrity and green washing remain in the market of green financing. Based on literature reviews that were mentioned, it can be learnt that green washing has evolved as an issue that is not merely a manipulation of a few rogue companies. The process itself has certain inherent problems regarding the disclosure writing, the manner the disclosure checks have been conducted, and manner in which the policies have been executed (Dempere et al., 2024; Lagoarde-Ségot, 2024).

These issues of credibility are aggravated by various ESG rating strategies, along with the wide adoption of voluntary disclosing, to mention a few. Since the rating factors cannot be rated consistently, as Berg et al. (2020) elaborated, the problem of selective reporting will arise in the future as the issuers strive to emphasize the good factors but ignore or redirect attention to the bad factors, including the externalities.

In a general sense, the paper argues that credibility is a structural facilitator of growth of green finance. Where there is no credibility, where there is no accountability, the market will have the bad meanings of dilution and implosion. On credibility, such topic is not pushed to the background.

6.3 Fragmented Taxonomies and Institutional Incoherence

Viewing the world through a global lens, there is a single obvious drawback to sustainable finance taxonomies: how we understand sustainability is splintered, and that schism is a practical impediment to cross-border green money and measuring actual impact. EU, China, and the emerging economies have different standards; it is harder and more expensive to comply with them, and the marketplace receives the invitation towards juggling the regulations. All this undermines consistency and trust in green financial markets Where labels lack consistency, investors become weary, and sustainability tags are no longer worthwhile indicators of actual development impact.

The research is not the idealistic ideal in terms of global standardization, it understands that total unification might not be practical since the goals of development, energy systems and institutional capacity are not interchangeable. It still stipulates the argument of increased harmonization on some of the main principles of sustainability. By arriving at mutual definitions of baseline, disclosure standards, and to set minimum environmental and social standards, it will become quite possible to increase transparency, and minimize the uncertainty of investors without disrupting national policy decisions. The convergence to some extent will facilitate comparability between economies with some options left to make at the local implementation level.

Finally, the discussion notes the extent to which institutional coordination is needed to deal with fragmented taxonomy. The multilateral bodies including OECD and UNEP Finance Initiative among others are essential in ensuring the consolidation of these connections as must critical forums of dialogue, harmonization of principles, and drivers towards a more sustainable governance of sustainable finance. These consolidations will have a crucial role to play in reshaping a rather piecemeal character of national strategies into a much more plausible and interoperable worldwide system of SDG-aligned green finance.

6.4 Implications

6.4.1 Policy Contribution

Turning to policy, it is one of the facts that are obvious because of the study that green finance should be incorporated into other developmental strategies at both the national and global levels. The results confirm what has been known since - that good regulatory standards, good taxonomy, and robust disclosure standards are needed in case we are to witness credible and scalable finance in line with the SDGs (IFC, 2022; OECD, 2020). Through its identification of governance deficient areas and those that exhibit the indications of fragmented policies, the report gives the policymakers a strict, systematic mandate to make any transformation of green finance a box-ticking activity and not a developmental one.

6.4.2 Contribution

In the case of banks, funds, and other organizations that invest as well, the implication of the study, as I would suggest, is that it needs to become not about checking the box when it comes to ESG; it needs to become about making a positive impact. The lessons of the case focus on how the element of high standards of sustained financial strength, positive image, and positive risk management practices depend on publicly visible sustainability performance-and not only on disclosures, as suggested by Flammer (2021). The paper describes the governance frameworks to realize good effects using green finance and provide the guidelines to attain investment alignment towards attainment of sustainability.

6.5 Concluding Reflections

To sum up, the example of the research indicates that green finance has the potential in terms of sustainable development but is hindered by the governance and biases and the lack of credibility. However, it is not sufficient to simply scale up green finance instruments, but that should be accompanied by desirable changes at the systemic level through appropriate regulation and actions that can define the outcome.

The connection between green finance and sustainable development agenda in the adoption of the 2030 Agenda will be more crucial than ever in the future. The findings reveal that the combination of government efforts with regulating bodies and the financial sphere is essential to reach a profound connection. Green finance is in need of development and emerge as a theme that is responsible and accountable to facilitate positive and balanced approach to sustainable development.

REFERENCES

Ahmed, S., Khan, M., & Rahman, A. (2023). Green finance and uneven sustainable development goal alignment: Evidence from emerging economies. *Journal of Sustainable Finance & Investment, 13*(4), 985–1006. DOI: 10.1080/20430795.2023.XXXXX

Berg, F., Koelbel, J. F., & Rigobon, R. (2020). Aggregate confusion: The divergence of ESG ratings. *Review of Finance, 24*(4), 919–975. DOI: 10.1093/rof/rfaa015

Climate Bonds Initiative. (2025). *India green finance and bond market update.* https://www.climatebonds.net

Dempere, J., Alamash, E., & Mattos, P. (2024). Unveiling the truth: Greenwashing in sustainable finance. *Frontiers in Sustainability, 5*, 1362051. DOI: 10.3389/frsus.2024.1362051

Flammer, C. (2021). Corporate green bonds. *Journal of Financial Economics, 142*(2), 499–516. DOI: 10.1016/j.jfineco.2021.01.010

Gupta, A., & Gupta, S. (2025). Sustainable finance in India: Progress, policy challenges, and the road ahead. *Journal of Development Policy and Practice, 10*(1), 45–67. DOI: 10.1177/24551333251366743

International Finance Corporation. (2022). *Country climate and development report: India.* World Bank Group. https://www.ifc.org

Lagoarde-Ségot, T., Le Quang, G., & Scialom, L. (2026). Sustainable economic policies: Exploring the effects of ecosystemic macroprudential regulations. *Journal of Post Keynesian Economics, 49*(1), 128–164. DOI: 10.1080/01603477.2025.2544047

Loiola, M., Kimura, H., & Souza, F. (2025). Green finance instruments and market evolution: A systematic review. *Journal of Sustainable Finance & Investment.* Advance online publication. DOI: 10.1080/20430795.2025.XXXXX

Mohanty, S., Das, P., & Sahoo, M. (2023). ESG integration and governance challenges in sustainable finance: A bibliometric review. *Finance Research Letters, 52*, 103476. DOI: 10.1016/j.frl.2023.103476

OECD. (2020). *Developing sustainable finance definitions and taxonomies.* OECD Publishing. https://www.oecd.org

Reserve Bank of India. (2023). *Report on climate-related financial risks.* https://www.rbi.org.in

Tranfield, D., Denyer, D., & Smart, P. (2003). Towards a methodology for developing evidence-informed management knowledge by means of systematic review. *British Journal of Management, 14*(3), 207–222. DOI: 10.1111/1467-8551.00375

United Nations. (2015). *Transforming our world: The 2030 agenda for sustainable development.* https://sdgs.un.org

United Nations. (2023). *Financing for sustainable development report.* https://www.un.org

World Bank. (2022). *Financing the SDGs: Global outlook.* https://www.worldbank.org

Zhao, X., Li, Y., & Wang, S. (2025). Mapping the evolution of green finance research: A bibliometric analysis. *Sustainability, 17*(3), 1124. DOI: 10.3390/su17031124

Compilation of References

Aarthi, S., Ravikumar, R. N., Sobirova, K., & Mamadiyarov, Z. (2025). Empowering a sustainable future through digital learning and the SDGs. In *Harnessing E-Learning to Create a Sustainable Future* (pp. 145–172). IGI Global Scientific Publishing., DOI: 10.4018/979-8-3373-0112-9.ch006

Abban, A. R., & Hasan, M. Z. (2021). Revisiting the determinants of renewable energy investment—New evidence from political and government ideology. *Energy Policy*, *151*, 112184. DOI: 10.1016/j.enpol.2021.112184

Abbass, K., Qasim, M. Z., Song, H., Murshed, M., Mahmood, H., & Younis, I. (2022). A review of the impact of global climate change, adaptation, and sustainable mitigation measures. *Environmental Science and Pollution Research International*, *29*(28), 42539–42559. DOI: 10.1007/s11356-022-19718-6 PMID: 35378646

Abhayawansa, S. (2022). Swimming against the tide: Back to single materiality for sustainability reporting. *Sustainability Accounting Management and Policy Journal*, *13*(6), 1361–1385. DOI: 10.1108/SAMPJ-07-2022-0378

Abhayawansa, S., & Adams, C. (2022). Towards a conceptual framework for non-financial reporting inclusive of pandemic and climate risk reporting. *Meditari Accountancy Research*, *30*(3), 710–738. DOI: 10.1108/MEDAR-11-2020-1097

Abiola-Adams, O., Azubuike, C., Sule, A. K., & Okon, R. (2025). Strategic liquidity management: Best practices for optimizing cash flows in multinational corporations. *Gulf Journal of Advance Business Research*, *3*(1), 143–156. DOI: 10.51594/gjabr.v3i1.71

Acar, E. (2024). ESG integration into financial markets: A comprehensive exploration of concepts and implementation. Çağ Üniversitesi Sosyal Bilimler Dergisi, 20(2), 133–147.

Acar, E. (2024). ESG Integration into Financial Markets: A Comprehensive Exploration of Concepts and Implementation. Çağ Üniversitesi Sosyal Bilimler Dergisi, 20(2), 133-147. https://dergipark.org.tr/cagsbd

Acquah, I. S. K., Baah, C., Agyabeng-Mensah, Y., & Afum, E. (2023). Green procurement and green innovation for green organizational legitimacy and access to green finance: The mediating role of total quality management. *Global Business and Organizational Excellence*, *42*(3), 24–41. DOI: 10.1002/joe.22183

Adeel-Farooq, R. M., Abu Bakar, N. A., & Olajide Raji, J. (2018). Green field investment and environmental performance: A case of selected nine developing countries of Asia. *Environmental Progress & Sustainable Energy*, *37*(3), 1085–1092. DOI: 10.1002/ep.12740

Adeel, M., Wang, B., Ke, J., & Mvitu, I. M. (2025). The nonlinear dynamics of CO_2 emissions in Pakistan: A comprehensive analysis of transportation, electricity consumption, and foreign direct investment. *Sustainability (Basel)*, *17*(1), 189. Advance online publication. DOI: 10.3390/su17010189

Adeneye, Y. B., Kammoun, I., & Ab Wahab, S. N. A. (2023). Capital structure and speed of adjustment: The impact of environmental, social and governance (ESG) performance. *Sustainability Accounting Management and Policy Journal*, *14*(5), 945–977. DOI: 10.1108/SAMPJ-01-2022-0060

Adwani, A. (2025). ESG investing trends in emerging markets: A behavioral finance perspective. SSRN *Electronic Journal*. https://doi.org/DOI: 10.2139/ssrn.5356746

Affolter, B., Ciarla, E., Meyer, J., & Sugandhita, S. (2024). Signaling sustainability: Differential reaction of the stock market following the announcement of sustainabilitylinked bonds. *Finance Research Letters*, *63*, 105261. DOI: 10.1016/j.frl.2024.105261

Aggarwal, S. (2025). SOCIALLY RESPONSIBLE INVESTMENT IN INDIA: A CONCEPTUAL FRAMEWORK Poonam. SSRN *Electronic Journal*. https://doi.org/DOI: 10.2139/ssrn.5206207

Ahmad, F., Boumaiza, A., Sanfilippo, A., & Al-Fagih, L. (2025). A comprehensive review on green finance and its impact on net zero energy transition: From the perspective of renewable energy development. *Energy Strategy Reviews*, *62*, 101948. DOI: 10.1016/j.esr.2025.101948

Ahmed, S., Khan, M., & Rahman, A. (2023). Green finance and uneven sustainable development goal alignment: Evidence from emerging economies. *Journal of Sustainable Finance & Investment, 13*(4), 985–1006. DOI: 10.1080/20430795.2023.XXXXX

Akala, C. S., Neuhaus, T., & Leary-Govender, I. O. (2022). A systematic review of sustainable investment approaches. *International Journal of Economics and Finance, 14*(12), 72. DOI: 10.5539/ijef.v14n12p72

Al frijat, Y. S., Al-Msiedeen, J. M., & Elamer, A. A. (2025). How green credit policies and climate change practices drive banking financial performance. *Business Strategy & Development, 8*(1). DOI: 10.1002/bsd2.70090

Alcorta, P., Escapa, M., & González, P. (2024). Investment risk under different renewable energy support schemes. *Environmental and Resource Economics, 86*(2), 223–249. DOI: 10.1007/s10640024009093

Alessi, L., & Battiston, S. (2022). Two sides of the same coin: Green Taxonomy alignment versus transition risk in financial portfolios. *International Review of Financial Analysis, 84*(102319), 102319. DOI: 10.1016/j.irfa.2022.102319

Alessi, L., Kuszewski, M., & Tettamanzi, P. (2024). Accounting for the EU Green Taxonomy: Exploring its concept, data and analytics. *Accounting Forum, 48*(3), 365–373. DOI: 10.1080/01559982.2024.2369343

Alfaro, L., Chanda, A., Kalemli-Ozcan, S., & Sayek, S. (2004). FDI and economic growth: The role of local financial markets. *Journal of International Economics, 64*(1), 89–112. DOI: 10.1016/S0022-1996(03)00081-3

Alharbi, S. S., Al Mamun, M., Boubaker, S., & Rizvi, S. K. A. (2023). Green finance and renewable energy: Worldwide evidence. *Energy Economics, 118*, 106499. DOI: 10.1016/j.eneco.2022.106499

Allen, F., Qian, J., & Qian, M. (2005). Law, finance, and economic growth in China. *Journal of Financial Economics, 77*(1), 57–116. DOI: 10.1016/j.jfineco.2004.06.010

Alshukri, T., Seun Ojekemi, O., Öz, T., & Alzubi, A. (2024). The interplay of corporate social responsibility, innovation capability, organizational learning, and sustainable value creation: Does stakeholder engagement matter? *Sustainability (Basel), 16*(13), 5511. DOI: 10.3390/su16135511

Álvarez-Ruiz, L., Echeverría King, L. F., Lafont Castillo, T. I., Moreno Garcia, D. E., Herazo Chamorro, M. I., Restrepo Ruiz, M., & De Luque Montaño, O. (2023). Collaboration for the internationalization of research and development: Opportunities for Colombia in the post-pandemic term. *Journal of Higher Education Theory and Practice*, *23*(18), 10–33423. DOI: 10.33423/jhetp.v23i18.6631

Amolo Dr Amolo Elvis Juma, P. (2024). Sustainable financing in infrastructure projects in Kenya. *International Journal of Research and Scientific Innovation*, *XI*(VIII), 597–601. DOI: 10.51244/IJRSI.2024.1108048

Andriuskevicius, K. (2025). Green Investments. In *Societal Challenges and Opportunities of Low-Carbon Energy Transformations* (pp. 333–375). CRC Press. DOI: 10.1201/9781003517481-8

Anku, J. E. (2025). Barriers to renewable energy adoption in Sub-Saharan Africa: a stakeholder perspective. Available at *SSRN* 5087846. DOI: 10.2139/ssrn.5087846

Archer, M. (2019). Sustainable Finance. In Archer, M. (Ed.), *Environmental Science*. Oxford University Press., DOI: 10.1093/obo/9780199363445-0117

Asongu, S. A., Pondie-Messie, T., & Ewolo Bitoto, F. (2025). What role can alternative finance play in Africa's sustainable development trajectories? *Business Strategy & Development*, *8*(3), e70217. Advance online publication. DOI: 10.1002/bsd2.70217

Auzepy, A., Bannier, C. E., & Fecht, F. (2023). Are sustainabilitylinked loans designed to effectively incentivize corporate sustainability? A framework for review. *Financial Management*, *52*(4), 643–675. DOI: 10.1111/fima.12437

Azam, I., Guo, Y., & Lau, C. K. M. (2025). Green finance and ESG readiness: Bridging the gaps in sustainability transitions. *Corporate Social Responsibility and Environmental Management, csr.70191*. DOI: 10.1002/csr.70191

Azhgaliyeva, D., Kapsalyamova, Z., & Saparbayev, A. (2023). Policy support in promoting green bonds in Asia. *Climate Policy*, *23*(4, S1), S1–S18. DOI: 10.1080/14693062.2023.2167800

Azuma, K., & Higashida, A. (2024). Climate change disclosure and evolving institutional investor salience: Roles of the Principles for Responsible Investment. *Business Strategy and the Environment*, *33*(4), 3669–3686. DOI: 10.1002/bse.3649

Babar, Z. N., & Wu, W. (2025). Advancing green finance through FinTech innovations: A conceptual insight into opportunities and challenges. *Journal of Excellence in Management Sciences*, *4*(1). Advance online publication. DOI: 10.69565/jems.v4i1.404

Batjes, N. H.. (2024). Towards a modular, multiecosystem MRV framework for soil organic carbon. *Carbon Management, 15*(1), 2410812. DOI: 10.1080/17583004.2024.2410812

Bauckloh, T., Schaltegger, S., Utz, S., Zeile, S., & Zwergel, B. (2023). Active first movers vs. Late free-riders? An empirical analysis of UN PRI signatories' commitment. *Journal of Business Ethics, 182*(3), 747–781. DOI: 10.1007/s10551-021-04992-0

Berg, F., Kölbel, J. F., & Rigobon, R. (2022). Aggregate confusion: The divergence of ESG ratings. *Review of Finance, 26*(6), 1315–1344. DOI: 10.1093/rof/rfac033

Bernards, N. (2024). Where is finance in the financialization of development? *Globalizations, 21*(1), 88–102. DOI: 10.1080/14747731.2023.2222481

Beteta Vejarano, G., & Swinkels, L. (2023). Social, Sustainability, and Sustainability-Linked Bonds. SSRN *Electronic Journal.* https://doi.org/DOI: 10.2139/ssrn.4420618

Bhattacharya, A., Meltzer, J. T., Oppenheim, J., Qureshi, Z., & Stern, N. (2016). *Delivering on Sustainable Infrastructure for Better Developemnt and Better Climate.* Global Economy and Development. https://www.brookings.edu/wp-content/uploads/2016/12/global_122316_delivering-on-sustainable-infrastructure.pdf

Bialkowski, J. P., Starks, L. T., & Wagner, M. (2024). Cultural values and cross-country differences in responsible investing sectors. SSRN *Electronic Journal.* https://doi.org/DOI: 10.2139/ssrn.4938888

Biktimirov, E. N., & Afego, P. N. (2022). Does investors' valuation of corporate environmental activities vary between developed and emerging market firms? *Finance Research Letters, 47*(102528), 102528. DOI: 10.1016/j.frl.2021.102528

Bloomberg, N. E. F. (2024). *Global trends in sustainable finance and investment.* Bloomberg Finance L.P.

Boffo, R., & Patalano, R. (2020). *ESG investing: Practices, progress and challenges.* OECD Publishing., DOI: 10.1787/8fca8c5f-

Bolton, P., & Kacperczyk, M. (2021). Do investors care about carbon risk? *Journal of Financial Economics, 142*(2), 517–549. DOI: 10.1016/j.jfineco.2021.05.008

Borensztein, E., De Gregorio, J., & Lee, J. W. (1998). How does foreign direct investment affect economic growth? *Journal of International Economics, 45*(1), 115–135. DOI: 10.1016/S0022-1996(97)00033-0

Bouchmel, I., & Omri, A. (2025). From loss to investment: How environmental monetary losses influence green investment in Eastern European SMEs? *Corporate Social Responsibility and Environmental Management, 32*(6), 7221–7234. DOI: 10.1002/csr.70086

Bougrea, A., & Vermeiren, M. (2025). Rolling out the Wall Street Consensus? Multilateral development banks and the trilemma of private capital mobilization. *Competition & Change, 10245294251343426*, 10245294251343426. Advance online publication. DOI: 10.1177/10245294251343426

Bouncken, R. B., Fredrich, V., Sinkovics, N., & Sinkovics, R. R. (2023). Digitalization of cross-border R&D alliances: Configurational insights and cognitive digitalization biases. *Global Strategy Journal, 13*(2), 281–314. DOI: 10.1002/gsj.1469

Bowley, T., & Hill, J. G. (2024). The global ESG stewardship ecosystem. *European Business Organization Law Review, 25*(2), 229–268. DOI: 10.1007/s40804-024-00316-7

Briera, T., & Lefèvre, J. (2024). Reducing the cost of capital through international climate finance to accelerate the renewable energy transition in developing countries. *Energy Policy, 188*, 114104. DOI: 10.1016/j.enpol.2024.114104

Buchanan, B., Silvola, H., & Vähämaa, E. (2024). Sustainability and private investors. *European Journal of Finance*, •••, 1–28. DOI: 10.1080/1351847X.2024.2362282

Buchner, B. K., Clark, A., Falconer, A., Macquarie, R., Meattle, C., Tolentino, R., & Wetherbee, C. (2019). *Global landscape of climate finance 2019*. Climate Policy Initiative.

Bunch, B., & Strauss, R. P. (2025). Evolution of U.s. state and local government green bond issuance. *Public Finance Journal, 2*(1), 56–72. DOI: 10.59469/pfj.2025.34

Bu, Y., Du, X., & Li, H. (2025). From digital finance to green growth: The role of FinTech in sustainable manufacturing. *Applied Economics*, •••, 1–17. DOI: 10.1080/00036846.2025.2560685

Bylo, A. (2025). Assessing the impact of green finance on sustainability in emerging markets: Trends, challenges, and future prospects (2000–present). *International Scientific Journal Monte, 10*(1). Advance online publication. DOI: 10.33807/monte.20253288

Cai, C. (2025). Crisis and Opportunity: Promoting Global Cooperation for Sustainable Development to Achieve a Greener Future. *Advances in Economics. Management and Political Sciences, 154*(1), 1–6. DOI: 10.54254/2754-1169/2024.19530

Calcaterra, M., Aleluia Reis, L., Fragkos, P., Briera, T., Boer, H. S., Egli, F., Emmerling, J., Iyer, G., Mittal, S., Polzin, F., Sanders, M., Schmidt, T. S., Serebriakova, A., & Steffen, B. (2024). Reducing the cost of capital to finance the energy transition in developing countries. *Nature Energy*, *9*(10), 1241–1251. DOI: 10.1038/s41560-024-01606-7 PMID: 39450347

Calcaterra, M., Ameli, N., & Hallett, T. B. (2024). Reducing the cost of capital to finance the energy transition. *Nature Communications*, *15*, 5469. DOI: 10.1038/s41467024506454 PMID: 39450347

Cao, Y., Li, H., & Su, L. (2024). A dynamic performancebased payment mechanism for PPP projects: An integrated principal–agent and multiobjective optimization model. *International Journal of Strategic Property Management*, *28*(2), 116–129. DOI: 10.3846/ijspm.2024.21183

Cao, Y., Li, H., Su, L., Zhang, W., & Zhang, C. (2024). Deciphering the difference puzzle of risksharing: A comparative analysis of infrastructure PPP development within China and US. *Project Leadership and Society*, *5*(2), 100135. DOI: 10.1016/j.plas.2024.100135

Casady, C. B., Cepparulo, A., & Giuriato, L. (2024). Public-private partnerships for low-carbon, climate-resilient infrastructure: Insights from literature. *Journal of Cleaner Production*, *470*, 143338. DOI: 10.1016/j.jclepro.2024.143338

Castelblanco, G., ArboledaCastrillón, L., & Bastidas, A. (2024). Financial system dynamics model for servicefee road PPPs. *Construction Management and Economics*, *42*(9–10), 893–912. DOI: 10.1080/01446193.2024.2335566

Caverzasi, E., & Godin, A. (2015). Stock-flow consistent modeling through the ages. *Cambridge Journal of Economics*, *39*(1), 157–181. DOI: 10.1093/cje/beu021

Cepparulo, A., Eusepi, G., & Giuriato, L. (2024). Public Finance, Fiscal Rules and Public–Private Partnerships: Lessons for Post-COVID-19 Investment Plans. *Comparative Economic Studies*, *66*(1), 191–213. DOI: 10.1057/s41294-023-00213-x PMID: 37359136

Chang, X., Fu, K., Jin, Y., & Liem, P. F. (2022). Sustainable finance: ESG/CSR, firm value, and investment returns. *Asia-Pacific Journal of Financial Studies*, *51*(3), 325–371. DOI: 10.1111/ajfs.12379

Chataraju, T. (2025). The evolution of sustainable finance in fixed-income indices: Challenges, opportunities, and future directions. *European Journal of Computer Science and Information Technology*, *13*(33), 30–42. DOI: 10.37745/ejcsit.2013/vol13n333042

Cheng, G., Ehlers, T., Packer, F., & Xiao, Y. (2024, June). *Sovereign green bonds: A catalyst for sustainable debt market development?* [BIS Working Papers No 1198]. Monetary and Economic Department, BIS. https://doi.org/https://www.bis.org/publ/work1198.pdf

Chen, R., & Zhang, T. (2025). Artificial intelligence applications implication for ESG performance: Can digital transformation of enterprises promote sustainable development? *Chinese Management Studies*, *19*(3), 676–701. DOI: 10.1108/CMS-11-2023-0653

Chen, R., Zhou, N., & Liu, Q. (2024). Impact of implicit government guarantee on the credit spread of urban construction investment bonds. *Financial Innovation*, *10*(1), 72. DOI: 10.1186/s40854-024-00722-3

Chen, S., & Fan, M. (2024). ESG ratings and corporate success: Analyzing the environmental governance impact on Chinese companies' performance. *Frontiers in Energy Research*, *12*, 1371616. Advance online publication. DOI: 10.3389/fenrg.2024.1371616

Chen, X., & Long, W. (2023). To enhance the credibility of the Green bond market through regulating GBERs: The case of China. *Laws*, *12*(6), 91. DOI: 10.3390/laws12060091

Chen, X., Weber, O., & Saravade, V. (2022). Does it pay to issue green? An institutional comparison of Mainland China and Hong Kong's stock markets toward green bonds. *Frontiers in Psychology*, *13*, 833847. DOI: 10.3389/fpsyg.2022.833847

Chen, Y., Che, Z., & Wan, D. (2024). How does the financial technology innovation of the regulatory pilot influence financial regulation? *Finance Research Letters*, *69*, 106255. DOI: 10.1016/j.frl.2024.106255

Cherkasova, V., Fedorova, E., & Stepnov, I. (2023). Market reaction to firms' investments in CSR projects. *Journal of Economics, Finance and Administrative Science*, *28*(55), 44–59. DOI: 10.1108/JEFAS-08-2021-0150

Chien, F., Chau, K. Y., Ady, S. U., Zhang, Y., Tran, Q. H., & Aldeehani, T. M. (2021). Does the combining effects of energy and consideration of financial development lead to environmental burden: Social perspective of energy finance? *Environmental Science and Pollution Research International*, *28*(30), 40957–40970. DOI: 10.1007/s11356-021-13423-6 PMID: 33772718

Chipalkatti, N., Le, Q. V., & Rishi, M. (2021). Sustainability and society: Do environmental, social, and governance factors matter for foreign direct investment? *Energies*, *14*(19), 6039. DOI: 10.3390/en14196039

Choy, S. K., Koci, I., & Wang, M. (2023). Does social capital foster sustainable investment? *European Financial Management*, *29*(3), 799–840. DOI: 10.1111/eufm.12376

Chrzan, S., & Pott, C. (2024). The steering effect of the EU taxonomy: Evidence from German institutional and retail investors. *Review of Financial Economics*, *42*(4), 349–375. DOI: 10.1002/rfe.1213

Chrzan, S., Sokolowska, E., & Dziwinski, P. (2024). Investor judgment based on the EU Taxonomy. *Review of Quantitative Finance and Accounting*, *63*(4), 1511–1548. Advance online publication. DOI: 10.1007/s11156-024-01297-x

Clark, G. L., Feiner, A., & Viehs, M. (2015). From the stockholder to the stakeholder: How sustainability can drive financial outperformance. *Available at SSRN* 2508281.

Climate Bonds Initiative. (2025). *India green finance and bond market update*. https://www.climatebonds.net

Climate Policy Initiative. (2024). *Global landscape of climate finance 2024*. https://www.climatepolicyinitiative.org/wpcontent/uploads/2024/10/GlobalLandscapeofClimateFinance2024.pdf

Climate Policy Initiative. (2025). Cost of Capital for Renewable Energy Investments in Developing Countries.

Cunha, F. A. F. de S., Meira, E., & Orsato, R. J. (2021). Sustainable finance and investment: Review and research agenda. *Business Strategy and the Environment*, *30*(8), 3821–3838. DOI: 10.1002/bse.2842

Dafermos, Y., Nikolaidi, M., & Galanis, G. (2016). A stock–flow–fund ecological macroeconomic model. *Ecological Economics*, *131*, 191–207. DOI: 10.1016/j.ecolecon.2016.08.013

Dafermos, Y., Nikolaidi, M., & Galanis, G. (2018). Climate change, financial stability and monetary policy. *Ecological Economics*, *152*, 219–234. DOI: 10.1016/j.ecolecon.2018.05.011

Danila, N. (2022). Random walk of socially responsible investment in emerging market. *Sustainability (Basel)*, *14*(19), 11846. DOI: 10.3390/su141911846

Darsono, D., Hersugondo, H., Yuniawan, A., Kusumaningrum, H. P., Latan, H., & Ali, M. (2025). Linking green finance to sustainability performance: the mediating role of CSR and the moderating effect of stakeholder pressures. *Journal of Economic and Administrative Sciences*, 1–20. DOI: 10.1108/JEAS-04-2025-0221

Dasinapa, M. B. (2024). The integration of sustainability and ESG accounting into corporate reporting practices. *Advances in Applied Accounting Research*, *2*(1), 13–25. DOI: 10.60079/aaar.v2i1.167

de Freitas Netto, S. V., Sobral, M. F. F., Ribeiro, A. R. B., & Soares, G. R. D. L. (2020). Concepts and forms of greenwashing: A systematic review. *Environmental Sciences Europe*, *32*(1), 19. DOI: 10.1186/s12302-020-0300-3

de Villiers, C., La Torre, M., & Molinari, M. (2022). The Global Reporting Initiative's (GRI) past, present and future: Critical reflections and a research agenda on sustainability reporting (standard-setting). *Pacific Accounting Review*, *34*(5), 728–747. DOI: 10.1108/PAR-02-2022-0034

Debnath, A., Panwar, M., Jategaonkar, S., Rathod, M., Neema, R., & Iqbal, R. (2024). Green investors' strategies and their role in supporting sustainable development through impact investing. *African Journal of Biomedical Research*, *27*(4S), 4675–4683. DOI: 10.53555/AJBR.v27i4S.4459

Demir, M., & Min, M. K. (2021). A comparative analysis of sustainability reports published by global enterprises: Standalone CSR versus integrated reporting. *The BRC Academy Journal of Business*, *11*(1), 23–51. DOI: 10.15239/j.brcacadjb.2021.11.01.ja02

Dempere, J., Alamash, E., & Mattos, P. (2024). Unveiling the truth: Greenwashing in sustainable finance. *Frontiers in Sustainability*, *5*, 1362051. DOI: 10.3389/frsus.2024.1362051

Demski, J., Dong, Y., McGuire, P., & Mojon, B. (2025). *Growth of the green bond market and greenhouse gas emissions* (BIS Quarterly Review) [Review]. BIS. https://www.bis.org/publ/qtrpdf/r_qt2503d.pdf

Dervi, U. D., Khan, A., Saba, I., Hassan, M. K., & Paltrinieri, A. (2022). Green and socially responsible finance: Past, present and future. *Managerial Finance*, *48*(8), 1250–1278. DOI: 10.1108/MF-11-2021-0561

Desalegn, G., & Tangl, A. (2022). Enhancing green finance for inclusive green growth: A systematic approach. *Sustainability (Basel)*, *14*(12), 7416. DOI: 10.3390/su14127416

Deschryver, P., & de Mariz, F. (2020). What future for the Green bond market? How can policymakers, companies, and investors unlock the potential of the Green bond market? *Journal of Risk and Financial Management*, *13*(3), 61. DOI: 10.3390/jrfm13030061

Devender, Kafila, & Manoharan, G. (2025). Green finance for sustaining tomorrow. In *Legal and Regulatory Considerations of Leveraging Sustainable Finance* (pp. 135–152). IGI Global. DOI: 10.4018/979-8-3373-0350-5.ch006

Devi, D. S. (2023). Green finance: A way towards sustainable India. *Asian Journal of Management and Commerce*, *4*(2), 231–237. DOI: 10.22271/27084515.2023.v4.i2c.214

Di Vaio, A., Hassan, R., Chhabra, M., Arrigo, E., & Palladino, R. (2022). Sustainable entrepreneurship impact and entrepreneurial venture life cycle: A systematic literature review. *Journal of Cleaner Production*, *378*, 134469. DOI: 10.1016/j.jclepro.2022.134469

Dikau, S., & Volz, U. (2021). Central bank mandates, sustainability objectives and the promotion of green finance. *Ecological Economics*, *184*, 107022. DOI: 10.1016/j.ecolecon.2021.107022

Dimpal Mohanbhai AhirRinkeshkumar Ganpatsinh Mahida. (2025). Green finance and sustainable investment strategies: Catalyzing a low-carbon global economy. *Vidhyayana*, *11*(si1), 72–95. DOI: 10.58213/8zrfw907

Distadio, L. F., & Johl, S. (2025). Shades of green in the bond market: The role of external verification reports. *The International Journal of Accounting*, *2541001*, 2541001. Advance online publication. DOI: 10.1142/S109440602541001X

Dutta, A., & Paul, B. (2023). Performance analysis of select ESG funds in India. *Management Journal for Advanced Research*, *3*(1), 1–7. DOI: 10.54741/mjar.3.1.1

Ecklu, J., et al. (2025). Digital MRV technologies for the voluntary carbon market. *ACS ES&T Letters*, *12*(x), e01048. https://doi.org/DOI: 10.1021/acs.estlett.4c01048

Edeminam, B., V., & Akpasoh, A. (2023). Climate finance landscape in Nigeria. *Resourceedings*, *3*(1), 13–21. DOI: 10.21625/resourceedings.v3i1.945

Egli, F. (2020). Renewable energy investment risk: An investigation of changes over time and the underlying drivers. *Energy Policy*, *140*, 111428. DOI: 10.1016/j.enpol.2020.111428

Elhady, A. M., & Shohieb, S. (2025). AI-driven sustainable finance: Computational tools, ESG metrics, and global implementation. *Future Business Journal*, *11*(1), 209. Advance online publication. DOI: 10.1186/s43093-025-00610-x

Emamian, S., Rahimian, F. P., Awang, M., & Dhingra, D. (2023). Unlocking the commercialisation process for academic ideas and their global market impact. *Law and Business*, *3*(1), 42–52. DOI: 10.2478/law-2023-0004

Emeka-Okoli, S., Nwankwo, T. C., Otonnah, C. A., & Nwankwo, E. E. (2024). Corporate governance and CSR for sustainability in Oil and Gas: Trends, challenges, and best practices: A review. *World Journal of Advanced Research and Reviews, 21*(3), 078–090. https://doi.org/DOI: 10.30574/wjarr.2024.21.3.0662

Emodi, N. V., Rekker, S., Greig, C., Wade, B., Inekwe, J. N., & Zakari, A. (2023). The contribution of cross-border capital flow towards decarbonisation. *Journal of Cleaner Production, 405*, 137040. Advance online publication. DOI: 10.1016/j.jclepro.2023.137040

Energy Transitions Commission. (2023). Financing the transition to a net-zero economy. *Etc.; a Review of General Semantics.*

Eskantar, M., Zopounidis, C., Doumpos, M., Galariotis, E., & Guesmi, K. (2024). Navigating ESG complexity: An in-depth analysis of sustainability criteria, frameworks, and impact assessment. *International Review of Financial Analysis, 95*(103380), 103380. DOI: 10.1016/j.irfa.2024.103380

European Commission. (2020). Study on environmental claims in the EU. https://environment.ec.europa.eu/topics/circular-economy-topics/green-claims_en

Ewis, H. F. M., & Ghanem, S. A. (2025). The economic implications of integrating green accounting practices in Middle Eastern financial institutions: Challenges and opportunities. *Edelweiss Applied Science and Technology*, *9*(3), 1299–1308. DOI: 10.55214/25768484.v9i3.5519

Eyo-Udo, N. L., Agho, M. O., Onukwulu, E. C., Sule, A. K., & Azubuike, C. (2024). Advances in green finance solutions for combating climate change and ensuring sustainability. *Gulf Journal of Advance Business Research*, *2*(6), 338–375. DOI: 10.51594/gjabr.v2i6.53

Farooq, B., Nazir, A., Farooq, M., & Anjum, S. (2025). Green Growth in Sustainable Environment and Future Outlook. In Parray, J. A., Shameem, N., & Haghi, A. K. (Eds.), *Environmental Landscape and Sustainable Biodiversity for Healthy Green Growth* (pp. 147–154). Springer Nature Switzerland., DOI: 10.1007/978-3-031-75405-0_15

Farounbi, B. O., Okafor, C. M., & Oguntegbe, E. E.Blessing Olajumoke FarounbiChizoba Michael OkaforEsther Ebunoluwa Oguntegbe. (2025). Macroeconomic modeling framework supporting strategic allocation of private credit across global markets. *International Journal of Advanced Economics*, *7*(9), 287–305. DOI: 10.51594/ijae.v7i9.2058

Feldhütter, P., Halskov, K., & Krebbers, A. (2024). Pricing of sustainability-linked bonds. *Journal of Financial Economics, 162*, 103944. DOI: 10.1016/j.jfineco.2024.103944

Feng, G.-F., Niu, P., Wang, J.-Z., & Liu, J. (2022). Capital market liberalization and green innovation for sustainability: Evidence from China. *Economic Analysis and Policy, 75*, 610–623. DOI: 10.1016/j.eap.2022.06.009

Fisher, S., Blau, A., Kantrowitz-Gordon, I., & Gendler, Y. (2024). Academic boycotts of Israel: A narrative review. *Israel Affairs, 30*(5), 1–13. DOI: 10.1080/13537121.2024.2394307

Flammer, C. (2020). Green bonds: Effectiveness and implications for public policy. *Environmental and Energy Policy and the Economy, 1*, 95–128. DOI: 10.1086/706794

Flammer, C. (2021). Corporate green bonds. *Journal of Financial Economics, 142*(2), 499–516. DOI: 10.1016/j.jfineco.2021.01.010

Fleta-Asín, J., & Muñoz, F. Fleta Asín. (2024). Risk allocation schemes between public and private sectors in green energy projects. *Journal of Environmental Management, 357*, 120650. DOI: 10.1016/j.jenvman.2024.120650 PMID: 38569262

Fligstein, N., & Huang, J. Z. (2025). Finance in sustainable transition: A comparative review across institutional investors, asset managers, venture capital, insurance, and bonds. *Wiley Interdisciplinary Reviews: Climate Change, 16*(4), e70012. Advance online publication. DOI: 10.1002/wcc.70012

Folqué, M., Escrig-Olmedo, E., & Corzo Santamaría, M. T. (2023). Contribution of sustainable investment to sustainable development within the framework of the SDGS: The role of the asset management industry. *Sustainability Accounting Management and Policy Journal, 14*(5), 1075–1100. DOI: 10.1108/SAMPJ-01-2022-0044

Fornasari, T., & Traversi, M. (2024). The impact of the CSRD and the ESRS on non-financial disclosure. *Symphonya Emerging Issues in Management, 1*(1), 117–133. DOI: 10.4468/2024.1.07fornasari.traversi

Frecautan, I. (2022). Performance of Green Bonds in Emerging Capital Markets: An Analysis of Academic Contributions. *Journal of Corporate Finance Research / Корпоративные Финансы | ISSN: 2073-0438, 16*(3), 111–130. https://doi.org/ DOI: 10.17323/j.jcfr.2073-0438.16.3.2022.111-130

Freudenreich, B., Lüdeke-Freund, F., & Schaltegger, S. (2020). A stakeholder theory perspective on business models: Value creation for sustainability. *Journal of Business Ethics, 166*(1), 3–18. DOI: 10.1007/s10551-019-04112-z

Friede, G., Busch, T., & Bassen, A. (2015). ESG and financial performance: Aggregated evidence from more than 2000 empirical studies. *Journal of Sustainable Finance & Investment*, *5*(4), 210–233. DOI: 10.1080/20430795.2015.1118917

Fu, C., Lu, L., & Pirabi, M. (2023). Advancing green finance: A review of sustainable development. *Digital Economy and Sustainable Development*, *1*(1), 20. Advance online publication. DOI: 10.1007/s44265-023-00020-3

Fu, J., & Ng, A. W. (2021). Scaling up renewable energy assets: Issuing green bond via structured public-private collaboration for managing risk in an emerging economy. *Energies*, *14*(11), 3076. DOI: 10.3390/en14113076

Gabor, D. (2021). The Wall Street Consensus. *Development and Change*, *52*(3), 429–459. DOI: 10.1111/dech.12645

Gambetta, N., Azcárate-Llanes, F., Sierra-García, L., & García-Benau, M. A. (2021). Financial institutions' risk profile and contribution to the Sustainable Development Goals. *Sustainability (Basel)*, *13*(14), 7738. DOI: 10.3390/su13147738

Gamso, J., & Dimitrova, A. (2024). Rewarding a friend: Does the World Bank direct noncommercial risk insurance to countries that support US foreign policy interests? *New Political Economy*, *29*(1), 159–172. DOI: 10.1080/13563467.2023.2230557

Gangi, F., Meles, A., D'Angelo, E., & Daniele, L. M. (2019). Sustainable development and corporate governance in the financial system. *Corporate Governance (Bradford)*, *19*(6), 1177–1198. DOI: 10.1108/CG-02-2019-0052

Garg, A., & Arora, S. (2023). The challenges of the impact investing: A systematic review of literature and future research agenda. *Russian Law Journal*, *11*(3), 760–793.

Garg, A., Goel, P., Sharma, A., & Rana, N. P. (2022). As you sow, so shall you reap: Assessing drivers of socially responsible investment attitude and intention. *Technological Forecasting and Social Change*, *184*(122030), 122030. DOI: 10.1016/j.techfore.2022.122030

Gatzert, N., & Kosub, T. (2017). Determinants of policy risks of renewable energy investments. *International journal of energy sector management, 11*(1), 28-45.

Gatzert, N., & Vogl, N. (2016). Evaluating investments in renewable energy under policy risks. *Energy Policy*, *95*, 238–252. DOI: 10.1016/j.enpol.2016.04.027

Gea, M., Sadalia, I., & Absah, Y. (2024). *Genealogy and implementation of green finance in Asia and Indonesia*. KnE Social Sciences., DOI: 10.18502/kss.v9i2.14926

Ge, H. (2025). Green Bond Policy and Corporate ESG Performance. *Advances in Economics. Management and Political Sciences*, *156*(1), 40–52. DOI: 10.54254/2754-1169/2025.20399

Geissdoerfer, M., Savaget, P., Bocken, N. M. P., & Hultink, E. J. (2017). The Circular Economy – A new sustainability paradigm? *Journal of Cleaner Production*, *143*, 757–768. DOI: 10.1016/j.jclepro.2016.12.048

George, T. E.. (2020). An evaluation of the environmental impact assessment system in Ghana. *Heliyon*, *6*(9), e04936. Advance online publication. DOI: 10.1016/j.heliyon.2020.e04758

Gevorkova, V., Sangiorgi, I., & Vogt, J. (2024). Cleansing investor's conscience: The effects of incidental guilt on Socially Responsible Investment decisions. *Journal of Business Ethics*, *193*(1), 89–114. DOI: 10.1007/s10551-023-05585-9

Gifford, J. L., Wang, Y., & Ma, H. (2024). What triggers PPP renegotiations? Evidence from U.S. highway concessions. *Public Management Review*, *26*(10), 1850–1877. DOI: 10.1080/14719037.2023.2200404

Giroud, A. (2024). World Investment Report 2023: Investing in sustainable energy for all. *J Int Bus Policy*, *7*(1), 128–131. DOI: 10.1057/s42214-023-00178-9

Globerman, S., & Shapiro, D. (2003). Governance infrastructure and US foreign direct investment. *Journal of International Business Studies*, *34*(1), 19–39. DOI: 10.1057/palgrave.jibs.8400001

Godley, W., & Lavoie, M. (2007). *Monetary economics: An integrated approach to credit, money, income, production and wealth*. Palgrave Macmillan. DOI: 10.1057/9780230626546

Goffetti, G., Böckin, D., Baumann, H., Tillman, A., & Zobel, T. (2022). Towards sustainable business models with a novel life cycle assessment method. *Business Strategy and the Environment*, *31*(5), 2019–2035. DOI: 10.1002/bse.3005

Gorski, A.-T., & Ranf, E.-D. (2024). Sustainability trends and dynamics: An integrative approach to economic, social, and environmental perspectives. *Science Bulletin*, *29*(1), 46–60. DOI: 10.2478/bsaft-2024-0006

Granoff, I., Hogarth, J. R., & Miller, A. (2016). Nested barriers to low-carbon infrastructure investment. *Nature Climate Change*, *6*(12), 1065–1071. DOI: 10.1038/nclimate3142

Grübler, A., Krey, V., & Napp, T. (2018). Technical and economic barriers for renewable energy deployment: The importance of infrastructure and coordination. *Energy Policy*, *113*, 1–10. DOI: 10.1016/j.enpol.2017.10.001

Guisande, D. P., Harjoto, M. A., Hoepner, A. G. F., & O'Sullivan, C. (2024). Ethics and banking: Do banks divest their kind? *Journal of Business Ethics*, *192*(1), 191–223. DOI: 10.1007/s10551-023-05476-z

Guo, X., Ma, J., Feng, Y., & Chen, B. (2023). Green credit policy and short-term financing for long-term investment: Evidence from China's heavily polluting enterprises. *Sustainability (Basel)*, *15*(24), 16804. DOI: 10.3390/su152416804

Guo, Y., Chen, C., Luo, X., & Martek, I. (2024). Determining concessionary items for "availability paymentonly" PPP projects: A holistic framework integrating value for money and social values. *Journal of Civil Engineering and Management*, *30*(2), 149–167. DOI: 10.3846/jcem.2024.20841

Gupta, A., & Gupta, S. (2025). Sustainable finance in India: Progress, policy challenges, and the road ahead. *Journal of Development Policy and Practice*, *10*(1), 45–67. DOI: 10.1177/24551333251366743

Haldar, S., Hoffman, J., Verma, M., Peddibhotla, A., & Bazaz, A. (2024). Reimagining energy infrastructure for justice: Power, politics, and institutional work in India's 2.05 GW Pavagada solar park. *Energy Research & Social Science*, *116*, 103645. DOI: 10.1016/j.erss.2024.103645

Hecht, A., & Lampenius, N. (2023). How do firms manage their foreign exchange exposure? *Journal of Risk and Financial Management*, *16*(8), 359. DOI: 10.3390/jrfm16080359

Hilbrandt, H., & Grubbauer, M. (2020). Standards and SSOs in the contested widening and deepening of financial markets: The arrival of Green Municipal Bonds in Mexico City. *Environment & Planning A*, *52*(7), 1415–1433. DOI: 10.1177/0308518X20909391

Hodge, G. A., & Greve, C. (2017). On Public–Private Partnership Performance: A Contemporary Review. *Public Works Management & Policy*, *22*(1), 55–78. DOI: 10.1177/1087724X16657830

Hong, J. (2025). The evolving role of ESG in investment decisions: From financing cost implications. *Advances in Economics. Management and Political Sciences*, *223*(1), 53–61. DOI: 10.54254/2754-1169/2025.GL27875

Hou, L., Yang, F., Liang, W., Wu, C., & Song, J. (2024). Government subsidy and benefit distribution mechanisms for transportation PPP projects: An evolutionary game perspective. *Journal of Environmental Management, 359*, 120981. DOI: 10.1016/j.jenvman.2024.120981 PMID: 38688132

Hovde Group. Charlotte, North Carolina, USA, Sikiru, A. O., Chima, O. K., Darden Business School, University of Virginia, USA; Otunba, M., Amazon, Seattle, WA, USA; Gaffar, O., Independent Researcher, USA; Adenuga, A. A., & McKinsey and Company, Nigeria; (2025). Navigating the regulatory trilemma - A framework for balancing U.s. tariffs, EU ESG directives, and cross-border capital controls. *Engineering and Technology Journal, 10*(08). https://doi.org/DOI: 10.47191/etj/v10i08.38

Huang, T., Zhou, W., Zhang, Y., Jia, X., Zhang, D., & Li, Z. (2023). An insight-based approach for batch water network with flexible production scheduling framework. *Journal of Cleaner Production, 385*, 135664. DOI: 10.1016/j.jclepro.2022.135664

Hueskes, M., Verhoest, K., & Block, T. (2017). Governing public–private partnerships for sustainability. *International Journal of Project Management, 35*(6), 1184–1195. DOI: 10.1016/j.ijproman.2017.02.020

Hu, X., Zhu, B., Lin, R., Li, X., Zeng, L., & Zhou, S. (2024). How does greenness translate into greenium? Evidence from China's green bonds. *Energy Economics, 133*, 107511. DOI: 10.1016/j.eneco.2024.107511

Ikevuje, A. H., Anaba, D. C., & Iheanyichukwu, U. T.Augusta Heavens IkevujeDavid Chinalu AnabaUche Thankgod Iheanyichukwu. (2024). Exploring sustainable finance mechanisms for green energy transition: A comprehensive review and analysis. *International Journal of Applied Research in Social Sciences, 6*(7), 1224–1247. DOI: 10.51594/ijarss.v6i7.1302

Inderst, G., Kaminker, C., & Stewart, F. (2012). Defining and measuring green investments: Implications for institutional investors asset allocations (OECD Working Papers on Finance, Insurance and Private Pensions, Vol. 24). OECD.

International Energy Agency. (2021). *Net zero by 2050: A roadmap for the global energy sector*. IEA. https://www.iea.org/reports/net-zero-by-2050

International Energy Agency. (2022). *World energy outlook 2022*. IEA.

International Energy Agency. (2023). *World energy investment 2023*. IEA.

International Energy Agency. (2024). *Renewables 2024: Analysis and forecast to 2029*. IEA.

International Finance Corporation. (2022). *Country climate and development report: India*. World Bank Group. https://www.ifc.org

International Finance Corporation. (2023). *Blended Finance for Climate Investments in India*. IFC.

International Finance Corporation. (2023). *IFC climate finance and investment report 2023: Aligning capital with climate-resilient development*. International Finance Corporation International Renewable Energy Agency (IRENA). (2022). *World energy transitions outlook: 1.5°C pathway*. IRENA.

International Monetary Fund. (2023). *Greening the financial system: Policy frameworks and innovation pathways*. International Monetary Fund.

International Renewable Energy Agency. (2020). *Renewable power generation costs in 2019*. IRENA.

International Renewable Energy Agency. (2020). *Renewable power generation costs in 2020*. IRENA.

International Renewable Energy Agency. (2022). *Global hydrogen trade to meet the 1.5°C climate goal*. IRENA.

International Renewable Energy Agency. (2024). *Renewable power generation costs in 2023*. IRENA.

IRENA. J. (2021). *World energy transitions outlook: 1.5° C pathway*. International Renewable Energy Agency.

Ivanisevic Hernaus, A., Zoricic, D., & Dolinar, D. (2023). How competitive is SRI in developing financial markets: The case of Central and Eastern Europe. *E+M. Ekonomie a Management*, *26*(2), 172–188. DOI: 10.15240/tul/001/2023-2-011

Jain, A., Islam, M. A., Keneley, M., & Kansal, M. (2022). Social contagion and the institutionalisation of GRI-based sustainability reporting practices. *Meditari Accountancy Research*, *30*(5), 1291–1308. DOI: 10.1108/MEDAR-06-2020-0917

James, S., & Quaglia, L. (2024). Emergent regime complexity and epistemic barriers in 'bigtech' finance. *New Political Economy*, *29*(6), 872–885. DOI: 10.1080/13563467.2024.2359940

Jenkins, K., McCauley, D., Heffron, R., Stephan, H., & Rehner, R. (2017). Energy justice: A conceptual review. *Energy Research & Social Science*, *11*, 174–182. DOI: 10.1016/j.erss.2015.10.004

Jeriji, M., Louhichi, W., & Ftiti, Z. (2023). Migrating to global reporting initiative guidelines: Does international harmonization of CSR information pay? *British Journal of Management, 34*(2), 555–575. DOI: 10.1111/1467-8551.12603

Ji, J., Liu, N., & Zhao, Y. (2023). Legal risk in transnational investment and its countermeasures. *Journal of Education. Humanities and Social Sciences, 24*, 477–481. DOI: 10.54097/ehnzj468

Jitmaneeroj, B. (2024). Value relevance of multifaceted corporate social performance: How do country-specific factors matter? *Humanities & Social Sciences Communications, 11*(1), 116. Advance online publication. DOI: 10.1057/s41599-024-02615-3

Jonwall, R., Gupta, S., & Pahuja, S. (2023). A comparison of investment behavior, attitudes, and demographics of socially responsible and conventional investors in India. *Social Responsibility Journal, 19*(6), 1123–1141. DOI: 10.1108/SRJ-08-2021-0358

Joshipura, M., Mathur, S., Joshipura, N., & Castelino, R. (2025). Decoding green bonds for sustainable development: A hybrid review and research agenda. *Journal of Economic Surveys, 39*(5), 2042–2056. DOI: 10.1111/joes.12687

Joshipura, M., Nasrallah, N., & Kedia, N. (2025). Green and climate finance for sustainability: Hybrid review and framework development. *Business Strategy and the Environment, 34*(3), 3618–3634. DOI: 10.1002/bse.4173

Josyula, H. P., & Vandanapu, M. K. (2024). Sustainable finance: Assessing environmental, social, and governance (ESG) factors in investment decisions. *SSRG International Journal of Economics and Management Studies, 11*(6), 7–14. DOI: 10.14445/23939125/IJEMS-V11I6P102

Kabderian Dreyer, J., Sharma, V., & Smith, W. (2023). Warm-glow investment and the underperformance of green stocks. *International Review of Economics & Finance, 83*, 546–570. DOI: 10.1016/j.iref.2022.10.006

Karpf, A., & Mandel, A. (2018). The changing value of the ‘green’ label on the US municipal bond market. *Nature Climate Change, 8*(2), 161–165. DOI: 10.1038/s41558-017-0062-0

Karumanchi, L. (2024). The role of green financing in accelerating sustainable economic development in emerging economies. *International Journal of Transformations in Business Management, 14*(3), 36–44. DOI: 10.37648/ijtbm.v14i03.004

Kathan, M. C., Utz, S., Dorfleitner, G., Eckberg, J., & Chmel, L. (2025). What you see is not what you get: ESG scores and greenwashing risk. *Finance Research Letters, 74*, 106710. DOI: 10.1016/j.frl.2024.106710

Kato, A. I., Chiloane-Tsoka, E. G., & Mugambe, P. (2024). Unlocking the potential: The influence of sustainable finance solutions on the long-term sustainability of small and medium-sized enterprises. *Cogent Business & Management*, *11*(1), 2391122. DOI: 10.1080/23311975.2024.2391122

Kaufmann, D., Kraay, A., & Mastruzzi, M. (2011). The worldwide governance indicators: Methodology and analytical issues. *Hague Journal on the Rule of Law*, *3*(2), 220–246. DOI: 10.1017/S1876404511200046

Keeley, A. R., Li, C., Takeda, S., Gloria, T., & Managi, S. (2022). The ultimate owner of environmental, social, and governance investment. *Frontiers in Sustainability*, *3*(909239), 909239. Advance online publication. DOI: 10.3389/frsus.2022.909239

Keeley, A. R., & Matsumoto, K. (2018). Investors' perspective on determinants of foreign direct investment in wind and solar energy in developing economies: Review and expert opinions. *Journal of Cleaner Production*, *179*, 132–142. DOI: 10.1016/j.jclepro.2017.12.154

Keser, N. S. (2025). Trend in sustainable finance metrics: A bibliometric literature review. *Pressacademia*, *2*, 2. Advance online publication. DOI: 10.17261/Pressacademia.2025.1983

Khalique, A., Wang, Y. C., & Ahmed, K. (2025). Europe's environmental dichotomy: The impact of regulations, climate investments, and renewable energy on carbon mitigation in the EU-22. *Energy Policy*, *198*, 114498. Advance online publication. DOI: 10.1016/j.enpol.2025.114498

Khan, M., Serafeim, G., & Yoon, A. (2016). Corporate sustainability: First evidence on materiality. *The Accounting Review*, *91*(6), 1697–1724. DOI: 10.2308/accr-51383

Khan, R. Z., Razak, L. A., & Premaratne, G. (2025). Green growth and sustainability: A systematic literature review on theories, measures and future directions. *Cleaner and Responsible Consumption*, *17*, 100274. DOI: 10.1016/j.clrc.2025.100274

Khan, S. A. R., Yu, Z., & Farooq, K. (2023). Green capabilities, green purchasing, and triple bottom line performance: Leading toward environmental sustainability. *Business Strategy and the Environment*, *32*(4), 2022–2034. DOI: 10.1002/bse.3234

Kilic, Y., Destek, M. A., Cevik, E. I., Bugan, M. F., Korkmaz, O., & Dibooglu, S. (2022). Return and risk spillovers between the ESG global index and stock markets: Evidence from time and frequency analysis. *Borsa Istanbul Review*, *22*, S141–S156. DOI: 10.1016/j.bir.2022.11.015

Kim, S., & Yoon, A. (2023). Analyzing active fund managers' commitment to ESG: Evidence from the United Nations Principles for Responsible Investment. *Management Science*, *69*(2), 741–758. DOI: 10.1287/mnsc.2022.4394

Koenigsmarck, M., & Geissdoerfer, M. (2023). Shifting the focus to measurement: A review of socially responsible investing and sustainability indicators. *Sustainability (Basel)*, *15*(2), 984. Advance online publication. DOI: 10.3390/su15020984

Kong, X., Li, Z., & Lei, X. (2024). Research on the impact of ESG performance on carbon emissions from the perspective of green credit. *Scientific Reports*, *14*(1), 10478. Advance online publication. DOI: 10.1038/s41598-024-61353-3 PMID: 38714797

Kopnina, H., Zhang, S. R., Anthony, S., Hassan, A., & Maroun, W. (2024). The inclusion of biodiversity into Environmental, Social, and Governance (ESG) framework: A strategic integration of ecocentric extinction accounting. *Journal of Environmental Management*, *351*(119808), 119808. DOI: 10.1016/j.jenvman.2023.119808 PMID: 38103427

Kouam, A. W. F. (2025). Navigating motivations and obstacles: Exploring the dynamics of foreign entrepreneurs in China's business landscape. *The International Entrepreneurship and Management Journal*, *21*(1), 12. Advance online publication. DOI: 10.1007/s11365-024-01040-x

Lagoarde-Ségot, T., Le Quang, G., & Scialom, L. (2026). Sustainable economic policies: Exploring the effects of ecosystemic macroprudential regulations. *Journal of Post Keynesian Economics*, *49*(1), 128–164. DOI: 10.1080/01603477.2025.2544047

Larsen, M. (2025). Any alternative to the Wall Street Consensus? Comparing the infrastructure financing models of the US, the EU, and China. *New Political Economy*, *30*(1), 34–47. DOI: 10.1080/13563467.2024.2373078

Larsen, M., & Henderson, I. (2019). Green and Sustainable Finance. In Leal Filho, W., Azul, A. M., Brandli, L., Özuyar, P. G., & Wall, T. (Eds.), *Responsible Consumption and Production* (pp. 1–10). Springer International Publishing., DOI: 10.1007/978-3-319-71062-4_75-1

Lauesen, L. M. (2019). Sustainable investment evaluation by means of life cycle assessment. *Social Responsibility Journal*, *15*(3), 347–364. DOI: 10.1108/SRJ-03-2018-0054

Leogrande, A. (2024). Integrating ESG principles into smart logistics:Toward sustainable supply chains. In *Preprints*. https://doi.org/DOI: 10.20944/preprints202411.1432.v1

Leonidou, L. C., Marinova, S. T., Marinov, M. A., Eduardsen, J. S., & Eteokleous, P. P. (2024). An enquiry into MNEs' CSR practices: Literature assessment, managerial implications, and academic perspectives. *MIR. Management International Review, 64*(5), 759–809. Advance online publication. DOI: 10.1007/s11575-024-00551-7

Li, J., Liu, B., Wang, D., & Casady, C. B. (2024). The effects of contractual and relational governance on public-private partnership sustainability. *Public Administration, 102*(4), 1418–1449. DOI: 10.1111/padm.12982

Li, J., Song, S., & Wang, Y. (2026). Green bond issuance and ESG performance. *Pacific-Basin Finance Journal.* Advance online publication. DOI: 10.1016/j.pacfin.2025.102949

Li, M., & Rasiah, R. (2024). Can ESG disclosure stimulate corporations' sustainable green innovation efforts? Evidence from China. *Sustainability (Basel), 16*(21), 9390. DOI: 10.3390/su16219390

Lindenberg, N. (2014). Definition of green finance. *German Development Institute Discussion Paper*, 23/2014.

Lingnau, V., Fuchs, F., & Beham, F. (2022). The link between corporate sustainability and willingness to invest: New evidence from the field of ethical investments. *Journal of Management Control, 33*(3), 335–369. DOI: 10.1007/s00187-022-00340-z PMID: 35719704

Linnenluecke, M. K. (2022). Environmental, social and governance (ESG) performance in the context of multinational business research. *Multinational Business Review, 30*(1), 1–16. DOI: 10.1108/MBR-11-2021-0148

Lin, Z., Liao, X., & Jia, H. (2023). Could green finance facilitate low-carbon transformation of power generation? Some evidence from China. *International Journal of Climate Change Strategies and Management, 15*(2), 141–158. DOI: 10.1108/IJCCSM-03-2022-0039

Liu, N., Liu, C., Xia, Y., Ren, Y., & Liang, J. (2020). Examining the coordination between green finance and green economy aiming for sustainable development: A case study of China. *Sustainability (Basel), 12*(9), 3717. DOI: 10.3390/su12093717

Liu, Y., Osterrieder, J., Hadji Misheva, B., Koenigstein, N., & Baals, L. (2023). Navigating the environmental, social, and governance (ESG) landscape: Constructing a robust and reliable scoring engine—Insights into data source selection, indicator determination, weighting and aggregation techniques, and validation processes for comprehensive ESG scoring systems [Version 1; peer review: 3 approved]. *Open Research Europe*, *3*, 119. Advance online publication. DOI: 10.12688/openreseurope.16278.1 PMID: 37840702

Li, W., Zheng, M., Zhang, Y., & Cui, G. (2020). Green governance structure, ownership characteristics, and corporate financing constraints. *Journal of Cleaner Production*, *260*, 121008. DOI: 10.1016/j.jclepro.2020.121008

Li, X., Song, Y., & Gan, X. (2024). Public–private partnerships and land value capture in urban rail. *Transport Policy*, *152*, 88–100. DOI: 10.1016/j.tranpol.2024.07.012

Li, Y., Zhang, D., & Zhang, C. (2024). Green finance and corporate performance. *Heliyon*, *10*(4), e25106. DOI: 10.1016/j.heliyon.2024.e25106 PMID: 38694050

Loiola, M., Kimura, H., & Souza, F. (2025). Green finance instruments and market evolution: A systematic review. *Journal of Sustainable Finance & Investment*. Advance online publication. DOI: 10.1080/20430795.2025.XXXXX

Lokuwaduge, C., & de Silva, K. (2020). Emerging corporate disclosure of environmental social and governance (ESG) risks: An Australian study. *Australasian Accounting Business and Finance Journal*, *14*(2), 35–50. DOI: 10.14453/aabfj.v14i2.4

Luo, W., Tian, Z., Zhong, S., Lyu, Q., & Deng, M. (2022). Global evolution of research on sustainable finance from 2000 to 2021: A bibliometric analysis on WoS database. *Sustainability (Basel)*, *14*(15), 9435. DOI: 10.3390/su14159435

Lusha, E. (2024). National and international collaboration and its impact on economic development. *Interdisciplinary Journal of Research and Development*, *11*(1), 76. DOI: 10.56345/ijrdv11n111

Madyan, M., & Widuri, S. K. (2023). Environmental, social, governance (ESG) performance and capital structure: The role of good corporate governance. *Jurnal Manajemen Teori Dan Terapan| Journal of Theory and Applied Management*, *16*(3), 560–570. DOI: 10.20473/jmtt.v16i3.47483

Ma, N. (2023). Integration of ESG factors in portfolio management: International trends and practices. *Frontiers in Business, Economics and Management*, *12*(2), 149–152. DOI: 10.54097/fbem.v12i2.14778

Maresca, A., Dal Maso, G., & Tripathy, A. (2023). Interpellating Finance – a dramaturgical model for green bond pricing. *Valuation Studies*, *10*(1), 90–117. DOI: 10.3384/VS.2001-5992.2023.10.1.90-117

Martini, A. (2021). Socially responsible investing: From the ethical origins to the sustainable development framework of the European Union. *Environment, Development and Sustainability*, *23*(11), 16874–16890. DOI: 10.1007/s10668-021-01375-3 PMID: 33841043

Marx, A. (2019). Public-Private Partnerships for Sustainable Development: Exploring Their Design and Its Impact on Effectiveness. *Sustainability (Basel)*, *11*(4), 1087. DOI: 10.3390/su11041087

Matome, G. K., & Fischer, T. B. (2024). Environmental assessment simplification in Botswana: A critical review. *Impact Assessment and Project Appraisal*, *42*(4), 1–12. DOI: 10.1080/14615517.2024.2363720

Matser, I., Fontrodona, J., & Van Wassenhove, L. (2023). Guest editorial: Driving impact through responsible investing and finance. *Sustainability Accounting Management and Policy Journal*, *14*(5), 917–921. DOI: 10.1108/SAMPJ-08-2023-606

Maula, M. V. J., & Lukkarinen, A. (2022). Attention across borders: Investor attention as a driver of cross-border equity crowdfunding investments. *Strategic Entrepreneurship Journal*, *16*(4), 699–734. DOI: 10.1002/sej.1424

Meng, J., Ye, Z., & Wang, Y. (2024). Financing and investing in sustainable infrastructure: A review and research agenda. *Sustainable Futures : An Applied Journal of Technology, Environment and Society*, *8*, 100312. DOI: 10.1016/j.sftr.2024.100312

Mertzanis, C., & Tebourbi, I. (2025). Geopolitical risk and global green bond market growth. *European Financial Management*, *31*(1), 26–71. DOI: 10.1111/eufm.12484

Michaelowa, A., Butzengeiger, S., & Schenuit, F. (2019). Policy risk and the economics of renewable energy projects: Lessons from Kenya and India. In *Climate Policy*

Minadakis, P., & Vega-Araujo, J. (2024). Rethinking the social license to operate? A theoretical exploration of its synergies with social acceptance and energy justice for a just transition. *Energy Research & Social Science*, *113*, 103552. DOI: 10.1016/j.erss.2024.103552

Minhas, A. S., Maqsood, N., Shahid, T. A., & Rehman, A. U. (2024). Investment performance in green finance: Assessing the impact of environmental social and governance integration. *IRASD Journal of Economics*, *6*(1), 27–44. DOI: 10.52131/joe.2024.0601.0192

Mohanty, S., Das, P., & Sahoo, M. (2023). ESG integration and governance challenges in sustainable finance: A bibliometric review. *Finance Research Letters*, *52*, 103476. DOI: 10.1016/j.frl.2023.103476

Mohanty, S., Nanda, S. S., Soubhari, T. N. V., Biswal, S., & Patnaik, S. (2023). Emerging research trends in green finance: A bibliometric overview. *Journal of Risk and Financial Management*, *16*(2), 108. DOI: 10.3390/jrfm16020108

Mol, M. J., & Lee, S. H. (2024). What produces corporate social irresponsibility in offshore outsourcing? The effects of interorganizational relationship governance and institutional distance. *Journal of International Business Studies*, *55*(5), 577–592. DOI: 10.1057/s41267-023-00664-5

Monasterolo, I., & Raberto, M. (2019). The impact of phasing out fossil fuel subsidies on the low-carbon transition. *Energy Policy*, *124*, 355–370. DOI: 10.1016/j.enpol.2018.08.051

Monkelbaan, J. (2019). Governance for achieving the Sustainable Development Goals in the electricity sector. *Sustainable Cities and Society*, *52*, 101779. Advance online publication. DOI: 10.1016/j.scs.2019.101779

Morshed, A. (2025). Sustainable energy revolution: green finance as the key to the Arab Gulf States' future. *International Journal of Energy Sector Management*. DOI: 10.1108/IJESM-10-2024-0007

Moshood, T. D.. (2024). Infrastructure digital twin technology: A new paradigm. *Technology in Society*, *76*, 102378. DOI: 10.1016/j.techsoc.2024.102378

Mudalige, H. M. N. K. (2023). Emerging new themes in green finance: A systematic literature review. *Future Business Journal*, *9*(1), 108. DOI: 10.1186/s43093-023-00287-0

Multilateral Investment Guarantee Agency. (2023). *Annual report 2023: Mobilizing private capital for development*. World Bank Group.

Nagesh, K. C., & Siva Murugan, K. (2025). Fintech and sustainable finance: Impact of digital finance in promoting green investments. *MLAC Journal for Arts, Commerce and Sciences (m-JACS) ISSN: 2584-1920, 3*(1), 30–38. DOI: 10.59415/mjacs.v3i1.246

Narayanan, S., & Pradhan, S. K. (2023). Exploring the research landscape of socially responsible investment through bibliometrics. *Multidisciplinary Reviews*, *7*(1), 2024022. DOI: 10.31893/multirev.2024022

Narayan, M., Kumar, N., Parida, V. K., & Kumari, P. (2025). Sustainable finance in emerging markets: Adaptive governance and environmental, social, and governance innovation for equitable climate resilience. *Development and Sustainability in Economics and Finance*, *8*, 100101. DOI: 10.1016/j.dsef.2025.100101

Nartey, E. K. (2024). Beyond profit: Ethical imperatives and the role of duty of care in sustainable investment strategies. *International Journal of Economics and Finance*, *17*(1), 22. DOI: 10.5539/ijef.v17n1p22

Nasta, L., Magnanelli, B. S., & Ciaburri, M. (2024). From profits to purpose: ESG practices, CEO compensation and institutional ownership. *Management Decision*, *62*(13), 46–68. DOI: 10.1108/MD-06-2023-0932

Nawaz, M. A., Seshadri, U., Kumar, P., Aqdas, R., Patwary, A. K., & Riaz, M. (2021). Nexus between green finance and climate change mitigation in N-11 and BRICS countries: Empirical estimation through difference in differences (DID) approach. *Environmental Science and Pollution Research International*, *28*(6), 6504–6519. DOI: 10.1007/s11356-020-10920-y PMID: 32997248

Nedopil, C., Dordi, T., & Weber, O. (2021). The nature of global green finance standards—Evolution, differences, and three models. *Sustainability (Basel)*, *13*(7), 3723. DOI: 10.3390/su13073723

Ngo, T., Le, T., Ullah, S., & Trinh, H. H. (2022). Climate risk disclosures and global sustainability initiatives: A conceptual analysis and agenda for future research. *Business Strategy and the Environment*. Advance online publication. DOI: 10.1002/bse.3323

Ng, T. H., & Tao, J. Y. (2016). Bond financing for renewable energy in Asia. *Energy Policy*, *95*, 509–517. DOI: 10.1016/j.enpol.2016.03.015

Nguyen, T. T., Grote, U., Neubacher, F., Rahut, D. B., Do, M. H., & Paudel, G. P. (2023). Security risks from climate change and environmental degradation: Implications for sustainable land use transformation in the Global South. *Current Opinion in Environmental Sustainability*, *63*, 101322. DOI: 10.1016/j.cosust.2023.101322

Nica, I., Chiri ă, N., & Georgescu, I. (2025). Triple Bottom Line in sustainable development: A comprehensive bibliometric analysis. *Sustainability (Basel)*, *17*(5), 1932. DOI: 10.3390/su17051932

Nichols, B. S., Kirchoff, J. F., Confente, I., & Stolze, H. (2023). When brands behave badly: Signaling and spillover effects of unethical behavior in the context of triple bottom line sustainability. *Journal of Product and Brand Management*, *32*(6), 908–926. DOI: 10.1108/JPBM-07-2021-3569

Nikiforos, M., & Zezza, G. (2017). Stock–flow consistent macroeconomic models: A survey. *Journal of Economic Surveys, 31*(5), 1204–1239. DOI: 10.1111/joes.12221

Nizamuddin, M., Mushir, N., & Thakur, M. (2024). Impact of environmental, social, and governance risk on the financial performance of selected Indian banks. *Educational Administration: Theory and Practice*, 6354–6364. DOI: 10.53555/kuey.v30i5.3944

Nogueira, E., Gomes, S., & Lopes, J. M. (2024). Financial sustainability: Exploring the influence of the triple Bottom Line economic dimension on firm performance. *Sustainability (Basel), 16*(15), 6458. DOI: 10.3390/su16156458

North, D. C. (1990). *Institutions, institutional change and economic performance*. Cambridge University Press. DOI: 10.1017/CBO9780511808678

NYU Stern Center for Sustainable Business. (n.d.). ESG and financial performance. New York University Stern School of Business. Retrieved December 22, 2025, from https://www.stern.nyu.edu/experience-stern/about/departments-centers-initiatives/centers-of-research/center-sustainable-business/research/research-initiatives/esg-and-financial-performance

Oduro, S. (2024). Eco-innovation and SMEs' sustainable performance: A meta-analysis. *European Journal of Innovation Management, 27*(9), 248–279. DOI: 10.1108/EJIM-11-2023-0961

OECD. (2020). *Developing sustainable finance definitions and taxonomies*. OECD Publishing. https://www.oecd.org

OECD. (2024). *FDI in figures: Green investment trends*. Organisation for Economic Co-operation and Development.

Ogundipe, F., Sampson, E., Bakare, O. I., Oketola, O., & Yusuf, R. A. (2022). Technology for a sustainable future: Unlocking the power of digital transformation. *Journal of Frontiers in Multidisciplinary Research, 3*(2), 146–156. DOI: 10.54660/.IJFMR.2022.3.2.146-156

Olatubosun, P., & Nyazenga, S. (2021). Greenwashing and responsible investment practices: Empirical evidence from Zimbabwe. *Qualitative Research in Financial Markets, 13*(1), 16–36. DOI: 10.1108/QRFM-12-2017-0125

Omri, A., & Ben Jabeur, S. (2024). Climate policies and legislation for renewable energy transition: The roles of financial sector and political institutions. *Technological Forecasting and Social Change, 203*, 123347. DOI: 10.1016/j.techfore.2024.123347

Organisation for Economic Co-operation and Development. (2023). *Innovative finance for sustainable development*. OECD Publishing., DOI: 10.1787/9789264963072-

Organisation for Economic Cooperation and Development. (2024). *Bridging the clean energy investment gap: Cost of capital and policy solutions* (ENV/WKP(2024)15/REV1). https://doi.org/DOI: 10.1787/ENVWKP(2024)15REV1en

Organisation for Economic Cooperation and Development. (2024). *Infrastructure for a climateresilient future*. OECD., DOI: 10.1787/a74a45b0en

Osuji, V. C., Okafor, C. M., & Dako, O. F.Vivian Chilee OsujiChizoba Michael OkaforOmoize Fatimetu Dako. (2025). Pioneering ESG-linked corporate finance programs to advance green finance, operational efficiency, and global sustainability goals. *Gulf Journal of Advance Business Research*, *3*(10), 1474–1494. DOI: 10.51594/gjabr.v3i10.169

Othman, K., & Khallaf, R. (2022). A REVIEW OF PUBLIC-PRIVATE PARTNERSHIPS FOR RENEWABLE ENERGY PROJECTS IN DEVELOPING COUNTRIES. *Proceedings of International Structural Engineering and Construction*, *9*(1). Advance online publication. DOI: 10.14455/ISEC.2022.9(1).ENR-01

Owen, R., Deffains-Crapsky, C., Hussain, J., & Mac An Bhaird, C. (2026). Financing SME green and sustainable innovation. *Venture Capital*, *28*(2-3), 1–12. DOI: 10.1080/13691066.2026.2643997

Owojori, O. M., & Erasmus, L. J. (2025). Public–private partnerships as catalysts for green infrastructure: A three-pronged analysis of economic, environmental, and institutional factors. *Frontiers in Sustainable Cities*, *7*, 1591278. DOI: 10.3389/frsc.2025.1591278

Paetzold, F., Busch, T., Utz, S., & Kellers, A. (2022). Between impact and returns: Private investors and the sustainable development goals. *Business Strategy and the Environment*, *31*(7), 3182–3197. DOI: 10.1002/bse.3070

Pal, S. (2026). Public-private partnership in energy investment and inclusive growth. *Energy Policy*, *210*, 115010. DOI: 10.1016/j.enpol.2025.115010

Pandey, A. (2025). Aligning green finance with climate governance. In *Designing Effective Public Policies to Address Global Warming* (pp. 157–184). IGI Global Scientific Publishing., DOI: 10.4018/979-8-3373-1310-8.ch007

Pan, Y., Fang, W., & Zhang, W. (2023). Development of an energy consumption prediction model for battery electric vehicles in real-world driving: A combined approach of short-trip segment division and deep learning. *Journal of Cleaner Production*, *400*, 136742. DOI: 10.1016/j.jclepro.2023.136742

Papafloratos, T., & Pantazi, T. (2025). A systematic review of the effects of mandatory corporate sustainability reporting. *Sustainability (Basel)*, *17*(12), 5336. DOI: 10.3390/su17125336

Papari, C. A., Polzin, F., Toxopeus, H., Bulkeley, H., & Menguzzo, E. (2024). Can the EU Taxonomy help upscale investments into urban naturebased solutions? *Environmental Science & Policy*, *151*, 103598. DOI: 10.1016/j.envsci.2023.103598

Paridhi, R., Ritika, , Arora, H., Arora, P., & Saini, N. (2024). Unlocking the path to sustainability: A hierarchical model for understanding corporate barriers to ESG reporting adoption. *Journal of Risk and Financial Management*, *17*(12), 527. DOI: 10.3390/jrfm17120527

Parveen, S., Coccorese, P., Umer, M., & Tahir, A. H. (2025). Synergizing financial inclusion and green finance: Advancing Sustainable Development Goals 2030 and 2050 in alignment with COP 29 commitments. *Sustainable Development (Bradford)*, *33*(S1), 48–76. DOI: 10.1002/sd.3553

Pasquino, M., & Lucarelli, C. (2025). Socially responsible investments inside out: A new conceptual framework for investigating retail investor preferences. *International Journal of Bank Marketing*, *43*(3), 449–475. DOI: 10.1108/IJBM-02-2024-0077

Patala, S., Juntunen, J. K., Lundan, S., & Ritvala, T. (2021). Multinational energy utilities in the energy transition: A configurational study of the drivers of FDI in renewables. *Journal of International Business Studies*, *52*(5), 930–950. DOI: 10.1057/s41267-020-00387-x

Pellegrino, R., & D'Apuzzo, M. C. (2024). Mitigating foreign exchange risk exposure with supply chain flexibility: A real option analysis. *Journal of Business Logistics*, *45*(1), 61–85. DOI: 10.1111/jbl.12338

Pepe, C. G. E., Fonseca, M. V. A., & Silva Marques, C. F. (2024). International collaboration towards innovation management: A network perspective and the Global Innovation Index. *Journal of Innovation and Entrepreneurship*, *13*(1), 32. Advance online publication. DOI: 10.1186/s13731-024-00384-6

Petri, I. (2025). Digital twins for dynamic LCA in the built environment. *The Science of the Total Environment*, *958*, 173025. DOI: 10.1016/j.scitotenv.2025.173025

Petucco, C., Schaubroeck, T., Gibon, T., Popescu, I.-S., & Benetto, E. (2025). On the validity of corporate green bonds' environmental claims: Is the environmental reporting of corporate green bonds reliable? *Environmental Research Letters*, *20*(6), 064007. DOI: 10.1088/1748-9326/add028

Pialli, G. (2023). The effects of limited exhaustibility of knowledge and geographical distance on the quality of R&D collaborations: The European evidence 2000–2012. *Journal of Evolutionary Economics*, *33*(4), 1125–1169. DOI: 10.1007/s00191-023-00831-9

Pinz, A., Roudyani, N., & Thaler, J. (2018). Public–private partnerships as instruments to achieve sustainability-related objectives: The state of the art and a research agenda. *Public Management Review*, *20*(1), 1–22. DOI: 10.1080/14719037.2017.1293143

Pizzi, S., Caputo, F., & de Nuccio, E. (2024). Do sustainability reporting standards affect analysts' forecast accuracy? *Sustainability Accounting Management and Policy Journal*, *15*(2), 330–354. DOI: 10.1108/SAMPJ-04-2023-0227

Pollin, R., & Callaci, B. (2019). The economics of a just transition: A framework for supporting fossil-fuel dependent workers and communities in the United States. *Labor Studies Journal*, *44*(3), 201–228. DOI: 10.1177/0160449X18787051

Polzin, F. (2017). Mobilizing private finance for low-carbon innovation – A systematic review of barriers and solutions. *Renewable & Sustainable Energy Reviews*, *77*, 525–535. DOI: 10.1016/j.rser.2017.04.007

Polzin, F., Egli, F., Steffen, B., & Schmidt, T. S. (2019). How do policies mobilize private finance for renewable energy? A systematic review with an investor perspective. *Applied Energy*, *236*, 1249–1268. DOI: 10.1016/j.apenergy.2018.11.098

Popovic, T., Lygnerud, K., Denk, I., Fransson, N., & Unluturk, B. (2024). Blended finance as a catalyst for accelerating the European heat transition? *Smart Energy*, *14*, 100136. DOI: 10.1016/j.segy.2024.100136

PRI. (2023). *A practical guide to ESG integration for equity investing*. Principles for Responsible Investment.

Priya, & Sharma, K. (2024). Global ESG fund evolution-an analysis of sustainable investment growth through comparison. *E3S Web of Conferences, 577*, 03003. https://doi.org/DOI: 10.1051/e3sconf/202457703003

Puaschunder, J. M. (2023). Kaur, H., Singh, K., & Kaur, A. (2024). Corruption and Environmental Degradation: Challenges and Solutions for Effective Climate Action. In *Modern Concepts and Practices of Climate Finance* (pp. 325-350). IGI Global.

Pudeyan, L., Zaporozceva, E., & Medvedskaya, T. (2024). "Green" bonds for financing environmental projects in Moscow. *BIO Web of Conferences, 141*, 04022. DOI: 10.1051/bioconf/202414104022

Pyka, I., & Nocoń, A. (2021). Responsible lending policy of green investments in the energy sector in Poland. *Energies, 14*(21), 7298. DOI: 10.3390/en14217298

Qu, Z. (2025). Research green finance and sustainable investment in China. *Advances in Economics and Management Research, 15*(1), 637. DOI: 10.56028/aemr.15.1.637.2025

Ramdhan, D. (2025). The role of ESG disclosure in attracting sustainable investment in Indonesia's capital market. *RIGGS: Journal of Artificial Intelligence and Digital Business*, *4*(3), 3384–3393. DOI: 10.31004/riggs.v4i3.2484

Ravikumar, A. S., Kalandarov, A., Djumaniyazova, M., & Habib, M. (2025). A roadmap to a sustainable future. In *Advances in Computational Intelligence and Robotics* (pp. 267–302). IGI Global Scientific Publishing. DOI: 10.4018/979-8-3373-3017-4.ch010

Ravikumar, R. N., & Aarthi, S. (2025a). Artificial Intelligence and IoT integration in supply chains. In *Leveraging Technology and Renewable Energy for Sustainable Supply Chains* (pp. 1–32). IGI Global Scientific Publishing., DOI: 10.4018/979-8-3373-3790-6.ch001

Ravikumar, R. N., & Aarthi, S. (2025b). Integrated cross-border renewable energy infrastructure for a green transition. In *Cross-Border Cooperation in the Age of Climate Change* (pp. 301–332). IGI Global Scientific Publishing., DOI: 10.4018/979-8-3373-3972-6.ch011

Ravikumar, R. N., Aarthi, S., Pardaev, J., & Shukla, P. (2025). Quantum computing for financial modelling. In *Quantum-Driven Financial Intelligence* (pp. 221–252). IGI Global Scientific Publishing., DOI: 10.4018/979-8-3373-2893-5.ch010

Raza, M. S., Wang, Y. S., Rauf, A., Aziz, N., Khan, M. A., & Hussain, A. (2024). Unveiling the green horizon: A bibliometric analysis of global foreign direct investment research and its emphasis on climate change. *Journal of Cleaner Production*, *446*, 141338. Advance online publication. DOI: 10.1016/j.jclepro.2024.141338

Reck, B. K., & Graedel, T. E. (2012). Challenges in metal recycling. *Science*, *337*(6095), 690–695. DOI: 10.1126/science.1217501

REN21. (2021). *Renewables 2021 global status report*. REN21 Secretariat.

Renewable Energy. (2021). Cross-border investment trends in renewable energy and grid modernization. *Renewable Energy, 170*, 1250–1265. DOI: 10.1016/j.renene.2021.02.045

Reserve Bank of India. (2023). *Report on climate-related financial risks.* https://www.rbi.org.in

Ringe, W.-G. (2023). Investor empowerment for sustainability. *Review of Economics, 74*(1), 21–52. DOI: 10.1515/roe-2023-0016

Rodrigues Loiola, R., Kimura, H., & Melo Souza, L. D. (2025). Sustainable Finance, Green Bonds and Financial Performance—A Literature Review. *International Journal of Financial Studies, 13*(4), 233. DOI: 10.3390/ijfs13040233

Rossoni, A. L., de Vasconcellos, E. P. G., & Sbragia, R. (2024). Influence of social capital, market orientation, and technological readiness on researchers' interactions with companies. *Future Business Journal, 10*(1), 69. Advance online publication. DOI: 10.1186/s43093-024-00359-9

Roy, P. K. (2023). Enriching the green economy through sustainable investments: An ESG-based credit rating model for green financing. *Journal of Cleaner Production, 420*, 138315. DOI: 10.1016/j.jclepro.2023.138315

Ryan, M., Popa, E., Blok, V., Declich, A., Berliri, M., Alfonsi, A., Veloudis, S., Costanzo, N., & Iannuzzi, M. (2024). Start doing the right thing: Indicators for socially responsible start-ups and investors. *Journal of Responsible Technology, 20*(100094), 100094. DOI: 10.1016/j.jrt.2024.100094

Sachs, J. D., Schmidt-Traub, G., Kroll, C., Lafortune, G., & Fuller, G. (2023). *Sustainable Development Report 2023.* Cambridge University Press.

Sadiq, R., Yasser, F., & Nawaz, F. (2025). Using AI to predict and mitigate green asset bubbles in financial markets. *The Regional Tribune, 4*(2), 170–190. DOI: 10.55737/trt/SG25.103

Sadoff, C. W., & Grey, D. (2002). Beyond the river: The benefits of cooperation on international rivers. *Water Policy, 4*(5), 389–403. DOI: 10.1016/S1366-7017(02)00035-1

Sakyi, J. K., Eboseremen, B. O., Adebayo, A. O., Essien, I. A., Okojie, J. S., & Soneye, O. M. (2024). Designing a sustainable financing model for emerging economies: Addressing climate goals through green bonds and ESG investments. *International Journal of Multidisciplinary Futuristic Development, 5*(1), 20–33. DOI: 10.54660/IJMFD.2024.5.1.20-33

Salehi, A. (2025). Economic Growth Theories: Comparative Analysis of Classical, Neoclassical, and Endogenous Models. *INTERNATIONAL JOURNAL OF SOCIAL SCIENCE HUMANITY & MANAGEMENT RESEARCH, 04*(12). Advance online publication. DOI: 10.58806/ijsshmr.2025.v4i12n05

Saravade, V., & Weber, O. (2024). Catalyzing the growth of green bonds: A closer look at the drivers and barriers of the Canadian green bond market. *Sustainability Accounting Management and Policy Journal, 15*(3), 605–627. DOI: 10.1108/SAMPJ-08-2023-0604

Saroglu, S. (2021). Geothermal energy investment and innovation in Turkey. *Renewable Energy, 170*, 1241–1252. DOI: 10.1016/j.renene.2021.02.012

Schmidt, T. S., Blum, N. U., & Wakeling, R. S. (2019). Attracting private investments into renewable energy: A review of policy instruments. *Energy Policy, 38*(1), 1–15. DOI: 10.1016/j.enpol.2009.08.035

Schoenmaker, D. (2017). *Investing for the common good: A sustainable finance framework.* Bruegel Essay and Lecture Series.

Scholtens, B. (2017). Why finance should care about ecology. *Trends in Ecology & Evolution, 32*(7), 500–505. DOI: 10.1016/j.tree.2017.03.013 PMID: 28457498

Shah, D. (2024). Sustainable Finance and ESG Investing. *International Journal for Research in Applied Science and Engineering Technology, 12*(2), 412–416. DOI: 10.22214/ijraset.2024.58346

Shimbar, A., & Ebrahimi, S. B. (2020). Political risk and valuation of renewable energy investments in developing countries. *Renewable Energy, 145*, 1325–1333. DOI: 10.1016/j.renene.2019.06.055

Siddik, A. B., Yong, L., & Sharif, A. (2024). Do sustainable banking practices enhance the sustainability performance of banking institutions? Direct and indirect effects. *International Journal of Bank Marketing, 42*(4), 672–691. DOI: 10.1108/IJBM-02-2023-0109

Silva, J. A., Pereira, V. J., & Abreu, M. (2023). Water supply and wastewater treatment and reuse in future cities. *Water (Basel), 15*(17), 3064. DOI: 10.3390/w15173064

Silvestri, R., & Kamerling, J. (2024). *CFA institute survey report on the ESG regulatory framework in the EU.* CFA Institute., DOI: 10.56227/24.2.10

Siri, M., Lamandini, M., & Muñoz, D. R. (2024). The current implementation of the sustainability-related financial disclosures regulation (SFDR). SSRN *Electronic Journal.* https://doi.org/DOI: 10.2139/ssrn.5042850

Sreepriya, Suprabha, & Prasad, K. (2023). Does GRI compliance moderate the impact of sustainability disclosure on firm value? *Society and Business Review, 18*(1), 152–174. DOI: 10.1108/SBR-06-2022-0172

Steckel, J. C., Jakob, M., Flachsland, C., Kornek, U., Lessmann, K., & Edenhofer, O. (2017). From climate finance toward sustainable development finance. *Wiley Interdisciplinary Reviews: Climate Change, 8*(1), e437. DOI: 10.1002/wcc.437

Steffen, B., & Schmidt, T. S. (2021). Strengthen finance in sustainability transitions research. *Environmental Innovation and Societal Transitions, 41*, 77–80. DOI: 10.1016/j.eist.2021.10.018

Stern, N., & Stiglitz, J. E. (2023). Climate change and growth. *Industrial and Corporate Change, 32*(2), 277–303. DOI: 10.1093/icc/dtad008

Suding, P. H., Engel, S., & Jones, A. (2015). Securing environmental standards in renewable energy investment. *Energy Policy, 86*, 331–338. DOI: 10.1016/j.enpol.2015.07.002

Sun, X., Zhou, C., & Gan, Z. (2023). Green finance policy and ESG performance: Evidence from Chinese manufacturing firms. *Sustainability (Basel), 15*(8), 6781. DOI: 10.3390/su15086781

Susskind, L., Chun, J., Gant, A., Hodgkins, C., Cohen, J., & Lohmar, S. (2022). Sources of opposition to renewable energy projects in the United States. *Energy Policy, 165*, 112922. DOI: 10.1016/j.enpol.2022.112922

Sverdrup, H. U. (2019). The global sustainability challenges in the future: The energy use, materials supply, pollution, climate change and inequality nexus. In Meadowcroft, J., Banister, D., Holden, E., Langhelle, O., Linnerud, K., & Gilpin, G. (Eds.), *What Next for Sustainable Development?* Edward Elgar Publishing., DOI: 10.4337/9781788975209.00013

Swaty. (2023). Green finance and sustainable development: Exploring dynamic causal links and global implications. *E3S Web of Conferences, 453*, 01053. DOI: 10.1051/e3sconf/202345301053

Syarkani, Y., Subu, M. A., & Waluyo, I. (2024). Impact of ESG performance on firm value: A comparison of emerging and developed markets. *Commercium : Journal of Business and Management, 2*(4), 204–219. DOI: 10.61978/commercium.v2i4.367

Szarka, J. (2004). Wind power, policy learning and paradigm change. *Energy Policy, 32*(12), 1625–1632. DOI: 10.1016/S0301-4215(03)00161-6

Taghizadeh-Hesary, F., & Yoshino, N. (2020). Sustainable Solutions for Green Financing and Investment in Renewable Energy Projects. *Energies, 13*(4), 788. DOI: 10.3390/en13040788

Tandan, P., Mishra, J., & Sarkar, S. (2025). FinTech and sustainable finance: Transforming traditional banking for a greener future. *International Journal of Economic Practices and Theories*, •••, 54–59. DOI: 10.52783/ijept.14

Tang, D. Y., & Zhang, Y. (2020). Do shareholders benefit from green bonds? *Journal of Corporate Finance*, *61*, 101427. DOI: 10.1016/j.jcorpfin.2018.12.001

Tawiah, V., Zakari, A., & Alvarado, R. (2024). Effect of corruption on green growth. *Environment, Development and Sustainability*, *26*(4), 10429–10459. DOI: 10.1007/s10668-023-03152-w

Teixeira, N. (2025). The evolution of sustainable investment: The role of decentralized finance and green bonds in the efficiency and transparency of green finance. *FinTech and Sustainable Innovation*, *1*, A1. Advance online publication. DOI: 10.47852/bonviewFSI52024817

Thacker, S., Adshead, D., Fay, M., Hallegatte, S., Harvey, M., Meller, H., O'Regan, N., Rozenberg, J., Watkins, G., & Hall, J. W. (2019). Infrastructure for sustainable development. *Nature Sustainability*, *2*(4), 324–331. DOI: 10.1038/s41893-019-0256-8

Tolliver, C., Keeley, A. R., & Managi, S. (2019). Green bonds for the Paris agreement and sustainable development goals. *Environmental Research Letters*, *14*(6), 064009. DOI: 10.1088/1748-9326/ab1118

Tonnarello, F., Vermiglio, C., Migliardo, C., & Naciti, V. (2025). The impact of EU Taxonomy for Sustainable Activities on European utilities' performance. *Business Strategy and the Environment*, *34*(3), 2848–2862. DOI: 10.1002/bse.4128

Trabacchi, C., & Stadelmann, M. (2015). Mobilizing private climate finance: Blended finance mechanisms and investment vehicles. *Climate Policy*, *15*(5), 1–17. DOI: 10.1080/14693062.2015.1022855

Tranfield, D., Denyer, D., & Smart, P. (2003). Towards a methodology for developing evidence-informed management knowledge by means of systematic review. *British Journal of Management*, *14*(3), 207–222. DOI: 10.1111/1467-8551.00375

Treepongkaruna, S., & Suttipun, M. (2024). The impact of environmental, social and governance (ESG) reporting on corporate profitability: evidence from Thailand. *Journal of Financial Reporting and Accounting*. https://doi.org/DOI: 10.1108/JFRA-09-2023-0555

Treepongkaruna, S., Au Yong, H. H., Thomsen, S., & Kyaw, K. (2024). Greenwashing, carbon emission, and ESG. *Business Strategy and the Environment*, *33*(8), 8526–8539. DOI: 10.1002/bse.3929

Tripathi, V., & Kaur, A. (2022). Does socially responsible investing pay in developing countries? A comparative study across select developed and developing markets. *FIIB Business Review*, *11*(2), 189–205. DOI: 10.1177/2319714520980288

Tuncay, M., & Dorjnaran, B. (2023). How do socially responsible investment and macroeconomic indicators interact with each other The case of selected developing countries. *Pressacademia*, *1*, 1. Advance online publication. DOI: 10.17261/Pressacademia.2023.1721

Udemba, E. N., & Alola, A. A. (2022). Asymmetric inference of carbon neutrality and energy transition policy in Australia: The (de)merit of foreign direct investment. *Journal of Cleaner Production*, *343*, 131023. Advance online publication. DOI: 10.1016/j.jclepro.2022.131023

UNCTAD. (2023). *World investment report 2023: Investing in sustainable energy for all.* United Nations Conference on Trade and Development. https://unctad.org/publication/world-investment-report-2023

UNCTAD. (2025). *World Investment Report 2025* (No. 2025; pp. 1–42). United Nations Conference on Trade and Development. https://unctad.org/system/files/official-document/wir2025_ch03_en.pdf

UNEP Finance Initiative. (2022). *Principles for responsible banking and investment.* United Nations Environment Programme.

United Nations Environment Programme. (2023). *Adaptation gap report 2023: Underfinanced. Underprepared.* United Nations Environment Programme. https://www.unep.org/resources/adaptation-gap-report-2023

United Nations. (2015). *Transforming our world: The 2030 agenda for sustainable development.* https://sdgs.un.org

United Nations. (2015). *Transforming our world: The 2030 agenda for sustainable development.* United Nations.

United Nations. (2023). *Financing for sustainable development report.* https://www.un.org

Usman, B. (2022). Sustainable Economies: A Review of Green Growth and Circular Models. *Journal of Business, IT, and Social Science*, *1*(2), 13–16. DOI: 10.51470/BITS.2022.01.02.13

Van Vu, N., Nazari, M. A., Dang, T., Muralev, Y., Mohanraj, M., Tran, T., & Hoang, A. (2025). Type of the paper*: Article*. https://doi.org/DOI: 10.2139/ssrn.5384374

Varsha. (2024). Fintech and sustainable finance: A review of environmental, social, and governance (esg) integration. *Educational Administration: Theory and Practice*, 6816–6824. DOI: 10.53555/kuey.v30i5.4019

Victoria, G.-M. (2023). *General Guidelines for the Implementation of Sustainability in Higher Education Institutions*. UNESCO.

Vietnam, B. A. of, & Bùi, H. T. (2025). A legal framework for promoting green finance: International lessons, current status, and recommendations for Vietnam. *T p Chí Kinh T - Lu t và Ngân Hàng, 27*(7). DOI: 10.59276/JELB.2025.07.2983

Villabruna, V. E., Hluszko, C., Rossi, D., Barros, M. V., Lam, J. S. L., & Lermen, F. H. (2024). Barriers and strategies for green investments in environmental, social and governance: A seaport companies' study. *Management of Environmental Quality, 35*(6), 1193–1212. DOI: 10.1108/MEQ-07-2023-0222

Volz, U., Böhnke, J., Knierim, L., Richert, K., Roeber, G.-M., & Derwisch, S. (2015). *Financing the green transformation.* German Development Institute. DOI: 10.1057/9781137486127

von Luepke, H., Neuhoff, K., & Marchewitz, C. (2024). *Bridges over troubled waters: Climate clubs, alliances, and partnerships as safeguards for effective international cooperation?* International Environmental Agreements Politics Law and Economics., DOI: 10.1007/s10784-024-09639-9

Wagenhofer, A. (2024). Sustainability reporting: A financial reporting perspective. *Accounting in Europe, 21*(1), 1–14. DOI: 10.1080/17449480.2023.2218398

Wall, R., Grafakos, S., Gianoli, A., & Stavropoulos, S. (2019). Which policy instruments attract foreign direct investments in renewable energy? *Climate Policy, 19*(1), 59–72. DOI: 10.1080/14693062.2018.1467826

Wang, K., Elahi, E., Zhang, Y., Wang, D., & Khalid, Z. (2022). A development of green finance and regional Eco-efficiency in China. *Sustainability (Basel), 14*(22), 15206. DOI: 10.3390/su142215206

Wang, Q., & Fan, Z. (2023). Green finance and investment behavior of renewable energy enterprises: A case study of China. *International Review of Financial Analysis, 87*, 102564. DOI: 10.1016/j.irfa.2023.102564

Wang, R. (2025). An empirical analysis of pricing determinants in China's green bond market: A study on risk mitigation effects through certification signals, rating analysis, and disclosure quality. *International Journal of Global Economics and Management, 8*(1), 232–260. DOI: 10.62051/ijgem.v8n1.26

Wang, S., Chen, S.-C., Ali, M. H., & Tseng, M.-L. (2024). Nexus of environmental, social, and governance performance in China-listed companies: Disclosure and green bond issuance. *Business Strategy and the Environment, 33*(3), 1647–1660. DOI: 10.1002/bse.3566

Wang, W., & Wang, X. (2023). Does provincial green governance promote enterprise green investment? Based on the perspective of government vertical management. *Journal of Cleaner Production, 396*, 136519. DOI: 10.1016/j.jclepro.2023.136519

Wang, X., Elahi, E., & Khalid, Z. (2022). Do green finance policies foster environmental, social, and governance performance of corporate? *International Journal of Environmental Research and Public Health, 19*(22), 14920. DOI: 10.3390/ijerph192214920 PMID: 36429642

Wang, Y. (2025). Issues and countermeasures in the implementation of Australian Corporations Act. *Advances in Economics. Management and Political Sciences, 228*(1), 225–231. DOI: 10.54254/2754-1169/2025.GL28390

Wang, Z., Teng, Y.-P., Wu, S., & Chen, H. (2023). Does green finance expand China's green development space? Evidence from the ecological environment improvement perspective. *Systems, 11*(7), 369. DOI: 10.3390/systems11070369

World Bank. (2012). *Inclusive Green Growth—Pathways to Sustainable Development*. World Bank.

World Bank. (2022). *Financing the SDGs: Global outlook*. https://www.worldbank.org

World Bank. (2022). *Global investment competitiveness report 2022: Rebuilding investor confidence*. World Bank Publications.

World Bank. (2024). *Green bond market development and impact measurement*. World Bank Publications.

Xiang, P., Chen, Y., & Xu, Y. (2022). Operational risk allocation in urban rail transit PPP projects: A cooperativegame approach. *Frontiers in Environmental Science, 10*, 900322. DOI: 10.3389/fenvs.2022.900322

Xiao, Y., Lin, M., & Wang, L. (2024). Impact of green digital finance on sustainable development: Evidence from China's pilot zones. *Financial Innovation, 10*(1), 10. DOI: 10.1186/s40854-023-00552-9

Xiao, Y., Yan, W., & Peng, B. (2023). Explore the complex interaction between green investment and green ecology: Evaluation from spatial econometric models and China's provincial panel data. *Sustainability (Basel), 15*(12), 9313. DOI: 10.3390/su15129313

Xu, L., Xie, L., Mei, S., Hao, J., Zhang, Y., & Song, Y. (2024). Corporate sustainability reporting and stakeholders' interests: Evidence from China. *Sustainability (Basel), 16*(8), 3443. DOI: 10.3390/su16083443

Yadav, R., Bhong, M., Aswal, U. S., Kumar, M., Reddy, C. V., Rajalakshmi, B., & Albazoni, H. J. (2023). Key enabler on efficient resource utilization: Technical and managerial investigations for sustainable materials and energy management. *E3S Web of Conferences, 453*, 01023. https://doi.org/DOI: 10.1051/e3sconf/202345301023

Yakovlev, I. A., & Nikulina, S. I. (2019). Indonesia's strategy for sustainable finance. *Financial Journal, 6*(6), 83–95. DOI: 10.31107/2075-1990-2019-6-83-95

Yáñez-Valdés, C., & Guerrero, M. (2024). Equity crowdfunding platforms and sustainable impacts: Encountering investors and technological initiatives for tackling social and environmental challenges. *European Journal of Innovation Management, 27*(7), 2326–2350. DOI: 10.1108/EJIM-03-2022-0127

Yao, F., Li, B., Lv, Y., & Qin, X.-D. (2025). Eco-labels and sales mode selection strategies for E-commerce platform supply chain. *MDE. Managerial and Decision Economics, 46*(2), 1278–1296. DOI: 10.1002/mde.4433

Yasmeen, R., Yao, X., Padda, I. U., Shah, W. U., & Jie, W. C. (2022). Exploring the role of solar energy and foreign direct investment for clean environment: Evidence from top 10 solar energy consuming countries. *Renewable Energy, 185*, 849–862. DOI: 10.1016/j.renene.2021.12.048

Ye, Z. (2024). Comparative analysis of global ESG information disclosure regulatory frameworks and challenges. In *Advances in Social Science, Education and Humanities Research* (pp. 942–950). Atlantis Press SARL. https://doi.org/DOI: 10.2991/978-2-38476-277-4_104

Ye, J., Moslehpour, M., Tu, Y.-T., Vinh, N. T., Ngo, T. Q., & Nguyen, S. V. (2023). Investment on environmental social and governance activities and its impact on achieving sustainable development goals: Evidence from Chinese manufacturing firms. *Ekonomska Istraživanja, 36*(1), 333–356. DOI: 10.1080/1331677X.2022.2076145

Yelnikova, J., & Kwilinski, A. (2020). Impact-investing in the healthcare in terms of the new socially responsible State Investment Policy. *Business Ethics and Leadership, 4*(3), 57–64. DOI: 10.21272/bel.4(3).57-64.2020

Yunus, Y. A., & Nanda, S. (2024). Exploring sustainable finance: A qualitative inquiry into Responsible Investment and ESG risk evaluation. *Golden Ratio of Finance Management, 4*(1), 01–13. https://doi.org/DOI: 10.52970/grfm.v4i1.429

Zaid, M. A. A., & Issa, A. (2023). A roadmap for triggering the convergence of global ESG disclosure standards: Lessons from the IFRS foundation and stakeholder engagement. *Corporate Governance (Bradford)*, *23*(7), 1648–1669. DOI: 10.1108/CG-09-2022-0399

Zatonatska, T., Soboliev, O., Artyukhov, A., Zatonatskiy, D., Balan, V., Wołowiec, T., & Woźniak, D. (2025). Sustainable energy investments: ESG-centric evaluation and planning of energy projects. *Energies*, *18*(8), 1942. Advance online publication. DOI: 10.3390/en18081942

Zeqiri, A., Ben Youssef, A., & Maherzi Zahar, T. (2025). The role of digital tourism platforms in advancing sustainable development goals in the industry 4.0 era. *Sustainability (Basel)*, *17*(8), 3482. DOI: 10.3390/su17083482

Zhang, F., & Gallagher, K. S. (2016). Innovation and technology transfer through global value chains: Evidence from China's renewable energy sector. *Energy Policy*, *94*, 191–203. DOI: 10.1016/j.enpol.2016.04.014

Zhang, L., & Lv, F. (2025). GREEN BONDS AND CORPORATE GREEN INNOVATION. *The Singapore Economic Review*, *70*(08), 2413–2437. DOI: 10.1142/S0217590825490268

Zhang, M., Zhang, C., Li, F., & Liu, Z. (2022). Green finance as an institutional mechanism to direct the Belt and Road Initiative towards sustainability: The case of China. *Sustainability (Basel)*, *14*(10), 6164. DOI: 10.3390/su14106164

Zhang, Y., & Colen, L. (2019). Fossil fuel divestment and renewable investment: Evidence from global capital flows. *Energy Economics*, *80*, 109–121. DOI: 10.1016/j.eneco.2019.01.009

Zhao, J., Liu, H. J., Love, P. E. D., Greenwood, D., & Sing, M. C. P. (2023). Value for money assessments for Public-Private partnerships: Characteristics, research directions, and policy implications. *Developments in the Built Environment*, *16*, 100246. DOI: 10.1016/j.dibe.2023.100246

Zhao, X., Li, Y., & Wang, S. (2025). Mapping the evolution of green finance research: A bibliometric analysis. *Sustainability*, *17*(3), 1124. DOI: 10.3390/su17031124

Zhao, X., Zhang, S., & Chen, Y. (2022). Global photovoltaic manufacturing and China's dominance. *Renewable Energy*, *181*, 1086–1098. DOI: 10.1016/j.renene.2021.09.098

Zhao, Y. (2024). Empowering sustainable finance: The convergence of AI, blockchain, and big data analytics. *Advances in Economics. Management and Political Sciences*, *85*(1), 267–273. DOI: 10.54254/2754-1169/85/20240925

Zheng, D., & Shi, M. (2017). Multiple environmental policies and pollution haven hypothesis: Evidence from China's polluting industries. *Journal of Cleaner Production, 141*, 295–304. DOI: 10.1016/j.jclepro.2016.09.091

Zheng, L., Zheng, Y., He, Q., & Xu, J. (2025). Environmental regulation, firm adaptation, and industrial land prices: Evidence from China's clean air policies. *Applied Economics*, •••, 1–21. DOI: 10.1080/00036846.2025.2540093

Zhou, M., & Fan, R. (2023). The Impact of Green Capital Structure on Enterprise Development and the Regulation of Technological Innovation under Carbon Peaking. *Sustainability (Basel), 15*(7), 5743. DOI: 10.3390/su15075743

Zhou, X., Liang, W., Wang, K. I.-K., Huang, R., & Jin, Q. (2021). Academic influence aware and multidimensional network analysis for research collaboration navigation based on scholarly big data. *IEEE Transactions on Emerging Topics in Computing, 9*(1), 246–257. DOI: 10.1109/TETC.2018.2860051

Zhu, Z. (2025). ESG regulatory intensity and investor behavior: An institutional explanation of rating signals. *Advances in Economics. Management and Political Sciences, 214*(1), 126–132. DOI: 10.54254/2754-1169/2025.CAU26829

Zournatzidou, G. (2025). Green Finance and Sustainable Development: Investigating the Role of Greentech Business Ecosystem Through PRISMA-Driven Bibliometric Analysis. *Administrative Sciences, 15*(4), 150. DOI: 10.3390/admsci15040150

About the Contributors

Siraj Kunjumuhammed is an experienced academic and quality assurance expert, currently serving as Assistant Professor at the Modern College of Business & Science, Sultanate of Oman. He is listed in the Register of External Reviewers at the Oman Authority for Quality Assurance of Education (OAQA), contributing to institutional quality assurance and accreditation processes. Dr. Siraj holds multiple professional certifications, including IRCA-certified ISO 9001:2015 Lead Auditor, and Certified Risk Professional for ISO 22301:2012 (Business Continuity Management), ISO 27001:2013 (Information Security Management), and ISO 31000:2018 (Risk Management Standards). Dr. Siraj earned his Ph.D. in Finance and Banking from Cochin University of Science and Technology (CUSAT, India) and holds MBA and MCom degrees in Finance from Mahatma Gandhi University, India. Dr. Siraj has edited and authored books on quality assurance, corporate finance, and sustainable finance, reflecting his interdisciplinary expertise in business education and financial governance. His research interests encompass corporate finance, bank asset quality and performance, and an interdisciplinary focus on quality assurance and entrepreneurship. He actively engages in sustainable finance research, exploring regulatory frameworks, financial stability, and governance mechanisms. Dr. Siraj has chaired national and international conferences and served as a session chair at several global academic forums, facilitating discussions on corporate finance, quality assurance, and sustainable finance

***

Duggirala Aravind is associated with ASET College of Science and Technology in the Department of Aviation. He is engaged in academic and professional activities related to aviation studies, with a focus on supporting students in understanding the technical, operational, and industry-oriented aspects of the aviation sector. His academic role reflects a commitment to developing student knowledge in areas such as aviation management, airport operations, airline services, safety practices, and emerging trends in the aviation industry. Through teaching, mentoring, and academic guidance, he contributes to building practical awareness and professional readiness among learners. Mr. Aravind is interested in encouraging disciplined learning, industry awareness, communication skills, and career-focused development among aviation students. His association with ASET College of Science and Technology highlights his contribution to aviation education and his role in preparing students for opportunities in the fast-growing aviation and allied service sectors.

Daisy Birir is a Research Scholar in the School of Management and Business Studies at Mahatma Gandhi University, Athirampuzha, Kottayam, Kerala, India. Her research interests include sustainable finance, green foreign direct investment, climate risk disclosure, and the role of finance in advancing the Sustainable Development Goals. She has presented papers at international conferences and is actively engaged in bibliometric analysis and systematic literature review–based research in sustainability and development finance.

Lenah Chelangat is a Research Scholar in the Department of Political Science, University of Kerala (Kariyavattom Campus), Trivandrum, India, and a Tutorial Fellow in the Department of Humanities and Social Sciences at the University of Kabianga, Kericho, Kenya. She is a Certified Secretary of Kenya (CSK) with over 10 years of professional experience and recently obtained a B2-Level Certification in French Language Pedagogy from Alliance Française, Montpellier, France. Her research interests include Political Economy, Governance, Development Studies, Media Framing, Communication, Law and Public Policy. She is engaged in teaching and interdisciplinary research with a focus on socio-political development in emerging economies.

Feruzbek Jumaniyozov is a faculty member in the Department of Accounting and Business Administration at Mamun University, Khiva, Uzbekistan. He is involved in teaching and academic activities related to accounting systems, business administration, and organizational management. His academic interests include financial accounting, managerial decision-making, business operations, and entrepreneurship education. He is committed to developing students' analytical, managerial, and practical skills through outcome-oriented and industry-relevant instruction. Feruzbek Jumaniyozov actively participates in academic and institutional initiatives aimed at strengthening business education, improving curriculum design, and promoting applied learning within higher education.

Latha K is an Associate Professor (Senior) at Saintgits Institute of Management, Saintgits College of Engineering, Kottayam, Kerala, India. Her academic and research interests include management studies, organizational performance, sustainability, and contemporary business practices. She has contributed to teaching, research, and academic development through publications and institutional engagement.

Khayrilla Kurbonov is a faculty member in the Department of Finance and Tourism at Termez University of Economics and Service, Termez, Uzbekistan. He is engaged in teaching and academic activities related to finance, tourism management, and economic development. His academic interests include financial analysis, tourism economics, destination management, and sustainable tourism practices. He is committed to integrating theoretical knowledge with practical applications to enhance students' professional competencies. Khayrilla Kurbonov also contributes to departmental and institutional initiatives focused on curriculum development, academic quality enhancement, and strengthening industry–academia linkages in finance and tourism education.

Rimi Mais is an academic specializing in Public Sector Accounting, CSR, and Sustainability Reporting. She currently serves as a lecturer and Head of the Institute for Research and Community Service at the Indonesian College of Economics, Jakarta, where she plays a key role in the Tri Dharma of Higher Education (October 2020). Her academic qualifications are extensive, including a Bachelor's degree in Economics and Accounting, a Master's degree in Accounting, and a Doctorate in Accounting from Brawijaya University, Malang. Rismawati is also a certified specialist in sustainability reporting (Certified Sustainability Reporting Specialist (CSRS) and a Certified Sustainability Reporting Assuror (CSRA). In addition, he has authored numerous publications on Social Accounting, Sustainability Accounting, Management Accounting, and CSR, making significant contributions to the academic community. His passion for reading and writing reflects his commitment to lifelong learning and professional growth in his field.

Kafila Md is a dynamic academic leader currently serving as Associate Professor and Assistant Dean (Academics) at the School of Business, SR University. She holds a Ph.D. in Finance and brings over two decades of experience in teaching, research, academic mentoring, and institutional leadership. Her areas of expertise include Finance, Human Resource Management, Financial Analytics, and Career Skills Development. She is a passionate advocate of experiential learning and industry-academia collaboration, having actively facilitated internship opportunities, MoUs with industry partners, and student projects with real-world relevance. Dr. Kafila is also a prolific researcher—recently authoring a Scopus-indexed paper on predictive modeling in health insurance (XANNLight: A Novel Hybrid Ensemble Model), and mentoring research scholars who have published in Springer (Q2) journals. Beyond research, she shares thought leadership through LinkedIn, regularly posting about career-readiness, remote internships, employability skills, and academic innovation. Her content often focuses on bridging the gap between campus and corporate, empowering students and early-career professionals with knowledge and confidence. She also engages in interdisciplinary research and digital transformation initiatives, and often collaborates with startup ecosystems to prepare students for the evolving demands of business and technology landscapes.

Munir Munir is an Assistant Lecturer (Assisten Ahli) at the Sekolah Tinggi Ilmu Syari'ah Al-Manar Jakarta, Jakarta, Indonesia, comparison of schools of thought. He holds a Bachelor of Sharia from the Imam Muhammad Ibn Suud Islamic Studies School in Riyadh, Saudi Arabia, Jakarta branch (Lc) and a Master of Islamic Law from Darul Ulum University, Jombang, Faculty of Islamic Law. In addition to his academic career, Munir is also known as a preacher in various offices and institutions. His research interests focus on Islamic Law Studies. He has actively published several scientific articles in accredited national journals. Many of his works explore topics such as Fiqh (Islamic jurisprudence), digital zakat payments, Islamic work ethics, and others. Munir is also registered as a member of the academic community through his profiles in SINTA (Science and Technology Index) under the Indonesian Ministry of Education, Culture, Research, and Technology, and Google Scholar, which document his academic activities and publications.

Ravikumar R. N. is currently a Postdoctoral researcher at Universiti Malaysia Perlis, Malaysia. Also, working as an Assistant Professor in the Department of Computer Engineering at Marwadi University, Rajkot, Gujarat. He has 14 years of national and international teaching experience. He completed his PhD at Amity University, Rajasthan, M.E at VMRF Deemed University, B.E at Anna University, Chennai. He is the co-founder of the Research Activities Club at Marwadi University and trains students on research activities, which leads to the various publications. He has published numerous research articles in Scopus, SCI journals, Book chapters, and Conference papers. Also, he hold several patents and authored books. His specialization is ML, DL, Federated Learning, Recommendation Systems, and Optimization Techniques.

Aarthi S is a dedicated Assistant Professor in Computer Science with over six years of teaching experience. She is currently pursuing her Ph.D. at Marwadi University, Gujarat, and holds an M.Phil. and MCA from Bharathiar University, Tamil Nadu. Throughout her academic career, Aarthi has specialized in programming languages such as C++, Java, and C, and contributed to research in recommender systems and AI-related data privacy. She has published journal articles, contributed to book chapters, and actively participated in technical workshops. Known for her student mentorship and engagement in academic events, Aarthi remains committed to fostering innovation and excellence in computer science education.

Elmurodov Shokhjahon is a faculty member in the Department of Finance at Kimyo International University in Tashkent, Tashkent, Uzbekistan. He is actively involved in teaching and academic activities in the areas of Finance, economic analysis, and applied business studies. His academic interests include economic modeling, development economics, and data-driven approaches to economic decision-making. He is committed to outcome-oriented teaching and the integration of theory with real-world economic applications. Elmurodov Shokhjahon contributes to academic research and institutional initiatives aimed at enhancing curriculum quality and strengthening economics education in higher education.

Ziyodullayev Sodiq is a faculty member in the Department of Finance and Tourism at Termez University of Economics and Service, Termez, Uzbekistan. He is engaged in teaching and academic activities related to finance, tourism management, and economic analysis. His academic interests include financial systems, tourism economics, sustainable tourism development, and applied financial planning. He is committed to integrating theoretical concepts with practical insights to enhance students' professional readiness. Ziyodullayev Sodiq also contributes to departmental and institutional initiatives focused on improving curriculum quality, industry relevance, and research engagement in finance and tourism education.

Ambati Suvarna is a full-time research scholar at SR University, focusing on the performance appraisal of SRI funds. With 16 years of teaching experience in HR and finance subjects, she has established herself as an experienced educator and researcher. Her academic contributions include three conference papers published in ISBN books, one paper published in SR University conference proceedings, and another presented at an international conference at Shinawatra University, Thailand. Additionally, she has authored multiple book chapters and published two research papers in academic journals. Her extensive teaching background, combined with ongoing research, demonstrates her commitment to academia and expertise in financial analysis and human resource management. Her work contributes valuable insights to the field of sustainable and responsible investing through comparative corporate performance analysis.

Roshna Varghese is an Associate Professor in the School of Management and Business Studies at Mahatma Gandhi University, Athirampuzha, Kottayam, Kerala, India. Her academic and research interests include sustainability, corporate finance, environmental governance, and responsible business practices. She has supervised postgraduate and doctoral research and has published in peer-reviewed journals while actively contributing to academic administration and research mentorship.

Index

A

B

C

D

E

G

I

L

M

P

R

S

T

V

www.ingramcontent.com/pod-product-compliance
Lightning Source LLC
LaVergne TN
LVHW081531300926
849161LV00006B/1380